T0301548

RESTRUCTURING PUBLIC TRANSPORT THROUGH BUS RAPID TRANSIT

RESTRUCTURING PUBLIC TRANSPORT THROUGH BUS RAPID TRANSIT

An international and interdisciplinary perspective

Edited by

Juan Carlos Munoz and Laurel Paget-Seekins

First published in Great Britain in 2016 by

Policy Press
University of Bristol
1-9 Old Park Hill
Bristol
BS2 8BB
UK
t: +44 (0)117 954 5940
pp-info@bristol.ac.uk
www.policypress.co.uk

North America office:
Policy Press
c/o The University of Chicago Press
1427 East 60th Street
Chicago, IL 60637, USA
t: +1 773 702 7700
f: +1 773 702 9756
sales@press.uchicago.edu
www.press.uchicago.edu

British Library Cataloguing in Publication Data
A catalogue record for this book is available from the British Library

Library of Congress Cataloging-in-Publication Data
A catalog record for this book has been requested

ISBN 978 1 44732 616 8 hardcover

Cover design by Policy Press
Front cover images kindly supplied by EMBARQ Brasil
Printed and bound in Great Britain by Marston Book Services, Oxford

Contents

List of figures and tables

Figures

Tables

Notes on the editors and contributors

Editors

Juan Carlos Munoz is the director of the BRT Centre of Excellence and sub-director of the multidisciplinary Centre of Sustainable Urban Development. He is the director of the Transport and Logistics Engineering Department at the Pontificia Universidad Católica (PUC) of Chile.

His research focus is on operational transport problems, but he has kept public transport design, operation and control issues as the core of his activity. He has been member of the board of Metro and advisor on public transport to the Chilean government. He believes that urban transport systems must be restructured urgently to reverse the trend in which urban space needed for moving people and freight and the resources consumed for these processes both grow. Space and resources should be devoted to life and social encounters, not traffic congestion. We, citizens, should pay much more attention to our actions and to our daily choices.

Laurel Paget–Seekins is a community organiser, turned academic, turned public transport administrator. She moved to Atlanta, Georgia, without a car and ended up with a PhD in civil engineering from the Georgia Institute of Technology with a focus on public transport. She was a postdoctoral researcher at the BRT Centre of Excellence in Santiago, Chile, for two years. Now she implements innovative projects and policies at the Massachusetts Department of Transportation. Laurel is passionate about interdisciplinary research and building community partnerships to change the way we think about transportation and urban public space.

Contributors

Cristina Albuquerque Moreira da Silva is a transportation engineer at EMBARQ Brazil. She is one of the coordinators of the data collection team for the BRTData.org website. She is also responsible for the users' satisfaction survey developed by EMBARQ Brazil to help cities to improve the quality of bus systems based on users' perspective. Cristina holds a master's degree in Transportation Engineering and a bachelor's degree in Industrial Engineering from the Federal University of Rio Grande do Sul (UFRGS).

José Manuel Allard attended the Corcoran School of Art in Washington, DC, received a master's degree from the California Institute of the Arts, and a PhD in industrial design and multimedia communication from the Polytechnic of Milan, Italy. His doctoral thesis addresses the design of public transportation maps and the complexity of their construction and interpretation. He is an associate professor and dean of the School of Design at PUC Chile. He consults on information design, wayfinding and navigation systems for public and private institutions. José believes understanding the perceptions and practices of users is the starting point to solve most public transport problems.

Marco Batarce is a professor in the School of Industrial Engineering at the Universidad Diego Portales in Santiago, Chile. His research fields include transportation economics, empirical industrial organisation and valuation of benefits of transport policies. He has participated in projects of urban and interurban transport planning, demand modelling, evaluation of transport projects for Chilean public institutions, such as the State Railway Company and the National Transport Planning Agency, and for international organisations such as the Inter-American Development Bank.

Felipe Delgado is an assistant professor at PUC Chile and a researcher in the multidisciplinary Centre of Sustainable Urban Development. His research focuses on the operation of air and public transport systems, but he has devoted most of his energies to developing control strategies to improve the level of service of public transport. He believes that a good public transport system is a way not only to travel but an opportunity to reduce social inequality, whereby citizens of different types meet, share and interact.

Fábio Duarte is professor of urban planning and urban mobility at the Pontificia Universidade Católica do Paraná, Curitiba, Brazil, and has been a visiting scholar at Massachusetts Institute of Technology (MIT) and research associate at Harvard Graduate School of Design. Duarte's main research focus is on urban mobility and how technological changes reshape urban life. Duarte is a CAPES fellow.

Nicolae Duduta is a transport planner at the World Resources Institute (WRI) in Washington, DC. Prior to joining WRI, he worked as a researcher for the Berkeley Center for Global Metropolitan Studies. He holds a Master of City Planning degree from the University of California at Berkeley.

Daniela Facchini is the director of projects and operations at EMBARQ Brazil and is responsible for managing projects related to sustainable mobility and urban development. Daniela also works with national policies to scale up sustainable initiatives, and participates as a speaker at events and roundtables around the country. Prior to joining EMBARQ, Daniela worked in Germany and Brazil in the European Community's projects to disseminate urban mobility practices. Daniela has a master's degree in transportation engineering and a bachelor's degree in civil engineering from the UFRGS.

Onesimo Flores Dewey holds a master's degree in public policy from the Harvard Kennedy School and a PhD in urban planning from the Massachusetts Institute of Technology (MIT). He is currently affiliated with the Harvard Graduate School of Design, where he lectures on transportation planning and serves as research associate for the Project for Transforming Urban Transport. His research explores the political conditions that enable or constrain decision making in the urban transport realm. Onesimo dreams of a world full of cities where people can easily access transportation alternatives that are faster, safer, more affordable and more convenient than driving a car.

Cristhian Figueroa is an architect, has a master's degree in urban projects from PUC Chile, and is a professor instructor at the PUC. His main research focus is pedestrian mobility and public space in vulnerable settlements.

Luis Neves Filipe has a degree in environmental engineering and a master's degree in transportation from Instituto Superior Técnico (IST) in Lisbon (Portugal), where he is studying information systems. He is currently doing his doctorate under the MIT Portugal Programme, at IST in Lisbon, studying the possibilities of using data on citizens as an instrument to manage urban mobility systems. In his dream city people walk and cycle every day, use public transport once a week and need their cars less than once a month.

Rosanna Forray is an architect with a master's degree and PhD in urbanism. She is associate professor in the faculty of Architecture, Design and Urban Studies at PUC Chile and academic staff of the Catholic University of Louvain. She is member of the Centre of Sustainable Urban Development at PUC. Her research focus is urban planning and design from public space and mobility perspectives, moved by the need to improve everyday life, space and time experience and equal opportunities in the city as a social, cultural and economic space.

Patricia Galilea is a lecturer in the Transport Engineering and Logistics Department at PUC Chile. She is a researcher at the Centre of Sustainable Urban Development and at the BRT Centre of Excellence. She is pursuing her PhD at University College London, analysing the success of public-private partnerships (PPPs) in transport. Her research interests also include the design of contracts and incentives for bus operators and bus drivers, how to tackle fare evasion, and the inclusion of wider economic benefits on cost-benefit analysis.

Bernardo Garcia has a degree in architecture and urbanism and a master's in transportation engineering from Universidade Federal do Ceará (Fortaleza, Brazil). He is currently doing a PhD in transportation systems at Instituto Superior Técnico (IST) in Lisbon, Portugal, studying the influence of transit maps on travel decisions. His research focuses are public transportation, passenger information systems, transit maps and travel behaviour. Other research interests are urban planning, sustainability and traffic calming.

Camila Garcia has a civil engineering degree and a master's in transportation engineering from Universidade Federal do Ceará (Fortaleza, Brazil). She is currently doing her doctorate in transportation systems in the Department of Civil Engineering, Architecture and Georesources at IST in Lisbon, Portugal, with a focus on accessibility planning. She has experience in urban mobility planning, mainly on mobility network modelling, spatial analysis, travel behaviour and public transportation information.

Ricardo Giesen is assistant professor in the Transport Engineering and Logistics Department at PUC Chile. He received his PhD in transportation systems from the University of Maryland, College Park, and a master's degree in transportation engineering and a bachelor's degree in Civil and Industrial Engineering from PUC. He specialises in the operation of transportation systems, public transit planning and operations, and logistics and distribution optimisation, particularly the use of information and communication technologies to improve transportation services. He is co-founder of TransitUC and RoutingUC.

David Hensher is the founding director of the Institute of Transport and Logistics Studies (ITLS), a federal government supported national centre of excellence at the University of Sydney. David is an economist and has received numerous awards (for example, IATBR lifetime achievement award) for contributions to the broad fields of transport, infrastructure, logistics and supply chain management. His most important contributions have been in methods to understand choice behaviour, especially in passenger and freight contexts. A long term desire is to take emotional ideology out of decision making in the transport sector and more generally in political choices.

Juan Carlos Herrera is an assistant professor at the Department of Transport Engineering and Logistics at PUC. He is also a researcher at the Centre of Sustainable Urban Development and at the National Research Centre for Integrated Natural Disaster Management, both at PUC. His main research interests include traffic flow theory, traffic control, and the use of advanced technology to manage and operate transportation systems. For this reason, he truly believes that technology plays a key role in developing a smart and sustainable city, in which agencies and (smart) citizens are provided with relevant information to take (smart) decisions.

Darío Hidalgo directs the integrated transport team at the WRI Ross Center on Sustainable Cities, with projects in India, Mexico, Brazil, Turkey, the Andean Region and China. He also coordinates the Observatory of the BRT Centre of Excellence. Dr Hidalgo has more than 23 years of experience as a transport expert, consultant, and government official. He has taken part in urban transport projects and taught training courses in various countries in Latin America, Asia and Africa. He holds PhD and master's degrees in transportation planning from Ohio State University, and a civil engineering degree from Universidad de los Andes, Colombia.

Rocío Hidalgo has a degree in architecture from the PUC and a PhD from the Universidad Politécnica de Cataluña, Barcelona, Spain. She is an assistant professor at PUC Chile, working through learning and research in the areas of urban design, public space and mobility. She is a member of the City and Mobility Laboratory, FADEU-PUC, and research collaborator at the Centre of Sustainable Urban Development at PUC.

Omar Ibarra is a postdoctoral researcher at the BRT Centre of Excellence. He has a PhD in systems engineering from the Autonomous University of Nuevo Leon in Mexico. His research is related to the implementation of operations research techniques for developing tools for the decision making process in transport systems. From his point of view, an efficient transport operation should meet a balance between flexibility and complexity of operation. This should be considered at the strategic, tactical and operational decision levels.

Homero Larrain is an assistant professor in the Transport and Logistics Engineering Department at PUC Chile. His main areas of expertise are logistics and public transport. In his PhD thesis, completed in 2014, he developed an algorithm for designing express services for BRT corridors and networks. He believes in public transport as a key element towards a sustainable city with a high quality of life.

Zheng Li is associate professor in transportation and logistics at the Department of Transportation in the University of Southwest Jiaotong University Hope College. Zheng's main research interests include willingness to pay valuation (for example, travel time variability), advanced nonlinear travel choice models and transport policy. Zheng has published over 30 journal articles, the majority of which are published in the top transportation and logistics journals (for example, *Transportation Research Parts A, B, D* and *E*; *Transportation Science*; *Transportation*), and has presented papers at a number of international conferences.

Luis Antonio Lindau is the director of the Brazil office of the WRI Ross Center for Sustainable Cities. He was one of the founders of the Brazilian Association for Research and Education in Transportation and implemented the Laboratory for Transportation Systems of the School of Engineering at UFRGS, where he is a professor. He led the development of the EMBARQ SimBRT that has been applied to evaluate the operations and potential of BRT systems around the world. Professor Lindau earned his PhD in transportation from the University of Southampton, where he wrote a microscopic model capable of representing high flow bus operations.

Rosário Macário has degrees in business economics, a master's degree and PhD in transportation systems, and a habilitation (DSc) in civil engineering. She is a professor and researcher in transportation at the Department of Civil Engineering, Architecture and Georesources at IST (Portugal) and guest professor at the University of Antwerp, Department of Transport and Regional Economics (Belgium). She is president of the Shareholder Assembly of TIS.PT. Her urban mobility research focuses are institutional setting, policy development and financing. She stands for a systemic and integrated view of urban mobility systems, prioritising accessibility as a value-capturing element and source of financing.

Corinne Mulley is the founding chair in Public Transport at the Institute of Transport and Logistics Studies at the University of Sydney. As a transport economist she leads research at the interface of transport policy and economics. Corinne has contributed to public transport policy of importance to New South Wales and the Australian government in the areas of investment appraisal, innovative funding mechanisms such as value uplift capture, new ways of looking at how to better allocate the road infrastructure and understanding the barriers to BRT implementation in a world where rail solutions predominate.

Juan de Dios Ortúzar pioneered the application of discrete choice models to determine willingness-to-pay for reducing externalities. He has published over 150 papers (archival journals and book chapters), and co-authored *Modelling Transport*, a Wiley book selling more than 17,000 copies. He is the co-editor in chief of *Transportation Research A* and editorial board member of another eight international journals. He believes sustainable cities must prevent the indiscriminate use of the car (through policies such as road pricing), have good integrated public transport systems and provide adequate infrastructure for increasing bicycle use.

Guillermo Petzhold is a transportation engineer at EMBARQ Brazil. His main focus of work is travel demand management at the corporate level. Among his areas of expertise are BRT systems (data collection and analysis, preparation for the launching of BRT corridors) and development and evaluation of sustainable urban mobility projects. He dreams of a city where people will live close to work thus spending less time in traffic and where transit is reliable, comfortable and attracts all kinds of people. Guillermo has a degree in civil engineering from UFRGS, Brazil, and he is currently pursuing a master's degree.

Sebastián Raveau is a postdoctoral associate at Singapore–MIT Alliance for Research and Technology (SMART), working in the Future Urban Mobility Interdisciplinary Research Group. He received his PhD in 2014 from PUC Chile, where he was also an associate lecturer. His research interests focus on travel behaviour, travel demand analysis and transport systems. He is a keen collector of public transport maps from across the world and hopes that one day passenger information systems will make travelling on public transport as easy as travelling on a map.

John Rose is research professor and co-director of the Institute for Choice at the University of South Australia. John's research interest is in the area of the econometrics of discrete choice modelling, with particular application to transportation, health and environmental economics. John's ideal urban mobility scenario is one in which he is retired and living within walking distance of both a beach and pub.

Lake Sagaris is an internationally recognised expert on cycle-inclusive urban planning, civil society development, and participatory planning theory and practice. She began her working life in Chile in 1980 as a freelance journalist. She holds a master's degree and PhD in urban planning and community development from the University of Toronto. Her current work uses participatory action research methods and community–government partnerships to advance towards more sustainable transport, with a strong focus on social justice, inclusion and resilience. These experiences have led to awards in Chile and abroad, and presentations in diverse venues around the world.

Maria Spandou is a researcher at the Technical University of Lisbon (IST), specialising in institutional issues related to public transport. She graduated from the Aristotle University of Thessaloniki (Greece) in rural and surveying engineering and also received a master's degree in planning, organisation and management of transportation systems. Currently, she is pursuing a PhD at IST under the MIT Portugal Programme, investigating the institutional and organisational determinants of metropolitan public transport. Her research interests focus on how hierarchies, markets and networks can contribute to a sustainable and people-oriented mobility system that adapts to the needs and promotes the development of cities.

Anson Stewart is a doctoral candidate in the interdepartmental programme in transportation at MIT. Drawing on international experience in transit planning and operations, he researches stakeholder engagement in transportation planning and how this engagement can be strengthened through interactive modelling, mapping and communication tools. He believes that more informed and open communication in planning processes can help build better connected cities.

Juan Miguel Velásquez is an associate in the Integrated Transport team of the WRI Ross Center on Sustainable Cities, where he supports research on project evaluation and finance, improving decision making for transit vehicles and fuels, planning sustainable urban transport solutions and supporting the BRT Centre of Excellence. Prior to joining WRI, he was a researcher and lecturer at the Regional and Urban Sustainability Research Group at Universidad de los Andes, in Bogotá, Colombia. He has a degree in civil engineering from Universidad de los Andes and holds a master's in transport from Imperial College and University College in London.

Jan Wampler, fellow of the American Institute of Architects, is a professor of architecture both at MIT and the University of South Florida. He has taught at MIT for over 40 years and is also a practising architect, for which he has received many awards. He has just finished his second book, *Notes for Young Architects*. He believes in a future environment that will be auto free with mass transit and pedestrianised.

Nigel Wilson is a professor of civil and environmental engineering at MIT. His research and teaching focuses on urban public transportation, including the operation, analysis, planning and management of transit systems. He has directed several long term collaborative research programmes with public transport agencies worldwide, including Transport for London and the Massachusetts Bay Transportation Authority, on using technology and data to control services effectively and to support long term planning. His dream for urban mobility is a system providing priority in resources to non-motorised alternatives and public transport with integrated customer information, including a wide range of service quality and price combinations.

Chris Zegras is associate professor of transportation and urban planning at MIT. His research and teaching focus on how planning, design, technologies and policies can lead to the co-creation of better mobility outcomes in the global north and south. He dreams of a future when, in every city around the world, people's first choice will be to move by bike or foot.

Carola Zurob is a professor at PUC Chile School of Design and a current student on a Master of Public Administration course at New York University. Her professional and academic experience focuses on qualitative research methods for design. She has been a consultant on information design for public services, such as the development of a passenger information system for Santiago's public transport. Carola dreams of a city where neighbours and authorities work hand in hand to create quality public spaces and appreciated transport systems.

Acknowledgements

Since this book is the culmination of the first five years of our Bus Rapid Transit Centre of Excellence, we want to acknowledge everyone who has been on this journey with us.

First we must thank the Volvo Research and Educational Foundations (VREF) for providing the financial resources needed for this project. The VREF has requested hard work and relevant results from us, but has been very flexible regarding what we do and made it very clear that our work is independent. They have been great partners, providing both feedback and new opportunities and challenges for us. As a VREF Centre of Excellence we are part of an amazing international community frequently interacting with researchers from the nine other Centres located on every continent.

We would not be an international and interdisciplinary Centre without all of our research teams at Pontificia Universidad Católica de Chile (Santiago, Chile), Massachusetts Institute of Technology (Cambridge, Massachusetts), Instituto Superior Técnico (Lisbon, Portugal), Institute of Transport and Logistics Studies at University of Sydney (Australia), and EMBARQ, part of the World Resources Institute Ross Center for Sustainable Cities. The team members have made significant efforts to keep this Centre alive through virtual means and by travel to conferences to share our visions and adjust our work roadmap.

Along the way we have also received critical feedback from Centre advisors and friends including Gerhard Menckhoff, Sam Zimmerman and Shivanand Swamy. We would like to especially thank the World Resources Institute who hosted our Annual General Assembly.

Most of our team members are represented by the authors of the chapters in this book, but we would like to acknowledge two members of our team who left us earlier than expected. Jose Viegas was a key player designing the structure of our Centre and its vision and left the Centre to work as Secretary General in the International Transport Forum, and Lucho Gutiérrez left us to lead SIBRT.

Along this five year trip we have enjoyed the permanent support of Ignacia Torres as the administrative leader of the Centre. Ignacia has been a pillar of the Centre from day one with her amazing skill in taking responsibility for any task and succeeding while keeping a calm and welcoming atmosphere around her.

Finally, as co-editors we would like to thank each other. Laurel would like to thank Juan Carlos for giving her the opportunity to edit this book and shape the narrative framework. Juan Carlos acknowledges that Laurel did the lion's share of the work in making this book happen and made sure it was completed on time. We also appreciate the work of all the internal and external reviewers for their valuable input.

The BRT Centre designed a roadmap that was impossible to achieve with the funding we were receiving from VREF. This is why chapters in this book need to acknowledge other funding sources for their work.

Chapter Four: This research is part of a larger project also funded by the Project for Transforming Urban Transport (TUT) hosted by Harvard's Graduate School of Design.

Chapters Seven and Eight: Marco Batarce acknowledges the support provided by the CONICYT through FONDECYT Project No. 3140327.

Chapter Nine: The fieldwork in India for this chapter was also supported by the Pontificia Universidad Católica de Chile. The author would like to thank Matías Fernández for conducting the interviews in Mexico City and Santiago, and Professor Geetam Tiwari at the Indian Institute of Technology in Delhi and Professor Shivanand Swamy at CEPT in Ahmedabad, India for facilitating the Indian site visits. Finally Laurel appreciates the participation of all the interviewees in the four cities.

Chapter Ten: The Workshop was carried out with additional financial support from MIT's Department of Urban Studies and Planning and the MIT-Chile Pontificia Universidad Católica (PUC) de Chile Seed Fund. We gratefully acknowledge the hard work of the MIT and PUC students who participated in the Workshop, upon which much of the chapter is based. We also thank the numerous government officials, citizen stakeholders, and fellow academics who contributed to the Workshop through many formal and informal meetings, discussions and presentations.

Chapter Eleven: This research was also support by the Australian Research Council.

Chapter Twelve: The authors are also grateful to Project Fondecyt 1110720, Project Fondef D10I1049, and the Inter-American Development Bank.

Chapter Fourteen: The author acknowledges Haris Koutsopoulos, professor of civil engineering at Northeastern University as effectively a co-author on this chapter through his major contributions to many of the ideas. Funding provided by Transport for London, MTR (Hong Kong) and the MBTA supported much of the research presented.

Finally Nigel would like to acknowledge the critical contributions of many MIT students to this work, including Michael Frumin, Jay Gordon, Meisy Ortega, Wei Wang, Dan Wood and Yiwen Zhu.

Chapter Fifteen: This research was also supported by the Centro de Desarrollo Urbano Sustentable (CEDEUS), Conicyt/Fondap/15110020, FONDECYT project # 11140443.

Chapter Sixteen: The first author would like to thank funding provided the Centro de Desarrollo Urbano Sustentable (CEDEUS), Conicyt/Fondap/15110020. This research was also support by the Australian Research Council.

Chapter Seventeen: This research was also supported by the Centro de Desarrollo Urbano Sustentable (CEDEUS), Conicyt/Fondap/15110020, FONDECYT project # 1150657, Corfo 13IDL4-18361.

Chapter Eighteen: This research was partially supported by Grants from FONDAP CEDEUS, FONDECYT (1110720/1120993/3140358), INNOVA-CORFO IDL4 18361, FONDEF-VIU 110065.

Chapter Nineteen: This research was made possible with funding support from Bloomberg Philanthropies.

ONE

The promise of BRT

Laurel Paget-Seekins and Juan Carlos Munoz

The promise of Bus Rapid Transit

Cities, or perhaps more accurately urban conglomerations, are the engines of economic growth and human development, but face numerous well documented challenges in the twenty-first century. Cities are increasingly forced to compete for capital in a globalised economy, but at the same time are the cradle of creativity and prosperity. Population and income are growing, and along with them motorisation rates, trips per capita, traffic congestion, inequality, and social segregation. These problems are compounded by a sense of urgency about the need to address climate change, air pollution, traffic injuries and deaths, and lack of physical activity.

Despite the seemingly insurmountable challenges, cities provide opportunities to shift urban development to a more liveable and sustainable pattern. Sustainable cities should continually reduce their environmental footprint, while shrinking social inequity and creating a stable long term economy that can meet the demands of the current and future population. Delivering on this triple bottom line agenda requires substantial changes to the existing design and management of urban space. As a major driver of urban space, transportation is a key element of both the problems and the solutions for urban sustainability.

Over the past 100 years, cities have increasingly been designed for the needs of cars – ample parking, capacity to meet peak-hour demand, roads designed to increase speed. At the same time land use has been planned for low density and single uses, forcing people to use cars, even for the simplest trips. However, a sustainable city should shape urban space around the needs of people, with transportation being for multiple uses and with multiple transportation modes possible.

The ability to meet peak-hour transportation demand is a key concern in urban areas. In the peak hours, when large numbers of people want to arrive in the same area at the same time, the car is clearly a problem from a social perspective. Cars do not use urban space efficiently (especially with the use of cars being underpriced in most cities), causing significant congestion and creating air pollution, particularly at low speeds. In order to avoid the problems associated with the use of cars during peak periods, cities need to have a high share of sustainable transport modes, including walking, cycling and public transport.

At the same time, cities face financial constraints, making it difficult to advance solutions for access at the required pace. In this context Bus Rapid Transit (BRT) can play a significant role as part of integrated public transport systems and is gaining support around the world in both developing and developed cities. BRT has shown its ability to carry large passenger volumes, while retaining the flexibility of a bus service, with low capital costs, fairly short implementation times, and significant greenhouse gas emission reductions.

The acronym BRT is increasingly being used as a generic term to describe any bus-based transit service with operational characteristics that improve on the speed of a traditional bus service. According to Transit Cooperative Research Program Report 90, BRT is a flexible, rubber-tired form of rapid transit that combines stations, vehicles, services, running ways, and Intelligent Transportation Systems (ITS) elements into an integrated system with strong identity (Levinson et al 2003). This very broad definition may fit almost any bus-based public transport service. According to the BRT Planning Guide, BRT is a high quality public transport system, which offers fast, comfortable, and low cost urban mobility. Its definition is more restrictive, requiring segregated lanes among other features (Wright and Hook 2007). More recently, the Institute for Transportation and Development Policy has developed a BRT standard assigning gold, silver, or bronze recognition to BRT corridors worldwide depending on what aspects of BRT are included – especially bus-only lanes, off-board ticketing, and distinctive image.

We recognise that BRT cannot be the same in every city. The most suitable public transport strategy will depend on the urban context, the demand pattern, the street width available, and the political will to make a radical transformation. In different situations different aspects of BRT will be implemented; not all BRT components may be appropriate or feasible. We consider the key elements of a BRT to be a *high frequency bus service* running on an (at least) partially segregated corridor with off-board fare payment (excluding specific stations with low demand or where the urban context prevents them) and level boarding. Key components for a reliable and fast service include limited intersections with local traffic or providing buses with significant priority and centralised control, and monitoring and dispatching buses to control headways and implement contingencies. For higher capacity systems, BRT may include multiple lanes or overtaking lanes at stations, allowing a mix of regular and express services and large buses. To meet the needs of passengers, static and dynamic passenger information and universal access principles are important.

In this book we are not making the case for BRT; instead we are exploring its potential to restructure the public transport provision in developing cities, to deliver high capacity transport, and to reshape urban space. A promise of BRT is that it can serve as a catalyst for embedding sustainable transport into the fabric of the city. As a surface mode it requires space and in order to provide high quality service, that space has to be dedicated to public transport. This means clear prioritisation for public transport vehicles and their users, including pedestrians and cyclists, in the design and enforcement of public street space.

Prioritising surface public transport means deliberately challenging the use of surface space by cars – in traffic or parked. Very often in cities where public transport is underground or elevated (that is, metro), the streets are left for cars. By reallocating street space, BRT can make car travel less attractive and public transport a more competitive and visible alternative. However, the prioritisation of the movement of people and not cars is also the most controversial and politically difficult aspect of BRT.

Since BRT invests in infrastructure, including dedicated lanes and pre-boarding stations, it indicates a commitment to high quality public transport service. While one benefit of the bus is its flexibility, this flexibility can mean services are easily moved or cut. BRT lays down a marker indicating a level of permanence for services. This permanence (sending a message of presence and visibility) is necessary to shape transit-oriented land use, which can help build ridership in the long term. This can occur regardless of the level of development of a city or existing public transport network.

In developing cities with informal bus service sectors, BRT is often used as a means to restructure public transport provision. An informal bus service is characterised by a large number of bus owners organised into collectives that control the routes. There are often limited barriers to entering the market and there are incentives to flood the market with buses. This often creates a high frequency service, but with high levels of bus congestion. The fierce competition for passengers often results not only in low profit margins, which affects environmental standards and maintenance of vehicles, but also aggressive driving and high crash rates. Drivers have poor labour conditions with long working hours in the informal economy without benefits or protections. Cities need to formalise the service in order to address the safety, congestion, and environmental problems caused by the informal sector.

High quality BRT helps the organisation of transit provision by requiring a level of institutional reform, while improving the travel experience of the users and the urban conditions of a given city. To deal with congestion, systems are designed as some variation of a trunk feeder network, which forces many passengers to transfer. This network structure requires fare integration with services designed to end on-street competition. Even though the number of kilometres driven and the necessary size of fleet in this system are often significantly lower than with the informal sector, the investment needed for high capacity buses with high emission standards are not possible under the existing bus owner regime. All of these changes require a larger public sector role in the provision and regulation of public transport service.

This change involves a significant restructuring of the bus industry and has impacts on all aspects of public transport provision. It creates the opportunity to improve service quality and efficiency, to plan public transport projects in coordination with land use plans built on effective public participation, and to develop passenger information systems and marketing to increase public transport mode share.

Cities are using different pathways for formalisation and for restructuring transit provision, but BRT corridors can act as a key element in moving to a fully integrated formal system. Not only can they serve as the main physical infrastructure for an integrated network design, but they can also serve as a stepping stone in the development of the necessary institutional and political infrastructure. In some cities higher capacity systems, like metro or commuter rail, may also be required, but BRT can play a role in the integrated network.

In cities with an already formalised transport network BRT can improve its quality of service and the overall functioning. In developed cities BRT is still considered an attractive method to expand the coverage of a public transport system at a lower cost than rail and rebuild ridership on buses by increasing frequency, reliability, and comfort.

In order for BRT to achieve its sustainability potential, it has to be considered as more than just a public transport mode. The goal has to be more than just increasing public transport mode share or carrying a certain number of passengers per hour; it has to be part of a restructuring of transportation and urban space. We have written this book to highlight the opportunities and challenges of meeting this potential and the current research addressing them.

This chapter serves as an introduction to both the current state of BRT and the process that created this book. First, we will briefly discuss the evolution of BRT and then the main challenges in both developing and developed cities. Then we explain the history of this project and the BRT Centre of Excellence. We end with an outline of the structure of the book.

Evolution of BRT

The evolution of BRT has been through several stages. The concept of dedicated lanes for buses is not new. They have been implemented in cities starting in the early 1970s. However, it was Curitiba (Brazil) that pioneered what is generally considered BRT with off-board ticketing stations, very large capacity buses, and land use planning around corridors. This example was replicated primarily in other cities in South America through the 1980s and 1990s. In 2000 Bogotá, Colombia introduced operational innovations that increased the passenger capacity further (up to metro standards), including overtaking lanes for express services. These successes were observed around the world and may be considered the 'tipping point' for the introduction of BRT corridors around the world.

In 2014 there were 186 cities in the world with some type of bus priority system in at least one corridor (of which BRT is the most complete), carrying nearly 32 million passengers daily. This represents 372 corridors with a total of almost 4,800 kilometres. Latin America

Figure 1.1: Growth of bus priority systems around the world

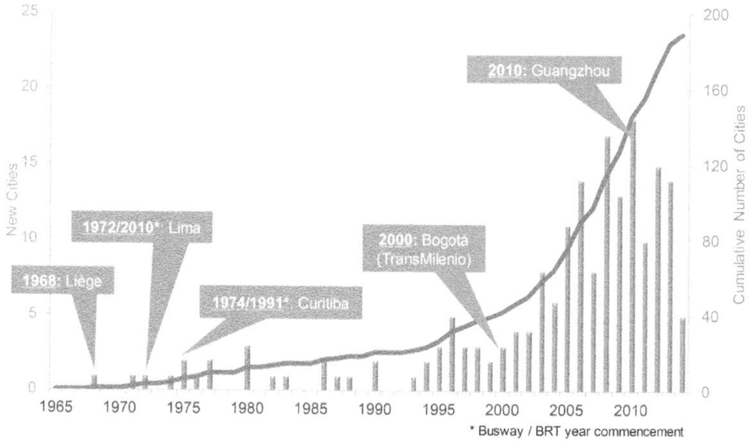

Source: data obtained from www.brtdata.org

remains in the forefront, with 32% of the world's cities with bus priority systems and 50% of the world's corridors, representing 62% of the global demand. But growth is also accelerating in Asia, with 20% of the world's cities with bus priority and just over a quarter of global demand.

BRT has evolved from simple bus priority measures to an integrated systems approach for enhanced service provision. The road has been full of difficulties and controversial projects. However, the long term trajectory of the industry is very positive, with lessons learned and some emblematic breakthroughs in BRT evolution in cities like Curitiba, Bogotá, Santiago, Istanbul, Guangzhou, and Mexico City. BRT is increasingly advancing urban transformations that go beyond the bus lane, including the formalisation and consolidation of the bus industry, renewal of the urban landscape, fare integration, fleet modernisation, smartcard payment systems, and bicycle and pedestrian infrastructure.

The cradle of BRT can be found in Curitiba, which in the early 1980s structured its transit network around backbone axes for linear urban development. Curitiba implemented longitudinally segregated median bus ways, tube shaped stations with fare prepayment and at-level access, physical and fare integration among diverse services with centralised fare collection. Curitiba's system can be considered the first 'surface metro' moving up to 13,000 passengers per hour per direction with a commercial speed of 21 kilometres per hour. Curitiba expansion was halted in the early 1990s after implementation of five corridors, some of them reaching capacity; a new corridor was introduced in 2009 using a former national highway, and a section of the system was overhauled, adding overtaking lanes, increasing capacity to 23,000 passengers per hour per direction and commercial speeds to 25 kilometres per hour. Buses are planned for high occupancy, which has resulted in user complaints and a shift to individual vehicles.

Bogotá in 2000 took the idea to a new level by enlarging the stations and adding a second lane for express services. Bogotá moves up to 45,000 passengers per hour per direction with a commercial speed of almost 30 kilometres per hour. However, now Bogotá's BRT performance has been a victim of its own success: the system became the most preferred transport mode in the city, but lack of expansion in coverage and capacity has resulted in significant overcrowding problems on its main corridors. The BRT system was planned to gradually replace all the dispersed public transport services in the city to achieve full integration in a 16-year period; the plans have not been met due to changes in priorities and cost escalation.

Santiago, Chile, took a different approach to improving transit service, skipping the development of BRT corridors, and instead implementing its fully integrated multimodal Transantiago system in 2007. The switch to the new system on a single day (the 'big bang' approach) was catastrophic and dramatically underlined the need for BRT-like infrastructure to be in place. Without the high speed bus corridors, the rise in transfers required by the integrated system increased passenger trip times and dissatisfaction with the new system. Despite the traumatic start, Santiago is in a privileged position to improve service now that full integration and formalisation of the industry have been achieved, a state that Bogotá is currently trying to reach.

The Istanbul BRT implemented in 2008 connects Europe and Asia through a central busway running in the middle of an expressway. The BRT is fully segregated from other traffic and operates with very long station platforms (90 metres) spaced 1.1 kilometres apart on average. This BRT provides the fastest operational speed in the world, reaching 42 kilometres per hour, and a very high peak throughput (30,000 passengers per hour per direction) and frequency (bus every 15 seconds) even though it has only a single lane per direction. On the downside, access to the BRT requires very long walks and the use of stairs and pedestrian bridges – not always providing universal access and connectivity.

Guangzhou in China implemented a BRT corridor in 2010 that defies the feeder trunk structure that is popular in Latin America. Instead, Guangzhou operates a direct service system in which routes enter the trunk corridor from adjacent neighbourhoods continuing on the trunk section and eventually leaving to serve different neighbourhoods. The Guangzhou Corridor has quite unique dimensions, with stations ranging from 55 metres to 260 metres. It allows up to 27,000 passengers per hour per direction, with 350 buses per hour and direction. The Guangzhou BRT is the corridor with the highest productivity in the world in terms of trips in the corridor per kilometre, reaching 35,500 passengers per kilometre. Having multiple routes on the same infrastructure provides very high capacity without transfers, but also entails an operational challenge as bus arrivals are less reliable than in a closed system. Some stations in Guangzhou face congestion and long queues.

Mexico City started implementation of BRT as a complement to its extensive metro network in 2005, and has been able to expand the system to 105 kilometres in just nine years. The network involves conventional BRT corridors (exclusive median lanes, median stations with off-board ticketing and level access operating with bi-articulated and articulated buses), and has high productivity with more than 3,000 passengers per bus per day in the initial Insurgentes Av. corridor. The system has also been able to adapt the design to different street layouts, using bus priority curbside lanes with 12 metre low-floor buses in the narrow streets of the historic district. While not traditional BRT, this approach using bus-only streets is an important addition to the set of context sensitive designs.

Systems in the developed world share some of the features of those in developing countries, but are usually smaller in capacity and have a stronger focus on technology (advanced vehicles and information systems). In this context bus corridors, BRT, or buses with high level of service (BHLS, mainly in Europe) need to focus on providing services that can attract new bus riders as opposed to serving the large existing ridership in developing cities. Some of the most interesting applications can be found in Australia (e.g. Brisbane and Sydney), France (Paris and Nantes), England (Cambridge), and the USA (for example Cleveland and Los Angeles). These projects are demonstrating that BRT can play an important role in established public transport networks.

These examples show that BRT continues to meet each city's specific needs and constraints. At the same time, innovations and best practices are being shared through city-to-city visits, non-government organisations, research centres, and development banks.

Current status of BRT

Despite the promise of BRT and its successful adoption around the world, the reality is that implementation challenges are numerous and exist on multiple levels. There are design and operational difficulties to creating a surface transit system that has to interact with mixed traffic, pedestrians, cyclists, and other users of public space and still provide high speed, high capacity service. Systems can be a victim of their own success, operating at very high occupancy levels, which results in increasing user complaints. Moreover, those challenges take place within difficult political and institutional contexts (local or regional) and are often accompanied by a negative perception of buses.

The challenges are specific to each city and potential BRT corridor, but commonalities exist both within developing cities and within developed cities. In the case of developing cities with an existing informal bus sector, government authorities first have to devise a strategy for what to do with the incumbents, who wield considerable political power in some cities. At the same time, authorities have to develop institutions to act as regulators and decide who will operate the service and design the necessary contracts and fare structures. Not only does the public sector often lack the capacity and experience for these types of projects, but they also have to find sources of funding for capital, and in some cases operating costs. To make things even more complicated, very often these cities lack a single authority that can address this project comprehensively. Instead local, metropolitan, and national authorities, which very rarely work together, must coordinate for successful implementation.

The operational challenges are also heightened in some developing cities as planners are not designing a single corridor, but developing the basis for an entire network structure. In cities with very high public transport demand, the service has to operate at very high frequencies, which requires strategies to address bus bunching and docking operations at stations reaching near-saturation rates. In all cities corridors have to be designed to accommodate multiple modes safely and efficiently with buses operating at high speeds. In addition, once a successful BRT is implemented, the demand on the corridor tends to grow, which leads to more challenging operations, including addressing overcrowding on buses and at stations.

Passengers have to be convinced of the value of the new service. In developed cities with low transit mode share, this means overcoming the prejudice against buses ('buses are boring, trains are sexy'; 'buses are for the poor and trains for the rich'), creating successful marketing campaigns, and developing transit-oriented land uses. In cities transitioning from an informal sector, this can mean ensuring a smooth conversion with adequate information about the new system and improvements in service quality to overcome the addition of transfers and maintain public transport mode share as incomes rise.

Finally, there are the political challenges of dedicating space and resources to public transport. Regardless of the city, there is always competition for the use of urban street space. It normally takes the form of cars versus all other users, but can pit public transport against pedestrians, cyclists, street vendors, and green space. Very often those living next to a BRT corridor are not the main beneficiaries of its promised high level of service. Instead, it is people living in the periphery and travelling through those neighbourhoods that will benefit the most. The decisions about where to put BRT corridors can come down to where capacity can be expanded in order to avoid converting general purpose lanes to bus-only lanes or removing parking. The unwillingness to inconvenience politically powerful car users or upset the status quo can also limit signal prioritisation and other operational enhancements.

The result of all of these challenges is that many BRT and new integrated transit systems are a reflection of a series of political compromises, trial and error planning methodologies, and limits on operational capacities. This can create BRTs on wide corridors that are unsafe and hard for pedestrians to cross and result in unappealing public spaces. Or a lack of commitment to funding and prioritisation can mean service that is only a minimal improvement over regular buses. Changing political leadership can mean delays in expansion plans and uncertainty in institutional relationships.

All of these challenges illustrate how critical it is to have an interdisciplinary approach to BRT research and decision making. BRT is an element in a transport system (or at a larger scale, an urban system). The outcomes of engineering models have to be calibrated with political realities and an analysis of institutional capacities. Corridors have to be designed within an existing urban context. But ultimately transport is about people, and understanding how potential passengers perceive and make decisions about public transport is critical. This requires a team with knowledge from the fields of engineering and economics, public policy and management, city planning and urban design, and sociology and human geography.

The Bus Rapid Transit Centre of Excellence

This book compiles the first five years of research from the Bus Rapid Transit Centre of Excellence (BRT CoE). This international and interdisciplinary research centre brings together academics and practitioners. The main goal of the Centre is to develop a new framework to plan, design, finance, implement, and operate BRT in different urban areas, giving clear guidelines to decision makers on when and how BRT projects can effectively enhance mobility and meet accessibility needs.

The BRT CoE is one of eight research centres funded by the Volvo Research and Educational Foundations (VREF) around the globe. It was established in May 2010 and is a consortium of five institutions led by Pontificia Universidad Católica de Chile (Santiago, Chile) and includes Massachusetts Institute of Technology (Cambridge, Massachusetts), Instituto Superior Técnico (Lisbon, Portugal), Institute of Transport and Logistics Studies at University of Sydney, and EMBARQ, part of the World Resources Institute (WRI) Ross Center on Sustainable Cities.

The objective of the Centre is to support the successful deployment of BRT, through the identification and effective communication of the conditions necessary for success at the strategic, tactical, and operational (STO) decision levels. Our focus is not only at the BRT project level, but also on how BRT projects interact with other elements of the urban system so that its complete mobility system is transformed and the whole city becomes more sustainable and attractive.

The BRT CoE has structured its work along four main dimensions.

- A BRT Observatory in which we gather, present and interpret BRT data from all around the world. The Observatory database collects key indicators that allow a comprehensive performance benchmark analysis among BRT and busways. In this database you can find several key indicators such as network extent, daily demand, number of cities, and evolution of number of systems since 1970.
- A BRT Laboratory, which is the bulk of our work. We develop in-depth research on the factors and relations underlying system performance, developing or improving analytical methods and their supporting instruments. Our focus ranges from the strategic to the tactical and operational, from political and financial aspects to controlling buses online.
- A BRT educational programme whose goal is to deploy the knowledge gained and support teaching, education, and training for regular and lifelong learning. We target not just graduate students at universities, but also professionals at public transport agencies, operators, consultants, financial institutions, and even journalists dealing with public transport projects.
- A BRT implementation support programme, which acts as a resource for cities looking for advice on what type of transformation is needed in their public transport system. This includes how to promote it among decision makers, citizens, and the media; and how to design, implement, and operate it.

With EMBARQ's staff on the ground in multiple countries and our work with SIBRT (the Latin American Association of Integrated Transport Systems and BRT), we are putting our research into practice by solving tangible problems at all stages of BRT implementation.

This book is the capstone of our five year project; it brings together all of our research projects to illustrate the big picture of the promise of BRT, but also the remaining challenges. We wrote it with the goal of reaching both academic and practitioner audiences, as these challenges will only be solved through the joint efforts of both communities working together.

Organisation of the book

This book is organised in three sections. The first section addresses the issue of institutional relationships. In particular the transition to formalised transit systems requires significant changes to institutions and the development of new capacity for the public sector. It transforms the relationships between the private operators, government authorities, and civil society. Depending on who is providing the service, new contracts have to be developed to govern these relationships. In addition to new challenges, these changing relationships create opportunities, such as an increased role for public participation and the setting for a debate about the proper level of subsidy and fares.

The second section recognises that any changes to the public transport network take place within a complex urban context. From the city to the individual passenger level change is difficult. Even for just a single corridor, political power, and perceptions of BRT shape the choice of mode and conflicts over public space for mobility. In both developing and developed cities planning land use around public transport corridors brings multiple challenges. For passengers, new service means having to learn new routes and this requires the design and implementation of passenger information system.

The third section examines the issues in operations and design. Clearly there are challenges to creating a surface rapid transit system, regardless of the type of city it is located in. But new technology is also bringing opportunities; automated data collection can improve service efficiency, planning, and real-time information to users. The switch to a formal system can improve working conditions and the efficiency of scheduling vehicles and driver shifts. An analysis of performance on BRT corridors can determine the factors that increase boardings, speed, reliability, and safety.

Each chapter outlines a challenge presented by BRT and the restructuring of public transport systems and then presents some of the research developed within the BRT Centre of Excellence to address this challenge. The chapters can stand alone, but we invite the readers to explore issues outside their areas of expertise. In the process of writing the book we discovered links we previously did not see between our diverse research areas.

Our goal with this book is not only to share the results of our research, but to provide a comprehensive framework within which to view the opportunities and challenges of BRT and sustainable transport moving forward. We believe our interdisciplinary and international approach contributes both academically and practically. We hope this book can both assist practitioners to solve problems on the ground and help students and researchers in multiple fields to see how their work fits together.

References

Levinson, H., Zimmerman, S., Clinger, J., Gast, J., Rutherford, S. and Bruhn, E. (2003) *Bus Rapid Transit – Volume 2: Implementation Guidelines*, Washington, DC: Transit Cooperative Research Program.

Wright, L. and Hook, W. (2007) *Bus Rapid Transit Planning Guide*, New York: Institute for Transportation and Development Policy.

TWO

Global overview of BRT and bus corridors

Luis Antonio Lindau, Cristina Albuquerque Moreira da Silva, Guillermo Petzhold and Daniela Facchini

Introduction

As discussed in the Introduction to this book, the acronym BRT (Bus Rapid Transit) is often used to describe a variety of infrastructure, operation and image improvements to local urban bus services. Different components of BRT have been implemented in both developed and developing cities around the world; not all BRT-like projects are called BRT and sometimes corridors without key BRT features are called BRT. That is why in this chapter we provide a global overview of bus priority schemes on a corridor basis and not just BRTs. We use the comprehensive database that the BRT Centre of Excellence has funded (www.brtdata.org) to develop comparative analyses ranging from more general aspects (such as geography, length and demand) to physical characteristics and performance in terms of demands and operating speeds. Finally we briefly compare the performance and costs of BRT to other modes.

Definitions

A BRT system is a mass transport system that couples the quality of railways with the flexibility of bus systems (Levinson et al 2003; Wright and Hook 2007; FTA 2009), including both infrastructure and operational characteristics that improve the level of service, as shown in Figure 2.1. The expectation is that BRTs can accommodate high demand especially when overtaking facilities allow for a combination of local, accelerated and express services. Given the many barriers to planning and implementing BRT systems (Lindau et al 2014), not every corridor incorporates all BRT elements.

Part of the issue when examining BRT is determining what defines a BRT or a 'good' BRT. Given the diversity of urban contexts, existing

Figure 2.1: BRT characteristics

Source: BRT Standard, ITDP 2014

public transit systems and institutional capacities, BRT is implemented differently around the world. The acronym is used for services in corridors that lack some of the elements that a BRT is generally considered to need. At a minimum, the most basic features of a BRT service are a segregated corridor and off-board payment stations, even though it is usually expected also to involve high frequency services, high capacity vehicles and clear branding.

In examining BRT systems around the world, it is clear that the system design characteristics are combined in a myriad of different ways, giving rise to a continuum of quality in self-named BRT corridors. There is also a range of terms for different BRT designs, including BRT 'lite', a term used in North America, buses with high level of service (BHLS), a term used for bus improvement projects in Europe, to full BRT. BHLS consists of a bus system offering better services than conventional bus lines in terms of frequency, travel time, reliability, comfort and accessibility, through adopting a segregated infrastructure with appropriate operational conditions (CERTU 2010). BHLS also aims to provide more comfort to users (COST 2011) in an attempt to attract new bus riders.

BRT involves both infrastructure and operational improvements over conventional bus services. However, some cities have only improved the infrastructure for buses by building bus corridors (and in some cases level boarding platforms). Some of the corridors can be open to all bus lines without coordinated operations, operating as a conventional service only with a special infrastructure.

There are different types of road infrastructure in bus priority corridors. Bus-only streets consist of streets just for buses, sometimes also bicycles and local traffic. Mexico City recently opened Linea 4 with bus-only streets through the historic district. Pereira and Bogotá in Colombia and Santiago in Chile have also implemented bus-only streets. Exclusive lanes are physically separated facilities for bus travel at all times with no level crossing opportunities for pedestrians and other vehicles (Vuchic 2007). Examples of exclusive lanes can be found in São Paulo (Expresso Tiradentes), or the BRT corridors in Istanbul. Segregated lanes are physically separated (for example by paint, curbs, or fences) from other traffic, allowing at-grade crossings for vehicles and pedestrians mostly at intersections (Vuchic 2007). Counterflow lanes are those where buses operate in the opposite direction to the rest of the traffic, as in the Lincoln Tunnel in New Jersey, US (Vuchic 2007; Duduta et al 2012).The more vulnerable segregation is (just paint) and the weaker enforcement is, the more likely it is that private motorised vehicles will invade the bus lane (in these cases cameras should be used to monitor the use of the lane). Finally, mixed traffic extensions define initial and final segments of priority corridors where buses operate without any form of road prioritisation.

The Institute for Transportation and Development Policy (ITDP 2014) has developed a BRT standard in which bus corridors worldwide receive gold, silver, or bronze ratings. This standard can provide authorities with recognition for high quality bus corridors in their cities and also help to identify which corridors have a set of minimum features to classify a system as a BRT. It also helps as a valuable checklist in planning higher quality bus corridors. Even though this standard is based on a set of quantifiable features, it must be interpreted carefully since it does not necessarily focus on performance and need, and it does not account for how operation is affected by its urban context.

BRT Data

The BRT Centre of Excellence created BRT Data (BRT Centre of Excellence et al 2014), a database of worldwide BRT, BHLS and bus priority corridors. It has been available to the public on the internet since April 2012. Its ultimate goal is to influence the design of future corridor projects by providing information on different attributes and indicators, including elements and aspects related to infrastructure, operational performance, fleet and road safety.

BRT Data is not fully exhaustive but is being continuously updated. Currently, it gathers information on 116 attributes and indicators of

378 bus based priority corridors located in 188 cities in 42 countries all over the world. Every day, more than 31 million passengers use these corridors, which cover a total length nearly of 5,000 kilometres. Our comparative analysis of bus priority corridors around the world uses BRT Data.

Geographic Distribution

South America is not only where BRT was invented (Lindau et al 2010), but also has the most corridors and highest demand. As seen in Figure 2.2, Latin America and the Caribbean are home to 33% of the total cities with bus priority systems and 49% of the world's corridors. Approximately 62% of the total global daily demand of passengers on bus corridors are in this region. Twenty per cent of cities in the database are located in Asia, which corresponds to approximately a quarter of the global demand. Europe has 28% of the cities in the database and 6% of the global demand.

As shown in Figure 1.1 (in the previous chapter), from the early 1970s, when the first bus corridors were built in the Americas, to 2000, when TransMilenio was inaugurated in Bogotá, the expansion of bus corridors was relatively modest. But after the turn of the millennium, the cumulative number of cities with bus corridors experienced exponential growth. It is expected that by 2019, 169 cities will be launching new or expanding existing bus priority systems adding 3,500 kilometres (EMBARQ Brazil 2014).

Figure 2.2: Global distribution of BRT and bus priority corridors

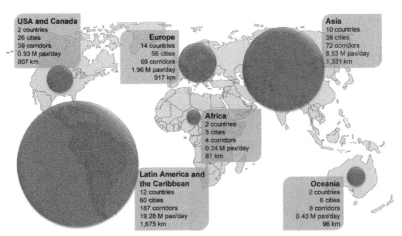

Countrywide data in terms of cities, corridors, lengths and daily demands are shown in Table 2.1. Brazil, China, France and the United States are the countries with the largest number of cities (from 33 to 18) with corridors where bus transit benefits from some form of physical priority. In Europe, France and the United Kingdom are the countries with the largest number of corridors, respectively 25 and 13. It is important to mention that many cities in the developed countries have significant rail based transit networks, most of them implemented last century.

While China has one of the fastest growing BRT networks, Mexico, Colombia and India also show noteworthy cases of expansion as a result of national policies that foster the implementation (Carrigan et al 2013). The United States, where private cars account for the great majority of urban trips, hosts the world's third largest length of bus priority corridors with a total of 555 kilometres. So merely having bus priority corridors of some sort does not necessarily translate into high bus ridership.

Table 2.1: BRT and bus priority including BHLS by country

	Number of cities	Number of corridors	Length (km)	Daily demand (1,000 pass/ day)	Corridors/ cities	km/ cities	Daily demand (pass/ day)/km
Brazil	33	119	827.9	11,766	3.6	25.1	14,212
France	20	25	236.9	444	1.3	11.8	1,875
China	18	32	567.9	3,978	1.8	31.6	7,005
United States	18	29	555.1	361	1.6	30.8	650
United Kingdom	13	13	158.6	162	1.0	12.2	1,024
Mexico	9	13	264.8	1,918	1.4	29.4	7,241
India	8	8	143.1	387	1.0	17.9	2,702
Canada	7	10	239.5	530	1.4	34.2	2,213
Colombia	6	18	201.5	2,868	3.0	33.6	14,237
Australia	5	7	89.5	407	1.4	17.9	4,549
Netherlands	5	6	137.9	108	1.2	27.6	783
Taiwan	5	3	89.7	1,202	0.6	17.9	13,408
Sweden	3	5	95.7	100	1.7	31.9	1,045
Germany	3	3	46.1	102	1.0	15.4	2,213
Iran	2	9	147.9	2,000	4.5	74.0	13,523
Ecuador	2	8	107.9	1,143	4.0	54.0	10,594
Argentina	2	7	48.1	970	3.5	24.1	20,166

(continued)

Table 2.1: BRT and bus priority including BHLS by country (continued)

	Number of cities	Number of corridors	Length (km)	Daily demand (1,000 pass/ day)	Corridors/ cities	km/ cities	Daily demand (pass/ day)/km
Italy	2	5	42.8	23	2.5	21.4	537
South Africa	2	3	58.5	42	1.5	29.3	718
Japan	2	2	28.5	9	1.0	14.3	316
Venezuela	2	2	18.3	60	1.0	9.2	3,279
Chile	1	14	91.9	341	14.0	91.9	3,710
Indonesia	1	12	206.8	370	12.0	206.8	1,790
Israel	1	3	40.0	N/A	3.0	40.0	N/A
Belgium	1	3	6.0	N/A	3.0	6.0	N/A
Guatemala	1	2	35.0	245	2.0	35.0	7,000
Spain	1	2	2.0	3	2.0	2.0	1,600
Turkey	1	1	52.0	750	1.0	52.0	14,423
Republic of Korea	1	1	43.0	400	1.0	43.0	9,302
Finland	1	1	27.5	30	1	27.5	1,091
Pakistan	1	1	26.0	130	1.0	26.0	5,000
Peru	1	1	26.0	350	1.0	26.0	13,462
Trinidad and Tobago	1	1	24.0	N/A	1.0	24.0	N/A
Nigeria	1	1	22.0	200	1.0	22.0	9,091
Thailand	1	1	15.3	10	1.0	15.3	654
Switzerland	1	1	11.0	14	1.0	11.0	1,273
Czech Republic	1	1	10.3	18	1.0	10.3	1,756
Panama	1	1	9.1	N/A	1.0	9.1	N/A
Ireland	1	1	8.4	34	1.0	8.4	4,048
Uruguay	1	1	6.3	25	1.0	6.3	3,968
New Zealand	1	1	6.2	23	1.0	6.2	3,694
Portugal	1	1	4.8	27	1.0	4.8	5,625

With almost 12 million passengers per day, Brazil is number one in terms of passengers benefiting from any form of bus priority corridor. The national daily demand totals three times the equivalent figure for China. As a proxy for estimating the use of built infrastructure, we divided the total nationwide daily demand, in terms of passenger volume using BRT and bus priority corridors, by the respective country's corridor length. Results presented in Table 2.1 indicate that systems operating in Argentina, Turkey, Brazil, Colombia, Iran, Peru and Taiwan exhibit the highest productivity – that is, more than

13,000 daily passengers per kilometre of implemented BRT and bus priority corridors. Of course this indicator should be considered carefully since systems where user trips are long will appear to be less productive than similar systems with short trips.

Comparative analysis

The database includes a range of bus priority features; some are implemented more frequently than others. Figure 2.3 shows the incidence of different types of bus lanes per total length of implemented corridors. The ease of implementation contributes to the strong prevalence of segregated over exclusive lanes, 80% as opposed to 6%. Counterflow lanes add to only 3% of the length of bus priority corridors. They are the most dangerous configuration for bus systems as many road users may not anticipate buses arriving from a counterflow direction (see Chapter Nineteen and Duduta et al 2012). Mixed traffic usually refers to road segments following the end of a busway. In many cases the suburban terminals are not located exactly on the busway, requiring buses to share space (under mixed traffic conditions) with other vehicles along sections of road before reaching the busway.

Some of the attributes registered in BRT Data have a stronger impact on the performance of the corridors in terms of transport capacity, operating speed and reliability. (These attributes are discussed in more detail in Chapter Sixteen.) Figures 2.4 and 2.5 depict the incidence of these attributes and design elements: (i) traffic signal priority for buses;

Figure 2.3: Incidence of different types of priority infrastructure

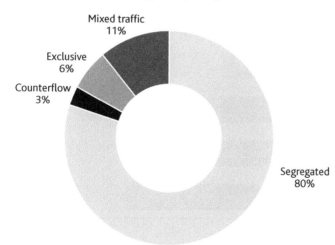

(ii) bus overtaking opportunities at stations and terminals; (iii) fare pre-payment to boarding; (iv) at-level boarding at stations and terminals; and (v) average distance between stations.

Traffic signal priority is key to increasing operating speeds and regulating headways along the route, thus preventing bus bunching (Delgado et al 2012). But more than 75% of the corridors do not have bus actuated traffic signals (Figure 2.4). Bus overtaking at stations and terminals not only provides greater transport capacity (FTA 2009), but also enables the operation of a combination of express, accelerated and local services. However, only 29% of the corridors allow overtaking under priority conditions along all (entire) or sections (part) of the corridor. Fare prepayment and at-level boarding allow shorter dwell times at stations (Weinstock et al 2011) and increase capacity (FTA 2009). The majority of the corridors do not have prepayment (55%); 38% offer prepayment along the entire corridor and 7% along part of the corridor. At-level boarding occurs in about 50% of the cases but, depending on prevailing docking manoeuvres, there can be gaps between platforms of buses and stations or terminals.

Distance between stations is crucial for the performance of any transit system. The greater the distance between consecutive stations, the higher the operating speeds (Kittlenson & Associates et al 2003; Lindau et al 2013) and the capacity of the corridor (FTA 2009). The most frequent average distance between passenger stations lies within the 600 to 700 metre range (Figure 2.5). The typical design of corridors connecting suburban to central areas along highways uses station spacing of over 1.5 kilometres. Shorter distances are associated

Figure 2.4: Incidence of design elements in bus priority corridors

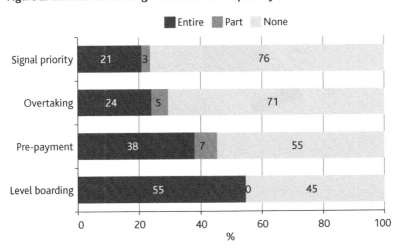

Figure 2.5: Average distance between stations

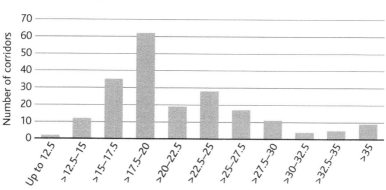

Average distance between stations (metres)

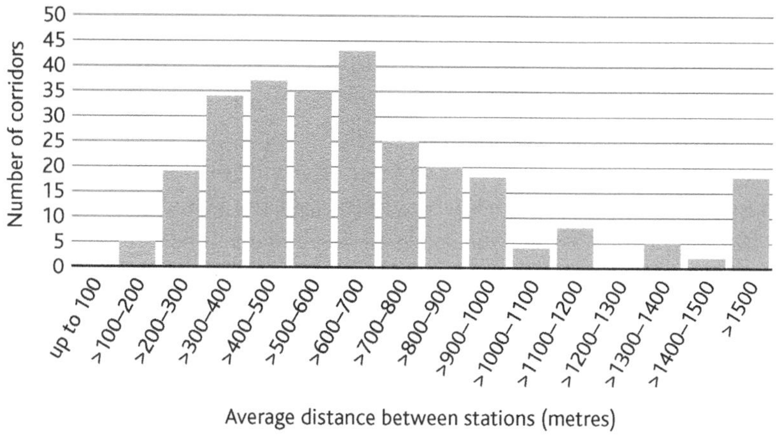

with corridors serving city centres and operated by multiple bus services.

The predominant average operating speed of the corridors is within the range of 17.5 to 20 kilometres per hour (km/h), as shown in Figure 2.6. Seventy per cent of the corridors have an operating speed from 15 to 25 km/h. As many bus priority lanes are located by the curb, interference with mixed traffic, such as right turns, loading operations and residents' parking, can reduce the operating speeds. A few corridors have very high average operating speeds, such as the Australian busways in Adelaide (80 km/h) (Currie and Delbosc 2013) and Brisbane (55 km/h) and the BHLS in Cambridge (60 km/h), benefiting from features like shuttle services, fully exclusive lanes, guided buses and traffic signal priorities.

Figure 2.6: Operating speeds

Average operating speed (km/h)

Mode comparison

Probably the biggest trade-off that needs to be faced when designing a public transport network has to do with the costs versus level of service to the user. The overall cost of a transit network is usually divided into two categories: capital costs and operating costs. The most important design elements of the level of service provided by a public transport network are the accessibility and the speed and capacity offered. Chapter Sixteen examines these elements for BRT corridors.

BRT, Light Rail Transit (LRT) and heavy rail can be alternatives to improve service on medium to high demand corridors or to serve as trunks in a trunk and feeder network. Cost, level of service to users and capacity vary, and these differences should be considered to determine the appropriate mode.

Table 2.2 shows a comparison of BRT against regular buses, LRT and heavy rail. The attributes shown for each one are capital costs, passenger capacity (measured in passengers per hour per direction, denoted as pphpd) and operating speeds. Ranges for each value are wide due to the impacts of the local economy on costs, and because of individual features within each system (for example, quality of stations, segregation from traffic and vehicle technology).

As Table 2.2 shows, standard bus systems are the cheapest option, but they are able to serve only low levels of demand. Their commercial speed is limited by the traffic conditions of the city, which makes them perform very poorly in congested areas. BRT systems provide, for a reasonable cost, a service with capacity and operating speed that can be higher than LRT. The speeds in BRT can also be improved, taking advantage of the flexibility buses have to skip stops. Heavy rail systems such as metro provide the highest quality service, with greatest capacity and operating speeds, but are by far the most costly alternative. They also take the longest to implement and are most rigid in terms of the type of service provided.

Table 2.2: Typical values of the performance indices for different transport modes

Type of transit mode	Capital costs (million US$/km)*	Capacity (pphpd)**	Operating speed (km/h)**
Standard bus	–	3,180–6,373	10–30
BRT	Up to 15	Up to 55,710	18–40+
LRT	13–40	Up to 30,760	18–40
Heavy rail system	40–350	52,500–89,950	20–60

* Adapted from Wright and Hook (2007); ** Adapted from Carrigan et al (2013).

A well designed BRT system combines the best aspects of other modes: the low costs from buses, and the high quality of service from LRT and heavy rail systems. Therefore, BRT systems may be a good alternative to increase system capacity at low cost in many scenarios.

Figure 2.7 depicts a comparison, in terms of productivity and operating speed, of the world's top ten BRT, LRT and metro systems with respect to daily demands, grouped into technological clusters (Lindau et al 2014; Petzhold 2012). The triangle, into which the BRT is clustered, represents the inherent flexibility of the mode. Under specific conditions, as presented by Istanbul and Guangzhou, BRT can achieve the same performance of subways both in terms of operating speed and productivity. Moreover, the results indicate that five BRT have a passengers per kilometre productivity within the range of the ten top metro systems while two (Istanbul and Bogotá) have operating speeds within metro range. The comparison with LRT is even more favourable, with five BRTs outperforming the ten top LRTs in terms of productivity, while the BRTs report similar LRT speed (with the exception of Istanbul's, which is significantly faster).

Figure 2.7: Comparing the performance of the world's top ten transit systems

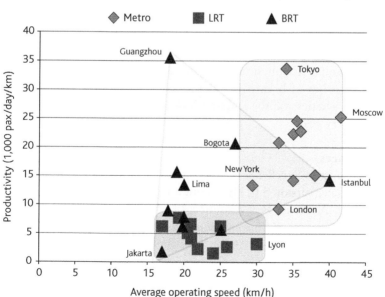

Source: Petzhold 2012; Lindau et al 2014

Discussion

There is quite a lot of diversity in bus priority corridors implemented around the world. Diversity derives from the inherent flexibility of bus systems that enables cities to implement bus based solutions to fit their particular mobility culture, needs and constraints (for example, financial, political, built environment and geography). It is also important to note that, while cities in developed countries may target improving bus services and infrastructure to increase transit ridership, developing cities still lacking mass transit networks implement BRT corridors to accommodate high demand. In every case, projects can be phased and be conceived to allow for expansion and promoting transit–oriented development.

By consolidating the worldwide BRT, BHLS and bus priority corridor experiences into a comprehensive database, we provide the means for more comprehensive analysis on the impact of project elements in the performance of different types of bus priority systems. Successful bus priority projects provide important insights for planning new systems. Benchmarking is key for designers and in preventing cities opting for the politically easy or less costly decisions. The image and quality of service can be severely compromised by wrong decisions at the conceptual stages. Bus priority systems providing more BRT and BHLS features show better performance and tend to attract more passengers.

One of the exciting aspects of BRT, BHLS and bus priority corridors is the environment they provide for continuous innovation. Gradually advocates, project designers and city leaders are finding ways to get around the physical and political obstacles that used to deter the expansion of high performance bus based transit systems. The number of cities and the length of bus priority corridors continue to grow every year.

References

BRT Centre of Excellence, EMBARQ, IEA and SIBRT (2014) Global BRT Data: version 3.0, http://www.brtdata.org

Carrigan, A., King, R., Velasquez, J.M., Raifman, M. and Duduta, N. (2013) *Social, Environmental and Economic Impacts of BRT Systems Bus Rapid Transit Case Studies from Around the World*, Washington, DC: EMBARQ.

CERTU (Centre for the Study of Urban Planning, Transport and Public Facilities) (2010) *Buses with a High Level of Services*, France: Centre for the Study of Urban Planning, Transport and Public Facilities.

COST (European Cooperation in Science and Technology) (2011) *Buses with High Level of Service*, Paris: European Cooperation in Science and Technology.

Currie, G. and Delbosc, A. (2013) 'Assessing Bus Rapid Transit system performance in Australasia', paper presented at the 13th International Conference on Competition and Ownership in Land Passenger Transport, Oxford, UK.

Delgado, F., Muñoz, J.C. and Giesen, R. (2012) 'How much can holding and/or limiting boarding improve transit performance?', *Transportation Research Part B*, 46(9): 1202–1217.

Duduta, N., Adriazola, C., Wass, C., Hidalgo, D. and Lindau, L.A. (2012) *Traffic Safety on Bus Corridors Guidelines for Integrating Pedestrian and Traffic Safety into the Planning, Design, and Operation of BRT, Busways and Bus Lanes*, Washington, DC: EMBARQ.

EMBARQ Brasil (2014) *Future Bus Priority Corridors around the World*, Porto Alegre: EMBARQ Brasil.

FTA (Federal Transit Administration) (2009) *Characteristics of Bus Rapid Transit for Decision-Making*, Washington, DC: Federal Transit Administration.

ITDP (Institute for Transportation and Development Policy) (2014) *The BRT Standard* (2014 edn), New York: Institute for Transportation and Development Policy.

Kittlenson & Associates, Inc., Kfc Group, Inc., Parsons Brinckerhoff Quade & Douglas, Inc. and Hunter-Zaworski, K. (2003) *Transit Capacity and Quality of Service Manual* (2nd edn), Washington, DC: Transit Cooperative Research Program, Report 100.

Levinson, H., Zimmerman, S., Clinger, J., Rutheford, S., Smith, R.L., Cracknell, J. and Soberman, R. (2003) *Bus Rapid Transit, Volume 1: Case Studies in Bus Rapid Transit,* Washington, DC: Transit Cooperative Research Program, Report 90.

Lindau, L.A., Hidalgo D. and Facchini D. (2010) 'Curitiba, the cradle of Bus Rapid Transit', *Built Environment*, 36(3): 269–277.

Lindau, L.A., Pereira, B.M., Castilho, R.A., Diogenes, M.C. and Herrera, J.C. (2013) 'Exploring the performance limit of a single lane per direction Bus Rapid Transit systems', paper presented at Transportation Research Board 92nd Annual Meeting, Washington, DC.

Lindau, L.A., Hidalgo, D. and Lobo A. (2014) 'Barriers to planning and implementing Bus Rapid Transit systems', *Research in Transportation Economics*, (48): 9–15.

Petzhold, G. (2012) 'Urban transit: a comparative analysis of high capacity systems', Dissertation in Portuguese, Engineering School, Universidade Federal do Rio Grande do Sul, Porto Alegre, Brazil.

Vuchic, V. (2007) *Urban Transit: Systems and Technology*, Hoboken, NJ: John Wiley.

Weinstock, A., Hook W., Replogle M. and Cruz R. (2011) *Recapturing Global Leadership in Bus Rapid Transit: A Survey of Select U.S. Cities*, New York: Institute for Transportation and Development Policy.

Wright, L. and Hook W. (eds) (2007) *Bus Rapid Transit Planning Guide* (3rd edn), New York: Institute for Transportation and Development Policy.

Section 1
Institutional Relationships

THREE

The path toward integrated systems

Darío Hidalgo, Juan Carlos Munoz
and Juan Miguel Velásquez

Introduction

The main goal of an urban transport system is to provide accessibility for the inhabitants of an urban region. As this book shows, Bus Rapid Transit (BRT) projects can play an important role in urban mobility, but they cannot stand alone. A combination of different transport modes is needed to serve the demand which varies across different times and geographical areas of the region. Residents have to navigate the transport system to reach their destinations. The service they receive depends on the characteristics of each of the segments they must follow (including the access to and egress from public transport) and the experience of transfer between them. The system will provide a higher level of service to its users if it is designed for passengers to move between trip legs as smoothly as possible, and if they understand the system's inherent complexity so as to be able to find their best possible route choice (see Chapters Twelve and Thirteen). The more convenient transfer experiences are within the system as a whole (for example, no additional fare and a short walk), the better the use that passengers will make of the available network of services. Alternatively, passengers may avoid certain service combinations due to inconvenient transfer experiences. Thus, users (and therefore the urban region) will always benefit from offering an integrated system with seamless transfers.

An integrated network that provides seamless access between all points is ideal; however, this is a complicated undertaking, especially when the system is fragmented into different authorities or decision makers, or when the starting point is an informal bus network, as described in Chapter Four. In this chapter we discuss the challenges faced by two integration pathways – sudden and gradual – and suggest a framework for advancing public transport integration which mitigates the main issues observed in these cases. The framework is designed for implementing integrated public transport systems in a context where regulation is insufficient and multiple private operators are involved. We found that this context is quite common, particularly in developing countries.

The issue of public transport integration

Integration has been a recurring topic in transport policy. Preston (2012) traces back the policies for transport integration in the UK to 1947 and in Europe to 1952, but indicates that integration has proven hard to achieve in practice due to the difficulty of defining and operationalising integration. He also shows an emerging body of evidence of successful practices which have not yet been mainstreamed (Givoni and Banister 2010). Hull (2005) suggests that integration is a ladder with an ascending order of organisational difficulty. The ladder's lower steps refer to horizontal integration of different aspects of the transport system (information; services; fares and ticketing; and infrastructure provision, management and pricing). The ladder's higher steps refer to vertical integration with aspects of governance and environmental, economic and social policies. In this chapter we concentrate on the horizontal integration of different aspects of the public transport system – the first steps, which are still rare in developing countries.

The success of integration comes from the pursuit of synergies (May et al 2006). Synergy implies reinforcement to achieve system objectives: better operational performance and integrated ticketing result in higher user perception and increased ridership. An integrated public transport system approach usually involves physical, operational and fare integration (see, for example, Mendeville et al 2006). The concept has been extended to the system image (brand), user information and management institutions, among other topics (see a literature review on the topic including case studies by GIZ 2010).

Integration of public transport systems has been elusive in developing countries as a result of dispersed institutional frameworks. As indicated by Flores Dewey (2013), public transport in many developing countries is characterised by 'a quasi-informal network of privately owned transport operators historically responsible for satisfying most of the public's mobility needs with minimal intervention from the state'. In the developed world, the levels of integration vary greatly from country to country. For instance, German cities have had fully integrated public transport systems for over 20 years (GIZ 2010), whereas British cities, with the exception of London, face significant barriers to integration in part due to the model of competition that they have adopted (Preston 2012). Similarly, cities in the United States show wide variations, with many cities unable to achieve high levels of integration as a result of governance hurdles typical of transit systems crossing multiple jurisdictions (Miller 2004).

Planners and decision makers in several countries have used mass transit as a tool for advancing institutions and regulation towards full integration (Preston 2012; Halcrow Fox 2000). In the developing world in particular, BRT has been the seed for larger integrated public transport systems (Flores Dewey and Zegras 2012; Hidalgo and Carrigan 2010). Some cities like Cali and Bogotá in Colombia, and Leon in Mexico, have decided to integrate public transport around the initial BRT corridors, to achieve citywide integration gradually (Hidalgo and King 2014). Other cities, like Santiago de Chile, have advanced integration in a single step, labelled as a 'Big Bang'.

Both approaches (gradual and sudden) have advantages and disadvantages, which we explore in this chapter. Our central question is whether urban regions should adopt a gradual or a 'Big Bang' approach for regional public transport integration. We also explore the underlying question of how regional integration may be advanced in urban regions starting with dispersed, quasi-formal public transport.

Methodology

We use two case studies to describe the sudden (or 'Big Bang') and the gradual approaches to regional public transport integration, Santiago and Bogotá, respectively, and indicate advantages and disadvantages of the two approaches. We also draw from the results of Hidalgo and Velasquez (2015), presenting a high level financial model summarising capital and operational costs of different integration scenarios to indicate the costs to government and operators of these alternative approaches to allow us to make general policy recommendations. The approach has some limitations as it generalises two case studies from a high level financial model, nevertheless, we still believe the analysis allows planners and decision makers to consider alternative approaches.

We use this working definition of regional public transport integration: physical, operational, fare, image and institutional integration in a city or metropolitan area (Hidalgo 2009). By physical integration we mean the opportunity for exchange of passengers between different types of services and transport modes. Operational integration refers to coordination of schedules, so passengers can transfer smoothly from one service to another (May et al 2006).

Fare integration, arguably the most important integration element, allows passengers to use different services with the same payment method, such as an electronic contactless card, and, hopefully, the total cost of travel is less than where services are not integrated. Fare integration cuts barriers to transit access, encourages participation in monthly pass programmes, and potentially serves as a new revenue source for transit agencies (Goldman and Gorham 2006). Fare integration also enables more sophisticated network designs in which passengers can take advantage of very efficient trip legs while not paying significantly more for their fare. In the case of Santiago, the metro system saw its demand almost double on a single day when transfers became free of charge (Muñoz et al 2009).

Image integration results in a common presentation of the system in a way which indicates that all the different services belong to the same system (Carrigan et al 2011). Institutional integration involves the management agencies coordinating the activities, hopefully under a single authority for strategic planning and oversight (see Chapter Five). This authority should be able to coordinate all transport modes over the whole metropolitan area. Some of the best examples of adequate institutional arrangements may be Transport for London, Syndicat Transport Ile de France (Paris), Consorcio Regional de Transportes de Madrid, and the Singapore Land Transport Authority (Meakin 2004).

Case studies: Santiago and Bogotá

Santiago and Bogotá have some similarities in their demographic and socioeconomic characteristics. The Santiago Metropolitan Area has 6,300,000 inhabitants in 984 square kilometres (km²) (6,402 persons/km²) (INE 2012); Bogotá has 7,878,783 inhabitants in 307 km² (25,663 persons/km²) (DANE 2013). Santiago has a higher GDP per capita (US\$21,393 vs US\$15,891) (Brookings Institution 2012). When both cities started to integrate their public transport, the structure of their services was fairly similar, with persistent bus oversupply, competition on the road, and a prevalence of individual ownership of buses. Both cities embarked on citywide transport reforms as described below.

Transantiago, Santiago

Bus services in Santiago were regulated until 1979 (fares, frequencies, vehicle types, among other elements). From 1980 to 1990 the national government implemented a free-market approach, which improved frequency and coverage, but inflated the number of buses in the city, increasing traffic congestion and pollution (Darbera 1993; Fernández and Muñoz 2007). After 1990 regulation was reintroduced (Koprich 1994). Routes were assigned through bidding processes; fares were adjusted; and bus operators were encouraged to renew bus fleets. Nevertheless, the basic structure in which buses were individually owned prevailed, resulting in inefficiencies and bus oversupply. Motorisation continued as the median income increased and service quality remained low; at the same time accident rates, pollution and congestion increased.

To overcome these difficulties, the national government started planning for an integrated public transport system in 2002. The new system, Transantiago, was intended to advance bus operations and integrate surface services with metro, under government control and regulation. At the time of system planning (2004) the city had 8,000 buses, operated by 120 organisations (more than 3,000 micro-entrepreneurs) and three metro lines (Etcheberry, 2004). Transantiago's objective was to maintain and increase the use of public transport in the city, improve the quality of the service, and improve sustainability from social, economic and environmental perspectives without subsidising the system's operations.

The system was launched on 10 February 2007, before most of the infrastructure and information systems were completed. Sudden implementation of most components in a single day, which was dubbed the 'Big Bang', resulted in chaos in the city. Users had little information on how to use the system (see Chapter Thirteen), and faced long waits due to the lack of service caused by reduction in the bus fleet to 4,600 buses and poorly designed incentives to operate them (see Chapter Seven). The confused users turned away from the buses onto the metro, which they could now access with the same fare, was the only system component that had not changed, was the most clear and visible place in the city to charge the electronic fare card, and had a reputation for fast and reliable service. Metro had some available capacity but not enough to accommodate the large number of new users, generating overcrowding. There were also user protests demanding better bus services and some of the users started evading payment.

To address the chaos the authorities increased the fleet by 1,500 buses, added a total of 90 kilometres of busways by the end of 2011, and renegotiated the contracts to improve control of service delivery. The result was an increase in bus frequencies and a decrease in travel times (Muñoz et al 2014).

Transantiago has achieved several of its goals. The quality of the service has improved but not enough to win the hearts of its users, despite it being ranked as one of the most advanced in the region (Mery and Astudillo 2014). Positive impacts on externalities are evident, and public transport is now integrated, and more formalised, organised and regulated. However, fare evasion remains very high. Regarding the main goal of increasing the modal share of public transport, the plan could be considered a failure since public transport demand instead dropped at the beginning of Transantiago and then remained stable as motorisation rates grew.

Integrated public transport system (SITP), Bogotá

Before the introduction of Bogotá's BRT system in 2000, the city's public transit comprised 21,000 buses, microbuses and minibuses affiliated to 68 different private companies, with scarce regulation by the local authorities (Ardila 2007). As in Santiago, bus drivers rented the bus daily from the vehicle owner and derived their income from the number of passengers. This created competition on the streets, called 'the war of the penny'. The road battle resulted in street chaos, increased traffic and pollution, high accident rates and frequent but poor quality of service.

The main strategy to overcome the appalling conditions of public transport in the city was the implementation of a feeder trunk system, TransMilenio. The trunk services operate on full BRT corridors inspired by the Curitiba system (Lindau et al 2010) with very high capacity due to a combination of dedicated busways, large stations and buses, off-board ticketing, level boarding and a combination of local and express services (Hidalgo et al 2013a).

TransMilenio started operations with 14 kilometres of BRT plus feeder services in one terminal in the northwest part of the city. It was an instant success, with very high public acceptance and good performance indicators (Hidalgo et al 2013b). The original plan stipulated TransMilenio would cover 85% of the city, with a total of 388 kilometres, by 2016 (CONPES 2000). However, expansion proceeded much more slowly than initially planned. By 2014 only 84 kilometres of BRT were completed. The level of service declined, due to difficulties with maintenance of busways and stations, and very high demand during peak hours.

In 2006, as a response to the severity of service decline, the city approved a mobility master plan which included the creation of an integrated public transport system (SITP in Spanish). The main goal of the new system was to organise public transport in the city through fare, operational, image and institutional integration, without waiting for completion of the original TransMilenio plan. The SITP, which comprises seven BRT corridors and a network of bus routes operating in mixed traffic, aspires to provide citywide coverage and seamless transfers to all users. All the operations would be organised under seven zone concession contracts, added to the 14 contracts of the initial TransMilenio system, and one contract for fare collection and information management.

The main goal of SITP was to eliminate the 'war of the penny'. In addition, the city was expected to gain in terms of safety, security, congestion and reduced emissions. The bus fleet would be reduced to 12,000 (30% of the 2006 fleet). All the vehicles less than 10 years old would be kept while older vehicles — about 2,800 – would be replaced by new Euro IV emission standard buses. Users had little information on the system and public participation in system planning was scarce. In 2012 it was already evident that there were gaps between the system goals and the user expectations (Kash and Hidalgo 2014). Users wanted comfortable, frequent and fast services at a reasonable cost; but the system was designed for high occupancy, less frequent buses (to save on fleet size and operational costs) and user fares would be similar to the official fares. The plan ignored that many users, especially those on low incomes, seek and obtain fare discounts from the bus drivers in the original system (Kash and Hidalgo 2014).

SITP started operations in September 2012 (TransMilenio 2012) with a plan for a gradual implementation over 18 months. The SITP promised to be fully operational in the first quarter of 2014; however, by June 2014, the SITP had implemented only 88 new routes (20% of the goal), 1,713 new buses (16%), 1,023 bus stops with shelters (63%), 2,797 simple bus stops (45%), 5,967 bus drivers retained (out of 26,750) and 32 old routes discontinued (out of 508) (Cubillos-Murcia 2013). Full implementation is expected in 2015 as several elements have caused undue delays. Contractual difficulties have resulted in issues for the integration of two different fare collection systems (the TransMilenio and the new SITP fare collection systems).

Removing traditional bus operators has been difficult because of the lack of clarity regarding the advantages for them to move to the new system; creating costly compensation mechanisms (see Chapter Four). Two large operators, formed by individual vehicle owners, turned into large operation companies, have faced severe financial difficulties and have required government intervention to help them comply with the contractual requirements. In addition, users have complained about the lack of information on the new system, particularly on the mechanisms and locations for recharging fare cards and about the new routes (see more on user information in Chapter Thirteen). In some cases direct services have been replaced and passengers have rejected the transfer experience (see Chapter Twelve). Regarding motorisation, Bogotá has been fairly successful as the modal share of private modes has remained below 20% over the last 16 years (Hidalgo and King 2014).

Summary lessons from Santiago and Bogotá

Each city adopted a different implementation approach to their ambitious plans for citywide integration of public transport. The final goal was similar: to change the institutional setup of public transport provision, from semi-formal, semi-regulated, to formal and well regulated services covering the entire urban area. Santiago opted for a swift change citywide (the 'Big Bang'), while Bogotá adopted a gradual approach – first with TransMilenio and then with the SITP.

The gradual approach used by Bogotá was chosen as a response to the difficulties seen and faced in Santiago. Protests in Santiago resulted in a political crisis; the Transport Minister had to step down and President Bachelet's popularity declined sharply. Due to the chaotic and visible difficulties in 2007, Transantiago is still labelled as the 'worst public policy ever implemented in Chile' (EMOL 2012).

Despite the initial chaos and very negative public perception, Santiago was able to complete the promise of an integrated service citywide with positive impacts on air quality and road safety. The cost has been significantly higher than initially expected. Planners sought a sustainable transport system, but service requirements resulted in a larger fleet than planned, pushing fares up around 25% in real terms between 2007 and 2014. Also, government introduced a permanent subsidy that, after discounts in student fares and a portion of metro infrastructure, covers the 5% operational deficit of the system.

The gradual implementation in Bogotá has not caused similar chaos, but delays have resulted in high implementation costs, estimated around US$400 million (Cubillos Murcia 2013). The delays resulted from overoptimistic timetables and changes in implementation pace after changes in the local administration (following democratic elections). The sum of technical difficulties and lack of adequate information systems have resulted in a loss of faith in the system by its users.

The two experiences do not suggest a preferred approach to citywide integration; both approaches have positive and negative results (Table 3.1). Santiago's 'Big Bang' approach has achieved integration, at a higher cost than initially expected and with very poor user perceptions of the system. Bogotá has not yet completed the implementation of

Table 3.1: Impacts of 'Big Bang' (Santiago) and 'Gradual' (Bogotá) approaches to citywide transit integration

	Santiago – Transantiago 'Big Bang'	Bogotá – TransMilenio & SITP 'Gradual'
Integration goal	Achieved (full fare integration metro and buses citywide)	Yet to be completed (expected in 2015)
Estimated implementation costs	Costs increased (subsidy was required), approximately US$500 million per year (student fares, metro infrastructure and operational subsidy)	Cost increased, approximately US$400 million required during the implementation phase, long term costs unknown
Time to complete	Implementation was sudden; adaptation took 12 months and then gradual improvements	Four years (expected) from initial expectation of 1.5 years
User acceptance	Very low (protests and high fare evasion); metro ratings remain high	Medium for the SITP and declining for TransMilenio BRT system
Impact on motorisation	High; at the beginning the system triggered more car trips; since adjustments in the first year, demand for public transport has remained constant (declining modal share for public transport)	Low; public transport share has remained stable over 15 years while population and activity keep increasing
Resistance of incumbent operators	High: existing operators staged riots but after legal action, process moved forward including proactive incumbent companies and international investors	High at the beginning (with TransMilenio), but all incumbent companies and a large fraction of bus owners participated in the SITP system
Externalities	High reduction in air pollutant emissions and decrease in traffic incidents. The war of the penny disappeared	

a citywide integrated system; protracted implementation has resulted in higher costs and lukewarm user perception. Bogotá has been better at managing motorisation than Santiago; and both cities have reduced emissions and traffic incidents.

Given these experiences, as well as other gradual implementation approaches (see for example Cali, in Hidalgo and King 2014, and São Paulo, in Hidalgo 2009), a recommendation on what approach to take is elusive. Sudden integration may be beneficial from the systems' perspective: areas with high density generating surplus are tackled simultaneously with areas of low density requiring subsidies and a rapid process would prevent incumbents from adopting protective positions. Nevertheless, the high risks of managing a complex process invites decision makers to prefer a gradual approach, which in turn faces management hurdles, particularly due to changes in political priorities. The next section attempts to provide an analytical framework to help answer this question.

Implementation pathways

This section discusses five implementation pathways, namely 'Big Bang Theoretical', 'Big Bang Actual', 'Gradual Theoretical', 'Gradual Actual' and 'Optimised', based on scenarios of a simplified financial model, for a city of a similar size and public transport modal share to Santiago, as presented by Hidalgo and Velasquez (2015). Using scenarios with a large set of assumptions, fairly compelling results are shown (Table 3.2). Nevertheless a particular application may require much more sophisticated financial modelling than indicated there. Scenarios are presented below; the reader is referred to the original analysis for further details.

Big Bang Theoretical: This scenario assumes that all the new buses are incorporated and the old buses scrapped in the first year. It also assumes demand increasing at a similar rate to population growth and low fare evasion (0.5%). The number of buses in this scenario (5,693) is calculated to have a net present value equal to zero (internal rate of return 12%). In theory, the scenario is very efficient: it results in the minimum number of buses (hence minimum costs) and no operational subsidies (Table 3.2); but it may also result in lower quality of service: lack of geographical coverage or insufficient peak section/peak hour

Table 3.2: Financial comparison of integration scenarios

| | Big Bang | | Gradual | | |
	Theoretical	Actual	Theoretical	Actual	Optimised
Implementation period (years)	1	1	3	5	3
Present value of operator costs (million US$)*	$9,400	$7,400	$7,000	$5,900	$10,000
Internal rate of return operator (%)	12%	12%	13%	12%	12%
Present value of government support (million US$)*	$0	$3,800	$0	$1,600	$800
Realistic	No	Yes	No	Yes	Yes

*All present values are estimated over 10 years with a discount rate of 12%.

service. In addition, a citywide Big Bang approach is extremely risky since in an integrated system each of its components is crucial to fulfil its goals and too many unforeseen events could trigger the delay or failure of one of these components. As a result, a demand–supply mismatch could be expected, harming quality of service and increasing system costs. Also, a Big Bang approach is very difficult for users to comprehend, even after developing significant participation processes and providing vast amounts of information through multiple channels.

Big Bang Actual: This scenario is derived from the difficulties of implementing the Big Bang Theoretical scenario. Given low coverage and frequency, fleet increases from 5,693 to 7,500 buses (31% increase). In this case it is assumed that implementation difficulties result in high fare evasion (20%) and that demand does not increase year by year.

Gradual Theoretical: Given the difficulties experienced with Big Bang, other cities try to go gradual and plan for implementation over a three year period. The theoretical result can be even more attractive than the initial scenario as indicated in Table 3.2. We assume low fare evasion (0.5%) and a 2% annual growth in demand. The result is a positive net present value (internal rate of return 13%). This makes the gradual proposition very attractive, but actual implementation has often proven protracted (especially as a result of political cycles and changes in the local authorities). Also assuming constant demand growth may not be realistic.

Gradual Actual: Introducing adjustments to the optimistic assumptions of the previous scenario shows large changes in the financial results. Rather than three years, full implementation is assumed to be in five years; the required fleet is 7,500 buses; there is zero growth of the demand over time and a higher evasion level (5%). To keep the operators afloat it is necessary for the government budget to cover the costs of depots, scrapping and subsidising the operation. Under the scenario assumptions it is necessary for government to assign US$1,600 million in present value at 12% over a period of 10 years. It is less than in the Big Bang Actual scenario, but is still a significant figure.

Optimised Scenario: We vary the assumptions to create a scenario of implementation in which the existing bus fleet is used and gradually replaced by new buses, considering operational improvements. We consider an intermediate total fleet size of 6,750 buses, zero demand growth, an intermediate level of evasion (2.5%) and a lower cost of operations for the existing fleet (due to the fact that the cost of capital has been already paid back).

The result for the Optimised scenario is promising (Table 3.2). While an operational subsidy is still required, it is much smaller than those under the realistic Big Bang and Gradual scenarios. The net present value of government support is estimated at US$800 million, which includes the cost of depots and scrapping, which are not charged to the user fare. This type of scenario analysis depends greatly on the assumptions, but the relatively large differences in the results (Table 3.2) indicate that an intermediate way between the Big Bang theory and optimistic gradualism may be a feasible course of action.

The proposed path towards integration

This optimised scenario requires taking a path that guarantees achieving the final goal, which is full citywide fare integration, but gets there very gradually. Thus, we suggest starting with fare collection integration for all the existing fleet and services. However, none of the service routes change in this process so for the user this will seem just like a system with much more travel opportunities paying the same fare. However, one can expect that many users will change their routes and modes, for more convenient trips (as observed in São Paulo, see Hidalgo 2009, or in Santiago, see Muñoz et al 2009). This should significantly change the load profile of each service. Some of them will become overcrowded while others will see their demand drop, especially in certain segments. Then, with this new information, the operation should be gradually adjusted: changing frequencies or type of vehicle on some routes, eliminating or shortening others, or adding new ones (especially express services). For this to happen contracts should allow some level of flexibility (or all the operation may be under a public agency). If specific services are contracted, this flexibility may be difficult.

This approach reduces the uncertainty and allows the authority to improve services without reducing existing coverage. It may require extra vehicles for a short time when service is being adjusted, an additional investment in fare collection equipment and a very good planning team, empowered to make the required adjustments as soon as possible.

Implementing integrated systems

From the case studies and the high level financial modelling we note that the implementation of an integrated system requires the recognition of the complexity of the problem and advancing an adequate process. In this section we discuss five elements planners and decision makers may consider important during this process: asking what people want; designing a system that is adequate to the local conditions and financial constraints; advancing an effective implementation strategy; accompanying the process with effective communications; and adapting the system to meet users' expectations.

Asking people what they want

Planners often plan transport systems at the outset based on a prescribed process: demand estimation, supply design, financial feasibility evaluation, legal analysis and implementation. Public participation is not necessarily part of the process and may be seen as obstructive by technocrats. The risk is to provide a system that may improve air quality, road safety and overall city organisation, but may not necessarily meet users' expectations.

To reduce the gap between system objectives and user expectations it is important to ask the people first. Kash and Hidalgo (2014) devised a methodology to elicit user expectations using open ended questionnaires and a qualitative analysis. This type of approach may be combined with other types of surveys, social media and community events. Advancing these processes will not only improve the understanding of what is important for the potential users in the planning process, but will also increase the probability of making the system closer to the hearts of the users. In the end successful implementation and long term sustainability depends on that. (See Chapter Six for a more in-depth discussion of public involvement.)

Systems should not be static; they need to continue improving. According to TCRP (2014) and Portal (2003) there are two fundamental dimensions of quality: availability and general convenience, which includes comfort. Availability means providing a real travel option for the users. Comfort and convenience are related to user satisfaction relative to the alternatives, and are key to maintaining user acceptance or to regaining users' faith if it was damaged during the implementation process. (See Chapter Twelve for a deeper analysis of factors affecting user perception.)

Designing the system

An adaptive system seems a more sensible approach than a thorough transformation of service provision. As public transport is important to the people, particularly in developing cities, making profound changes is not only complex, but highly risky (as the experience of Santiago indicates). But a protracted implementation also carries difficulties, especially derived from lack of commitment of successive city administrations. An intermediate process, suggested in this chapter, entails an adaptive design in which direct services are gradually replaced by a combination of trunk (BRT and metro corridors) services, intermediate bus priority corridors (such as BHLS), feeder services and integration with non-motorised transport and emerging services like car and bike sharing. (See Chapter Fifteen for more discussion on network design.)

Placing too much faith in technical models ignores the fact that urban systems entail large uncertainty (Flyvbjerg 2007). While it is important to use available tools (demand and transport analysis models), more emphasis seems to be required on the evaluation of alternatives than prediction of long term results. Spending too much time and effort on the planning process may be counterproductive, as the window of opportunity may be lost if studies take too long. We suggest a balanced approach. The proposed approach for implementing integrated systems achieves this by letting the demand adapt to fare integration before services are completely transformed. Thus, planning models will be used intensively once the uncertainty faced by planners is lower.

Advancing an effective implementation strategy

Implementation requires objective driven management. Creating an independent and empowered implementation team has proven effective (Hidalgo and Carrigan 2009). The team must combine multiple professionals from different disciplines to tackle the administrative, legal, political, environmental, economic, financial and technical aspects of the project. Ideally the implementation team will evolve into an established institution. (See Chapter Five for more discussion of institutional policy arrangements.)

Effective communications

One of the key aspects in project success is advancing educational and media campaigns that allow the users and general public to know what the transformation entails, and to feel part of the whole process. Carrigan, Arpi and Weber (2011) prepared a creative guide to advance public transport systems based on multiple successful and failed processes. They recommend eight components of such an strategy: (1) brand and identity; (2) user education; (3) marketing campaigns; (4) user feedback systems; (5) internal communication; (6) user information systems; (7) public relations and external communications; and (8) online engagement.

The purpose of such strategies is to attract new users that currently use private transport such as cars and motorcycles; retain existing public transport users who might feel compelled to buy a private vehicle; and secure political and financial support from government officials. The authorities should resist the temptation of transmitting an image that will be impossible to achieve. User satisfaction is directly linked to expectations, creating too high expectations will quite likely prove fatal. (See Chapter Thirteen for more discussion on designing customer information systems.)

Conclusion

We documented the difficulties experienced by the Latin American cities of Santiago and Bogotá, as paradigmatic cases of Big Bang (very fast large scale implementation) and Gradual (protracted approach). Neither of these models adequately achieved the goal of an integrated system. While Santiago was able to complete its large scale integration project in a short time, it came at a very high cost for users (in the form of low quality services and enormous inconvenience) and the government (not only financially through unexpected subsidies that were institutionalised, but politically: the prestige of the national administration was severely affected).

In the other case, Bogotá is trying to complete a large scale integration of public transport services gradually, but difficulties with the financial model for incumbents (particularly former small owners of public transport vehicles) and lack of continuity in local policies is extending the timetable and undermining the confidence of the general public.

Based on the results of a high level financial model, we propose an intermediate approach in which integration starts with the fare collection system and citywide fare integration and then is adapted over time. Such an approach may require less financial support from the government than the alternatives (Big Bang or Gradual), but a high planning and institutional capacity is still necessary to advance the different components. We recognise that higher quality and formalised services may require subsidies. On top of the financial advantages, such an approach may be more acceptable for the transport users since it is less disruptive, while the operational changes would follow actual (not modelled) route selection fostered by the integrated fares. This may be less risky and unforeseen costs would be reduced as well.

References

Ardila, A. (2007) 'How public transportation's past is haunting its future in Bogota, Colombia', *Transportation Research Record: Journal of the Transportation Research Board*, 2038(1): 9–15.

Brookings Institution (2012) *Global Metro Monitor*, www.brookings. edu/research/interactives/global-metro-monitor-3

Carrigan, A., Arpi, E. and Weber, E. (2011) *From Here to There: A Creative Guide to Making Public Transport the Way to Go*, Washington, DC: EMBARQ.

CONPES (Consejo Nacional de Política Económica y Social) (2000) *Sistema de Servicio Público Urbano de Transporte Masivo de Pasajeros para la Ciudad de Santa Fé de Bogotá – Seguimiento*, Concejo Nacional de Política Económica y Social, Ministerio de Transporte y Departamento Nacional de Planeación, República de Colombia.

Cubillos Murcia, N. (2013) 'Implementación del Sitp le costará *$750.000 millones a los Bogota*nos', *La República, Economía, Infraestructura*, www. larepublica.co/infraestructura/implementaci%C3%B3n-del-sitp-le-costar%C3%A1-750000-millones-los-bogotanos_42046

DANE (Departamento Administrativo Nacional de Estadística) (2013) www.dane.gov.co/

Darbéra, R. (1993) 'Deregulation of urban transport in Chile: what have we learned in the decade 1979–1989?', *Transport Reviews*, 13(1): 45–59.

EMOL (El Mercurio On Line) (2012) 'Gobierno califica al Transantiago como "la peor política pública" aplicada en Chile', www.emol. com/noticias/nacional/2012/02/10/525683/gobierno–califica–al–transantiago–como–la–peor–politica–publica–aplicada–en–chile.html

Etcheberry, J. (2004) *Presentation, 21 Septiembre de 2004*, Ministro de Obras Públicas, Instituto de Ingenieros de Chile, Chile.

Fernandez, J.E. and Muñoz, J.C. (2007) 'Privatisation and deregulation of urban bus services: an analysis of fare evolution mechanisms', *Journal of Transport Economics and Policy*, 49: 25–49.

Flores Dewey, O.A. (2013) *Expanding Transportation Planning Capacity in Cities of the Global South: Public-private Collaboration and Conflict in Chile and Mexico*, Thesis, Department of Urban Studies and Planning, MIT, http://dspace.mit.edu/handle/1721.1/84427

Flores Dewey, O. and Zegras, P.C. (2012) 'The costs of inclusion: incorporating existing bus and paratransit operators into Mexico City's BRT', paper prepared for the *12th Conference on Advanced Systems for Public Transport,* July, Santiago, Chile.

Flyvbjerg, B. (2007) 'Cost overruns and demand shortfalls in urban rail and other infrastructure', *Transportation Planning and Technology,* 30(1): 9–30.

Givoni, M. and Banister, D. (eds) (2010)*Integrated Transport: From Policy to Practice* (1st edn), New York: Routledge.

GIZ (2010) *Public Transport Integration, Recommended Reading and Links,* GIZ Division 44 Water, Energy and Transport www.sutp.org/component/phocadownload/category/87–rl–pti?download=146:rl-pti-en

Goldman, T. and Gorham, R. (2006) 'Sustainable urban transport: four innovative directions', *Technology in Society,* 28(1): 261–273.

Halcrow Fox (2000) *Department for International Development: World Bank Urban Transport Strategy Review – Mass Rapid Transit in Developing Countries*, http://siteresources.worldbank.org/INTURBANTRANSPORT/Resources/uk_mass_transit_halcrow.pdf

Hidalgo, D. (2009) 'Citywide transit integration in a large city', *Transportation Research Record: Journal of the Transportation Research Board,* 2114(1): 19–27.

Hidalgo, D. and Carrigan, A. (2010) *Modernizing Public Transportation: Lessons Learned from Major Bus Improvements in Latin America and Asia*, Washington, DC: EMBARQ and The World Resources Institute.

Hidalgo, D. and King, R. (2014) 'Public transport integration in Bogotá and Cali, Colombia – facing transition from semi–deregulated services to full regulation citywide', *Research in Transportation Economics,* 48: 166–175.

Hidalgo, D. and Velásquez, J.M. (2015) 'Evaluating public transport integration scenarios', Working Paper, BRT Centre of Excellence, www.brt.cl/

Hidalgo, D., Lleras, G. and Hernández, E. (2013a) 'Methodology for calculating passenger capacity in bus rapid transit systems: application to the TransMilenio system in Bogotá, Colombia', *Research in Transportation Economics*, 39(1): 139–142.

Hidalgo, D., Pereira, L., Estupiñán, N. and Jiménez, P.L. (2013b) 'TransMilenio BRT system in Bogota, high performance and positive impact – main results of an ex-post evaluation', *Research in Transportation Economics,* 39(1): 133–138.

Hull, A. (2005) 'Integrated transport planning in the UK: From concept to reality', *Journal of Transport Geography,* 13(4): 318–328.

INE (Instituto Nacional de Estadísticas) (2012) *Censo 2012,* Instituto Nacional de Estadísticas – Chile, www.censo.cl/

Kash, G. and Hidalgo, D. (2014) 'The promise and challenges of integrating public transportation in Bogotá, Colombia', *Public Transport,* 6(1-2): 107–135.

Koprich, D.F. (1994) 'The modernization of Santiago's public transport: 1990–1992', *Transport Reviews,* 14(2): 167–185.

Lindau, L.A., Hidalgo, D. and Facchini, D. (2010) 'Curitiba, the cradle of bus rapid transit', *Built Environment,* 36(3): 274–282.

May, A.D., Kelly, C. and Shepherd, S. (2006) 'The principles of integration in urban transport strategies', *Transport Policy,* 13(4): 319–327.

Meakin, R. (2004) *Sustainable Transport: A Sourcebook for Policy-makers in Developing Cities. Module 1b Urban Transport Institutions; Sustainable Transport,* GIZ.

Mendeville, F., Cortes, P., Fuentes, R., Cantillana, A., Malbrán, H. and Barrientos, R. (2006) 'Infraestructura especializada para buses en Transantiago (Chile)', *Carreteras, Revista Técnica de la Asociacion Española de la Carretera,* 146: 103–111.

Mery, V. and Astudillo, D. (2014) 'Estudio evalúa al transporte público de Santiago como el mejor de Latinoamérica', *La Tercera,* www.latercera.com/noticia/nacional/2014/10/680-599800-9-estudio-evalua-al-transporte-publico-de-santiago-como-el-mejor-de-latinoamerica.shtml

Miller, M.A. (2004) *Assessment of Service Integration Practices for Public Transportation: Review of the Literature,* California Path Program, Institute of Transportation Studies, University of California, Berkeley.

Muñoz, J.C., Batarce, M. and Hidalgo, D. (2014) 'Transantiago, five years after its launch', *Research in Transportation Economics,* 48: 184–193.

Muñoz, J.C., Ortúzar, J. de D. and Gschwender A. (2009) 'Transantiago: the fall and rise of a radical public transport intervention', in W. Saleh and G. Sammer (eds) *Travel Demand Management and Road User Pricing: Success, Failure and Feasibility.* Farnham: Ashgate Publishing, 151–172.

Portal (2003) *Benchmarking and Quality Management in Public Transport,* EU Funded Urban Transport Research Projects.

Preston, J. (2012) *Integration for Seamless Transport*, Discussion Paper No. 2012-01, International Transport Forum, OECD (Organisation for Economic Co-operation and Development).

TCRP (Transit Cooperative Research Programme) (2014) *Report 165: Transit Capacity and Quality of Service Manual* (3rd edn), Washington, DC: Transportation Research Board.

TransMilenio (2012) *SITP Boletín 001: A partir del 29 de septiembre operan dos rutas urbanas del SITP*, www.sitp.gov.co/publicaciones/a_partir_del_29_de_septiembre_operan_dos_rutas_urbanas_del_sitp_boletin_001sitp_pub

FOUR

BRT as a tool for negotiated re-regulation

Onesimo Flores Dewey

Introduction

Government authorities in cities across the global south embrace disruptive technologies, such as Bus Rapid Transit (BRT) and system integration (see Chapter Three), not only as lower cost alternatives to heavy rail, but as mechanisms 'to establish effective regulatory control over largely privatized transit systems' (Hook 2005, p. 184; see also Corporación Andina de Fomento 2010, p. 24; Hidalgo and Huizenga 2013, p. 76). In many of these cities, loosely regulated consortia of vehicle owners are entrenched as the dominant suppliers of services, and their operations contribute to many urban ills, such as pollution, accidents, congestion, noise and petty crime. In turn, authorities are limited by severe budget constraints and by weak enforcement capacity. Where this combination arises, the adoption of new transit technologies like BRT can serve as a tool to restructure the existing industry and renegotiate agreements governing service. The growing appeal of these technologies is at least partly based on two critical assumptions: (1) that the savings resulting from the rationalisation of routes, vehicle fleets and administrative functions will suffice to cover costs currently ignored by existing private operators (such as timely vehicle maintenance, fleet replacement, cleaner fuels, driver training and benefits, taxes, parking and maintenance facilities); and (2), that most users care about transport externalities enough to accept at least some inconveniences (for example, having to make additional transfers, walk greater distances to stops, board more crowded buses or spend more time waiting).

While project planners frequently accept these assumptions, they usually relax initial expectations when confronted with cost and performance tradeoffs. In most cases, such as Cape Town and Johannesburg, South Africa, the potential disruption and cost implications of an envisioned citywide transit reform has constrained implementation to a few showcase corridors, leaving the vast majority of transit trips to be served with little change in the incumbent providers. In a few other cases, such as Leon, Mexico, Seoul, Korea and Santiago, Chile, authorities set out to rationalise the entire public transit network, but adjusted their aims once the financial cost to taxpayers and inconvenience to users became evident. Paradoxically, authorities rely on the continued involvement of at least some of the same private operators that they initially sought to replace, not only to defuse their opposition to implementation, but also as a means to lower the costs of formalisation and to reduce the strain on users. This may suggest that contrary to an often espoused idea held by planners and regulators, the resilience of a private, fragmented and loosely regulated transit industry may be a tool rather than an obstacle to reform efforts, and that a successful transition may depend more on securing their collaboration than their eviction.

To illustrate this point, this chapter explores public transit reform efforts in Mexico City and Santiago, Chile. This research draws from 74 interviews with consultants, government officials and private transport operators involved in reforms leading to the implementation of Metrobús, Mexico City's BRT system, and of Transantiago, the integrated system in the Chilean capital (for the full study, see Flores Dewey 2013). While these projects differ in scope, they were designed with the same purpose: to re-establish government authority over planning and regulation of public transit. For the purposes of this chapter I highlight how an evolving cycle of public–private conflict and collaboration led proponents to reframe the participation of incumbent private operators as a tool to be leveraged rather than as a malaise.

The chapter is organised as follows. First I describe the challenge of planning and regulating public transit in cities of the global south. Then I introduce the cases, describing how both cities arrived at a fragmented, loosely regulated and privatised public transit system, and how previous 'modernisation' plans gave way to an incremental, consensual approach to reform. Third, I briefly outline the implementation of Metrobús and Transantiago, highlighting that the success of these projects hinged more on the ability of government authorities to forge accountable partnerships with incumbent private operators and less on their efforts to optimise the existing system. I draw lessons from both cases and conclude with implications for policy makers.

The challenge of planning and regulating public transit in the global south

Private consortia of vehicle owners, who coordinate their operations but retain individual management over critical functions, are the main suppliers of public transportation services in many cities in the global south. These consortia usually fight in the streets for the right to supply services, and only later obtain permits from the state. Many of the rules governing vehicle standards and driver behaviour emerge from market demand and from negotiations within and between these organisations, rather than from government specifications. These consortia are often vilified as the cause of many problems that plague service provision, and authorities frequently embrace their replacement with corporatised, professionally managed and better capitalised firms as an implicit goal of BRT and system integration.

Their vehicles are often under-maintained and highly polluting. Their drivers compete curbside for passengers, and their reckless behaviour frequently causes accidents. Routes are usually long and circuitous, and tend to overlap in a few places, causing congestion. Operators like to stay as long as possible in high demand stops, and sometimes skip stops patronised by students or seniors if they are allowed to pay lower fares. They have no incentive to serve low density neighbourhoods or maintain agreed frequencies during the night or at weekends. Joint use infrastructure, such as terminals, is usually of very low quality.

The fragmented ownership structure of this industry complicates coordination and decision making, diffuses accountability, and bars operators from accessing long term, lower cost financing. Increased government intervention *is* justified. However, these private consortia of vehicle owners also make distinct contributions to mobility in cities of the global south. They provide ubiquitous service at a relatively affordable cost to a vast transit dependent population, demanding little if any financial contributions from the state. They are quite effective at managing fare evasion. They complement and expand the otherwise limited reach of more regulated transit modes, such as subways and public buses, and flexibly adapt to changes in the travel patterns of cities. As noted by Cervero and Golub (2007, p. 456), these transport operators 'are consummate gap fillers'. While observers point to the resilience of this fragmented, loosely regulated and privatised industry structure as evidence of the failure of government efforts to 'modernise' public transit service, their contribution cannot be ignored.

The desire of government officials to intervene is thus tempered by the need to retain the positive traits of the existing setup. Pragmatic authorities must ensure a proposed intervention will not (a) require substantial fare increases or large government subsidies, (b) leave a significant proportion of users with worse service, or (c) prove hard to monitor and police. Prior to innovations like BRT, affordable, high performing, feasible alternatives to the status quo seemed unavailable. Instead, local governments frequently adopted a hands-off approach, limiting regulatory oversight to a few easy to monitor variables (such as the price of fares and the maximum age of vehicles) and in some cases focusing their resources on sustaining publicly owned and operated modes, which serviced only a small proportion of total trips.

The combination of low labour costs, low labour conditions and relatively low capital investment required to participate ensures that a dense and frequent route network develops organically, reaching the farthest corners of these cities. Even when fully licensed small scale operators retain many of their 'informal' traits, government authorities have little incentive to enforce or tighten existing regulation, partly because the capacity of these operators to offer cheaper fares depends on avoiding costs internalised by 'formal' public or private competitors. Strict observance could put pressure on the level of fares, trigger demands for subsidies or drive them out of the market. In other words, the resilience of the apparently chaotic system may not be due to the lack of political commitment to improve surface transit, but a calculated consequence of authorities choosing not to meddle with a system that supplies minimally acceptable service without demanding much in the form of government subsidies.

The prevalence of overwhelmed, disempowered, under-resourced and perhaps even captured authorities can certainly help explain why governments in cities of the global south frequently seem incapable of making significant progress. However, the difficulties of balancing public and private goals in settings where administrative and financial limitations make private sector collaboration indispensable to sustain affordable and ubiquitous service across vast territories should not be underestimated.

Transportation planning bureaucracies develop distinct sensibilities as a result of constant interactions with these entrepreneurs. They learn to act strategically. They know that private operators will react to proposed improvements by threatening to stop services or by demanding a fare increase. What frequently ensues from such standoffs is rarely strong enforcement, but a period of negotiation in which both sides come to terms: a smaller fare increase or a small public subsidy in exchange for the adoption of a relaxed version of the proposed rules, such as allowances on the maximum age for vehicles. Given a history of such interactions, transportation ministry bureaucrats in these cities have much more developed skills for political negotiation than for technical transport planning, and the resulting service standards are better understood as a collection of ad hoc deals than as part of a coherent plan.

Further, the goal in these cities 'is much less that of how to maintain a public transport service as an alternative to the car through the deployment of subsidies and much more that of how to best serve the needs of the poor without subsidy' (Gwilliam 1997, p. 173). Of course, the needs of the poor have tended to be framed merely as maintaining a minimally acceptable transport alternative, while more ambitious social objectives such as improving air quality, lowering accident rates and mitigating congestion are jettisoned. Lacking financial and regulatory 'muscle' to establish more stringent policies, and lacking an affordable alternative capable of sustaining comparable levels of service – such as those promised by BRT – authorities in many cities of the global south tolerate (and even encourage) what Bayliss (2000) called 'the para-transit domain'.

The emergence of paratransit in Mexico City and Santiago, Chile

In the late 1970s, Mexican authorities coupled subway construction efforts with comprehensive plans to reorganise bus services across the city. When the private bus operators that dominated the industry resisted the proposed changes, the Mexican government revoked their permits and established a publicly owned bus company, *Ruta 100*, to replace them. This move was justified as part of a larger effort to 'optimise public services' (Departamento del Distrito Federal 1981), to 'provide clean and efficient service, operating at fixed stops, with good maintenance practices, an integrated fare policy, and well defined routes and hierarchies' (Angel Molinero, cited in Gakenheimer et al 2002, p. 240), and to 'coordinate service supply segments' (Figueroa 1990a, p. 227).

A parallel story can be found in Santiago. In 1968, the Chilean national government approved a comprehensive plan to build a subway system comprising five lines and 62 kilometres of track by 1980 (Ministerio de Obras Públicas y Transportes 1968; see also Morales 1988). This plan included a complete reorganisation of bus services in this city, with participation of Empresa de Transportes Colectivos del Estado (Collective Transport Company of the State) (ETCE), the publicly owned bus company. While full government takeover of the private bus industry was not deemed viable in Santiago, the relationship between the Chilean government and the private bus industry prior to the 1973 military coup was just as adversarial as it would be in Mexico (see Rojas 1976, pp. 111–15; Kaufman 1988, pp. 108, 200; Figueroa 1990b).

For a brief period of time, authorities in both cities felt empowered to force their plans on private operators. However, the dreams of leaving behind 'the ad-hockery of yesteryear' (Ward 1990, p. 110) were soon abandoned as their implementation increased the financial and administrative burden of sustaining affordable, high performing services. Authorities in Mexico City and Santiago adjusted their planning and regulatory strategy, shifting from comprehensive visioning to incremental muddling through, and their relationship with private operators evolved from adversarial to negotiated correspondence.

By the early 1980s Mexican authorities had successfully reorganised all bus routes in Mexico City into an 'orthogonal network' that complemented rather than competed against the subway, and implemented a multimodal ticket allowing users to transfer without paying a second fare. They extended the subway network in Mexico City to include five lines, 79.5 kilometres of track and 80 stations (Islas Rivera 2000, p.287), and operated *Ruta 100* with a fleet of 4,300 buses, slated to grow to 9,360 by 1988 (Legorreta 1995, p. 78). The Mexican government financed many of its capital investments with debt in foreign currency. However, when the price of oil dipped, a massive debt crisis plunged the country into an economic crisis (see Krauze 1999). This, combined with sustained conflict with the militant bus workers union, forced subsequent governments to slow down subway expansion and to limit financial support for *Ruta 100*. Fare-box revenue accounted for 14% of *Ruta 100* expenditures, while subsidies (local and national) were slashed by 38% in real terms between 1984 and 1988 (Islas Rivera 2000, p. 273).

Plans to increase, renew and maintain *Ruta 100*'s bus fleet were continuously postponed, and 'more than 3,000 buses were soon out of service, stopped by technical difficulties like insufficient spare parts and workshops, and obsolete tools to repair them' (Lajous et al 1988). With few new vehicles to replace those that routinely broke down, in 1988 only 52% of the total fleet remained in operating conditions, down from 76% in 1982 (Islas Rivera 2000, p. 263). As a result, the 'high frequency' bus routes in the orthogonal network remained high frequency only in name.

As the Mexican federal government reduced financial support to Mexico City's transit system, local authorities found little alternative to increasing fares and taking on more debt. The subway became the largest debt producing item in Mexico City's budget, siphoning resources not only from *Ruta 100* but also from other urgent priorities, despite serving a small percentage of total trips. In 1987 public transportation outlays accounted for 37.8% of total city budget (including own revenues and federal transfers) (González 1988, p. 81). This massive burden, combined with previous debt incurred to build the subway, widen roads and renew the bus fleet of *Ruta 100*, was 'fiscally devastating' (Davis 1994, p. 249). To keep the city moving, authorities turned a blind eye to *taxis colectivos* (collective taxis) that offered unauthorised services to disgruntled *Ruta 100* users. Mexico City officials are on record defending this unofficial policy as early as December 1983, merely two years after the creation of *Ruta 100*. As they explained, they had to 'tolerate' these services, 'since the insufficiency of service made them necessary' (Lajous et al 1988). Mexico City authorities began 'regularising' collective taxis in 1985, not only granting them permits, but also using 'the instruments of control and regulation at their disposal with some flexibility, with the aim of not interfering in the growth of the supply of this now indispensable service' (Islas Rivera 2000, p. 309).

Official estimates for the metropolitan area of Mexico note a surge of collective taxis, from 4,530 in 1979 to 98,000 in 1988 (Legorreta 1995, p. 162). The organic emergence of a dense collective taxi network rendered comprehensive government plans mute. Government capacity to set standards also weakened, as 'the make, model and physical conditions of the vehicles did not matter ... the only condition was getting approval from an organization leader to join' (López Zaldívar 1997, p. 81). With competition growing, fewer users patronised *Ruta 100* and subway services. Pressure to increase subsidies or raise fares mounted. Before *Ruta 100* was dissolved in 1995, collective taxi operators served 54% of all vehicular trips in Mexico City's metropolitan area, while the share for subway and public buses decreased to 16% and 10% respectively (González and Vidrio 2011, p. 30). The dream of a multimodal, integrated, publicly provided public transport system was gone.

A somewhat similar process took place in Santiago. Construction of the first two lines of the subway began in 1969 and 1973 respectively, just as authorities announced their intention to strengthen ETCE and tighten regulation on private buses. Taking advantage of a closed vehicle and spare parts import market, the Chilean government attempted to maintain a firm grip over this industry, even amidst a severe fiscal crisis and a polarised political environment. Regulatory disputes in this period were embedded in the larger political conflict that led to the military coup of 1973. Public transport operators in Santiago unsurprisingly joined the national transportation lobby in denouncing President Allende for seeking 'to liquidate all privately owned means of transport, beginning in Aysén and ending in Arica' (Alexander 1978, p. 303). Whether or not this was Allende's long term goal, his government was never able to develop ETCE into a viable alternative. By the time of the military coup, the public bus company operated with an insufficient fleet of 710 buses, approximately 35% of which was routinely out of service waiting for repairs and spare parts (see González Pino and Fontaine Talavera 1997, p. 645; Coeymans et al 2008). Despite the high hopes of government authorities, this period was characterised by 'chronic shortage and low quality of services' (Estache and Gómez-Lobo 2005, p. 140). Similar to Mexico City, the underperformance of the publicly owned bus company was masked by the emergence of approximately 2,500 buses and 1,500 'taxi-buses', operated by hundreds of small entrepreneurs, each owning an average of 1.5 vehicles (Fernández and Muñoz 2007, p. 28).

The dominance of private operators grew after the military coup. The combination of rising costs and ideological distaste for government-run endeavours led the regime to cancel the surface transport component from the 1968 transport plan, and to slow down subway construction. The first 8 kilometres of Line 1 did not open to the public until 1975. That year, subway construction costs absorbed 29.7% of the total national public works budget, and similar proportions would persist in subsequent years (Morales 1988). Line 2 would not open until 1978, and Line 3 was postponed indefinitely after the 1982 devaluation of the Chilean peso (Collier and Sater 1996, p. 371). In turn, ETCE's budget was slashed, and the company dissolved in 1981. The military regime had opted for surface transport deregulation. By December 1979, anyone with a suitable vehicle could enter the market, design routes and determine service frequencies. After 1983, private operators were free to set their own fares. This process was paired with Pinochet's land reform, which opened vast swaths of farmland to development. Massive *comunas* (neighbourhoods) emerged in Santiago's periphery (Oppenheim 1999, pp. 152–5), and private taxi-bus entrepreneurs swiftly covered their transportation needs. According to one of them, "the only rigidity of the system was applying to operate a service, practically always authorised. Absolutely nothing else. Controls over service quality were non–existent, and there was no supervision over our operations. Everything was non-regulated" (Personal interview, Simón Dosque, 15 June 2012).

Between 1977 and 1990, the number of buses and taxi-buses in Santiago surged from 4,760 to 12,678 (Paredes et al 2001),[1] while passenger demand remained relatively stable at an average of 1,050 million passenger trips per year (Fernandez 1994). The transport sector employed approximately 35,000 people, including drivers, mechanics and route assistants. The transit network expanded from 80 bus routes in 1979 to 110 *plus* 325 variants in 1989 (Darbera 1993), and the average route length increased 28% from 1976 to 1984 (Morales 1988, p. 38). The network became so dense that it was possible to hail a bus after waiting an average of only 3 to 4 minutes on any corner (Estache and Gómez-Lobo 2005, p. 142; Figueroa 2013, p. 90), and to reach most major destinations without transferring to a different bus. Average vehicle capacity utilisation was reduced to 55% for buses and to 32% for the smaller taxi-buses (Cruz 2001). This meant that while the service became less profitable for individual vehicle owners, users were much more likely to find a seat. And perhaps most importantly, these noticeable improvements were mostly achieved without government subsidies.

Similar to Mexico City, this expansion in service supply came at a significant social cost. Buses expelled large amounts of exhaust fumes due to poor quality fuel and inadequate maintenance. By 1989 no visitor could fail to notice 'that the Santiago smog was one of the most noxious in the western hemisphere – caused partly by the sheer rise in the number of automobiles (approaching 1.5 million in Chile by the mid 1990s) and partly by an uncontrolled increase in bus traffic' (Collier and Sater 1996, p. 375). Transport modes became alternatives rather than complements, and little was left from the integrated system envisioned in 1968. Relatively wealthier *santiaguinos* paid a premium to board half empty subway cars, while on the surface hundreds of buses fought curbside for passengers. At peak hours roughly 1,500 buses and taxi-buses ran over the same corridor served by Line 1 of the Santiago subway (Alvarez 1991). This resulted in a grossly underutilised and expensive subway system, and in surging air pollution, congestion and accident rates on the surface.

New political coalitions promising to increase government oversight of public services were elected to government in Chile in 1990 and in Mexico City in 1997, but the existing setup proved resilient. Despite stated goals, democratically elected authorities realised that they could not dispense with the existing operators if they hoped to meet the mobility needs of the population. Financial resources were scarce, particularly in Mexico City, where local authorities could no longer count on the financial backing of the federal government. Regulatory and planning capacities in the bureaucracy were weak, especially in Chile, where the Transport Ministry had been hollowed out by a dictatorship committed to a small government. And to complicate matters, well capitalised professional private companies were not willing to enter these markets without substantial financial guarantees and regulatory protection from unauthorised competition. Several public tenders (1996 and 1998) organised in Mexico City failed to elicit sufficient interest and were eventually cancelled. Similarly, public tenders to award route based contracts organised in Santiago (1991, 1993 and 1998) only attracted bids from groups already in control of those routes, and functioned merely as instruments to negotiate marginal improvements and regularise their operations.

Most of the problems planners sought to solve failed to elicit a sense of public urgency. Pollution levels, accident rates and congestion certainly preoccupied the residents of these cities, but few mobilised politically against the existing system since it met most transport needs at an affordable price. In contrast, bus operator organisations resisting change were well organised, and offered a base of political support for amicable governments. They supplied foot soldiers and financial support for political campaigns. For these reasons, and at least until reforms like BRT and integrated systems emerged as alternatives capable of lowering the cost of sustaining high quality services, government authorities in Mexico City and Santiago settled for an incremental, non-disruptive, mostly negotiated reform strategy, which nonetheless yielded important gains, given the context.

While the transit industry in both cities was fragmented in ownership, it developed a conveniently hierarchical organisation. In both cities, vehicle owners controlling a particular route coalesced as organisations ('rutas' in Mexico City, and 'líneas' in Santiago) with elected leaders. These organisations accepted new members and expanded their territorial reach, colonising new routes. Interactions (and clashes) with rival organisations and with government authorities were frequent. To strengthen their position vis-à-vis rivals and to better represent their interests when dealing with authorities, route-based organisations gradually joined a handful of citywide consortia, which had their own leadership structure ('cúpulas' in Mexico city, and 'federaciones' in Chile).

Vehicle owners looked to the leaders of route organisations for guidance, and these in turn followed the leaders of citywide consortia offering the most direct access to the highest level of government decision making. These leaders, such as Demetrio Marinakis in Santiago and Francisco Aguirre in Mexico City, went around regulators and negotiated transportation policy directly with transportation ministers, mayors and even presidents. As one operator summed up when interviewed, "leaders could fix things". They could boycott regulatory proposals, but could also enforce discipline among the rank and file of their organisations, violently if necessary. They often instigated citywide strikes, heightening the tone of their rhetoric to maintain credence within their organisations. They 'sized up' incoming transport ministers, reminding them that in the event of conflict, they were more likely to prevail. Despite the growing power of these actors, government officials recognised their value as conduits to govern an otherwise chaotic system, and learned to work with them to gradually enhance service (or, admittedly, to pursue less legitimate goals). Over time, regulators built trusted relationships with some of these leaders, which would greatly facilitate policy making. By brokering agreements with only a few of such individuals, government authorities could implement policies that would be observed and accepted by thousands of vehicle owners.

It was through this process of negotiated re-regulation that the fleet service in these cities gradually homogenised, phasing out older, more polluting and smaller vehicles and introducing microbuses with catalytic converters. In Mexico City, the microbus (capacity 20–25 passengers) replaced the combi (capacity 8–10 passengers) as the most prevalent public transport vehicle. Taxi-buses in Santiago were similarly phased out and banned from entering downtown areas. Public transit vehicles were painted in the same colour (yellow in Santiago, green and grey in Mexico City). Authorities in both cities also succeeded in limiting the number of vehicles offering service.

Mexico City authorities finally curtailed the exponential growth of the authorised public transit vehicle fleet (which remained roughly at 42,000 between 1988 and 1994, falling to approximately 30,000 by 2000), and banned vehicles coming from neighbouring municipalities from picking up passengers outside subway stations. In Santiago, private operators agreed to take thousands of excess vehicles out of service. The number of public transit vehicles in this city fell from a peak of 13,353 in 1991 to 8,179 in 2001. As a result, capacity utilisation rates in Santiago doubled, and the number of passengers transported per day per bus rose from 268 to 523 (Díaz et al 2004). Between 1988 and 1997, the average age of the buses running in Santiago fell by more than half, from 12.1 to 5.1 years (Paredes et al 2001, p. 37). Of course, all of these programmes depended on the support of consortia leaders and kept the market closed to outside interests. They also required significant government subsidies. In the case of Mexico City, the government underwrote loans to purchase the new microbuses and, starting in 1998, offered a subsidy of approximately US$10,000 for each replaced vehicle. In Santiago, the national government established a fund in 1991 to purchase and destroy older buses and taxi-buses. Owners were paid between US$2,669 and US$7,710 dollars per vehicle, depending on the age. Redundant workers were also compensated.

To some observers, no 'modernisation' could take place without breaking the corporative and clientelistic control that consortia leaders held over the industry (for example, see Navarro Benítez 1993). However the governments of these cities depended on these hierarchical structures to maintain their ability to govern the system.

Authorities in Mexico City and Santiago bridged the recurring problem of insufficient financial and regulatory capacity by empowering consortium leaders. Only when these leaders chose not to cooperate and/or when the government had little to give as compensation, did the alternative of conflict and system reinvention gain traction. Through frequent interactions, authorities learned to recognise whom among their counterparts were trustworthy, whose voice really carried weight within the trade, and who had the willingness to explore alternative business models. Perhaps the most important outcome of this interim period is the strengthening of negotiating capacity within transportation ministry bureaucracies, and the development of relations of reciprocity with key leaders with real authority over the industry *and* willing to experiment with alternative business models.

Government authorities learned to advance their agenda by leveraging the limited resources under their control. This often implied empowering, rather than fighting, consortia leaders. As Germán Correa, former Transport Minister of Chile, confided, "I gave more information to the leader that most supported my modernization plans than the rest. I knew he was trying to convince the most backward members of his organization of the positive aspects of the policies pursued by the government" (Personal interview, 13 June 2012). Armando Quintero, former Transport Minister of Mexico City, similarly reflected "the government chose to strengthen leaders [of bus operator organisations] who supported its policies by helping [these leaders] solve the problems of [their] organisation's members. When facing someone that was not friendly to the administration, we withdrew our support, and his leadership would suffer" (Personal interview, 21 May 2014). The implication is that leaders of organisations who did not support government policies had significantly more difficulties to personally access transport regulators, which significantly limited their capacity to effectively represent their organisation's members. This may strike some readers as suggestive of undesirable practices. However, it was precisely through such strategic interactions that authorities laid the groundwork for, and later sustained, ambitious projects like Metrobús and Transantiago.

Metrobús and Transantiago: new chapters in a history of negotiated re-regulation

Metrobús is Mexico City's BRT system, was inaugurated in 2005. It began operation with a single, 20-kilometre corridor, and has since expanded to form the longest BRT network in Latin America, with six lines and 125 kilometres. Current Mexico City authorities recently announced several additional lines, including one on Avenida Reforma. A key feature of Metrobús is that many of the small entrepreneurs that used to operate in these corridors became stockholders of the companies that own and operate BRT vehicles. As former Transport Minister Luis Ruiz explained, "we were not displacing them, not taking advantage of them. Our quest was to find a healthy equilibrium, which allowed them to participate on good terms. That was our commitment. The data, the financial runs, everything was structured to honour this commitment" (Personal interview, 1 March 2011). To participate, operators agreed to void their individual permits, and to scrap their old vehicles under a 'cash for clunkers' programme. The money from this governmental programme and a small contribution from each entrepreneur were pooled as down-payment for a fleet of new, articulated buses. Participants became stockholders of new companies that own the buses and hold a 10-year concession to operate BRT services (for details see Flores Dewey and Zegras 2012).

Transantiago is Santiago's integrated transport system, inaugurated in 2007. It includes all bus services in Santiago, the subway and an electronic fare collection mechanism. Its implementation included renewal of a significant share of the bus fleet and a reorganisation of the route network to eliminate redundancies and foster multimodal coordination (for a good summary see Muñoz and Gschwender 2008). The project implied significant industry transition. The Chilean government declared void all pre-existing *route* based contracts, and awarded 14 new *area* based contracts (five 'trunk' and nine 'feeder' areas) via public tender. While government authorities initially designed this process to be competitive, in the end the terms of the tender were adjusted to ensure most contracts would be won by firms owned by pre-existing operator consortia. The characteristics of the required fleet, the length of the contracts, and the capital required to participate were strategically fixed to 'nudge' new entrants towards the two larger contracts in play (Flores Dewey 2013, pp. 249–56). Further, the project originally called for the exit of 4,575 of the 7,279 buses that operated in Santiago previous to the reform,[2] but these terms were revised soon after implementation to allow the majority of these vehicles back into the system.

Why would proponents of projects that seek industry 'modernisation' turn to the arguably 'pre-modern' organisations of vehicle owners for help? Why would they craft frameworks that almost guaranteed their inclusion and permanence? This approach seems inconsistent with the optimisation assumptions that often justify bus improvement reforms like BRT and integrated systems (explained in Chapter Three). The efficiencies achieved by these reforms, promoters frequently argue, will be sufficient to finance not only the purchase of new rolling stock and facilities, but also to internalise the 'costs of formalisation', such as payment of taxes, fixed driver salaries, social security contributions, and so on. The transition away from the existing system is therefore typically framed as a battle against the inefficient, the informal and the 'pre-modern'. However, the cases of both Metrobús and Transantiago fail to back this narrative. In fact, a closer look suggests that the long term success of these reform efforts hinged on making use of previous investments in vehicles and human capital, on flexibly adapting the projects to nurture private cooperation, and on strategically leveraging 'inefficient' redundancies provided by incumbent operators.

Authorities in Mexico City guaranteed incumbent operator inclusion as they implemented their new BRT system. This decision was partly driven by sheer political calculation. Officials understood the whole industry was watching, and that the operators' experience in the maiden BRT corridors would reverberate in future negotiations with transport operator consortia across the city, BRT related or not. For good reason, officials saw little point in straining their relationship with the only organisations seemingly capable of serving the mobility needs of residents *across the city* without operational subsidies.

To secure existing operator inclusion, authorities willingly forwent economic efficiencies that presumably could result from inviting better capitalised, more professional operators to compete for Metrobús contracts. The flawed legacy of *Ruta 100* made local authorities humble in their goals, and strategic in their interactions. They realised that the underlying goal of the Metrobús project was not merely optimising transport supply within a few corridors, but demonstrating to the leaders of thousands of private transport operators elsewhere in the city that bus reform does not mean displacement. Even more important than improving the transportation experience of users of BRT corridors was signalling to the industry that it made good business sense to cooperate with future reform plans. For this reason, the first Metrobús operating contracts guaranteed each stockholder a monthly earning similar to their income as an individual operator. All stockholders would receive a payment akin to a salary, informally treated as a fixed cost, independent of any profits achieved by the firm through efficiencies. Claudia Sheinbaum, the minister spearheading this project stated the government's logic succinctly: "You can't offer a business opportunity to anyone by saying 'you'll earn less than what you earn today'" (Personal interview, 11 March 2011).

This approach, if sustained as the system expands, risks negating the optimisation benefits of BRT. However, by casting BRT as a pathway to modernisation with limited displacement, Mexico City authorities have fostered a transformative momentum that led to the voluntary substitution of over 900 underutilised, individually owned microbuses for 230 articulated, company owned buses. It also facilitated the transition from several quasi-informal organisations into nine more professional and accountable private firms. The Metrobús 'model' has even expanded to non-BRT corridors, as several route organisations have voluntarily corporatised, rationalised and professionalised their services and renewed their vehicle fleets. Service has improved along the affected corridors, with reduced travel times and safer and more reliable trips. And perhaps most importantly, the public sector's role as regulator of public transport has been clarified and reasserted.

In the case of Santiago, project promoters eventually realised that their original aim of replacing existing operators and eliminating redundant routes came at significant performance and financial cost. Potential new entrants to the market were mostly interested in select high demand corridors – the 'crown jewels' – and demanded significant revenue guarantees to participate. Further, officials concluded "a system that relied only on new buses essentially meant doubling the fare" (Personal interview, Guillermo Díaz, former Under Minister of Transport, 4 August 2012). To hedge against the risk of not attracting competitive bids, and to craft a financial model that would not trigger a significant fare increase or a subsidy requirement, the participation of many of the incumbent operators re-emerged as a necessity. As confided by Javier Etcheberry, the Chilean Transport Minister at the time, "I did not side with those that wanted to replace existing operators with new, modern firms, that would magically do everything right ... To keep all types of costs manageable, we needed their participation" (Personal interview, 12 July 2012). The process was not initially amicable. Chilean authorities first had to demonstrate their commitment to the project by prosecuting consortia leaders that instigated a two-day citywide strike and street blockade in opposition to Transantiago. And while the tendering rules extended an opportunity for most operators to remain in the system, this did not imply authorities would overlook noncompliance with new regulations. While most pre-existing consortia of vehicle owners succeeded in winning a Transantiago contract after the bidding process, only those that performed with excellence have survived and thrived. Several organisations tried to operate under the same business practices of the past, with leaders extracting rents rather than promoting productivity, and went bankrupt soon after. Others thrived by creating a hybrid model, making vehicle owners responsible for vehicle maintenance but holding them accountable by centralising labour relations, accounting and planning functions (for details, see Flores Dewey 2013, pp. 321–3).

The importance of the pre-existing industry to the survival of Transantiago became clearest as the February 2007 launch date approached. Funding limits placed on the project by the central government resulted in postponing planned bus priority infrastructure, such as 25 kilometres of BRT corridors, 70 kilometres of repaved streets, 35 transfer stations, and two large multimodal stations (see MOPTT 2004). Without this infrastructure, average wait times originally estimated by technical advisors Fernández y de Cea at 4–5 minutes would be at best 10–12 minutes, and average capacity utilisation would surpass 90% (see Briones 2009, p. 77 and Quijada et al 2007). These well-regarded technical advisors concluded that without a larger vehicle fleet and redundant routes, trips would take longer and be more uncomfortable relative to the previous system. With only weeks before the launch, authorities realised that Transantiago needed 1,405 buses more than required in the signed contracts. This, among other implementation flaws, soon transformed Transantiago into a major political crisis.

Authorities scrambled for months for a solution. Incorporating *new* vehicles was not a viable option, as it would add significant pressure to a rapidly sprawling financial deficit. Also, buses needed to be equipped with fare validating devices, which rapidly turned into a bottleneck, as these devices were not readily available. The best vehicles from the previous system had already been cherry-picked by the incumbent consortia, leaving only older, more polluting vehicles as a possibility. Authorities relaxed their original requirements to keep the new system afloat. They renegotiated the new contracts, allowing companies to 'temporarily' introduce these lower quality vehicles lacking fare-validating equipment to their fleets. According to the new terms, 'requisites about bus ownership, terminals, average vehicle age and emissions, will only be verified and enforced when and if the Ministry establishes their permanent incorporation to the fleet' (MTT 2007, pp. 4–5). Authorities also realised that without the promised infrastructure, users walked long distances or were forced to make an unacceptable number of inconvenient transfers. In order to appease growing protests, they modified the new network, prolonging routes and making them more circuitous. Not only did this mean softening the optimisation principles that originally guided the design of Transantiago, but it also required requesting companies to increase fleet sizes again to maintain acceptable frequencies. Service improved notably, but *only* after reincorporating the vast majority of the buses that had participated in the previous system, and after committing a monthly subsidy that soon reached US$50 million per month, and that remains to this day.[3]

Conclusion

These case studies exemplify practical challenges faced by authorities seeking to restructure surface urban transport. 'Modernising' an existing system – even through reforms like BRT – is a balancing act, where visions of a planned and regulated system must be weighed against the need to retain desirable financial, social and operational attributes of the status quo. Striking this equilibrium forces governments to choose between committing significant financial resources and tolerating lower service standards to encourage private sector compliance. The cases included in this paper demonstrate how authorities temper their espoused views and self-interestedly attempt to foster collaboration with incumbent operators. The reason is that governments in many cities of the global south depend on a vibrant local private sector to meet the transportation needs of the public, particularly in the context of resource constraints, weak institutions, and demographic and spatial urban growth. Seen jointly, the Santiago and Mexico City cases suggest that gradual and negotiated re-regulation continues to be the key, even amidst the implicit promises of innovations like BRT and integrated systems.

These cases also suggest, however, that as the aims of public authorities extend from simply preserving a minimally acceptable public transit option for the masses, towards also advancing broader social objectives such as improving air quality, mitigating congestion and reducing accident rates, the public–private relationship becomes more demanding and contentious. The pursuit of such wider goals requires costly investment, more intrusive government oversight, optimised operations and more efficient business models. They also require the active involvement of citizens (see Chapter Six). Even if at the end only a fraction of the stated goals are likely to be achieved, shrewd political strategy is necessary to move reform efforts forward. When committed to large, transformative goals, government officials need to be much more creative and proactive, not only to lay out technically and financially viable plans, but also to ensure private operators come to the table to discuss them constructively, aware that cooperation is in their own relatively autonomous interest.

Such conditions need to be manufactured. They require the existence of a 'table' – an institutionalised forum where public and private actors discuss terms and make binding commitments, and through which trust, defined as the willingness to take increasing risks on behalf of the reform project, and fear, defined as the awareness that non-collaboration is costly, can develop. Such a 'table' has long existed in Transportation Ministries of cities featuring loosely regulated, private and fragmented transit industries, like Santiago and Mexico City. Often dismissed as corrupt and inefficient, officials working in these agencies know how to negotiate marginal improvements to the existing service, choose and test their counterparts, and selectively influence their behaviour with targeted subsidies or other 'informal' enticements. These negotiations are often dismissed as a black box, inconsistent with reputable transportation planning practice. However, anyone truly interested in restructuring public transport in the global south should focus their attention on deeply understanding this cycle of conflict and collaboration. Why does it happen? How can authorities reduce the time required to build trust? How can they identify and strengthen credible partners? Which features of proposed interventions lead to more accountable and durable partnerships?

The implementation of BRT and integrated systems represents a viable path to restructuring public transit in the global south, but only to the extent that they help strengthen public–private collaboration and deliver more acceptable equilibria of cost and performance. It is this possibility that makes bus improvement reforms like BRT exciting and worthy of continued research.

Notes

[1] Figures reflecting the size of the bus fleet in Santiago vary, but trends are consistent. Other sources are Figueroa (1990b), Díaz et al (2004), and Estache and Gómez-Lobo (2005).

[2] These figures are from documents shared by Isabel Guzmán, Coordinator of the Transantiago project in 2006.

[3] To be fair, a substantial share of this subsidy is now used to cover student fare discounts and pay for one-third of the investment needed for new metro lines.

References

Alexander, R.J. (1978) *The Tragedy of Chile, Contributions in Political Science*, Westport, CT: Greenwood Press.

Alvarez, D. (1991) 'La Florida en unos minutos', *APSI* [Agencia Publicitaria de Servicios Informativos], 397: 58–60.

Bayliss, D. (2000) 'Review of urban public transport competition', Topic Review Paper prepared for the World Bank Urban Transport Strategy Review, London: Halcrow Fox.

Briones, I. (2009) 'Transantiago: un problema de información', *Estudios Públicos*, 116(Spring): 37–91.

Cervero, R. and Golub, A. (2007) 'Informal transport: a global perspective', *Transport Policy*, 14(6): 445–457. doi: 10.1016/j.tranpol.2007.04.011

Coeymans, J.E., Allard, P., Basso, L., Covarrubias, A.L., de Cea, J., de Grange, L., Doña, J.E., Fernández, José Enrique, Fernández, Rodrigo, Hutt, Gloria, Munizaga, Marcela and Muñoz, Juan Carlos (2008) *Diagnóstico, análisis y recomendaciones sobre el desarrollo del transporte público en Santiago*, Santiago: MTT.

Collier, S. and Sater, W.F. (1996) *A history of Chile, 1808–2002*, second edition. Cambridge Latin American Studies series, 82. Cambridge: Cambridge University Press.

Corporación Andina de Fomento (2010) *Observatorio de movilidad urbana para América Latina*, edited by E. Vasconcellos, Bogotá, Colombia: CAF.

Cruz, C. (2001) *Transporte urbano para un nuevo Santiago*, Santiago, Chile: Ministerio de Transportes y Telecomunicaciones.

Darbera, R. (1993) 'Deregulation of urban transport in Chile: what have we learned in the decade 1979–1989?', *Transport Reviews*, 13(1): 45–59.

Díaz, G., Lobo, A.G. and Velasco, A. (2004) 'Micros en Santiago: de enemigo público a servicio público', *Estudios Públicos*, 96(Spring): 5–48.

Davis, D.E. (1994) *Urban Leviathan: Mexico City in the Twentieth Century*, Philadelphia: Temple University Press.

Departamento del Distrito Federal (1981) 'Resolución mediante la cual se revocan todas las concesiones otorgadas con anterioridad a particulares para la prestación del servicio público de transporte urbano de pasajeros en autobuses en el Distrito Federal', Mexico City: Diario Oficial de la Federación, 30 September.

Estache, A. and Gómez-Lobo, A. (2005) 'Limits to competition in urban bus services in developing countries', *Transport Reviews*, 25(2): 139–158.

Fernández, D. (1994) 'The modernization of Santiago's public transport: 1990–1992', *Transport Reviews*, 14(2): 167–185.

Fernández, J.E. and Muñoz, J.C. (2007) 'Privatisation and deregulation of urban bus services: an analysis of fare evolution mechanisms', *Journal of Transport Economics and Policy*, 41(1): 25–49.

Figueroa, O. (1990a) 'La evolución de las políticas de transporte urbano colectivo en la Ciudad de México entre 1965 y 1988', *Estudios Demográficos y Urbanos*, 5(2): 221–235.

Figueroa, O. (1990b) 'La desregulación del transporte colectivo en Santiago: balance de diez años', *EURE Review*, XVI(49): 23–32.

Figueroa, O. (2013) 'Four decades of changing transport policy in Santiago, Chile', *Research in Transportation Economics*, 40(1): 87–95.

Flores Dewey, O. (2013) 'Expanding transportation planning capacity in cities of the global south: public–private conflict and collaboration in Chile and Mexico' (PhD dissertation), Cambridge, MA: Massachusetts Institute of Technology. Available at: http://dspace.mit.edu/handle/1721.1/84427

Flores Dewey, O. and Zegras, P.C. (2012) 'The costs of inclusion: incorporating existing bus and paratransit operators into Mexico City's BRT', paper prepared for the *12th Conference on Advanced Systems for Public Transport,* July, Santiago, Chile.

Gakenheimer, R., Molina, L.T., Sussman, J., Zegras, C., Howitt, A., Makler, J., Lacy, R., Slott, R., Villegas, A., Molina, M.J. and Sánchez, S. (2002) 'The MCMA transportation system: mobility and air pollution', in L.T. Molina and M.J. Molina (eds) *Air Quality in the Mexico Megacity: An Integrated Assessment*, Dordrecht: Kluwer Academic Publishers.

González, A. and Vidrio, M. (2011) *Evaluacion del diseño e instrumentación de la política de transporte público colectivo de pasajeros en el Distrito Federal,* Mexico City: PUEC-UNAM.

González, O. (1988) 'El metro de la Ciudad de Mexico', *Revista Eure,* XIV(42): 63–82.

González Pino, M. and Talavera, A.F. (1997) *Los mil días de Allende, Vol. 1,* Santiago de Chile: Centro de Estudios Públicos.

Gwilliam, K.M. (1997) 'Can developing countries learn from our mistakes?', *Annals of the American Academy of Political and Social Science,* 553: 168–179.

Hidalgo, D. and Huizenga, C. (2013) 'Implementation of sustainable urban transport in Latin America', *Research in Transportation Economics,* 40(1): 66–77.

Hook, W. (2005) 'Institutional and regulatory options for Bus Rapid Transit in developing countries: lessons from international experience', *Transportation Research Record: Journal of the Transportation Research Board,* 1939(1): 184–191.

Islas Rivera, V. (2000) *Llegando tarde al compromiso: la crisis del transporte en la Ciudad de México,* México City: El Colegio de México, Centro de Estudios Demográficos y de Desarrollo Urbano, Programa sobre Ciencia, Tecnología y Desarrollo.

Kaufman, E. (1988) *Crisis in Allende's Chile: New Perspectives,* New York: Praeger.

Krauze, E. (1999) *El sexenio de López Portillo,* Mexico City: Clío.

Lajous, A., Beltrán, U., Cárdenas, E. and Portilla, S. (1988) *Las Razones y las obras: El gobierno de Miguel de la Madrid, crónica del sexenio 1982–1988* (1st edn), Coleccion Tezontle, Mexico City: Presidencia de la República, Unidad de la Crónica Presidencial, Fondo de Cultura Económica, www.mmh.org.mx/nav/node/166.

Legorreta, J. (1995) *Transporte y contaminación en la Ciudad de México* (2nd edn), Mexico City: Centro de Ecología y Desarrollo.

López Zaldívar, I. (1997) *Nadie está satisfecho: Los derroteros del transporte público concesionado en el D.F. Mexico,* Mexico City: UTEHA Acomex.

Ministerio de Obras Públicas y Transportes (1968) *Estudio del Sistema de Transporte Metropolitano de Santiago de Chile.* Santiago: Ministerio de Obras Públicas y Transportes.

Morales, Sergio (1988) 'El Metro de Santiago', *Revista Eure,* XIV(42): 19–41.

MOPTT (Ministerio de Obras Públicas, Transportes y Telecomunicaciones) (2004) *Prospecto de Inversión, Transantiago Súbete,* Santiago, Chile.

MTT (Ministerio de Transportes y Telecomunicaciones) (2007) 'Modificación de contrato de concesión de uso de vías de la Ciudad de Santiago para la prestación de servicios urbanos de transporte público remunerado de pasajeros mediante buses – Su Bus Chile', Santiago, 9 February.

Muñoz, J.C. and Gschwender, A. (2008) 'Transantiago: a tale of two cities', *Research in Transportation Economics*, 22(1): 45–53.

Navarro Benítez, Bernardo (1993) 'Dialéctica contradictoria del transporte en el Valle de México', in A. Bassols and G. González (eds) *Area Metropolitana del Valle de México*, Mexico City: Departamento del Distrito Federal/UNAM.

Oppenheim, L.H. (1999) *Politics in Chile: Socialism, Authoritarianism, and Market Democracy* (2nd edn), Boulder, CO: Westview Press.

Paredes, R., Sánchez, J.M. and Sanhueza, R. (2001) *Participación Privada en Proyectos de Infraestructura y Determinantes de los Arreglos Contractuales Observados: El Caso de Chile*, Washington, DC: Interamerican Development Bank.

Quijada, R., Tirachini, A., Henríquez, R. and Hurtubia, R. (2007) *Investigación al Transantiago: Sistematización de declaraciones hechas ante la Comisión Investigadora, resumen de contenidos de los principales informes técnicos, información de documentos públicos adicionales y comentarios críticos*, Santiago, http://ciperchile.cl/wp-content/uploads/Reporte_Transantiago.pdf.

Rojas, R. (1976) *The Murder of Allende and the End of the Chilean Way to Socialism* (1st edn), New York: Harper & Row.

Ward, P. (1990) *Mexico City: The Production and Reproduction of an Urban Environment*, London: Belhaven.

FIVE

Institutional design and regulatory frameworks

Rosário Macário, Maria Spandou and Luis Neves Filipe

Introduction: the complexity of urban environments

Urban areas have been recognised for decades as complex systems (North 1990), akin to organic structures (Simon 1997). Both comparisons aptly acknowledge the dynamics and interactions at play in cities and metropolitan areas, complexities which tend to scale up with population and size. Transportation is a key component of the development and management of increasingly large and complex cities because it provides the means to move goods and people along mobility chains. Ideal urban mobility systems provide access to activities as quickly and conveniently as possible.

High quality urban transport generally requires the participation of multiple organisations across different elements of the system. While political entities define objectives to be achieved, planning agencies design the system (for example, operations, infrastructure). Different types of operators oversee vehicle operation, infrastructure, traffic management, parking, and so on. Regulating agencies establish and monitor market rules; other agencies undertake the enforcement role. The success of transportation interventions, especially the implementation of Bus Rapid Transit (BRT) services, depends on all these entities acting in concert, and this is where complexity is born. Lack of consistency between these entities will inevitably lead the system to underperformance or even to collapse. Each time a new economic agent (or actor) enters the system, new interactions develop, either with other private agents, or with public entities, or both, and readjustments are needed. As noted by Macário (2011), in mobility systems the mutual dependence between actors requires the system to have structural consistency. It is this consistency that provides alignment between operational results and planning objectives and between these and the strategic vision of the city.

The implementation of a BRT system is always done in cities where an urban mobility system already exists, however informal. Implementation can often be disruptive to this pre-existing system, whether due to lack of intermodal adjustment, inequitable situations between new and incumbent operators, and conflicts over tariffs, or to gaps in information systems. Examples of such disruptions are reported in several cities, such as Bogotá, Santiago, Léon and Mexico City (Flores and Zegras 2012; Kash and Hidalgo 2012) and are also addressed in Chapter Four of this book.

Despite these examples, BRT implementation does not need to be disruptive. The implementation of BRT can in fact be a transformative opportunity to smooth mobility chains by integrating walking, cycling and motorised modes, enhance overall quality of urban spaces, and improve the accessibility of those spaces. It is indeed a change process (that is, a new actor entering the system) that requires an adjustment (for example, ensuring complementarity between modes) so that consistency is preserved in the city and the urban mobility system.

This chapter suggests which institutional and policy elements, given the context of urban complexity, should be addressed in the BRT implementation process and their relevance for the performance of the mobility system. It presents an interdisciplinary framework that defines the spectrum of institutional, organisational and regulatory settings and performance interactions that support the best combination of policy measures to pave the way for successful introduction of BRT into established mobility systems.

The discussion first considers the need for structural consistency at the strategic, tactical and operational decision and planning levels for BRT implementation, and how decision making at these three levels can be conducted to facilitate effective design of institutional and regulatory frameworks. The subsequent section addresses the relation between institutions, regulatory frameworks, organisations and system performance. The fifth section builds on the process of implementing policy measures. The sixth section presents an evaluation framework for policy measures. The last section offers conclusions.

Structural consistency for BRT implementation

Institutions have been defined in various ways (Williamson 2000; Aoki 2001). We adopt the prevailing definition by North, defining institutions as 'the rules of the game in a society, or, the humanly devised constraints that shape human interaction. In consequence they structure incentives in human exchange, whether political, social or economic' (1990, p. 3). It is worth noting the distinction he establishes between institutions, identified as rules of the game, and their players. Furthermore, he defines these players as organisations, 'groups of individuals bound by a common purpose to achieve an objective ... a major role of institutions in a society is to reduce uncertainty by establishing a stable (not necessarily efficient) structure to human interaction' (North 1990, p. 6). However, it is also this interaction structure that enables the creation of constraints in the relation between actors, largely through codes of conduct, norms for social and institutional behaviour and conventions. Literature usually divides these rules into formal and informal constraints. Formal rules include political (and legal) rules, economic rules and contracts (North 1990, p. 46).

Three levels of decision making are relevant for transit interventions (Viegas and Macário 1998):

- At the strategic level, long term concerns include defining: general mobility policy, market shares, desired cost recovery, geographic areas of intervention, levels of accessibility for different areas at different times, the social service character of services to be provided and the resources allocated to the provision of those services, and the degree of intermodality provided by the system. In brief, the strategic level provides a long term vision of where we want the system to be, or what we want to achieve. The introduction of a BRT system affects the overall structure of the mobility system, and the roles and interactions between agents and modes, as well as the levels of accessibility provided to the citizen, which is the most critical element of performance. Level of accessibility is clearly a political decision. The strategic level is where targets of public intervention measures are formulated for application by the other decision levels.

- At the tactical level, the main concerns are medium term decisions related to the configuration of system supply, individual service definition to match the different market segments and detailed specifications, such as type of vehicle, routes, timetables, different fares. In brief, the tactical level provides the plan that defines how the system must be organised to reach the strategic goals. These changes are especially visible through the organisation of the intermodal network, dividing the roles of trunk and feeder services. The relation with land use is also consolidated at this level of planning and decision making, allowing transit-oriented development (see Chapter Ten). Contracts with operators are an important element at this decision level (see Chapter Seven).

- At the operational level, concerns are mostly short term and related to management of services and resources. This is the level where the service is carried out, but also where operational performance monitoring is undertaken, providing feedback on whether the strategic vision and plan produced adequate results, outcomes and impacts over time. Depending on the degree of integration of activities, all these functions can be allocated to one or several entities, in different ways as defined in the regulatory framework.

Structural consistency entails a horizontal and a vertical dimension. Horizontal consistency concerns actions of different agents[1] with a recognised common purpose, which, in the case of urban transportation, is providing mobility and accessibility. Vertical consistency seems to be more complex and involves the following attributes, linking the three levels described above:

- System coherence is an attribute given by the alignment of decoupled objectives down through the different decision levels (Viegas and Macário 1998), ensuring that strategic level goals will be well translated into adequate objectives for the tactical and operational levels. Coherence requires, for example, that BRT have a well specified role within the overall network of the mobility system.

- System efficiency represents how well basic resources (that is, the means that were allocated through strategic decisions) are translated into service outcomes. Efficiency can be achieved through specifications made at the tactical level, and further down into consumption units, leading to efficient performance at the operational level. Such efficiency is often considered the ultimate objective for the implementation of a BRT system. However, efficiency must be balanced with other objectives, namely accessibility of the urban space, which provides the need to integrate with other modes and services.

- Accountability constitutes a main instrument for management control, and is provided through a double feedback loop between field results and strategic decisions, assessing where strategic objectives require revision in face of changes in the current system and future scenarios, and assessing whether tactical choices and operational and control decisions made are in fact providing the desired results and impacts.

A typical illustration of lack of vertical consistency is found in cities where sustainable development and priority for public transport, such as through BRT investments, are stated as strategic objectives, but at the tactical level, parking is promoted in the city centre, effectively favouring private motor cars. This example reveals a lack of capacity to perceive systemic cause–effect relations within the urban mobility system. Obviously mistakes are not intentional; they frequently result from policy interventions with other purposes that have not been properly articulated (for example, parking measures are often the result of a second best congestion control policy). The same problem can also occur due to horizontal inconsistency through divergent action of the two agencies in charge of transit and parking planning.

Disregarding the multidimensional character of policy objectives and neglecting the need to articulate policy measures is also a frequent remote cause of unfavourable performance outcomes. The cross-effects between horizontal and vertical specialisation in a mobility system leads to a complex network of organisations, mirroring the complexity of the urban environment, with different degrees and forms of interaction. Ideally, all of these organisations should be linked by a set of performance objectives. Given this tight network of interactions, fitness of purpose and action is important, indeed a truly indispensable attribute that can only be assured by a continuous adjustment and articulation of institutional and organisational design, policies and regulatory interventions. Structured organisational networks emerge from these cross-effects and demand that each mode and service have a specific role. For BRT to play an effective mass transit role, vertical coherence is required across strategic decisions to adopt BRT, tactical planning to ensure intermodal coordination and appropriate feeder services, and efficient operational control.

Objectives and policies for urban mobility devised by authorities worldwide reveal a high degree of variation (ICCR 2002). In many urban areas, the urban mobility concept is not yet perceived as a systemic one and in others, despite evidence of having understood the concept, it has not been implemented using an integrated organisational and management structure covering all the decision levels (Macário 2006). In fact, even in the latter cases, the most common situation is a scattered distribution of responsibilities to several entities, sometimes backed up by an integrated policy document, but often without any provision ensuring that decision processes actually reflect integration purposes (ICCR 2002). Even where the systemic character of urban mobility is recognised, there is often a misfit between the existing institutional design (principles, rules, and so on) and the organisational requirements for the management of such a complex system. This results in non-articulated policies, deviations from the original assignments for diverse reasons, and inconsistencies that negatively impact on the overall performance of the transport system.

The configuration of the transportation network, despite requiring a high level of technological knowledge, is influenced by economic, financial, social and political factors that have to be reconciled due to conflicting goals that emerge from public pressure. Some factors and popular opinions weigh more than others, depending on the context and time, and often override strategic decisions (Macário 2005). Accountability plays an important role in inducing performance improvements and ensuring clear relationships with stakeholders (Käyhkö 2011)

Institutions, organisations and decision making

As stated by Parsons (1995, p. 536), 'policy-making takes place in conditions of uncertainty, flux, unpredictability and variation'. That is, the analysis of policy design and implementation requires the understanding of a multi-agent complex system, often with multiple levels of government, different interests and overlapping authority and decision making. Several authors note that in policy analysis we ought to apply percolation theory by studying the properties of the overall institutional and organisational setting instead of looking only at its single elements (Capra et al 2007). Planning and decision processes reach the complete network of organisations. The policy making approach and the underlying policy process are instrumental for the success of any efficient intervention. Irrespective of institutional and governance settings, policy intervention requires acting simultaneously in different domains (Macário 2011). This is best achieved through smart combinations of measures, or 'policy packages'. The package building process often means 'cherry picking' components governed by different public sector areas to assemble the required measures, calling for negotiation, coordinated action and co-decision whenever hierarchies are absent (Macário 2000).

The role that decision making plays in this problem cannot be ignored. Decision making processes define the flow of interactions between agents – the 'flux' conditions of policy making. While the governance structure underlying a decision making process (for example, centralisation, state intervention) is a fundamental characteristic that can influence and, to a certain extent, dictate the features of the strategic decision making process (interest group influence, conflict resolution, knowledge and information availability, and so on), the process also extends to tactical and operational levels (Macário 2005, 2011).

The quality of the decision making process is a challenge in most countries and can face serious hurdles where transparency of processes has not yet been achieved. Good policy initiatives can be seriously jeopardised by politicians aiming to influence decision making processes. Despite the amount of knowledge in this domain, there is also strong empirical evidence (for example, Sha 2006) that policy making in most parts of the world has been more about 'muddling through' rather than a process in which social or policy sciences have had an influential part to play (Parsons 1995). The aim of developing more effective and efficient policy packages in a sector like transport is to try to enhance quality of governance and public interventions. As a more detailed discussion of political structures is beyond the scope of this chapter, we adopt a broad definition of governance, appropriate for both the developed and developing world (Kaufmann et al 1985, p. 3) as 'the traditions and institutions by which authority in a country is exercised'. This definition includes the process of selecting, monitoring and replacing governments and their sector representatives, delegating effective power, governmental capacity to effectively formulate and implement sound policies, and citizens' recognition and trust in their capacity.

The understanding of interests and behaviours of the various private economic agents and public entities, as well as their roles and position of power, at the different decision levels, is fundamental for a successful implementation process. Moreover, any BRT implementation requires managing change. Institutional stability is an important parameter when facing transition processes, like integration of informal services. This is the case of paratransit processes in many developing countries where the services have been reformulated to feed consolidated trunk services, such as BRT systems (see Chapter Three for a detailed discussion).

Justice is also an important consideration in decision making. Rothstein (1954, in Rawls 2005, p. 12) asserts that 'specifying political procedures that can be motivated by norms of justice will give policy outcomes a greater chance of being beneficially and morally just'. This is a highly relevant regulatory aspect of how economic agents are given the opportunity to access and explore markets, and their relations with competitors, incumbents and especially users. This element of justice is materialised on one hand, in relation to incumbents or newcomers, through fair competition rules enabling market initiative as well as through the terms of contractual agreements, and on the other hand by access conditions (physical and financial) offered to the users. It should be noted that operator ownership (public or private) by itself is only relevant whenever state aid to publicly owned operators is practised, representing a form of biasing the market.

Furubotn and Richter (2000) state that an institutional equilibrium representing a complete institutional arrangement implies that an original set of formal rules remains in active use despite the fact that a supplementary set of informal rules and enforcement characteristics has emerged to complete the total structure. They also identify two states of institutional equilibrium: (i) when new informal rules evolve to reach a stable endpoint without destroying the original formal framework, and (ii) after disturbance of an initial institutional equilibrium a new equilibrium will be reached (Furubotn and Richter 2000). These states reflect the frequency of change in rules and norms indicated in Williamson (2000) and shown in Table 5.1, and these

Table 5.1: Economics of institutions and change processes

Transport framework setting	Functional description (according to Williamson 2000)	Objective (purpose)	Frequency of change (according to Williamson 2000)
Contextual	**Emdeddedness:** Informal institutions, customs, traditions, norms, religion	Nonspecific	More than 100 years
Institutional (i.e. rules, principles and norms)	**Institutional environment:** Formal rules of the game	Obtain an institutional environment that enables correct market stimulus	Between 10 and 100 years
Strategic decision and planning level	**Governance:** The game play. Aligning governance structures with transactions	Obtain a correct governance structure	Between 1 and 10 years
Tactical decision and planning level	**Resource allocation:** Prices, quantities, incentives, and so on	Obtain correct marginal conditions	Continuous

varying timescales in turn suggest that whenever a BRT system is adopted, not all of the institutional and organisational setting is immediately taken into account. Later adjustments must be made to ensure vertical consistency with the higher level institutions (such as constitutions, framework laws). The main pitfall we observe in the field is the introduction of the BRT system without aligning the institutional environment and governance structures with the new reality and new interactions.

Furubotn and Richter (2000) also argue that the general perception of institutional change is that it results from the institutional instability caused by bad institutional design, but in reality this instability might emerge as a consequence of economic growth/decline, or shortage of financial means, or even technical, intellectual and cultural shifts (Furubotn and Richter 2000). North (1992, p. 6) identified five propositions on institutional change (below in italics, with commentary following):

- *The continuous interaction between institutions and organisations in the economic setting of scarcity, and hence competition, is the key to institutional change.* Institutions are the rules of the game and organisations are the players. Organisations' ultimate objective is survival, whether profit maximisation for a firm or re-election for a political party, because all live in a world of scarce resources and consequently a competitive environment.

- *Competition forces organisations to continually invest in skills and knowledge to survive. The kinds of skills and knowledge individuals and their organisations acquire will shape evolving perceptions about opportunities and hence choices that will incrementally alter institutions.* The ubiquity of competition in the overall economy induces organisations to invest in improving their efficiency. If competition is neutralised organisations have no incentive to invest and in consequence rapid change is not induced.

- *The institutional framework provides the incentives that dictate the kinds of skills and knowledge perceived to have the maximum payoff.* If the highest rate of return in a city is from informal transport it is to be expected that organisations will invest in skills and resources to provide better informal transport and neglect any investment in other modes of transport.

- *Perceptions are derived from the mental constructs of the players.* In a world of 'complete' information about the consequences of choice, individuals with the same utility function will converge to a common equilibrium. However, as information is imperfect, divergence occurs.

- *The economies of scope, complementarities and network externalities of an institutional matrix make institutional change overwhelmingly incremental and path dependent.* Large scale change generates much opposition and benefits can only overcome costs under a situation of gridlock.

These propositions should guide the implementation of a BRT system, enhancing the techniques of managing and controlling the policy making process that leads to institutional change and should also guide public engagement. Tolerance to change, or public acceptability, shapes the process of implementation of a new mode. We have observed the problem of resistance to change in all BRT implementation processes, such as in Santiago or Lima, where large protests have characterised the implementation process due to the perception of unfair treatment, towards local residents, citizens or incumbent operators.

Regulation and organisational structures versus performance

Defining the roles of principals and agents

Organisations are agents that play a main role in the institutional relations discussed in previous sections. In urban mobility systems there are several levels of nested principal–agent relations:[2] between the government (principal)[3] and the regulator (agent); between the regulator (principal) and the organising authorities (agent), which, in the case of decentralised governance, can be a municipality or an established consortia of municipalities, which is often the case in metropolitan areas; and between each organising authority (principal) and the several agents acting at the operational level, where the operation of BRT systems is visible, and where the individual citizen, who can choose between transport facilities, is also one of those agents. Moreover, even the operator of transport services can play the role of principal whenever part or the totality of the services is subcontracted.

Previous research consolidated the evidence that it is important to have a clear definition of an agent's roles in line with the strategic, tactical and operational decision levels described above (Macário 1998). Feedback between the three decision levels ensures the vertical consistency of the system. A wide diversity of elements exist that can affect the operation of a BRT system. Several of this volume's other chapters are dedicated to these elements. Among the main difficulties observed (Macário 2014), we see strategic decisions advanced at the tactical level without being explicitly adopted and reflected with transparency and rigour in the corresponding allocation of resources and the respective limits. Moreover, fragmentation of authorities by mode has led to a clear dilution of responsibility and lack of coherence, and this is a situation found all too often in BRT systems.

Changing the paradigm implies, first and foremost, accepting that the territorial definition of the urban transport system requires the use of variable institutional geometry so that the interactions between land use, multimodal mobility and energy use can be effectively leveraged. Institutional design should thus be guided by a network logic. This will enable provision of service related (and associated decision making) continuity in the administrative and jurisdictional setting of the organisation holding responsibility for the territorial management of urban mobility.

As noted by Macário (2005), before any discussion of formal or informal interactions between organisations and their institutional environment, it is worth understanding the meaning of interdependence[4] and where we should look for it while observing the dynamics of an urban mobility system. Information flow materialises transactions and interactions between organisations. The nature and scope of interaction depends on roles and missions and occurs in such a way that each organisation depends on the other for pursuing its own goals, although not necessarily in a subordinate role. All changes may hinder established interests and conflicts arising can be prospectively solved through incentive mechanisms or reactively solved through negotiation.

Barriers

Barriers to coordinated decisions might lead to adjustment of resources, as a way of mitigating opposition. According to Rouwendal et al (2003), a 'barrier' is a factor, typically exogenous, that limits the decision maker's ability to implement the most desired policy. These barriers are sometimes imposed by external factors not controlled by the body willing to implement a given measure or policy. Among other reasons, the driver for adjustment can lie on the interaction with other government bodies and resulting lack of consensus and/or lack of public acceptance. There were several examples of this during the creation of Transantiago in Santiago, Chile, where government and city bodies were coordinated by the Ministry for Public Works and Transport in developing the system, but were unable to reach consensus in some areas of the project (for example, land use, integration with private transport modes) during its development.

Furthermore, the transport system is affected by the behavioural, social and cultural background of its various actors (or stakeholders, or agents). According to their ability to influence decision making, these players accept, promote, cooperate, participate and learn from one another, or not, causing barriers (that is, constraints) to the implementation of decisions, objectives, strategies and policy measures. Several background studies have exhaustively identified and assessed the transport related barriers and constraints for different types of cities (Crain & Associates, Inc and Pacific Consulting Group 1996; Rietveld and Stough 2005; TIS.PT 2003 (MARETOPE); May et al 2006; NEA 2006 (METEOR); Rayle 2008), but the absence of a comprehensive framework clarifying roles and interactions between organisations and their institutional context was not found in the literature. Building upon previous work, Spandou and Macário (2010) identified a set of barriers with two main blocks, one organisational and another behavioural, including social and cultural, which are further divided into a number of subcategories, as presented in Figure 5.1. The identification of these barriers when implementing a BRT system facilitates design of policy measures that can overcome these constraints.

The institutional and organisational setting and the barriers to decision making interfere directly with overall system performance. An important claim of this work is that the cause of poor performance does not always lie in the individual behaviour of an agent but, instead, is the malfunction of the system itself. The purpose of developing a performance management framework is primarily the identification of the parameters that lead to a system functioning worse than anticipated – that is, risk factors – while another aspect of performance management is the motivation of stakeholders towards better performance, through incentive or penalty initiatives – that is, inducement factors. Furthermore, accountability is also directly related to performance management and is gaining more importance as an effective inducement factor (Käyhkö 2011).

Performance management

According to Poister (2003), over time useful performance measures facilitate the actual improvement in an organisation or a programme. In

Figure 5.1: Barrier classification and interrelations

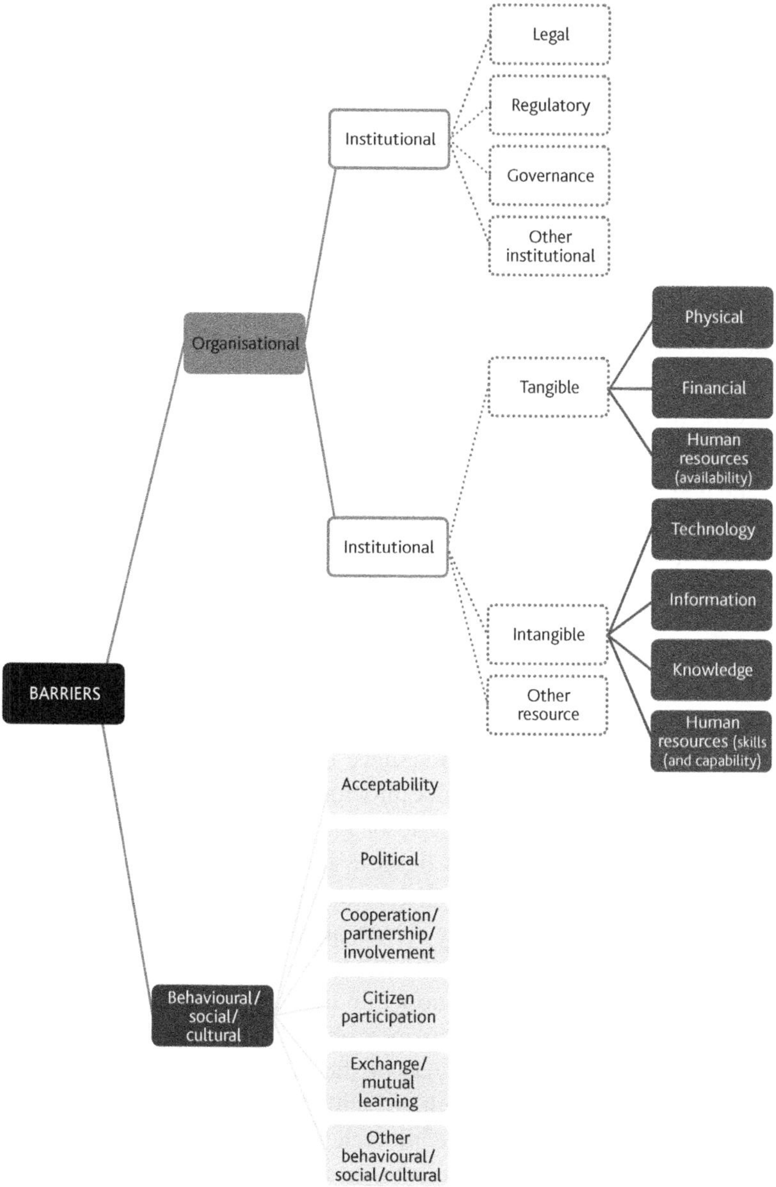

Source: Spandou and Macário (2010)

order to be useful, a measurement system must be designed to serve the needs of the particular management process it is intended to support. A framework that relates institutional and organisational structure and performance, and which has been the traditional approach in industrial organisations for years, is the structure–conduct–performance (SCP) paradigm, which assumes a stable, causal relationship between the structure of an industry, the individual conduct of organisations, and market performance (Lipczynski et al 2005). Based on this SCP rationale, Spandou and Macário (2010) propose a conceptual framework for institutional and organisational performance as presented in Figure 5.2, primarily having in mind the transportation industry in general and the BRT case in particular. The column heading 'structure' contains three levels of structure: the institutional setting (that is, formal and informal principles and enforcement rules) that forms the contextual background where a BRT system is implemented; the governance arrangements, represented by different organisations (public, private, hybrid, and so on) in different regulatory settings (for example centralised, decentralised) and the contractual frameworks linking these organisations; and last, but not least, the individuals taking different roles, skills and competencies in a society that can be managed with different degrees of citizen participation. The column 'conduct' provides the several possible actions to be taken by the organisations embedded in the structure. Each action has both a given potential to achieve certain objectives and a cost. Finally, the column 'performance' provides the aspects to be monitored and accountable to either private or public or both types of agents. The claim represented in this figure is that performance depends on institutional and organisational structure and a set of actions. Good performance is not necessarily a consequence of the merit of a single agent.

Consequently, it is of foremost importance that whenever a BRT system is implemented performance objectives are defined from the outset, considering the life cycle of the project and what is needed beyond the BRT system itself to achieve those objectives. Worth noting is the importance of the life cycle of the project to the expected performance. While immediate outcomes like passengers carried may be apparent soon after inauguration, broader impacts like land use change and urban restructuring may take many years. One of the main pitfalls that can be observed is the political promise wrapping up a BRT system and managing it within the typical four year period of a political cycle, neglecting the evidence that in systems where human behaviour is the driver, good performance has a correlation with the maturity of

Figure 5.2: Conceptual framework for institutional performance analysis based on the Structure–Conduct–Performance paradigm

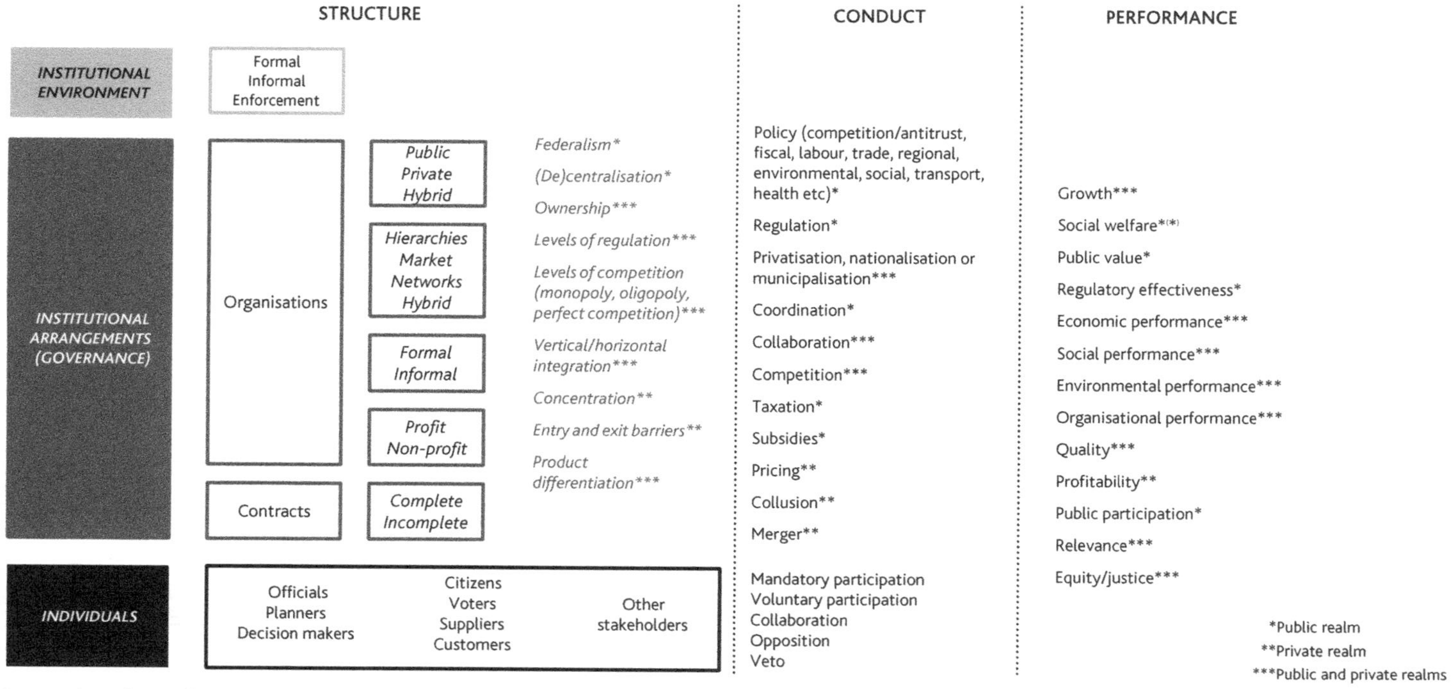

STRUCTURE

Formal
Informal
Enforcement

Organisations

- Public
- Private
- Hybrid

- Hierarchies
- Market
- Networks
- Hybrid

- Formal
- Informal

- Profit
- Non-profit

Contracts

- Complete
- Incomplete

- Officials
- Planners
- Decision makers

- Citizens
- Voters
- Suppliers
- Customers

- Other stakeholders

Federalism*
(De)centralisation*
Ownership***
Levels of regulation***
Levels of competition (monopoly, oligopoly, perfect competition)***
Vertical/horizontal integration***
Concentration**
Entry and exit barriers**
Product differentiation***

INSTITUTIONAL ENVIRONMENT

INSTITUTIONAL ARRANGEMENTS (GOVERNANCE)

INDIVIDUALS

CONDUCT

Policy (competition/antitrust, fiscal, labour, trade, regional, environmental, social, transport, health etc)*
Regulation*
Privatisation, nationalisation or municipalisation***
Coordination*
Collaboration***
Competition***
Taxation*
Subsidies*
Pricing**
Collusion**
Merger**

Mandatory participation
Voluntary participation
Collaboration
Opposition
Veto

PERFORMANCE

Growth***
Social welfare**(*)
Public value*
Regulatory effectiveness*
Economic performance***
Social performance***
Environmental performance***
Organisational performance***
Quality***
Profitability**
Public participation*
Relevance***
Equity/justice***

*Public realm
**Private realm
***Public and private realms

Source: Spandou and Macário 2010

the system and the stages of the life cycle. The message embodied in Figure 5.2, that performance is dependent on structure and on action, recommends that a strategic long term lens be used when BRT is implemented so that its full potential can be effectively developed.

Necessary elements for a BRT policy package

> Changing behaviour (managing demand) rather than catering for it (supply to meet demand) and pursuing several objectives (the tripartite goals of sustainability) rather than one (to meet demand) has been the major shift in transport policy over the last two decades, and this in turn has required the use of policy packages. (Givoni et al 2013, p. 4)

The implementation of BRT systems all over the world always emerges as a result of different policy packages, which depend on the cultural, political, institutional and technical backgrounds of the cities. The design of the packages, in turn, influences the performance of these systems. This becomes evident when analysing the literature about the subject or comparing case studies (such as the database described in Chapter Two). An example of this is the different urban mobility approaches taken in South America and Asia, where systems are usually designed to face huge demand for public transport in a context of scarce economic resources, and in Europe or the US, where 'close to BRT' systems tend to privilege passenger comfort and reliability and are not designed to face such high levels of demand.

The so-called policy packages are sets of public measures that together aim to achieve a predetermined objective. These may include a wide range of possibilities, from operational to regulatory measures. Thus, the agents involved in the final package may vary depending on the measures and policies considered. One fundamental question is: what are the categories of policies needed for successful implementation and management of BRT systems?

A BRT policy package is thus a combination of policy measures aimed at successful implementation of BRT systems, created in order to improve the positive impacts of such a system, minimise its possible negative side effects and/or facilitate its implementation and acceptability. The ultimate objective of such a package should be to achieve levels of accessibility and enhance patronage at levels of service that are attractive for both demand and supply, leading to a smooth introduction of BRT in an existing urban mobility system, overcoming most, if not all, barriers.

The policy package framework presented here aims to serve as a self-evaluation instrument to guide implementation of BRT systems in different scenarios, considering the diversity of agents, interactions and potential barriers previously discussed. For this purpose it is critical to have a flexible framework that can be adjusted to different degrees of maturity, different stages of the BRT life cycle and even to different types of BRT. It is worth clarifying that despite this book being BRT centred, any policy package addressing BRT implementation must also address the urban mobility system in general and public transport in particular.

Table 5.2 summarises and explains all the items considered, several of which are dealt with in the subsequent chapters of this book.

A decision framework for building BRT policy packages

Evaluation of transport projects is a broad topic that will not be extensively addressed in this chapter. Instead, responding to the need for guidance in package building and based on the reflections on the systems approach previously presented, supporting the evidence that policy making requires a multicriteria analysis setting, this chapter provides the structure of a proposed assessment framework and the guidelines for its utilisation by decision makers, planning agencies and investors. It is meant to be a self-evaluation tool, used by the entity designing the policy packages in comparing alternatives.

According to the considerations discussed previously, a decision process on the implementation of a policy package must consider the following steps:

- Diagnosis of the situation in the city concerned.
- Establishment of a potential policy package (using Table 5.2).
- Selection of the relevant stakeholders for analysis of the policy packages.
- Adjustment of the evaluation matrix proposed here for the city concerned.
- Running a Delphi process[5] of convergence with independent scores allocated by each actor.
- Interpretation of the results considering the proposed scoring matrix (the individual components of the proposed package are given a score, then multiplied by the weights in the scoring matrix).
- Discussion of scores and project attributes and readjustment of the policy package if needed.

Table 5.2: Explanation of the measures to include BRT policy packages

Aspect	Items to address	Explanation for Bus Rapid Transit (BRT) and other modes/services
BRT service integration	Logical integration	Policy measures aimed at integrating the information flows from the system to passengers and vice-versa with that of other modes. The final outcome should be a network where BRT is fully integrated with other modes. Investment in information assets is required in all modes
	Physical integration	Policy measures aimed at providing space (network, stations, technology) and time integration within the BRT system and between the BRT and other modes. Physical integration must be done in users' perspective considering not only public transport but also individual forms of mobility, both motorised and non-motorised (for example walking and cycling)
	Tariff integration	Policy measures promoting fare integration, or at least coordination between modes, and revenue sharing mechanisms between BRT and other public transport (PT) modes and also with parking facilities to encompass individual motorised mobility in multimodal chains and promote the partial modal shift towards public transport
Policy integration	Institutional and regulatory regime	Policy measures promoting the institutional and regulatory integration of the BRT system within the existing institutional and regulatory frameworks. Introduction of BRT should be inclusive and not discriminatory, otherwise the system will be running in parallel to the other modes and services and so disrupting the mobility chain
	Intersectoral policy concertation	Combined measures bringing together two or more policy sectors in a common action, namely energy and land use, taking into consideration the life cycle of implementation of BRT and expected outcomes, results and impacts accruing from its integration into the urban mobility systems considering all modes
	Transit-oriented development	Policy measures that promote transit-oriented development (TOD) – commercial and residential densification around areas served by the BRT, and also by other PT structuring modes. Densification should be carried out having in consideration the public transport network

(continued)

Table 5.2: Explanation of the measures to include BRT policy packages (contd.)

Aspect	Items to address	Explanation for Bus Rapid Transit (BRT) and other modes/services
Funding and financing	Private transport externalities	Policy measures that account for monetisation of externalities caused by private transport and their transfer to financing PT in general and BRT (for example congestion charging, fuel taxes) in particular. Ex ante appraisal of the project is recommended, containing the effects of BRT implementation in the other modes/services
	Value capture from other sectors	Policy measures that promote the capture of the value added by the BRT to other sectors (such as land use) and promote its application to the financing of the BRT system. This should be done for all mobility modes and service as well, although when assessing a BRT project the focus should be on this particular service and mode
	Other budgetary measures	Policy measures regarding any other budgetary items that promote the PT's economic sustainability in general and BRT in particular
Stakeholder involvement	Before implementation During implementation After implementation	These items refer to any policy measures that aim at involving all stakeholders prior, during and after the project implementation – the latter should not only contribute to management accountability but also address future project improvements. These measures include items like public awareness campaigns, stakeholder meetings, public discussions, monitoring and information dissemination. While stakeholders' involvement in assessment of BRT projects is of utmost importance, for reasons of public acceptability the procedure should be generally applied to all modes
Business model	Cost structure	Policy measures defining the cost structure and cost coverage requirements for the BRT and other PT systems
	Revenue streams	Policy measures related to the revenue streams of the BRT and other PT systems (including fare policies) might be related to the tariff integration mentioned above (diversification of revenue sources, and so on)
	Subsidies	Policy measures defining the levels and form of subsidies, award of subventions and any other subsidy related issues to public transport
	Partnerships	Policy measures which intend the establishment of partnerships between operators, creation of operation consortia or other types of partnerships related to the functioning of the BRT and its relation with other modes

(continued)

Table 5.2: Explanation of the measures to include BRT policy packages (contd.)

Aspect	Items to address	Explanation for Bus Rapid Transit (BRT) and other modes/services
Business model (contd.)	Quality certification	Policy measures related to quality of service and certification requirements for transport systems in general
Infrastructure	Traffic management	Policy measures that influence traffic management (priority rules and signalling, grade separation, and so on) to favour public transport services
	Accessibility	Policy measures to improve the accessibility to BRT stations by soft modes (cycling, walking or other) as a way to increase patronage and the catchment area of the system
	Stations and terminals	Policy measures intended to facilitate access (passenger and goods) and transfer of passengers in buses
	Land availability	Policy measures intended to facilitate land availability for the implementation of the project – corridors and stations
Technology	Intelligent Transport Systems (ITS) technologies and applications	Policy measures that are related to the use of ITS and other 'smart technologies' generally applied to PT services and specifically considered in the implementation of a new BRT system (Global Positioning System [GPS], smartcards, smartphone apps, and so on), which makes it very relevant for investment assessment purposes.
	Energy requirements	Policy measures related to the energy consumption of public transport (energy certification, alternative fuels, and so on). Might be related to environment as well
	Environmental requirements	Policy measures related to the environmental performance of the BRT system (emission standards, use of alternative fuels, and so on) aligned with those imposed on other PT modes/services. Might be related to energy.

The evaluation matrix presented here is a template to show how the matrix can work – that is, as a scaffold that should be adjusted for the city using this framework, and that does not provide guidance on how an individual measure is scored in a given city. The lines in the evaluation matrix show all the policy categories that were defined in the BRT implementation package of the previous section. The columns show four different illustrative BRT development contexts:

- Single corridor as a pilot for further extensions or as a completed project.
- Complementary form of mass transport if the city already has some type of mass transport which BRT will complement.
- Primary form of mass transport if the city currently has no form of mass transport. The BRT will serve this goal.
- Disruptive intervention if the transport system of the city is defective in many ways. BRT will be implemented as a replacement solution.

The score points that can be found on the intersection of each 'Category' row and 'Context' column represent the potential (maximum) score assigned to that category for that particular context (for example, the category 'BRT service integration' has a potential score of 200 for the first and second contexts, 175 for the third and 125 for the last context). The score represents only a weight for comparing across measures and is independent of how the individual measure is evaluated. The score points for the 'groups of measures' within each category are simply a breakdown of that category's subtotal.

Table 5.3 presents the scores empirically obtained in an exploratory exercise using a small group of experts in an example evaluation. These are the first order weights to be attributed through a Delphi process. For each development context the total potential score is always 1,000 points.[6] For each context, the category considered to be the most important was assigned a potential score of 200. The remaining 800 points in each context are distributed among the other six categories according to the results of the Delphi process. The distribution of the potential score of each category by the different groups of measures is done by assigning a percentage to each group (that is, second order weight of the Delphi convergence process, in first column, between brackets). The sum product of first order and second order weights returns the overall weight, which is the global maximum score (see Table 5.3).

As an illustration, take the 'business model' category: if BRT is implemented as a single corridor, as a pilot for further extensions or as a completed project then the design of the business model may be a critical aspect to show its feasibility either in the case of a pilot project or in comparison to other mass transit alternatives, justifying higher scores of 175 or 100, respectively. Alternatively, if the BRT is implemented in a city where no mass transit exists, the business model is less important to demonstrate the feasibility and merit of the system, hence a lower score of 75. The context reflects also the maturity and path dependency and its interaction with the institutional environment

Table 5.3: Sample BRT policy package's evaluation matrix

(Second order weights)	Single corridor	Complementary form of mass transport	Primary form of mass transport	Disruptive intervention
	First order weights			
BRT service integration (100%)	200	200	175	125
Logical integration (30%)	60	60	52.5	37.5
Physical integration (40%)	80	80	70	50
Tariff integration (30%)	60	60	52.5	37.5
Policy integration (100%)	50	150	150	175
Institutional and regulatory regime (40%)	20	60	60	70
Intersectorial policy concertation (40%)	20	60	60	70
Transit-oriented development (20%)	10	30	30	35
Funding and financing (100%)	150	125	200	100
Private transport externalities (40%)	60	50	80	40
Value capture from other sectors (40%)	60	50	80	40
Business model (100%)	175	100	75	100
Cost structure (20%)	35	20	15	20
Revenue stream (30%)	52.5	30	22.5	30
Subsidies (30%)	52.5	30	22.5	30
Partnerships (10%)	17.5	10	7.5	10
Quality certification (10%)	17.5	10	7.5	10
Stakeholder involvement (100%)	125	175	150	200
Before implementation (50%)	62.5	87.5	75	100
During implementation (35%)	43.75	61.25	52.5	70
After implementation (15%)	18.75	26.25	22.5	30
Business model (100%)	175	100	75	100
Cost structure (20%)	35	20	15	20
Revenue streams (30%)	52.5	30	22.5	30
Subsidies (30%)	52.5	30	22.5	30
Partnerships (10%)	17.5	10	7.5	10
Quality certification (10%)	17.5	10	7.5	10

Context (type of intervention) of the BRT (first order weights). Growing intensity and scope of intervention.

(continued)

Table 5.3: Sample BRT policy package's evaluation matrix (continued)

(Second order weights)	Context (type of intervention) of the BRT (first order weights)			
	Single corridor	Complementary form of mass transport	Primary form of mass transport	Disruptive intervention
	Growing intensity and scope of intervention →→→			
	First order weights			
Stakeholder involvement (100%)	125	175	150	200
Before implementation (50%)	62.5	87.5	75	100
During implementation (35%)	43.75	61.25	52.5	70
After implementation (15%)	18.75	26.25	22.5	30
Infrastructure (100%)	150	125	150	150
Traffic management (30%)	45	37.5	45	45
Accessibility (30%)	45	37.5	45	45
Stations and terminals (25%)	37.5	31.25	37.5	37.5
Land availability (15%)	22.5	18.75	22.5	22.5
Technology (100%)	150	125	100	150
ITS technologies and applications (40%)	60	50	40	60
Energy requirements (30%)	45	37.5	30	45
Environmental requirements (30%)	45	37.5	30	45

= highest scores

and the reality in the city and this is why scores must be adjusted for the different cities and no universal formula would be recommended.

This framework contributes to the systematisation of the decision process by providing a list of relevant elements to consider (like a 'checklist') and a method of weighting the importance of the different elements, but is of course not free of criticism. In fact it uses a compensatory mechanism where poor scores in one category can be compensated by good scores in another, which is often not possible in the real world.

An important aspect of this framework lies in its flexibility. It can be used as a self-assessment tool in the design of the policy package, or to assess from the outset the potential of a city for smooth implementation of BRT or simply to provide a basis for a comparative assessment. It can be used in different degrees of maturity of the BRT system given by the different context, recognising the path dependency of the learning process in every city. As in the majority of quality assessment frameworks, the scoring system can also be adjusted according to the system's maturity. It is often the case that these types of frameworks with a score ranging between 0 and 500 points are used at the start and after some experience progress to the more demanding score range of 0–1,000 points. Overall this flexible framework provides a guidance instrument for both design and analysis of policy packages for implementation or expansion of BRT systems. Transport operators, authorities and regulators, for example, can use this assessment framework to ensure that a broad range of policy measures are being appropriately considered and weighted.

Conclusions

This chapter addresses the main elements related to the institutional, regulatory and organisational setting underlying an urban mobility system and having direct responsibility in the performance of the overall system. BRT is considered a component of the urban mobility system and thus affected by its symbiotic characteristic and interactions. For this reason proposed policy interventions always consider the systemic approach to urban mobility

The following steps are recommended for institutional and regulatory design to follow in the process of BRT implementation or expansion:

1. Assess the consistency of the institutional and organisational setting, identifying who is who and their respective responsibilities in the framework of the three structural decision levels (strategic–tactical–operational).
2. In the initial ex ante appraisal of the system, take into account metrics reflecting the strategic objectives and avoid moving forward without having these objectives clearly defined with identification of expected outcomes, results and impacts along the implementation and consolidation path.
3. Assess barriers and establish a sound strategy towards acceptability of the new mode by stakeholders in general and incumbents in particular. Drive the acceptability process towards integration, assuming different roles for different agents.
4. Establish management instruments to maintain a continuous assessment of the system – such as contracts, information databases, self-assessment frameworks – and identify accountable agents to maintain it.

5. Establish feedback mechanisms through information and rigorous metrics allowing assessment of the relation between the backstage structure, incentives to stimulate agent behaviour and performance of the overall system. This feedback mechanism should allow the organisations at the different decision levels to understand the effects of their actions and reflect upon the need to introduce any change.
6. Design inclusive policy packages that tackle all relevant elements involved in a BRT implementation or expansion, including a decision process framework that in parallel promotes coherence and buy-in from different stakeholders

It is critical that we understand in our analysis and design of BRT systems that there is an invisible part which forms the backstage structure where all agents interact. Policy measures and decision making can induce the action of all the entities involved in this complex system, but their success is conditioned by the proper functioning of the invisible institutional and organisational structure. Neglecting to take account of the synergetic conditions that will affect the success of the implementation of a BRT has proved to be a critical issue, and there is evidence of these consequences around the world.

The current chapter is focused on the setting of that structure and the constraints for its development, as well as on the guidance for designing policy packages. There are various elements to consider in the performance of a BRT and other chapters in this volume address them.

Notes

[1] All these agents are mobility providers, although acting at different times and with different roles in the supply chain, linked through identical purposes and quality objectives that define the level of service they must provide.

[2] Any arrangement in which one entity (principal) appoints another (the agent) to act on its behalf and to accomplish a number of objectives.

[3] To be exact, we have (in democratic countries) the Parliament (the principal), that represents the people, and the government, which is the executive body complying with determination of the former (a delegated principal). In the most correct institutional design the regulator should have a direct nomination from the Parliament so that it can act with full independence as required. This is, however, not the case in many countries and the regulators depend on government nominations.

⁴ We distinguish between interdependence and interaction. The latter representing only the coherent transfer of information between any two basic elements of the system.

⁵ The Delphi technique aims at generating consensus. It requests opinions from groups of experts in an iterative process of answering questions. Responses are summarised after each round and redistributed for discussion in the next round. A process of convergence leads to consensus by involving the identification of common trends and interpretation of outliers.

⁶ The global dimension of 1,000 points is inspired by auditing processes.

References

Aoki, M. (2001) *Toward a Comparative Institutional Analysis*, Cambridge, MA: MIT Press.

Capra, F., Juarrero, A. and Van Uden, J. (2007) *Reframing Complexity*, Mansfield, MA: ISCE Publishing.

Crain & Associates, Inc and Pacific Consulting Group (1996) *Institutional Barriers to Intermodal Transportation Policies and Planning in Metropolitan Areas*, Transportation Research Board National Research Council, TCRP Report 14, Washington, DC.

Filipe, L.N. and Macário, R. (2013) 'A first glimpse on policy packaging for implementation of BRT projects', *Research in Transportation Economics* 39: 150–157.

Furubotn, E.G. and Richter, R. (2000) *Institutions and Economic Theory: The Contribution of the New Institutional Economics*. Ann Arbor, MI: University of Michigan Press.

Flores, O. and Zegras, C. (2012) 'The costs of inclusion: Incorporating existing bus and paratransit operators into Mexico City's BRT', Conference on Advanced Systems in Public Transport, July 2012, Santiago, Chile.

Givoni, M., Macmillen, J., Banister, D. and Feitelson, E. (2013) 'From policy measures to policy packages', *Transport Reviews: A Transnational Transdisciplinary Journal*, 33(1): 1–20.

ICCR Foundation (Research for Society, Economy and Policy) (2002) 'TRANSTALK – policy and project evaluation methodologies', 4th RTD Programme, European Commission.

Kash, G. and Hidalgo, D. (2012) 'The promise and challenges of integrating public transportation in Bogotá, Colombia', Conference on Advanced Systems in Public Transport, 2012.

Kaufman F.X., Majone G. and Ostrom V. (eds) (1985) *Guidance, Control and Evaluation in the Public Sector: The Bielefeld Interdisciplinary Project*, Berlin/New York: Walter de Gruyter.

Käyhkö, E. (2011) 'Public accountability to citizens: from performance measures to quality thinking', 2011 Public Management Research Conference, Syracuse, NY.

Lipczynski, J., Wilson, J. and Goddard, J. (2005) *Industrial Organization: Competition, Strategy, Policy* (2nd edn), Englewood Cliffs, NJ: Prentice Hall.

Macário, R. (2000) 'Upgrading quality in urban mobility systems', *Managing Service Quality Magazine*, 2(2): 93–99.

Macário, R. (2005) 'Quality management in urban mobility systems: an integrated approach', Dissertation. Instituto Superior Técnico, Universidade de Lisboa, Portugal.

Macário, R. (2006) 'Towards a reform of urban transit systems: topics for action', in *Privatisation and Regulation of Urban Transit Systems*, Paris: OECD/ITF.

Macário, R. (2011) *Managing Urban Mobility Systems*, London: Emerald Group Publishing.

Macário, R. (2014) 'Access as a social good and as an economic good: is there a need of paradigm shift ?', in E. Sclar, M. Lonnroth and C. Wolmar (eds), *Urban Access for the 21st Century: Finance and Governance Models for Transport Infrastructure*, London: Routledge.

May, A.D., Kelly, C. and Shepherd, S. (2006) 'The principles of integration in urban transport strategies', *Transport Policy*, 13(4): 319–327.

NEA, European Commission, EC (2006), 'Final Report', METEOR (Monitoring and Evaluation of Transport and Energy Oriented Radical) Strategies for Clean Urban Transport, Fifth Framework Programme, Competitive and Sustainable Growth, DG TREN.

North, D.C. (1990) *Institutions, Institutional Change and Economic Performance,* Cambridge: Cambridge University Press.

North, D.C. (1992) 'Institutions and economic theory', *American Economist*, Spring: 3–6, John R. Commons lecture given at the American Economic Association meeting, January 1992.

Parsons, W. (1995) *Public Policy: An Introduction to the Theory and Practice of Policy Analysis*, Aldershot: Edward Elgar Publishing.

Poister, T.H. (2003) *Measuring Performance in Public and Nonprofit Organizations*, San Francisco: Jossey-Bass.

Rayle, L. (2008) 'Tracing the effects of transportation and land use policies: a review of the evidence', SOTUR Working Paper, MIT-Portugal Program.

Rawls, J. (2005) *Political Liberalism* (expanded version), New York: Columbia University Press.

Rietveld, P. and Stough, R. (2005) *Barriers to Sustainable Transport*, London: Spon.

Rothstein, B. (1954) *The Quality of Government: Corruption, Social Trust and Inequality in International Perspective*, Chicago: University of Chicago Press.

Rouwendal, J., Borger, B., de Palma, A., Lindsey, R., Niskanen, E., Proost, S. and Verhoef, E. (2003) 'Pricing of urban and interurban road transport: barriers, constraints and implementation paths – deliverable 4. Implementation of marginal cost pricing in transport – integrated conceptual and applied model analysis (MC-ICAM)', www.transport-research.info/Upload/Documents/200608/20060821_163039_38707_MC-ICAM%20Final%20Report.pdf

Rouwendal, J. and Verhoef, E.T. (2006) 'Basic economic principles of road pricing: from theory to applications', *Transport Policy*, 13(2): 106–114.

Sha, A. (2006) *Local Governance in Developing Countries, Public Sector Governance and Accountability Series*, Washington, DC: World Bank Institute.

Simon, H.A. (1997), *Administrative Behaviour*, New York: The Free Press (1st edn 1945).

Spandou, M. and Macário, R. (2010) 'Institutional framework and performance of mobility systems: a review of funding and financing in public transport systems', presented at 12th WCTR – World Conference in Transportation Research, in Lisbon, July 2010.

TIS.PT (Consultores em Transportes, Inovação e Sistemas, s.a.) (2003) 'Managing and assessing regulatory evolution in local public transport operations in Europe', 5th RTD – Transport Programme EC DGTREN.

Viegas, J. and Macário, R. (1998) 'Pricing and financing schemes in the different regulatory and organisational frameworks for urban transport system in Europe', presented at TERA 98 Congress in Milan, Italy.

Williamson, O.E. (2000) 'The new institutional economics: taking stock, looking ahead', *Journal of Economic Literature*, 38(3): 595–613.

SIX

Strategic participation for change

Lake Sagaris

Introduction: bringing context into focus to understand the power of participation

As discussed elsewhere in this book, transport planners seeking to build more sustainable urban transport systems generally view Bus Rapid Transit (BRT) as an option that offers substantial advantages, in terms of flexibility, implementation, public–private arrangements, capacity and other elements. Moreover, when treated as the articulator of a whole transport system and major contributor to resilience overall, BRT can also enhance health, environmental quality, social integration and equality, among other benefits.

Often these benefits are not realised, despite planners' and politicians' efforts to position BRT as an alternative to better known approaches, such as metros/subways, trains and light rail. In these conditions, traditional participation methods, which primarily involve vertical delivery of information to passive recipients, do not help and can hurt. Often, citizens see these as largely hollow rituals that do not genuinely consider the needs and desires of diverse, often marginalised groups (Bickerstaff et al 2002). With a few exceptions, BRT has provoked indifference, hostility and rejection among the general public and political leaders. This is highly problematic, given that for BRT to accomplish the larger/sustainability goal of transforming street/public space it requires active support from the public, particularly vocal and respected organisations, committed public health officials, transit riders, cyclists and pedestrians, given the prevailing bias favouring car use in many cities.

This chapter examines issues of public buy-in, focusing on experiences in Santiago, Chile. Unlike traditional views, which examine participation largely from a process-centred perspective, this chapter starts by examining issues of democratisation in established, post-World War II democracies (Canada, the US, most of Europe), and in newly democratising countries, particularly in Latin America, as these affect the relevant policy making environment.

Terminology is complex, with 'citizen engagement' being the most common in the English-language literature, based primarily on experiences in North America and Europe, while *participación ciudadana* (citizen participation) is widely used in Latin America.

Although analogous, the terms enclose a world of difference. The first refers to permanent procedures for citizen involvement, practised in the context of established democracies, with diverse civil society actors and elected 'public servants' at the local and regional levels. Their relationships tend to be relatively horizontal, although there are many exceptions. The second refers to a highly controversial component of public policy making, in contexts where civil society actors tend to be weak or non-existent. In these contexts, the prevailing relationship with 'the authorities' tends to be clientelistic, in Taylor's sense (Taylor 2004), and therefore distorted by interest in short term and individual benefits over long term and more widespread social benefits. This complexity is often compounded by extreme authoritarian practices, including threats and violence, which influence citizen–government relations. In many cases, privatisation also raises questions about transparency of information and citizens' 'right' to play a role in decision making.

Issues of democratisation, equality and social justice are central to the social component of the sustainability trio (society, economy, environment), but social sustainability is seldom the centre of debates and planning and is poorly understood. Without significant levels of democratisation, equality and social justice – that is, social sustainability – progress toward greater economic or environmental sustainability will remain precarious.

These considerations are important to BRT because this new, hybrid and complex human–technological phenomenon offers many benefits when measured within a framework of sustainability overall, but particularly where it can mobilise urban potentialities that favour *social* sustainability and the inclusion of certain groups with the most needs. For example, BRT can not only move massive numbers of people relatively efficiently. It can also save much-needed physical space, currently being devoured by cars (parking, mobility, and so on) and make it available for walking, reforestation, food gardens and/or social space in areas with enormous deficits.

Again, context is crucial, given high levels of car use in Canada, the US and Europe (with modal shares up to 80% cars, 20% other). This is not the case elsewhere, even in rapidly changing Chile (22%

cars, 78% other). In developing countries, where the vast majority do not have cars, car-centred planning is extremely unjust. Moreover, 'automobility' (Urry 2004) – that is, the car as industrial, financial and socio-cultural icon – worsens exclusion in spatial, but also in cultural and political terms.

Developing countries typically enjoy a set of conditions that could be mobilised in favour of sustainable transport and BRT: high modal shares for walking, cycling and public transport; deeply rooted urban traditions such as the street fairs that supply neighbourhoods with fruit and vegetables on a weekly basis; cycle taxis and other amenities. Potentially, BRT could serve as an umbrella policy that responds well to diverse needs, attracting widespread support from citizens, and positive leadership from politicians, along with funding and other resources (priority access to roads and other public space, as discussed in Chapter Nine).

Unlike the car, sustainable transport and particularly BRT requires coordination between different modes, to provide door-to-door service. Because the vast majority of users access the system by walking, cycling or some other intermediate mode (for example, auto rickshaws in India), which also involves some walking, public transport is arguably an integral part of active transport, affording mobility and access to destinations beyond the scope of walking (0–3 kilometres) or cycling (2–10 kilometres), within a typical 30-minute trip.

Paratransit systems, such as cycle taxis, bikeshare, tricycles and other modes common in developing countries are vital to a healthy, sustainable transport ecology and the families that depend on these microbusinesses where they exist. Buses, running on the surface without the endless stairways common to underground systems, offer countless advantages: daylight, views, bike racks, easier to implement universal access. Stops and intermodal stations, moreover, could offer crucial services that reinforce public health campaigns: microbusinesses offering freshly squeezed juices, cycle parking combined with news kiosks, washrooms that are sorely lacking among public amenities in many cities. To date, few transit agencies consider the importance of these complementary services to their own success, focusing their operations and infrastructure solely on elements directly concerned with buses. They seem to ignore the fact that their success depends on the entire trip chain, from door to door, which is where their competitor, the car, excels. Essentially, successful transit agencies must integrate a range of modes and services. Without meaningful user input, agencies may fail to consider this, and lose political support.

Because buses, particularly in BRT systems, are more efficient than cars, in terms of service, space and energy consumption, they promise savings that should translate into better conditions for pedestrians and cyclists, but also for the public realm. In cities pressed for environmental services, trees to reduce the heat island effect, soil to absorb and store runoff, and food to improve nutrition and offer a buffer against major emergencies are crucial not only to sustainability but to resilience – a community's capacity to survive the shocks of earthquakes, oil shortages, fires and floods. Thus, in theory BRT could advance a whole chain of measures to absorb the effects of climate change. People who advocate for BRT tend to perceive these benefits. But they are seldom achieved, particularly where political considerations force planners to build for BRT, while maintaining facilities for space-hogging cars.

Realising the benefits that sustainable cities need from BRT requires major changes in what people know, how they feel, the way they think, their daily habits. To do so requires involving people in processes where they can learn, experience and understand more deeply the benefits of BRT, and that, in turn, calls for participation that goes beyond the information-based rituals that form the bulk of participation today.

If the majority in developing cities use public transport, walk or ride bicycles, why is there not more public support? Can we, by comparing different kinds of participation, extract some salient lessons for BRT? And based on these lessons, can we develop a strategic approach that goes beyond simplistic, short term events to build ongoing processes and influential constituencies of BRT-friendly citizens, among walkers, cyclists and public transport users alike?

To answer these questions, this chapter examines the broader context of citizen involvement in transport, considering lessons from anti-highway movements, cyclists and other urban movements as they could be applied to facilitate BRT implementation and improve overall results, particularly in terms of public space. Its focus is primarily on experiences over the past 20 years in Santiago, Chile, although many of the conclusions reflect ongoing conversations with colleagues, field visits and exchanges in diverse cities. It does not, therefore, focus on participation as communications techniques, involving large public meetings or surveys. Strictly speaking, these are informational exercises and do not entail the kind of two-way, mind changing and conviction building 'deliberation' (as defined below) necessary to achieve a sea change in perceptions among diverse, highly relevant publics.

Case study and experimentation in the 'living laboratory' of Santiago, Chile

The joys and the pitfalls of citizen engagement in public policy are the object of hot debates, particularly in the fields of planning (Carp 2004; Forester 1999; Healey 2006; Innes and Booher 1999; Yiftachel and Huxley 2000) and development (Cooke and Kothari 2001; Hickey and Mohan 2004; Mohan and Stokke 2000).

This study examines issues of participation within a broader framework of democracy, democratisation and civil society, particularly in terms of healthy 'ecologies' of robust citizen actors, usually groups, and the importance of ''civic capacity' (De Souza Briggs 2008). Rather than using Arnstein's (1969) classic ladder, which is excellent for measuring process quality, I have preferred Susskind and Elliott's (1983) categories of paternalism, conflict and coproduction. These are based on studies in Europe in the 1970s, a time when new democracies were developing quickly, and automobility was on the rise, analogous to conditions in Chile and many developing countries today.

Susskind and Elliott (1983, p. 6) identify paternalistic forms of participation as centralised processes 'in which advice from citizens is either restricted or closely prescribed'. These can help citizens complain, plan, give and receive advice. Nonetheless, paternalism rarely leads to 'substantial alterations in the distribution of power'. As discussed below, participation in Santiago's bus system reflected a particularly limited version of paternalistic participation.

Conflict occurs when 'open struggle by citizen action groups or political parties has led public officials to change policies, redesign programs, or accede to other resident or consumer demands' (Susskind and Elliott 1983, p. 8). It may take the form of a long range strategy or a short term tactic. In this case, the citizens' coalition, *No a la Costanera Norte*, led a conflict against a highway project, in conditions in which there were few provisions and no experience with effective citizen participation.

Coproduction involves sharing decision making power among public officials and citizen groups, but also, significantly, sharing responsibility for results. Cycling engagement in Santiago began as conflict in the late 1990s. By the period covered in this study, however, more sophisticated groups were emerging, able to generate diverse tactics and strategies for influencing policy. This study focuses on an initiative that involved virtually all relevant public, citizen and some private actors, through a process we have classified as coproduction.

Like Arnstein's ladder, these concepts consider process quality, but they also bring into focus the importance of context, institutional arrangements and more or less authoritarian/democratic cultures. They widen the definition of participation beyond state initiated and controlled instances (paternalism), by examining key aspects of governance: citizen and government action, contents, procedures and results. These concepts are useful, among other reasons, because they encompass processes, but also the interactions between governance and citizen organisations.

These categories provide insight into the interactions between social movements, citizens' associations, governments and others. They bring into focus the need for citizen *organisations*, to generate continuity, credibility and the consensus necessary for more sustainable transport. In this light, probably the most significant difference between North America and Europe as compared to newly democratising countries is the lack of a robust ecology of civil society organisations, and the pervasive clientelism that marks most citizen–government relations.

Case study work in Santiago involved extensive interviews with key actors and participatory action research methods. Some concepts from complexity theory were useful, particularly the role of nested scales in diffusing ideas through an entire urban system and thereby enabling exponential changes, even when relatively small numbers of actors were involved. Similarly, despite the complexity of city and planning systems, it was possible to identify relatively simple interactions that can work across scales to shift the whole system.

These experiences were complemented by interviews and observation of cycling initiatives in the Netherlands and Denmark, and transport debates in Toronto, Montreal and Vancouver. Colleagues' reflections from Bogotá and New Delhi underlined the relevance of the quality of communication.

Collaborative planning theory and practice focuses on communication, of course, and particularly the importance of deliberation or authentic dialogue (Innes and Booher 2010) to generate 'strategic conviction' (Healey 1997) – that is, the social consensuses that make change accepted and, eventually, habitual, in ways that improve how people live together. In the case of BRT, strategic participatory processes must engage citizens in general, but also generate Kingdon's (2003) 'policy entrepreneurs', to position it suitably in public imaginaries and on political agendas. Some specific components, as currently being developed in Santiago, are discussed.

Conflict, paternalism and coproduction: lessons from transport debates in Santiago

First identified in Europe in the 1980s, three categories of citizen involvement (paternalism, conflict and coproduction) recur pretty frequently around the world. This reflects common patterns of mobility, concerns about road safety and mortality, and a resilient passion for utility cycling among an often small, but persistent segment. This section summarises lengthy and complex processes, to highlight the foundations for the observations and conclusions in the following sections.

An anti-highway revolt: citizenship learning through participation as conflict

In 1997, seven years after the end of the Chilean military regime (1973–1990), 25 citizen organisations on the wrong side of the Mapocho River organised to oppose the country's first urban highway concession, the *Costanera Norte*, whose proponent was the powerful ministry of public works, led by Ricardo Lagos, an ambitious politician on the way to the national presidency. The three-year campaign saw neighbourhood leaders pursue intense training from diverse sources on the costs and impacts of highways and generate significant debate not only about highways and public transport, but also about the role of citizens in government policy and decision making. Despite threats, intimidation and media campaigns against them, these groups, known as the *Coordinadora No a la Costanera Norte*, successfully demanded an environmental impact assessment, and then achieved equal conditions for citizen participation.

Although the highway was eventually built, its design changed significantly, with central portions running through the *Coordinadora's* neighbourhoods being located under the Mapocho River, a decision that left three of the four neighbourhoods untouched. The fourth, two extremely poor communities in the Independencia municipal sector, saw those affected – owners, renters, homeless people boarding with family members (*allegados*) – compensated, and relocated elsewhere in the city.

For the communities that organised, the experience was a lesson in working across very diverse values, socioeconomic and other differences (Sagaris 2014b). Approximately half of the 25 organisations represented very poor and lower middle class families, either as residents or as precarious fruit, flower and vegetable sellers. The coalition proved to be a genuine school for civic capacity, as leaders learned to read plans, to speak directly to ministers and other power figures, to deliberate, strategise and plan together, to fundraise and to generate a common set of goals based on initially disparate agendas (Pinnington and Schugurensky 2010).

When environmental nongovernmental organisations (NGOs) advising the coalition suggested that market vendors' agendas were not legitimate, since they were based on economic survival rather than environmental priorities, the coalition's leaders shared a round of opinions, before deciding that the coalition was about working together on a combined social, environmental and pro-democracy agenda. When public works staff – after over a year of requests for a meeting with the minister – told the coalition only three people could meet, the coalition took a delegation of 20 people, including leaders from each organisation and expert advisors. When media insisted on highlighting only the upper class leadership, the *Coordinadora* began to assign spokespeople to specific subjects and refused to accept a model where just one or two people spoke for all.

The *Coordinadora* involved local community through massive hugs of the neighbourhoods, using ribbons, balloons and long lines of neighbours holding hands around areas scheduled for destruction. It reached out to architectural, medical and other professional organisations, published its own newspaper in the form of a large wall poster, and developed additional media as technologies advanced. Moreover, it blended physically moving events, such as on-street activities, music, art auctions and shared meals, creating a multidimensional strategy to draw in and hold support from people in different social classes.

Leadership included people with pro- and anti-regime positions, a combination virtually unheard of in post-Pinochet Chile, and meetings typically took place around kitchen tables, in people's living rooms and in church halls.

The political leaders who led the campaign in favour of the highway project started from highly contemptuous stances, often reflected in media headlines, for example threatening leaders with the burden of all court costs when a writ of habeas corpus froze the first attempt to tender the project. Nonetheless, the public works minister, Ricardo Lagos, went on to become president of Chile, and proclaimed in several public speeches his conviction that the country needed more active citizens like those who opposed the highway project. Public transport entered presidential debates, at least partly as a result of the *Coordinadora's* campaign.

Lagos himself issued a presidential decree requiring all ministries to contemplate some form of citizen participation (Lagos 2000), and with the years, the issue of how to include citizens remained the subject of considerable debate, and eventually two highly significant pieces of legislation: a law governing participation itself (GobiernoChile 2011) and a right to information law (GobiernoChile 2005).

Other grassroots organisations have since emerged, also in opposition to highway projects around the city, with the majority of these forming a Coalition for Transport Justice in 2013. Among their demands, calls for better public transport, particularly metro and cycling facilities, are emphasised, and some protest events have included activities such as the inauguration of an imaginary metro station in the route intended for a highway. Thus, conflicts over highways have generated new, autonomous and increasingly effective citizens' movements, which in turn have helped to put new representatives on city councils and in the national congress.

From conflict to coproduction: placing cycling high on political agendas

As the highway conflict drew to a close in 2000, neighbourhood leaders founded *Ciudad Viva* (Living City), a citizen-controlled foundation to continue to fight for neighbourhood improvements, inclusive recycling, transport for equality, respect for local identities and empowerment of citizens. Several projects won significant awards for innovation in planning and active citizenship, leading to important improvements to the neighbourhoods and acting as a significant point of reference regarding the usefulness of citizen participation (Valle 2003).

From 2007 to 2010, Living City joined forces with other emerging, pro-cycling organisations, the regional government and the regional office of the national transport ministry, to bring in Dutch experts (Interface for Cycling Expertise) and organise a series of trainings, working groups, participatory mapping and other sessions to update Santiago's cycling plan. This combined effort generated a fund of US$48 million for infrastructure, debate about new standards and locations for cycle routes, and new policies to fund cycle promotion, car-free and other initiatives, including a women's cycling school.

As a result, cycling moved out of its stigmatised position as a poor man's ride. Cycling facilities quadrupled in length and proportion of women cyclists rose. Cycle counts reveal that, since 2007, the number of cyclists on the main routes has soared, by 15–20% annually (Sagaris and Olivo 2010), and transport authorities estimate its modal share has risen from 3% (2006) to 6% (2012).

The Cycling Roundtable, which articulated these diverse initiatives, was co-chaired by a citizen representative and the regional governor and proved highly effective (Sagaris 2014a). Its procedures ensured that citizen groups working on specific initiatives (a gender study, mapping cycling routes or danger points, and so on) presented first, followed by government officials. This eliminated a common pattern, in which senior officials pronounce vague opening speeches and then leave citizens to talk among themselves (or with low-level technical staff). In this case, both political authorities and technical staff listened, then responded to well-prepared reports, diagnoses and proposals from mixed public–citizen–private working groups or citizen organisations. At a typical roundtable meeting, citizens would present and government officials would respond, announcing, for example, new cycle parking in metro stations, new funding for cycle promotion through sports and cultural programmes, new rural cycling infrastructure, private initiatives to create a cycle path along the main irrigation channels and, ultimately, an updated master plan for the city, based on a round of participatory events throughout the metropolitan region.

One of the working groups established a new set of standards for cycle facilities, based on the Dutch manual (De Groot, 2007), which was then integrated into a proposal for new road designs (REDEVU 2010), but was delayed by the housing ministry, before serving as an input into new design guidelines now being applied (as of 2014). Working groups, such as this one, were the backbone of the process, generating serious deliberation and trust among diverse actors. Small in size (typically 5–25 people), altogether these working groups mobilised more than 1,500 people over a three-year period. Workers, recyclers, street vendors, professionals, men and women, girls and boys: participants led in their own policy niche, whether community, government office, institution. The result was a series of initiatives for change at local, regional, neighbourhood and national levels, most of which continued after the process itself ended in early 2010.

Cycling civil society also expanded: in terms of skills, numbers and diversity. In 1997, there was only one organisation, the *Movimiento de los Furiosos Ciclistas* (MFC), whose main activity was a monthly cycle ride modelled on New York's Critical Mass, with 200–300 participants. By 2012, not only were more than 1,000 people participating in the MFC ride, thousands more were cycling to celebrate heritage, happiness and urban cycling all over the capital region. The women's cycling school has now held over a dozen sessions, with more than 300 graduates who continue to cycle. Most universities have cycle parking policies and active pro-cycling groups, and there have been some modest pilot programmes in schools. The *Bicicultura* festival has become an active advocacy group, with an online map-your-ride service, and several government commissioned studies to its name, covering cycling safety, legal issues and other subjects.

Living City itself developed, with other organisations elsewhere in Chile, a national citizens' agenda for sustainable, socially just cities, and in 2012 persuaded candidates from all political parties to endorse its goals and commit to meeting them, if elected, as many were in key municipalities. A former Living City president, Josefa Errazuriz, became mayor of the emblematic Providencia municipal council, and more than 10% of the population of metropolitan Santiago now lives in areas governed by mayors committed to this agenda.

Conditions for cycling remain far from ideal, but progress is evident in the swarms of cyclists visible along the main cycle routes throughout the city, in positive media coverage and the bicycle's presence as a new trendy advertising icon.

Paternalism: Transantiago as the paradigm for public policy disaster

In 2001, two leaders of the newly founded Living City were able to visit Bogotá and study its innovative transport policies, particularly the bus rapid transit system, TransMilenio, and its network of cycle facilities. This led Living City to launch a 'Citizens' Agenda for Sustainable Transport' (2001) in conjunction with the government's new 'Sustainable Urban Transport Plan' (also 2001). Despite this auspicious beginning and the Plan's own commitment to participation, regional planners issued no further invitations and ignored Living City's demands for citizen involvement.

In the ensuing years, government officials came and went, promising a first-rate public transport system as they battled with the mafia-like organisations of the private transport operators. On two occasions, planners organised formal presentations of the plan, but discussions were so limited that even questions from the floor had to be presented in writing. When the new system was implemented in February 2007, it proved a political and technical disaster (see Chapter Three), which almost brought down the Bachelet national government. While the lack of participation can hardly be blamed for this failure, it was certainly a powerful symptom of the government's refusal to consider the opinions of citizens and external experts alike.

Six years later, the system works considerably better, but suffers from high levels of fare evasion and vandalism, a clear indication of citizens' contempt. Rather than providing the enclosed stations typical of the Curitiba and Bogotá bus rapid transit systems, Santiago's open-air platforms with their railings and ramps resemble livestock loading areas. Seven years into implementation, segregation of bus lanes remains incomplete, even along the major routes. Overcrowding, lack of seats, the increase in transfers and other elements have generated the image that Transantiago users, mostly from low and middle income households, are second class citizens. Although after a huge effort the transport ministry managed to obtain a necessary subsidy from congress, improvements have been minimal, with most funding going to subsidise student fares and non-bus infrastructure (metro). Perhaps not surprisingly, most Transantiago users aspire to getting into their own cars, as quickly as possible.

Plans for a major corridor reaching from the city's centre to its southern edge have been on hold since massive protests in the 2000s, and similar plans for another corridor provoked major opposition from citizens, the city council and other leaders on the north side of Santiago. Notwithstanding, new efforts to reposition Transantiago as crucial to the sustainable, friendly and safe city to which most Santiaguinos aspire are apparent in cooperation to develop a major new initiative along the Alameda–Providencia corridor in the city centre. The latter began with a 'participatory' workshop that brought together government and university experts in a groundbreaking process, but no citizen organisations were invited.

Contrasting results, depending on the kind of participation

Table 6.1 summarises the results of the three experiences with participation. Limited participation in Transantiago's development failed to create buy-in or citizens' voices favouring the new system. In contrast, the anti-highway campaign reflected a classic bottom-up citizens' rebellion, while citizen–government collaboration produced genuine improvements favouring cycling.

A thorough examination of the reasons behind these different responses is beyond the scope of this chapter, but the evidence suggests that, as Banister (2008) suggests, transport is more than a derived demand: people walk, cycle and drive to reach a destination, but also because they enjoy the co-benefits these provide. Where buses are so overcrowded people can hardly breathe, never mind read or enjoy the view, these co-benefits vanish and so does affection for the mode.

Table 6.1: Participatory modes contrasted

Transport issue	Costanera Norte Hwy (1997–2000)	Transantiago (2001–2007)	Cycling (2007–2010)
Participation	Conflict	Paternalism	From conflict (1990s) to coproduction (2007–2010)
Communication	Dissension and debate	Information delivery	Deliberation and consensus
Hierarchy	Bottom up	Top down	'Middle out'
Planning paradigm	Rational technical	Rational technical	Collaborative
Who	Local groups, organisations, academics, government actors, media, citizens	General public, organisations (but with no specific role or recognition)	Outside experts, regional government, citizen-led planners and civil society allies
How	Formal participatory process complemented by marches, media, other movement and advocacy tactics	One-off informational sessions, with large audiences (100 or more)	Collaborative process, with plenary and small groups co-chaired by civil society and regional government actors
Main impacts			
On citizens	Living City recognised as major citizen organisation and new organisations emerging with similar agendas	No buy-in from citizens. No groups campaigning in favour. Widespread but temporary protests	Multiple diverse ad hoc groups, small companies, NGOs, and so on, each pushing a cycling agenda from diverse perspectives.
Policy impacts	Transport policy expanded beyond cars to consider other transport modes	Controversy over subsidies and poor implementation. High fare evasion	High priority nationally and for key local governments, infrastructure increased fourfold
Political impacts	Amplified dissenting voices (citizens, academics, internal government), pollution and sustainable transport discussed, but little change	Bachelet government almost fell, Transantiago hotly debated, overwhelming reference for negative urban policy	Consensus between diverse actors, new positive image of cycling, a priority across party lines and political scales (municipal, regional, national)

(continued)

Table 6.1: Participatory modes contrasted (continued)

Main impacts (continued)			
Social impacts	Car remains king	Public transport users perceived as second class, captives of the bus system	Cycling is trendy and a frequent positive image in both advertising and news media
Transport impacts	Dozens of new conflicts, as citizens increasingly organise against new highway projects	Those on low incomes aspire to have car (become first class citizens)	Cyclists soaring by 20% per year on main routes. Major expansions of infrastructure, with quality improving

Source: Own elaboration, based on interviews, participant observation and media analysis.

Anti-highway revolts reflect (and build) strong local identities, while cycling too comes with powerful positive identifiers that build social cohesion and capital.

Transantiago, in contrast, impacted on the whole city at once and in a very short period of time (its 'Big Bang' implementation in 2007). While this generated some spontaneous outbreaks of anger and organising, it did not grow into a more ongoing citizen capacity. The anti-highway movement, moreover, had more time, well before implementation, especially once it forced the public works ministry into a formal participatory process, through the environmental impact assessment system. Transantiago did not undergo a complete impact assessment, which under Chilean law requires participation. The first anti-highway groups were able to question the highway, pulling in other citizens, academics and perspectives. They had three years to learn how to influence policy, and build personal and collective skills that enabled them to address the planning system on multiple levels.

Leaders of the anti-highway campaign went on to found a citizen-led planning organisation, Living City (in 2000), which attempted to apply its newly acquired expertise to Transantiago. In 2001, with its Citizens' Agenda for Sustainable Transport, Living City demanded (and sometimes got) an opportunity to participate, at least in the early stages of Santiago's urban transport plan (2001–2004). As implementation advanced (2005–2007), however, the government reneged on promises of participation, and Living City focused more on neighbourhood recovery, cycling and other initiatives.

Indeed, through a modest network of new, pro-cycling organisations, *Ciclistas Unidos de Chile*, Living City and its allies worked with government staff to build a cycling initiative that mobilised actors in different niches of the policy environment – local and regional government, diverse citizen groups, some private sector. This initiative achieved a dynamic that was neither top down nor bottom up, but rather 'middle out': involving coproduction and generating co-responsibility.

In terms of nourishing more effective citizen organisations and achieving more cycle-friendly policies, this was the most effective of the three kinds of participation. This is consistent with Booher and Innes' (2002) study of 'network power', which can shift traditional power relations when diverse groups, bound by a compelling common interest, are able to develop the 'authentic dialogue' necessary to enable meaningful collective action.

The second half of the table considers the main impacts: on citizens' skills and level of organisation; in terms of policy, political support, social support, and transportation itself. These reveal the value of considering 'wild' (nongovernment initiated) along with 'tame' (government initiated) citizen engagement methods and particularly coproduction by citizens and government for optimum results.

In democratising contexts, both conflict and coproduction develop skills, credibility and co-responsibility among interested citizens, all necessary for continuity. In today's rapidly changing policy environments, they also provide 'quick data', instant information from participants' networks, which facilitates early detection of problems and opportunities. These are important when planners seek to address sustainability in a world threatened by global climate change, high energy prices, inequality and exclusion, and the social unrest these generate.

These experiences also suggest the importance of 'citizen planners', especially when innovation is required, as with sustainability. It is difficult for government staff, trained to respect the regulations and norms of professional practice, to 'think outside the box' or pioneer innovation. Their job is to apply the rules, not break them, even when these are unsuited to changing circumstance. At the least, organised citizens can support politicians and technical staff when they challenge accepted wisdom.

In this case, the anti-highway campaign forced politicians to move from a highways 'yes or yes' stance, to consider critiques, and from there to give higher priority to both public transport and, more recently, cycling. Moreover, in post-Pinochet Chile the *Coordinadora's* insistence on citizens' right to have their needs and opinions reflected in final planning decisions also contributed to shifts in both public and elite opinion.

The cycling initiative illustrates the effectiveness of well-prepared citizens' organisations in mobilising actors in diverse niches of a transport policy environment – national and local transport planners, private consultants, private firms involved in cycling or other related areas, diverse citizens organisations, cultural and sports groups – in this case in favour of more cycle-inclusive urban policies and projects.

It is not that citizens alone advocated and achieved these results. Rather, as their skills increased and their participation evolved, they acted as catalysts, mobilising supporters among the public and in government, and resources, and tracing a route to change that involved multiple dimensions: design standards, investment funds, promotion by civil society and other groups, local municipal as well as national transport leadership, and so on. The result was considerable innovation, although Santiago remains far from exemplary when it comes to integrated and sustainable transport planning.

Discussion: understanding the role of 'ecologies' in policy undertakings

Evans (2002) notes that major change is unlikely to emerge from civil society organisations alone. He sees 'ecologies of agents', consisting of 'local communities, translocal intermediary organizations such as NGOs and political parties, and last but not least, the variegated collection of organizations that constitute the state' (Evans 2002, p. 14) as bringing about the paradigmatic changes required to make cities more sustainable. The citizen–government roundtable in favour of cycling illustrates how a participatory planning process, designed and implemented by organised citizens and political–technical leadership, successfully drew in actors from local neighbourhood associations, environmental groups, municipal governments, national transport and infrastructure planning offices, and some private sector actors. By making the most of knowledge held by actors in these diverse 'niches' of the policy environment, pro-cycling forces were able to take it from its stigmatised position as a 'poor man's ride' to its status as a national priority, under both the Bachelet and the subsequent Piñera governments.

Increasingly, theorists are calling for new metaphors to help humanity work with the complexity of modern planning challenges (Lakoff and Johnson 2003). In this case, it was useful to think about people's interrelationships not in terms of the more technological metaphor of the network, but rather in terms of relational trees, requiring nourishment and acting on different levels, at and below the surface of formal interactions. By bringing people together in small working groups these became relational forests, dense and able to both nourish and communicate shifts in positions relatively distant from the central nucleus where leaders were located. The roundtable plenary involving political leaders, technical planning staff, diverse citizen and other groups met several times a year. This reinforced transparency, rewarding concrete measures favouring cycle inclusion and drawing in and assigning new values to previously marginalised players, particularly the recyclers (wastepickers) who ply their trade in the city on tricycles.

This was possible because by 2007, several citizen organisations were emerging that were able to demand participation and elaborate a collaborative approach to cycling-inclusive urban planning, which drew in Dutch expertise, but also ran it through the filters of local planners, consultants, cyclists, environmentalists and neighbours, to produce consensuses that made sense in the Chilean planning environment. Civil society as it related to urban issues was growing in sophistication and complexity.

The 'furious cyclists' movement' (MFC) born in 1997 was a single issue, single tactic group, focusing almost exclusive on the monthly cycle ride. It eschewed democratic structures and ended up with a set of de facto leaders. For several years, this ad hoc leadership discouraged the emergence of new leadership among women cyclists and other groups. In 2005–2006, these aspirations led to the creation of the women's cycling group, the *Macletas*, the *Bicicultura* festival and the *CicloRecreovia* open streets initiative. Living City's focus on diverse urban issues affecting people of all ages and social classes, meanwhile, led to its rejection by the 'traditional' cycling group, at the same time as it was highly instrumental in bringing cycling to a much broader population. In early 2007, these newer organisations formed *Ciclistas Unidos de Chile* (United Cyclists of Chile), a loose network that cooperated on specific issues and events.

Divisions and reorganisation reflected different priority, strategic and even identity issues, and occur worldwide. In New York, Critical Mass continues to lead a monthly cycle ride, while other organisations, like Transportation Alternatives, focus on planning, participation and other issues. Batterbury's article detailing efforts by the Ealing Cycling Campaign in London (Batterbury 2003) rightly notes that the cycling 'community' is really a social network. Some groups form bonds mainly from like-to-like, Putnam's bonding social capital, while others build relationships mainly across difference, bridging social capital (Putnam 2000).

Different groups show different levels of complexity (Table 6.2). This diversity is taken for granted in the Netherlands, Canada, the

Table 6.2: Organisational complexity matrix, cycling

	1–2 issues	More than two issues
1–3 tactics	MFC, Arriba la Chancha, territorial cycling groups	Macletas (gender and cycling), CicloRecreovia (cycling, walking, health)
More than three tactics	Bicicultura (cycling, culture)	Living City

Source: Own elaboration.

US or the UK, where they have long been part of the democratic landscape. In newly democratising countries such as Chile, however, there are fewer such groups. While most organisations start out in quadrant 1 (the MFC, the *Coordinadora*), they face significant barriers to further development. Quadrant 1 groups deliver visibility and often large numbers, while those in quadrants 2 and 3 represent more diverse approaches. Quadrant 4, where Living City is located, offers the most ability to link diverse actors across a wide range of issues, all related to rights, justice and sustainability, using a broader range of techniques, occasionally large numbers but more often focused in small groups favourable to the political deliberation that fosters genuine change.

It is not that one kind of group is 'better': this diversity is necessary and important to the civil society ecology overall. As the citizen side of cycling's political ecology developed, different groups filled different niches: cycling events large and small, cycling education, open streets initiatives spreading through the city, the development of cycle-friendly mapping, technical knowledge, and so on. The accumulative effect was that, despite sometimes fierce debates, they successfully positioned cycling as a desirable urban goal for health, education, gender, inclusion, social justice, urban efficiency and other reasons, among a very diverse public.

When considering ways of organising citizen engagement in transport planning, planners would do well to consider the kinds of civil society groups present (and absent) from the relevant policy ecology, and ways of nurturing more and better civil society actors. Diverse funding mechanisms are needed, to encourage 'starter', 'intermediate' and 'advanced' groups, provide continuity and foster the extensive, credible and effective networks needed to exchange information, introduce new knowledge, and ensure that credible information reaches those who require it.

These experiences illustrate the links between 'wild' as well as 'tame' citizen engagement and building social capital favourable to sustainable urban transport, and underline the need for investment in a robust civil society. This may seem outside the mandate of a transport planning agency. Nonetheless, these factors are crucial to results, at a time when institutions, citizens and other players increasingly seek agreement on more sustainable and socially beneficial transport policies, which often challenge the prevailing automobility.

A review of knowledge about cycling and behaviour change as managed by both practitioners and the growing academic literature, reveals three key 'levers' for change: shifts in urban design and policies (such as traffic calming or parking charges); education, promotional campaigns and other behavioural change initiatives, in both formal and informal educational systems; and a 'cycling economy' – that is, the development of key products and services that support new users.

Public transport, particularly BRT, has worked hard to get the infrastructure and necessary institutional arrangements into place, but invested little in educational and promotional campaigns, or complementary economic aspects (which in fact are far from clear, and require closer study). While roads, often lined with car dealerships, parking, repair and other services, attest to the diverse economic aspects of automobility, planners have only recently considered equivalent measures for public transport.

Thus, there are few 'natural' actors who feel they have a strong stake in public transport. The lack of more substantial participatory processes has also left the vacuum in civil society activism virtually untouched, although there are some exceptions in developed cities. Certainly the US based global NGOs Embarq and Institute for Transportation and Development Policy (ITDP) have worked to develop pro-BRT policies in many cities around the globe. Their efforts, however, focus on local and regional governments, rather than building civil society.

Conclusions: key lessons for participation to obtain better BRT systems

The what

The contrast between limited participatory processes in paternalistic, government controlled modes used for Transantiago and the results achieved by participation from autonomous citizen organisations, through conflict, in the case of the anti-highway protests, or through collaboration, in the case of cycle inclusion, is striking and informative. These experiences underline the need, particularly in a democratising context, for individual citizen learning. But they also point to the importance of civil society *organisations*, able to accumulate skills, knowledge, credibility and other elements necessary to create powerful citizen voices in favour of new approaches to transportation.

The why

Participatory processes are extremely important to position a new BRT initiative and to gain support from a critical group of policy actors, in the citizen, public and private spheres. The Santiago experiences suggest key elements must be present for participatory strategies to deliver: citizens must have real access to decision makers and decisions must reflect consensuses developed through deliberation in small, mixed groups. Participation must also produce noticeable change, in response to observations and proposals from citizens.

The when

Participation is a process and not a one-off or short term event. Different kinds of participation should enrich a new initiative throughout the project cycle, evolving through the use of different kinds of groups, activities and requirements as projects move from diagnosis, to planning, implementation and evaluation. These should start with widespread and deep participation to establish a vision, goals for the public transport system in the urban context, and consensuses regarding funding priorities and other issues. They should provide new information and nourish powerful deliberative experiences among diverse, representative players, deeply embedded in their own extensive networks. They should build lasting ties amongst different actors and include the resources necessary to develop and stabilise civil society organisations.

These 'foundational' processes should evolve into both ongoing and ad hoc participatory tools throughout the planning system: problem-solving instances such as special commissions to deal with challenges such as fare evasion, vandalism or drivers' disenchantment; ongoing commissions mixing citizens with private and public officials for planning and evaluation; outreach processes and territorial commissions for new projects.

In 2013–2014, Transantiago began to develop a coproduction based participatory process to establish a general vision for the system and the city. The first phase aimed to develop, using participatory methods, a participatory component throughout the institution; define goals for achieving positive impacts on public space; and improving cycle integration for better door-to-door service. This umbrella process was also designed to contribute to building a sustainable transport *constituency*, favourable to funding, urban policy and other measures necessary to ease Transantiago's further development.

Once these broad consensuses and participatory methods have been defined, planners, citizens and politicians can move ahead more quickly on specific projects. But where participation only occurs in the context of individual projects, these gains are not possible. Agencies attempt to move ahead 'quickly', but founder for lack of these basic agreements. Leaving out these foundation building processes does not save time: it merely postpones conflicts until later in the planning process. The later these occur, the more expensive and time-consuming they become. Hence, the recommendation is for early, deep participation and ongoing participatory instruments throughout.

The who

It is essential to stop planning for an average, male user travelling from home to office. Women with packages, people with children, the elderly in a context of ageing populations: trips for reproduction related (education, child and elderly care, and so on) as well as production related activities should become central to BRT planning. These require cycle taxis, electric bicycles and tricycles, public and private bikeshare programmes, medium and long term cycle parking and other measures to genuinely meet passengers' door-to-door needs. The simplest way to integrate these challenges and opportunities, as they arise, is through effective participatory policies that build long term relationships with effective, diverse and representative citizens' organisations.

Generating planning processes that nourish leadership from neighbourhood organisations, which are typically led by women, and contemplate gender and age specific policies (such as the inclusion of washrooms at key transit nodes) would go a long way to taking public transport out of the category of necessary evil, and turning it into a prized public good. Influencing public spaces to improve walkability, encouraging green areas that take into account local movements for kitchen gardens and other resilience enhancing measures: these policies can enhance the image of public transport in the eyes of both direct and indirect users, the people who climb onto buses every day, and those who benefit or suffer from their impacts on neighbourhoods.

The how

To get the most out of citizens, both citizens and processes themselves must be truly representative, in the sense of both delivering information to those who are represented and bringing in ordinary citizens at specific moments of the process, through activities such as plenary events, on-street demonstrations of planned changes, with plenty of time for people to get used to them, express their own fears and suggest their own improvements. Chile's environmental impact assessment system originally encouraged organisations to register, nominate and vote for candidates to act as citizen representatives on specific bodies. Supplemented by basic protocols regarding communication, and funding to assist citizens' representatives from low income groups, this approach could be extremely effective.

Studies such as those by Giering (2011) and Hull (2010) reveal diverse tools for involving the public used by North American transit agencies, among them permanent commissions. These should exist at different scales (local, regional, national), involving local players, citizens, but also municipal staff, business groups, street fairs, recyclers and other crucial stakeholders.

Depending on the scope of a policy, validation through process plenaries or plebiscites, as have become effective in Switzerland for example (Beatley 2000), become more effective as part of an overall strategy rather than a standalone measure for citizen participation.

Fostering robust, independent civil society organisations is necessary, to mobilise support and ensure sufficient resources. Jacobsen et al's (2009) work on barriers to walking and cycling – the two main ingress and egress modes – is crucial to understanding the importance of agencies seriously working to maintain modal share, but also to make BRT systems leaders in sustainable transport overall. This can foster goodwill – building alliances with cyclists, public health and other urban players.

Participatory processes must be strategic in the sense that they mobilise these desires and link them to specific transport solutions, support citizens' organisations advocating for them, and build them into planning and implementation. This way, the benefits of public transport and particularly BRT can move from theory into planning practice, and onto city streets that make it clear that public transit benefits everyone.

References

Arnstein, S. (1969) 'A ladder of citizen participation', *Journal of the American Institute of Planners*, 35(4): 216–224.

Banister, D. (2008) 'The sustainable mobility paradigm', *Transport Policy*, 15(2): 73–80.

Batterbury, S. (2003) 'Environmental activism and social networks: campaigning for bicycles and alternative transport in West London', *Annals AAPSS (American Academy of Political and Social Science)*, 590: 150–169.

Beatley, T. (2000) *Green Urbanism: Learning from European Cities*, Washington, DC: Island Press.

Bickerstaff, K., Tolley, R. and Walker, G. (2002) 'Transport planning and participation: the rhetoric and realities of public involvement', *Journal of Transport Geography*, 10: 61–73.

Booher, D.E. and Innes, J.E. (2002) 'Network power in collaborative planning', *Journal of Planning Education and Research*, 21: 221-236.

Carp, J. (2004) 'Wit, style, and substance: how planners shape public participation', *Journal of Planning Education and Research*, 23: 242.

Cooke, B. & Kothari, U. (2001) *Participation: The New Tyranny?*, London/New York: Zed Books.

De Groot (ed.) (2007) *Design manual for bicycle traffic*, Utrecht, The Netherlands: CROW.

De Souza Briggs, X.N. (2008) *Democracy as Problem Solving: Civic Capacity in Communities across the Globe*, Cambridge, MA: MIT Press.

Evans, P.B. (2002) *Livable Cities? Urban Struggles for Livelihood and Sustainability*, Berkeley, CA: University of California Press.

Forester, J. (1999) *The Deliberative Practitioner: Encouraging Participatory Planning Processes*, Cambridge, MA: MIT Press.

Giering, S (2011) *Public Participation Strategies for Transit: A Synthesis of Transit Practice*, Washington, DC: Transportation Research Board.

GobiernoChile (2005) *Ley de Transparencia 20.285, Artículo 8 de la constitución*, Government of Chile, Santiago, Chile.

GobiernoChile (2011) *Sobre Asociaciones y participación ciudadana en la gestión pública*, Ministerio Secretaría General de Gobierno, Santiago, Chile.

Healey, P. (1997) *Collaborative Planning: Shaping Places in Fragmented Societies*, Basingstoke, Hants/New York: Palgrave Macmillan.

Hickey, S. & Mohan, G. (2004) *Participation, from tyranny to transformation?: Exploring new approaches to participation in development*, London/New York: ZED Books; Palgrave Macmillan.

Hull, K. (2010) *Transit Cooperative Research Program (TCRP) Synthesis 85: Effective Use of Citizen Advisory Committees for Transit Planning and Operations*, Washington, DC: TCRP.

Innes, J. and Booher, D. (1999) 'Consensus building and complex adaptive systems: A framework for evaluating collaborative planning', *Journal of the American Planning Association*, 65: 412–423.

Innes, J. and Booher, D. (2010) *Planning with Complexity*, London and New York: Routledge.

Jacobsen, P.L., Racloppi, F. and Rutter, H. (2009) 'Who owns the roads? How motorised traffic discourages walking and bicycling', *Injury Prevention*, 15: 369–373.

Kingdon, J.W. (2003) *Agendas, Alternatives, and Public Policies* (2nd edn), Longman Classics in Political Science, New York: Longman.

Lagos, R.P. (2000) Instructivo Presidencial de Participación Ciudadana Presidency of Chile, Santiago, Chile, www.guiadigital.gob.cl/guiaweb_old/recursos/documentos/InstructivoPresidencialParticipacion.pdf (accessed 2 September 2015)

Lakoff, G. and Johnson, M. (2003) *Metaphors We Live By*, Chicago: University of Chicago Press.

Mohan, G. & Stokke, K. (2000) 'Participatory development and empowerment: the dangers of localism', *Third World Quarterly*, 21: 247–268.

Pinnington, E. and Schugurensky, D. (2010) *Citizenship Learning and Participatory Democracy throughout the World*, Oxford: Cambridge Scholarly Press.

Putnam, R.D. (2000) *Bowling Alone: The Collapse and Revival of American Community*, New York: Simon & Schuster.

REDEVU (Recomendaciones para el Diseño de Elementos de Infraestructura Vial Urbana) (2010) *Revisón capítulo bicicleta*, Santiago, Chile: SECTRA (Secretaría de Planificación de Transporte).

Sagaris, L. (2014a) 'Citizen participation for sustainable transport: the case of "Living City" in Santiago, Chile (1997–2012)', *Journal of Transport Geography*, 41(December): 74–83.

Sagaris, L. (2014b) 'Citizens' anti-highway revolt in post Pinochet Chile: catalyzing innovation in transport planning', *Planning Practice and Research*, 29(3): 268–286.

Sagaris, L. and Olivo, H. (2010) *El Plan Maestro de Ciclo Rutas del Bicentenario*, Santiago Regional Metropolitan Government, Interface for Cycling Expertise, Living City, Santiago, Chile.

Susskind, L. and Elliott, M. (1983) *Paternalism, Conflict, and Coproduction: Learning from Citizen Action and Citizen Participation in Western Europe, Environment, Development, and Public Policy*, New York: Plenum Press.

Taylor, L. (2004) 'Client-ship and citizenship in Latin America', *Bulletin of Latin American Research*, 23(2): 213–227.

Urry, J. (2004) 'The system of automobility', *Theory, Culture and Society*, 21(4–5): 25–39.

Valle, M. (2003) 'Reciclar es vivir mejor: Gestión de residuos sólidos en La Chimba', in A. Surawski and J. Cubillos (eds), *Ampliando la ciudadanía, promoviendo la participación: 30 innovaciones locales, Instituto de Asuntos Públicos & Fundación Nacional para la Superación de la Pobreza*, Santiago, Chile: Programa Ciudadanía y Gestión Local.

Yiftachel, O. & Huxley, M. (2000) 'Debating Dominance and Relevance: Notes on the "Communicative Turn" in Planning Theory', *International Journal of Urban and Regional Research*, 24(4): 907–913.

SEVEN

Designing bus concession contracts

Patricia Galilea and Marco Batarce

Introduction

Authorities of an urban area with regulatory control over the mass transport have to decide whether to operate the service with a publicly owned agency, contract the service to private companies, or create a framework for a deregulated market. This decision is necessary in both developing cities transitioning from an informal mass transport sector and developed cities exploring deregulation of existing public services. There are technical components, but the decision primarily takes place in the political realm.

As explained in Chapters Three and Four Bus Rapid Transit (BRT) is being used as a tool to formalise informal bus services in developing cities. But how to phase that transition and what to do with the existing informal operators is politically complicated. These complications play into the decision of whether to operate the service publicly or to contract it to private companies. Even if the authorities decide to contract the service, the way they handle the incumbents and include them (or not) in the tendering process may affect the success of a new bus service.

While BRT is not possible under completely informal conditions, contracting operations to private operators is not necessary. In developed and developing countries there are BRT services operated by public operators. Many factors, such as the role of incumbents, institutional and regulatory capacity of the government, and the legal and political context, play into the decision. However, contracting service to private operators is part of the model of BRT service being promoted around the world by various nonprofits and development banks.

This makes the issue of contract design central and relevant for BRT decision making in both developing and developed cities. Contracting is complex since it seeks to align public and private interests and it should be done carefully because renegotiating is expensive and complicated. After the initial round of contracts, the incumbent operators have advantages that can make competitive rebids difficult.

Why contracts are necessary

Contracting between the public and the private sector in order to provide a public service has been employed in a wide range of projects in the transport sector (Bernardino et al 2010; Galilea and Medda 2010; Medda and Carbonaro 2007). This type of relationship between a transport authority and a private operator when providing a bus service also involve a duality in their conception that may endanger its success (Grout 1997; Hart 2003; Laffont 2001; Laffont and Martimort 2002): the goal of the public body and of the private may prove to be in conflict: for example, to achieve social goals versus to maximise profits. Therefore, the partnership's success is not assured and a contract is needed.

A contract must reflect the needs of both parties and secure their convergence. Hence, getting contracts right is very important to the success of any provision. The aim of this chapter is to study the elaboration and implementation of contracts for BRT systems, through the analysis of recent experiences across the world. We will focus on the identification of relevant variables and incentives that should be taken into account in order to have a successful outcome, given each city's context.

Another important issue in the success of a partnership is the expertise each partner has in the business. Generally speaking, there is an asymmetry of information between the public transport authority (principal) in charge of tendering, implementing, and monitoring a bus concession contract and the operator (agent) (Gagnepain and Ivaldi 2002). This relationship can be modelled through the principal–agent model (Laffont and Tirole 1986), where the operator has a better knowledge of the real costs involved in the operation of the bus concession and decides how much effort to make to reduce costs. Thus, the design of efficient regulatory schemes becomes a critical issue to take into account when designing a contract. Moreover, this asymmetry tends to increase when authorities do not have much experience in contracts and/or bus concessions (which might be the case with authorities that change frequently) or when authorities decide to formalise an informal system and have to develop an institutional capacity without experience in bus operations.

What authorities seek through a contract

Contracts should always aim to achieve social goals (efficient service provision, maximisation of social welfare), but should also take into account the needs of the private operator. Contracts should always aim to achieve financial sustainability for the system (Hook 2005). There are transit systems that operate with government subsidies, while others are financially self-sufficient (fares cover the costs). By financial sustainability we mean that the system operates financially as it was designed (operator covers its costs thanks to fare and/or subsidy and it is also aware of its operation costs and has the correct incentives in order to control them). Here, it is important to note that this financial sustainability is especially relevant in developing countries (where many cities have limited financial resources) and it should be accounted for in the design of the whole system. For example, the design of routes is crucial, because the achievement of financial self-sufficiency may require route restructuring.

Financial sustainability not only helps to build credibility in the new transportation system, but it is crucial to get operators and suppliers to act as expected. Thus, the financial conditions become an active restriction for every possible value proposition the system may offer to any stakeholder. Contracts may also be used to generate incentives towards certain behaviour from the operators, depending on authorities' goals. In this chapter we will show how a contract can induce operators to innovate and improve service quality and/or operational efficiency.

We start by describing the types of contracts used for the private provision of bus services. Then we will discuss some key decisions that a contract should address, such as risk sharing, paying per passenger or per kilometre, level of service, division of responsibility between operators and authority. We will also present how some cities have implemented different kinds of contracts, and, finally, we address the challenges and potential problems that cities face when implementing bus concession contracts.

Types of contracts

To analyse the types of contracts, we use economic theory. Contracts may be classified according to a cost reimbursement rule. This rule is the extent of cost sharing between the firm and the transport authority representing consumers or taxpayers.

There are two main cost reimbursement rules. One is to pay the private operator a fixed amount of money for the provision of transit services, independently of the cost incurred. Contracts based on this rule are called *fixed-price contracts*. Another rule is to pay the private operator for the cost of provision plus a fee. This type of contract is called *cost-plus contract*.

Fixed-price contracts

With the fixed-price contract the operator is the residual claimant[1] for its cost savings. Therefore, private operators have incentives to reduce cost and provide the transit services efficiently. In this case, the operator not only benefits from the cost savings, but also bears the risk of cost overruns.

Cost-plus contracts

With cost-plus contracts the operator does not bear the cost risk, as the regulator reimburses the total cost of provision of the transit services. Under this type of contract the operator has no incentive to reduce costs and the transport authority bears the risk of cost overruns.

Gross-cost versus net-cost contracts

Contracts may also be classified into two types: *gross-cost* (or full-cost) and *net-cost*. In a gross-cost contract the transportation authority receives the fare revenues and transfers to the operating firm a negotiated payment for supplying a specific level of service, independent of the actual number of passengers. Since in most cases this payment is based on an anticipated cost, the private operator bears the costs of service provision, making the contract a fixed-price contract.[2] Under gross-cost contracts, the transportation authority bears the risk for revenue and demand changes.

Under net-cost contracts, the operator receives the fare revenues and pays the cost of provision. The transport authority pays an amount to cover the difference between revenues and costs, which may also be zero. Usually, the payment from the transport authority is fixed on the basis of the anticipated cost; therefore the contract is of a fixed-price type.[3] Under net-cost contracts, the operator bears the revenue risk since profits depend on the actual number of passengers. Table 7.1 presents a typology of contracts.

Table 7.1: Typology of urban public transport delegation contracts

Contractual form		Production risk borne by	Revenue risk borne by
Fixed-price contract	Net cost contract	Operator	Operator
	Gross cost contract	Operator	Transport authority
Cost-plus contract		Transport authority	Transport authority

Source: Adapted from Quinet and Vickerman (2004)

Different types of contracts incentivise operators to exert effort in different aspects of operation. For instance, fixed-price contracts incentivise efforts to reduce costs whereas net-cost contracts incentivise operators to increase patronage (by improving service quality, for example). It would seem that net-cost contracts should be preferred because they lead to efficient provision and increased ridership. However, the most suitable contract type depends on the transport authority's objectives and the city's characteristics.

For instance, in Great Britain, contracts for bus services are net-cost type, except in London, where they are gross-cost contracts (Hensher and Wallis 2005). In France, 51% of the contracts are gross-cost type, while 27% are net-cost type and the rest is a mix of both types of contracts (Roy and Yvrande-Billon 2007). In Germany, 90% of the contracts are gross-cost type (Augustin and Walter 2010). In Italy, net-cost contracts are the most widely used (Boitani and Cambini 2006).

As said before, when deciding the type of contract a city's context is relevant. In cities in developing countries a large proportion of the population has no alternative to public transportation, and thus the demand has very low elasticity to price and to quality (that is, changes in price or quality do not greatly affect consumption of public transport). Therefore, under a fixed-price contract, bus service operators have incentives to increase profit by reducing cost at the expense of quality of service. Even if the demand is elastic to quality, operators will reduce quality for cost savings under gross-cost contracts. Consequently, in developing countries, if the quality of service is a concern for the transport authority, it should consider cost-plus contracts (Laffont and Tirole 1993).

Alternatively, if quality is contractible (if the contract is able to include all aspects of the service quality and, therefore, it can be enforced), the fixed-price contracts should be the best option for the transport authority. For instance, in London, quality incentives have been introduced in the contracts since 2001. These contracts are mainly gross-cost contracts and stipulate bonuses and penalties depending on the observed service quality. In the case of London, quality has improved since the introduction of these contracts; however, the operating costs increased too (Amaral et al 2009). These quality incentive contracts encourage improved service quality, rather than volume of kilometres per bus run (which is determined in the initial contract specification), through setting targets for excess waiting times and bonus payments. For instance, to improve reliability, one means is to increase layover time at each end of the route. A route requiring 10 vehicles at a given frequency might be increased to 11 to provide this margin, the extra costs being justified by passenger benefits through reduced waiting time. This will cause a significant increase in costs – on British cost structures, by about 8% both for the total, and unit cost per bus-kilometre. Pyddoke and Andersson (2010) simulate the effect of net-cost contracts augmented with a subsidy per passenger for bus operators. Their results indicate that such contracts may incentivise operators to improve frequency (as ridership is increased), but may become costly to the transport authority.

Contracts such as those implemented in London or simulated by Pyddoke and Andersson (2010) are called quality contracts or performance based contracts (Hensher and Wallis 2005). This type of contract consists of a payment for a minimum service level and a patronage growth incentive payment rate. Payment for patronage growth is linked to quality of service.

Which contract is better

Empirical evidence is not clear about which fixed-price contract is better. White and Tough (1995) report that gross–cost contracts resulted in lower bids in tendering contracts in Britain. Net–cost contracts are more expensive for the transport authority because bids include risk premiums due to the revenue risk bore by the operator. By contrast, Muren (2000) concluded that net-cost contracts give, in principle, the possibility of achieving the desired level of service quality at a lower transfer to the operator. However, if demand is uncertain because exogenous factors (such as fare evasion), the advantages of net-cost contracts over gross–cost contracts reduces due to the risk premium required by the operators.

Roy and Yvrande-Billon (2007) study the incentive power of contracts to produce efficiency in the French urban transport sector. Their results indicate that operators under cost-plus contracts exhibit a higher level of technical inefficiency than operators under fixed-price agreements. In addition, operators regulated by gross–cost contracts reach the highest technical efficiency among several reimbursement rules implemented in France.

Most of the existing literature on the contracting of bus transport services is in the context of developed cities. Since the growth of BRT systems is primarily in developing cities, the issue of contracts for BRT in developing cities presents new issues that we will be addressing in the rest of the chapter.

Key decisions

When designing a contract, the transport authority must decide on several aspects that comprise the contract beyond the reimbursement rule.

Contracts may set lump-sum payments based on anticipated or actual cost and contracted subsidy. Also, contracts may define unit payments based on the quantity of supply or the actual passenger demand. For instance, a unit payment based on supply is the payment per kilometre and a unit payment based on demand is the payment per passenger.

Payment per kilometre

When a transport authority decides on a supply based payment, the contract is a gross-cost type. The contract transfers production risk to the operating firm and revenue risk to the authority. Indeed, the firm has no incentive to improve the service quality because its profits do not depend on the ridership. Therefore, supply based payments should be complemented with other contractual conditions. For example, if quality is contractible, monitoring measures should be agreed to verify the fulfilment of quality standards. This approach implies the implementation of compliance measures, which may be costly, both technologically and monetary, in the case of large cities with a large number of bus lines and high frequency.

If quality is not contractible or monitoring is difficult and costly, the contract may include incentives to improve quality. This means that the transport authority should implement a performance based contract. In doing so, authorities also need to define quality measures and monitoring procedures. However, ridership is the best measure of quality (Hensher and Wallis 2005), the incentives may be associated with measures of increasing demand. Passenger demand is easy to measure and does not require additional information collection because the transport authority has the control of revenue and passengers in the gross-cost contract. Contract may allow the operating firm to set fares and frequency to some extent to increase ridership (Pyddoke and Andersson 2010). However, developing countries (or public transport systems with low elasticity to fare and quality) are not suitable for performance based contracts because passengers are captives of public transport and passenger demand it is not a good measurement of quality. In this case, a better alternative is to set other measures of quality, for instance those defined for Santiago de Chile: measures for the number of seat/standing places per hour, frequency, and regularity (for more details see Beltrán et al 2013).

Payment per passenger

Payment per passenger implies transferring the revenue risk to the operating firm. In this case the contract adopts the form of a net–cost contract. This type of contract is more costly than a gross–cost contract for the transport authority, because it must pay for the risk premium. Payment per passenger provides incentive for quality improvements, as explained before. Nevertheless, in cases of inelastic demand or a large proportion of the population being captive to public transport, these contracts provide incentive to reduce costs at the expense of quality. Again, the monitoring of quality is necessary for the system to operate at minimum standards.

In summary, both payment per kilometre and payment per passenger require implementation of monitoring measures, included in the contracts along with the penalties and bonuses for compliance with the contracted supply or minimum standards.

Other key decisions

There are other key decisions when a contract is designed; however, they are related to the management of the contract rather than the design itself. Some of these decisions are the division of responsibilities between operators and authority: fare evasion, ownership of terminals, construction of infrastructure, information systems, and control systems. Whenever these decisions involve monetary costs, they may be included in the contracts.

Fare evasion is the only responsibility that may affect the contract design. Indeed, financial responsibility to control fare evasion is defined at the time of choosing the type of contract. If the contract puts revenue risk on the operating firm, the firm must be responsible for fare evasion. However, control of evasion requires the legal authority to force passengers to pay the fare and/or fine them for fare evasion, and such ability is usually in the hands of the public authority. In some countries, the transfer of this authority to transportation firms is (almost) impossible because it needs legal arrangements, including modifications to the law. In these cases, the transport authority must be responsible for controlling fare evasion.

Case studies

In this section we will review implementation of four bus concessions: TransMilenio (Colombia), Transantiago (Chile), TransJakarta (Indonesia), and Delhi (India). We will give a brief description of each bus system and we will discuss some key decisions made by authorities, focusing on risk sharing (between local authority and operator), how operators are paid (fixed payment, per person and/or per kilometre), and monitoring.

TransMilenio (Bogotá, Colombia)

TransMilenio is one of the most famous and successful BRT in Latin America. It has one of the highest operational speeds for BRT and carries over 185,000 passengers in the morning peak time. TransMilenio is an example of a well-planned BRT (Hidalgo et al 2013). The design process started with a high investment in demand and traffic studies that offered enough confidence in the system to attract operators to a competitive tendering process in order to gain the monopoly on a trunk line and associated feeder services. The BRT changed the whole transportation scheme in Bogotá as it gradually implemented a trunk feeder scheme from an old system of approximately 35,000 small, private bus operators offering point-to-point services. (See Chapter Three for a discussion of this process and its limitations.)

Bogotá's tendering process for the initial stages of TransMilenio was a great innovation, as not only was it used to minimise the amount of money the government would have to pay to operators, but also to force the renewal of the rolling stock and other policy goals. So far a tender like this has not been seen in any other studied system (Hook 2005).

Contracts stated that operators would assume part of the risk over the demand of the system as a way to keep their incentives aligned with the objectives of the BRT. But this condition made it difficult for operators who won the tender to find the initial financing they needed in order to acquire new buses in Colombia, since banks were not confident in the success of the BRT and saw it as too risky an investment. The government did not offer any financial assistance, so operators had to look for loans in Brazil. The fact that the buses were being made in that country helped the Colombian operators find financing there. These loans were completely repaid and operators have not faced any problems in obtaining finance to renew the fleet, as the system has proved successful.

In order to maintain a high quality service, authorities can fine operators up to 10% of their monthly income for service failures. As operators are paid by kilometre driven, fines are applied by modifying the weekly schedule for buses, which establishes the number of buses and their daily schedule. This simple mechanism has allowed TransMilenio to achieve a good quality service with high operational speed and regular frequency in an efficient way (Hidalgo et al 2013). Nevertheless, it should be noted that if fines reduce the amount of kilometres driven, it worsens the system's quality and the operator reduces its income, but also operation costs. Nowadays, TransMilenio faces passenger protests due to the overcrowding of the system (which is not included as an indicator of service quality). Therefore, new measures for quality are required in the contracts. It should also be noted that the successful contracts for TransMilenio were on the corridors with the highest ridership and therefore the most likely to be financially successful. Now that Bogotá is extending the contracting scheme to the entire city some operators are having financial difficulties.

Transantiago (Santiago, Chile)

Transantiago was a big change for Santiago's transportation system as it completely modified the transportation scheme for the whole city from one day to another (Muñoz and Gschwender 2008; Muñoz et al 2014). It is not a complete BRT system, since it does not have corridors on every bus route, but it is a citywide feeder trunk system (see Chapter Three).

Before Transantiago was implemented, bus services were controlled by a cartel of small private operators that worked in an almost unregulated market. So when the new system went into the planning stage, authorities set the goal of breaking this cartel and bringing in foreign investors as operators (see Chapter Four). In order to achieve this goal, policy makers decided that individual operators would be responsible for only a small percentage of the demand risk of the system, guaranteeing up to 90% of the estimated income and building a low-risk business (Beltrán et al 2013). Thus Transantiago's contracts with the bus operators were, in practice, fixed-price contracts. This ended up with operators having no incentives to transport passengers, which caused many problems when the new system started in February 2007.

The contracts established certain fines in case operators did not achieve their operational goals. Once an operator accumulated a certain amount in fines, it would automatically lose its concession and a new tendering process would be called for its area/trunk service. But when Transantiago started, there were so many problems that almost all operators would have lost their concession only months after the start of the system. As it was impossible for the authorities to simultaneously change all operators, renegotiations had to be conducted in order to guarantee public transportation in Santiago.

After intense negotiations with operators, guarantees were reduced and new performance indicators came into effect that had an impact on the operator's income. Beltrán et al (2013) describe the evolution of compliance indicators in Santiago. This programme of compliance measures started by mid-2007 and increased the operating fleet from 4,600 to 5,800 buses in only five months, thus increasing the service level (with a bigger fleet operators could offer more frequency and less crowding in buses and at bus stops). The compliance measures focus on the number of seat/standing places per hour (measured through Global Positioning System [GPS]), frequency, and headway regularity. As shown by Batarce and Galilea (2014), the introduction of the first compliance measure led the firms to improve quality and to increase their efforts to reduce costs.

Transantiago's contracts have had major renegotiations at least five times. A detailed review of clauses related to operator's payment, their effects, and evolution can be found in Briones and Gómez-Lobo (2013). During 2009 there were contract renegotiations in order to include formally the set of indices designed to improve bus operation. Afterwards new problems started to arise: evasion and buses not stopping at bus stops to pick up passengers (drivers were more aware of being on time at the terminal end of their route in order to fulfil operational indices than serving passengers at stops).

During 2010 and 2011, there were other renegotiations of contracts in order to give operators more incentives to control passenger evasion by increasing the demand risk faced by operators.

Jakarta, Indonesia

Transjakarta BRT today has medium to high operational speeds and a very low patronage, with the buses sharing the segregated lanes with buses from the previous system and competing for passengers with them. The high number of both BRT and existing buses sometimes makes the segregated lanes congested, affecting operational speed and quality of service (Deng and Nelson 2013).

At the beginning, local authorities decided that the government would be responsible for acquiring the whole fleet of new buses for the system. Operators would then need to rent the number of buses they needed each day. The authorities' idea was that operators would have to maintain the buses, but this responsibility was not formally written into the contracts signed with them. Since operators are not directly affected by non-operational buses and do not directly benefit from maintaining them, they have reduced costs by omitting maintenance almost completely. This has greatly reduced the quality of the service provided, making it difficult to improve ridership levels and offer a quality service (Hidalgo et al 2007).

Delhi, India

Non-motorised transportation in India is still the main mode of mobility and the authorities wanted to improve conditions for most of the population while encouraging the use of public transport. The government of Delhi used the construction of the BRT as a way to completely renovate the urban landscape (Mohan 2012). The Delhi pilot did not just use segregated lanes for buses, but also built new special lanes for non-motorised vehicles, new footpaths, and improved the city landscape around the corridor (Tiwari and Jain 2010).

The authorities in Delhi got around the issue of contracts by implementing an open BRT corridor. In an open BRT corridor all buses regardless of operator are able to use the segregated lanes and boarding platforms. This means buses operated by a public agency or operated by private companies use the corridor under the existing regulations; no operating contracts are needed.

While open BRT corridors simplify the need for contracts there are operational impacts. (See Chapter Fifteen for more discussion of open and closed BRT corridors.) Currently, Delhi's BRT has a high patronage level but its operational speed is quite slow. In part the low speed is caused by the bus lanes being shared by all buses. Without contracts there are no controls over the maintenance and buses break down in the lanes (Hook 2005). There also are no controls over other service quality issues.

Challenges and potential problems

As stated in Gómez-Lobo and Briones (2014) the design of effective bus concession contracts is difficult, and it is especially difficult for extensive citywide bus systems. Therefore, policy makers should plan a gradual implementation (in time and space), leaving room for a trial and error approach.

Renegotiations

No bus concession contract will be perfect since there are conflicting tradeoff objectives: demand risk borne by the operator versus the system's financial affordability. Consequently, it is likely that contracts will be renegotiated (unless they could be shorter and/or more flexible) and this should be recognised at the design stage of a concession contract. For instance, Transantiago contracts have been renegotiated at least five times in seven years.

One important weakness in these renegotiation processes is that even if the transport authority wants to remove an operator that has performed poorly, in practice it is difficult to do. At least in Transantiago's case, authorities have not had a good alternative because of the complexity of the procurement process in the public sector, taking at least a year and a half to prepare, tender, award, and start up a contract with a new operator. Hence, current operators know that they are in a safe position and behave accordingly. Who owns the terminals and bus depots is also a factor in making the future market contestable.

What should be done with incumbents

When a public authority is thinking about implementing a BRT (or any bus concession contract), it has to make a decision regarding the incumbents, especially if the actual operators are part of an informal market. Authorities may decide to include them in the new tendering process (Metrobús in Mexico City), mix them with the new bus concessions (TransMilenio has incumbents as feeders of TransMilenio, while Delhi's BRTs share its corridors with them), or not include them at all. Each one of these options has its advantages and disadvantages. (Chapter Four covers this issue in detail.)

Type of contracts

Generally speaking, it would seem that net-cost contracts should be preferred because they lead to efficient provision and increased ridership. However, the most suitable contract type depends on the transport authority's objective and the city's characteristics; there are successful examples of each type of contract. Gómez-Lobo and Briones (2013) and Briones and Gómez-Lobo (2014) also acknowledge that the contract decision depends on the extension of the public transport reform (whether it is a BRT or a citywide reform) and the technological capacity that the authority has to control bus operations. A citywide system that does not have a monitoring technology able to effectively control bus performance will face severe problems because bus companies will be more tempted to underperform. This was the case of Transantiago between 2007 and 2009.

If the quality of service is a concern for the transport authority, it should consider cost-plus contracts. If the city has an inelastic demand to public transport quality (the case in many developing countries), it should be careful in the use of fixed-price contracts. When contracts are incomplete and service level is not adequately incorporated into the contract, fixed-price contracts may not be efficient. So, authorities are advised to design contracts that allow a certain level of quality monitoring when deciding on fixed-price contracts. Also, monitoring proves to be an effective tool to incentivise cost reduction efforts without hindering the service level (as was done in Transantiago). Also, optimal bus contracts should include important performance based bonuses (or discounts) in order to incentivise good quality service provision.

Allocation of demand risk

Gómez-Lobo and Briones (2014), after looking in detail at the experience of bus concessions in Latin America, recommend that operators face some demand risk, so they cater to demand with an adequate service level. Nevertheless, they also conclude that it is unavoidable to shield operators from demand risk (to some extent).

Institutional capacity of the public authority to monitor contracts

As it has been shown in the previous sections, authorities should design contracts that allow them to monitor the quality of the service and should also have the institutional capacity to enforce fines and penalties, which in turn should be credible and useful as an incentive mechanism (Gómez-Lobo and Briones, 2013)

Notes
[1] Since the operator is receiving a fixed amount of money, regardless of the number of passengers served, any improvements in terms of costs will be savings that will benefit it alone.

[2] However, if the negotiated payment is based on the incurred cost plus a fee, it leads to a cost-plus contract.

[3] But if the payment is contingent on realised operator's cost, the contract is a cost-plus type.

References

Amaral, M., Saussier, S. and Yvrande-Billon, A. (2009) 'Auction procedures and competition in public services: the case of urban public transport in France and London', *Utilities Policy*, 17(2): 166–175.

Augustin, K. and Walter, M. (2010) 'Operator changes through competitive tendering: empirical evidence from German local bus transport', *Research in Transportation Economics*, 29(1): 36–44.

Batarce, M. and Galilea, P. (2014) 'Power of incentive schemes, provision of quality and monitoring: the case of the public transit system in Santiago de Chile', Proceedings of the 2014 Annual Conference of the International Transportation Economics Association (ITEA), Toulouse, https://editorialexpress.com/cgi-bin/conference/download.cgi?db_name=ITEA2014&paper_id=46.

Beltrán, P., Gschwender, A. and Palma, C. (2013) 'The impact of compliance measures on the operation of a bus system: the case of Transantiago', *Research in Transportation Economics*, 39(1): 79–89.

Bernardino, J., Hřebíček, Z. and Marques, C. (2010) 'Applying social marginal cost pricing in rail PPPs: present state, drawbacks and ways forward', *Research in Transportation Economics*, 30(1): 59–73.

Boitani, A. and Cambini, C. (2006) 'To bid or not to bid, this is the question: the Italian experience in competitive tendering for local bus services', www.openstarts.units.it/xmlui/handle/10077/5921

Briones, J. and Gómez-Lobo, A. (2013) 'Incentive structure in transit concession contracts: the case of Santiago, Chile, and London, England', Washington, DC: Policy Paper prepared for the Clean Air Institute.

Deng, T. and Nelson, J.D. (2013) 'Bus Rapid Transit implementation in Beijing: An evaluation of performance and impacts', *Research in Transportation Economics*, 39(1): 108–113.

Gagnepain, P. and Ivaldi, M. (2002) 'Incentive regulatory policies: the case of public transit systems in France', *RAND Journal of Economics*, 33(4): 605–629.

Galilea, P. and Medda, F. (2010) 'Does the political and economic context influence the success of a transport project? An analysis of transport public–private partnerships', *Research in Transportation Economics*, 30(1): 102–109.

Gómez-Lobo, A. and Briones, J. (2014) 'Incentives in bus concession contracts: a review of several experiences in Latin America', *Transport Reviews*, 34(2): 246–265.

Grout, P.A. (1997) 'The economics of the private finance initiative', *Oxford Review of Economic Policy*, 13(4): 53–66.

Hart, O. (2003) 'Incomplete contracts and public ownership: remarks, and an application to public–private partnerships', *The Economic Journal*, 113(486): 69–76.

Hensher, D.A. and Wallis, I P. (2005) 'Competitive tendering as a contracting mechanism for subsidising transport: the bus experience', *Journal of Transport Economics and Policy*, 39(3): 295–322.

Hidalgo, D., Custodio, P. and Graftieux, P. (2007) 'A critical look at major bus improvements in Latin America and Asia: case studies of hitches, hiccups, and areas for improvement: synthesis of lessons learned', Report produced with the Assistance of TRISP, a partnership between the UK Department for International Development and the World Bank.

Hidalgo, D., Pereira, L., Estupiñán, N. and Jiménez, P. L. (2013) 'TransMilenio BRT system in Bogota, high performance and positive impact – main results of an ex-post evaluation', *Research in Transportation Economics*, 39(1): 133–138.

Hook, W. (2005) 'Institutional and regulatory options for BRT in developing countries: Lessons from international experience', *Transportation Research Record: Journal of the Transportation Research Record*, 1939: 184–191.

Laffont, J.J. (2001) *Incentives and Political Economy* (Clarendon Lectures in Economics), Oxford: Oxford University Press.

Laffont, J.J. and Martimort, D. (2002) *The Theory of Incentives: The Principal–Agent Model*, Princeton, NJ: Princeton University Press.

Laffont, J.J. and Tirole, J. (1986) 'Using cost observation to regulate firms', *Journal of Political Economy*, 94(3): 614–641.

Laffont, J.J. and Tirole, J. (1993) *A Theory of Incentives in Procurement and Regulation*, Cambridge, MA: MIT Press.

Medda, F. and Carbonaro, G. (2007) 'Growth of container seaborne traffic in the Mediterranean basin: outlook and policy implications for port development', *Transport Reviews*, 27(5): 573–587.

Mohan, D. (2012) 'Translating policy into action', in: The Volvo Research and Educational Foundation (ed.), *VREF: 10 years with the FUTProgramme* (1st edn). Göteborg: Swedish National Road and Transport Research Institute, VTI, pp. 22–31.

Muñoz, J.C. and Gschwender, A. (2008) 'Transantiago: a tale of two cities', *Research in Transportation Economics*, 22(1): 45–53.

Muñoz, J.C., Batarce, M. and Hidalgo, D. (2014) 'Transantiago, five years after its launch', *Research in Transportation Economics, Competition and Ownership in Land Passenger Transport*, 48: 184–193.

Muren, A. (2000) 'Quality assurance in competitively tendered contracts', *Journal of Transport Economics and Policy*, 34(1): 99–111.

Pyddoke, R. and Andersson, M. (2010) 'Increased patronage for urban bus transport with net-cost contracts', Working paper from Swedish National Road and Transport Research Institute.

Quinet, E. and Vickerman, E. (2004) *Principles of Transport Economics*, Cheltenham: Edward Elgar.

Roy, W. and Yvrande-Billon, A. (2007) 'Ownership, contractual practices and technical efficiency: the case of urban public transport in France', *Journal of Transport Economics and Policy*, 41(2): 257–282.

Tiwari, G. and Jain, D. (2010) 'Bus Rapid Transit projects in Indian cities: a status report', *Built Environment*, 36(3): 353–362. doi:10.2148/benv.36.3.353

White, P. and Tough, S. (1995) 'Alternative tendering systems and deregulation in Britain', *Journal of Transport Economics and Policy*, 29(3): 275–289.

EIGHT

Fare structures

Marco Batarce and Corinne Mulley

Introduction

Customers pay fares for the services they consume on public transport and fares are the means by which operators receive a contribution to the cost of service provision. This simple exchange belies a complex set of decisions in every urban area which have far reaching impacts beyond the operation and use of the public transport system. It affects the accessibility of citizens and ultimately impacts on urban form.

A fare system is defined by its structure, its collection method and the fare level. The objectives for public transport guide how these three elements are combined. For instance, a transport authority may use fares as a tool to meet policy objectives such as demand management to reduce congestion or subsidy allocation to promote equity or social inclusion. In this chapter, we are concerned with the fare finally paid by the user in contrast to the technical fare (BRT Planning Guide (ITDP 2007)), which is related to the amount per passenger received by the operator and how this is related to efficiency and incentives (Laffont and Tirole 1993), which is more properly considered as a part of the contract design (see Chapter Seven).

The implementation of a BRT system as new infrastructure offers an opportunity to reinforce government objectives because the process usually introduces regulations and contractual agreements that allow the authority to set fare fixing criteria consistently. In the case of urban areas with unregulated bus transport systems, such as many cities in developing countries, BRT implementation is also an opportunity to harmonise transport in the city by regulating the fares of previously unregulated operators either by offering a substitute mode with a regulated fare, which could be lower, or by giving incentives to complementary services to agree an integrated fare system. New BRT or integrated systems are however different from the many unregulated services they replace since the latter typically operate without subsidy and behave like typical 'firms'.

It is important to understand the overarching goal of a BRT system – whether the objective is to maximise the number of passengers, maximise the revenue or to reach some other specific goals such as commercial cost recovery or to benefit some sector of the community, such as the socially excluded. It is clear that cities cannot expect to meet all these goals at the same time and that they will have different implications for fare levels in particular. These objectives are linked to the institutional setting of the country in which the city is located, with revenue based objectives being more likely in a deregulated market and passenger based objectives being more likely in a public transport system aimed at delivering accessibility.

At this point it is worth discussing why letting the market fix the fare level is not a good policy. There are two main reasons. The first is the existence of externalities in the provision of public transportation, which leads to distortion in the market price. One such externality is a reduction in average waiting time as more people use public transportation because more passengers require an increase in frequency. When a user decides to use public transportation they consider their average waiting time, but their decision will lead to an increase in the frequency and a reduction in waiting time for the rest of the users.

A second reason is the existence of search costs in the 'consumption' of bus services. As users have to wait for the bus with the lowest fare, they undergo a cost of searching, which is their waiting time. As the arrival of the buses at the stop are uncertain (in frequency based services), users choose the first bus even if it does not have the lowest fare. This search cost is used by bus operators to set the prices over marginal cost, leading to inefficient equilibrium, with reduction in social welfare. For a detailed explanation of this problem see Fernandez and Muñoz (2007) and Gómez-Lobo (2007). Thus, the implementation of a BRT system is also an opportunity to correct through its fare system some of the market distortions that have developed in the urban bus transport market over time.

This chapter is organised in five sections, including this introduction. The next section describes the components of a fare system. Section three presents the microeconomic theoretical framework for fare computation. The fourth section applies the pricing principles presented in the third section to the bus system in Santiago de Chile. The final section discusses some policy implications of common fare structures and concludes.

Components of a fare system

This section describes the three components that determine a fare system: the fare structure, fare collection and the fare level.

The fare structure

Fare structures fall broadly into three categories: flat fares, distance based fares, zonal fares and travel passes There are a number of criteria for the evaluation of the fare structure, including the ease of understanding for passengers, the simplicity of collection, the ability of the fare structure to generate the required revenue, how easy it is to control fares (particularly from evasion by passengers), how equitable it is and its attractiveness to passengers.

Flat fares do well on a number of these criteria (ease of understanding, simplicity of collection and attractiveness to passengers). However, the major disadvantage is that a flat fare does not relate to the 'quantity' of travel that is purchased and so it is often argued that it is inequitable as long journey travellers consume more than short journey travellers. Perhaps more seriously, a flat fare can mean that very short rides are not taken and are substituted by walking; thus revenue can be reduced (and this is why in some cases a 'short hop' fare is additionally in place).

Exact distance based fares are rare, with some European railway systems charging by the kilometre. But for urban bus systems, distance based fares are usually charged by 'fare stages' or 'fare sections', with passengers paying for the number of stages that are traversed. Distance based fares are normally related to the line of travel rather than geography, as with zonal fares. Distance based fare structures are often 'capped' with a maximum fare. Distance based fares do not score well on ease of understanding for passengers or passenger attraction, and policing distance based fares can be difficult as there is a requirement to know the origin and destination of the traveller. However, many of the disadvantages of distance based fares can be overcome with more technologically based fare collection systems when a distance based fare can be seen as providing an equitable payment system. Many cities have distance based fares because of the need to raise revenue to support public transport.

Zonal based fares are a form of distance based fare, but usually more crudely graduated by distance. Normally a single fare applies to all intra-zonal journeys, with higher fares becoming payable as passengers travel in multiple zones. The best zonal fare structures are those which have natural boundaries between zones, such as rivers. Zonal boundary construction needs to take into account the typical journeys of the city in question so that short trips do not end up crossing zone boundaries. As compared to flat fares, zonal fares introduce more distance based fares and therefore more complexity and make it more costly to ensure passengers pay the correct fare. From a passenger understanding, it is more complicated than a flat fare and requires a spatial understanding of the journey to be undertaken. However, unlike distance based fares, zonal fares are based on the geographical relationship between origin and destination rather than the line distance travelled in the public transport system, which does make zonal systems more attractive.

Discounted fares are typically offered irrespective of the baseline structure of the fare. The discounted fares come in multiple formats, including travel passes (giving unlimited travel or giving discounts). Discounted fares are used either to increase revenues to the operator or to meet other objectives (increase use of public transport by the unemployed or those on low incomes). Discounted fares and their collection are inextricably linked and are discussed more below.

Fare collection

How fares are collected are influenced by the form of payment (whether cash or pre-payment) and whether it is made at the time of travel or in advance and whether it is purchased on or off-vehicle. While cash payment was a previous standard, in many cities this has been replaced by prepayment schemes of different kinds for many reasons, including the operational simplification it brings to bus operation (drivers not having to handle cash), and operating cost and travel time savings through the reduction in dwell times. Payment methods are increasingly made by passengers on a self-service basis with very many cities moving towards or having already achieved payment using smart cards or some other automated system. Smart cards – or their less smart predecessors with magnetic strips – offer a way of sophisticated fare collection (as well as providing a wealth of information on the travel patterns of passengers (see Chapter Fourteen). Discounted tickets are often linked to specific forms of fare collection, such as a 'strip' of tickets or a travel pass.

As identified above, the critical element in terms of fare collection is where the fare is collected in relation to the travel undertaken. The movement away from cash and towards smarter means of fare collection have been motivated by operational savings as discussed in the previous paragraph. But there are also some infrastructural considerations in fare collection linked to where the fare payment is made. The more that fares are taken off vehicles, thus speeding up passenger boarding, the more sophisticated the off-vehicle infrastructure needs to be to make sure passengers pay before boarding to ensure revenue collection.

The fare level

The fare level adopted in a city is influenced by the objectives set for the public transport sector; the method of financing and in particular how much of the public transport system cost needs to be covered by fare revenue; the costs of operating the system and the costs of competing modes; and the user characteristics, in particular their elasticity of demand which may vary by different urban contexts and in different operational contexts. In the UK, for example, the rule of thumb is that the price elasticity for bus travel is −0.4, with the value being slightly lower at around −0.35 for Europe as a whole. In Santiago de Chile, estimated price elasticity for bus travel is around −0.6 (Batarce and Ivaldi 2014), which is higher than that in the UK because of the comparatively lower household income in Chile. As a result of the higher service quality it is likely that price elasticities for BRT will be more inelastic but still less than one in absolute value. In any case, these values suggest that cities must be careful about raising fares in absolute or real terms as revenue will decrease as a result.

In terms of the relationship between costs and fares, this will depend on what the revenue from fares needs to cover. Clearly, if the fares need to cover the full costs, including construction, the fare level will have to be higher than if required to cover only operational costs. Moreover, the way in which the fare level is determined is important: fare levels could be driven by a mark-up over marginal costs, by market pricing or by some sort of yield management approach to maximise income.

Operationally, public transport costs are driven by the peak costs and BRT operation is no different. It is an important decision in a city as to how much of this additional peak cost should be transferred to fares for peak travellers. Many cities use their fare levels to encourage travel outside peak times for those passengers who are able to do so by including an off-peak fare as this is a more palatable approach than charging a 'peak' fare. However, it should be noted that the way in which costs are driven by peak requirements means that many of the time limited tickets (travel passes and season tickets) which reward frequent travel are rewarding frequent travel in the peak as these tickets are commonly used for commuting. This is, of course, directly opposed to charging a fare that is related to costs. As identified above, the introduction of a new BRT system offers the opportunity to correct for distortions which have been historically implemented and this is another case in point.

The above suggests that the relationship between costs and fare levels is not straightforward and yet there are more market segments that can be used to differentiate fare levels. Different types of service (express versus local services) might be charged at a different fare level because the quality of service is different. Commuters, despite travelling at peak times when the services cost more to provide, could justifiably be given a discount if they commit money upfront for a significant period.

Many cities also offer discounts to students, unemployed people and older people, and how these are interpreted requires a bit more care. In many societies, it is hoped that low or free fares will improve the accessibility of older people and, as a result, the government or funding body makes up the difference between the fare older people pay and the normal adult fare. This is called a concession fare. Lower fares for children come into this same concession category. However, cheaper fares for students and unemployed people are not usually made up by the funding body because this is a form of price discrimination. Students and unemployed people have a more elastic demand and so the practice of offering a lower fare is to encourage greater travel. This is therefore a market pricing response where the decision to discount the fare to these low income categories of travellers is an attempt to increase revenues through more travel. In practical terms how concessions versus price discriminatory discounts for travellers with more elastic demand are treated will depend on the contractual relationship for service provision. Operators are much more likely to support market related fare discounts when they are operating on net cost contracts, retaining all the fare revenue.

The role of objectives

The choice of fare structure, fare collection and fare level is inextricably linked to the objectives for the public transport system and is often a trade-off between conflicting aspirations or objectives which are subject to constraint. Objectives are usually set by government or transport authorities, and in those cities where this does not include the actual fare level and ticket types it is the operator who is left with the task of turning these into an operational fare system.

Since there are multiple conflicting objectives, fare systems are often a compromise. For example, an urban form which has low income earners living a significant distance from the areas of main employment may employ either a low fare level or a distance based fare structure with a low maximum fare. However, this can lead to a reinforcement of undesirable land use patterns where low income workers trade more space for low rents on the fringes of city and 'pay' for this by travelling longer distances.

Pricing theory

The starting point to understand and analyse the mechanisms for fixing the fare level is the economic theory. In the following, we present the basic principle of first–best pricing, which has as a goal to maximise the social welfare of public transport users. We also present the second-best pricing policy, which also maximises users' welfare, but subject to some constraint such as the firm breaking even. Next, we discuss some implication of the theory on the fare structure.

Theoretical fare level

Generally speaking, first-best pricing, originally proposed by Pigou (1920) and Knight (1924), consists of charging the full marginal cost to users (consumers). The cost includes the production cost as well as external effects like congestion, pollution, noise, and so on. In other words, first-best pricing tries to make individuals pay all the cost they cause to society. In the case of public transportation, the average social cost, which includes operation cost plus users' cost (travel, waiting, and access time), decrease as more individuals use public transport. Mohring (1972) shows that the operating cost and users' waiting time decrease with the total demand. This is known as the 'Mohring effect' and implies that there are economies of scale in the provision of public transportation.

Mathematically, if $m(Q)$ is the marginal operation cost function, which depends on the travel demand Q, and $p(Q)$ is the inverse demand function, in equilibrium, individual willingness to pay should equal the generalised transport price (fare plus monetary value of average travel, waiting and access time). Total welfare (W) is equal to the aggregate users' benefit (B) minus the total costs (C). Total costs include the users' cost plus operation cost. Users' cost is $Qc(Q)$, where $c(Q)$ is the average user cost (travel, waiting and access time).

Therefore, the welfare to maximise is:

$$W = B - C = \int_0^Q p(q)\,dq - Qc(Q) - \int_0^Q m(q)\,dq$$

The first-order condition to maximise the total social welfare is:

$$p(Q) - c(Q) - Q\frac{\partial c}{\partial Q} - m(Q) = 0 \qquad (1)$$

The first term is the total price paid by the user: the fare plus the cost experienced by the user when travelling. Therefore, the latter should not be included in the fare charged, $f(Q)$. The second to fourth terms are equal to the social marginal costs ($m_s(Q)$), leading to the condition:

$$p(Q) = f(Q) + c(Q) = c(Q) + Q\frac{\partial c}{\partial Q} + m(Q) \qquad (2)$$

Thus

$$f(Q) = Q\frac{\partial c}{\partial Q} + m(Q) \qquad (3)$$

Since the average user cost decreases with the total demand because of the Mohring effect, the first term on the right hand side is negative, and the fare is lower than the operational marginal cost. In transport systems with high demand the benefits of increasing demand may be reduced because of congestion on buses and at stops (or stations). For instance, in the Santiago metro system waiting time has increased because the crowding in both trains and stations prevents people boarding the first train to arrive. In Bogotá, the BRT system experiences congestion at the stations because of the high frequency of buses required to meet the demand. Therefore, even if the long term social cost should reduce with the demand, the economies of scale vanish for high levels of demand in the short and medium term.

If the positive externality due to the demand for public transportation vanishes, the optimal fare equals the marginal cost of operation. In the short run the marginal cost of carrying an additional passenger should be very low, since the route structure is unchanged and the fleet does not increase. However, in the long run marginal cost should include both changes in routes and additional fleet required. Proper pricing policy should be based on long term marginal costs. On top of that, the operational cost usually exhibits constant returns to scale. This means the average cost equals the marginal cost. Thus, the optimal fare coincides with average-cost pricing.

The previous discussion does not consider the effect of public transport fares on demand for alternative transport modes. If the authority intends to maximise social welfare, taking into account the cross-price elasticity of demand, the resulting public transportation fares will include a correction term proportional to the difference between marginal cost and price charged in all transport alternatives (Jara-Diaz 2007). For instance, consider the case of two alternatives for transportation: bus and car. The planner fixes the fare level of the bus by maximising the social welfare of all transport users (car and bus). Therefore, the optimal fare is:

$$f(Q_b) = m(Q_b) + Q_b \frac{\partial c}{\partial Q_b} + \frac{Q_a}{Q_b} \frac{\varepsilon_{a,b}}{|\varepsilon_{b,b}|} (p_a - m_a) \qquad (4)$$

where Q_b and Q_a are the demand for bus and car respectively, $\varepsilon_{a,b}$ is the cross-price elasticity of car demand to bus price, $\varepsilon_{b,b}$ is the price elasticity of bus demand, p_a is the generalised price paid by car users (including the operational cost of a car and the travel time in money units), and m_a is the total marginal cost of car travel.

As private transport is often underpriced, because car users do not internalise congestion effects, the optimal bus fare results in below operational marginal cost. Again, subsidies for public transport are justified on grounds of social welfare maximisation. Therefore, welfare maximisation implies bus fares lower than the marginal operational cost. If marginal cost is equal or lower than average cost, it is necessary to give subsidies to the operators. (Usually firms operating public bus services exhibit constant returns to scale, which means marginal cost equals average cost.) This pricing policy is called second-best price.

In general, any public policy trying to maximise social welfare under any kind of restriction will be called a second-best pricing policy, and was first described for general situations by Lipsey and Lancaster (1956) and Baumol and Bradford (1970), among others. In the case of a limited budget for subsidies, the expression for welfare maximising fares only changes by including a term related to the cost of public funds, called the Ramsey index. For pricing bus fares without considering competing modes, the fare is given by:

$$f(Q) = Q \frac{\partial c}{\partial Q} + m(Q) + \frac{\lambda}{1+\lambda} \frac{Q}{\dfrac{\partial Q}{\partial f}} \qquad (5)$$

From equation (5), the optimal fare keeps the same structure as the first-best prices. That is, internalisation of the positive externality, due to economies of scale.

In the case of competing modes, the fare is given by a more complex expression; however, it is also composed of the marginal cost of provision, internalisation of the externality, and the distortion in related markets, due to underpriced transport alternatives. Interested readers can see Jara-Díaz (2007) for a more detailed exposition of this type of pricing scheme.

Even though maximising social welfare seems to be the preferable criterion for fixing fares for public services, the authority may use something else. For instance, the transport authority may allow operators to maximise profits, or may want to maximise patronage subject to the firm breaking even. The former case is common in some public–private partnership for road infrastructure provision where the objective is revenue generation to make the private investment profitable. The latter case has a goal to exhaust available capacity, and to be a more profitable public investment.

It is worth noting that in all cases the fare should be computed as the result of equilibrium between fare, marginal cost and demand. This computation needs to know the inverse demand and marginal cost functions, which should be estimated for every city. If a transport model is available for the city, including a transit assignment model, a more detailed fare computation may be done by using the model. The planner's objective function should be specified using as variables the model outputs (demand levels, and travel, waiting and access time). Then the maximisation of the objective function is subject to the variables from the transport model. This approach is attractive because of the internal consistency and the possibilities for a detailed network representation; however, the fare computation needs to solve complex bi-level mathematical programming.

Practical issues of implementation of theoretically consistent fares

The fare structure will be related to the optimal fare if the fares in use distinguish between different costs of provision for different lengths of travel and for different periods of the day. Therefore, maximising social welfare by trying to have the fares reproduce the actual production cost involves defining a fare structure that distinguishes distances, origin and destination, time of day, and so on. In this sense, zonal fare structures and distance based fares are theoretically consistent with welfare maximisation.

However, for practical reasons, the structures usually implemented cannot strictly meet the economic rationale behind the theory outlined above. Indeed, distance-based fares are not consistent with low cost collection systems, although the available technology could allow this type of fare to be implemented with the help of satellite positioning systems (GPS) and electronic payment cards (and is increasingly an option when brought together with smart card technology). In the case of BRT systems, payment before boarding the bus allows the operator to charge distance based fares by installing control machines at the exits, as in some metro systems. As identified above, this is an advantage of systems with dedicated infrastructure although it imposes an additional cost in infrastructure provision.

Another source of variation in costs, which should be reflected in the fares, is the time of day. Indeed, at peak hours the marginal cost of a trip by public transport should include the cost of increasing the system's capacity. This means including the capital investment cost, both buses and infrastructure, which is necessary to provide an additional trip. As in the off-peak hours demand does not meet the available capacity of buses and infrastructure, the marginal cost of a trip only considers operating costs. This is because the additional demand in off-peak hours can be augmented with increases in frequency or scheduling of larger vehicles, if there are available buses of different size for operation.

The theoretical structure suggests the fare structure should include higher rates for peak-hours. This also helps to manage demand so as to encourage users to travel in off-peak hours and avoid inefficiencies due to accumulation of idle capacity and high capital costs. However, as discussed above, charging for peak travel is often controversial and charging off-peak fares is used to encourage travel outside peak times by those able to do so.

Different modes of public transport or services with special features should have different fares, as the cost of providing each is different. Thus the implementation of express services should reflect the marginal cost of using them. The same criterion applies for metros and trams. This provides the opportunity in a city with a BRT system to calibrate the fare for the BRT differently from the other modes of transport in the city.

However, an integrated fare system provides the opportunity to take advantage of economies of scale in transport systems that promote the combined use of different modes or bus services. Therefore, the fare should be calculated based on the cost of the combined system. For this we can apply the same models as previously, where social welfare or the firm's profit is maximised, but the decision variable is only one fare and the costs are those for the entire system. This approach requires knowledge of the users' behaviour in terms of their propensity to combine modes. In this case, the best approach might be one demand model based on a model of the transportation network.

Finally, travel passes are normally determined by political criteria and based on trial and error. However, there is an economic basis for determining the optimal value and the number of trips offered on a travel pass. The origin of this fare structure is second-degree price discrimination or nonlinear pricing. In simple terms, nonlinear pricing attempts to create a discount structure so that users can select: (i) the one that maximizes their welfare, and (ii) the one that maximizes the objective function of the planner, either social welfare or the firm's profits. Thus, nonlinear prices are a type of second-best pricing, because they are the result of constrained maximisation. Carbajo (1988) presents a detailed microeconomic foundation of travel passes, which goes beyond the scope of this chapter.

Case study

The case study in this section illustrates the above with two alternative fares for financing the bus system in Santiago de Chile. Our analysis is based on the paper by Batarce and Galilea (2013). In the first case, we determinate the balanced budget fare assuming no subsidy. In the second case, we assume that the amount of available subsidy is fixed by the Chilean government and we calculate the balanced budget fare accordingly. Strictly speaking, the welfare measure we use is not total welfare because we do not consider externalities, either positive or negative, of bus operation and the effects of bus fares on car demand. However, the case illustrates well the procedure for fixing fares in an integrated bus system. The public transport system also includes a metro network, but for the case study we focus on buses only.

The bus system in Santiago has an integrated payment system, where users pay only once for a trip with up to two transfers. Therefore, the fare needs to finance the cost of the complete trip even if the users travel on more than one bus line. To estimate the fare by trip, we use the average number of legs per trip in the system, which is empirically determined at 1.605 for 2011. Therefore, the fare will be 1.605 times the optimal payment per leg. We price legs because the cost of provision depends on the number of users that board the buses.

Batarce and Galilea (2013) model the cost and demand functions and these are used in the analysis of the different fare systems in this case study.

In the first case (balanced budget fare without subsidy), the value of the fare equals the average cost of the system, which is the outcome of an equilibrium problem, since the firm's costs depend on the demand, which in turn depends on the value of the fare. The balanced budget fare and associated demand are shown in Table 8.1. The second case (balanced budget fare with fixed subsidy) assumes the transport authority gives an annual subsidy of US$715.4 million for the operation of Transantiago. After removing the student fare subsidy (US$367.4 million) only US$348 million can be used as subsidy for the operation of the bus and metro systems. As bus transport accounts for two-thirds of all trips in the city, and the modelled firms represent 65% of the bus segments, the corresponding subsidy is estimated proportionally. Thus, the available annual subsidy for the group of modelled firms is US$150.8 million, which reduces the fixed cost of the system and also the average cost of the system. The new equilibrium shows a balanced budget fare of US$1.00 (Table 8.1), which is 92% of the current fare of the bus system. The 8% difference between this balanced fare with a fixed subsidy and the fare currently charged in Santiago may be because actual bus operators are less efficient than the modelling assumes.

Table 8.1: Fare, monthly demand and annual subsidy for the cases analysed

Case	Fare (US$)	Annual subsidy (million US$)	Monthly demand (million trips)
Current fare (December 2011)	1.08	150.8	60
Balanced budget fare without subsidy	1.27	0	55
Balanced budget fare with fixed subsidy	1.00	150.8	63

Policy implications of fare structure

Even though the theory gives us the guidelines for fixing both the level and structure of fares, there are several aspects that policy makers must consider when setting fares on public transport systems. For instance, limited information on demand leads to fixing fare levels based on approximated measures of the demand price elasticity. Likewise, when operators are responsible for determining the fares and they have limited information on costs, this prevents them from charging fares close to the theoretical ones. Policy makers often only have limited information even when the service is owned or run on their behalf since costs are very complex and it is difficult to have good enough information on costs to apply the theoretical models. This is clearly shown by the case study.

As mentioned, fares should reflect the marginal cost of producing the service provided and, therefore, vary according to distance travelled and the time of day. However, besides practical implementation reasons, there are reasons of equity based on the lack of travel alternatives, urban segregation or inadequate income distribution that may require a flat fee structure to be fixed or discounts to be provided to specially identified groups of passengers (the aged, the unemployed, and so on).

Equity is very important in developing countries, where a significant portion of the population are without cars and whose only motorised travel alternative is public transportation and where family spending on public transport may represent a large proportion of disposable income. For example, in Santiago, spending on public transport amounts to 15% of the city's average family income. For many low income users, the demand for travel in the peak hours is inelastic to the fare because users must travel to work. Applying a maximum welfare criterion leads to high fares for peak periods so the peak-load fare structure needs be accompanied by a policy of flexible work hours to increase the elasticity of demand or to provide some specially targeted subsidy.

However, the discussion of equity in the previous paragraph must recognise the welfare loss trade-off between the users travelling at peak hours and those travelling in off-peak hours. Indeed, a high fare during rush hour harms those who must travel at that time, but also allows a lower fare in off-peak times because fares are being related to costs. Most likely, a fair pricing policy should allow planners to set cross-subsidies between peak and off-peak times and to use their judgement as to how to encourage off-peak use where appropriate.

Issues of equity are also highlighted by spatial segregation which mitigates against a distance based fare structure. In cities where low income users are displaced to neighbourhoods far from centres of employment and service, charging by distance increases inequality among the inhabitants of the city, with distance based fares accelerating the gentrification processes and worsening the situation of the poorest inhabitants. In large cities of developing countries, this phenomenon cannot be reversed in the long run because the value of land in the city centre is so high that the low cost of low transport fails to induce relocation of low-income users. This is often an issue with the implementation of a new BRT system in a developing country.

As discussed above, travel passes are useful for increasing demand. However, their implementation can present drawbacks. Operators receive reduced fare revenue because users have unlimited travel for a fixed price, so that the more trips made, the lower the unit cost of the trip. However, the literature provides a solution to this problem through the recognition that travel passes have lower price elasticity than normal fares and so these passes should enter the market with a low price and high normal rates. Therefore, users widely prefer passes over the regular fares (Gschwender 2007). Once introduced, the price of the passes can be gradually increased and, given the low price elasticity, users will keep choosing the passes, and operators will eventually avoid reductions in fare revenue.

However, operators and authorities need to be clear that increasing demand can lead to an increase in cost, once capacity is reached. With new BRT systems it is crucially important to understand the likely demand during peak operating hours since this is when the system is likely to be at full capacity and where an increase in demand would require investment in new vehicles and labour to maintain service quality. As BRT systems approach full capacity, operators and authorities should consider what further elements of optimal pricing, as discussed in this chapter, might be appropriate to switching demand from peak to off-peak times rather than reducing demand, which then switches to less sustainable modes.

In conclusion, although fares differentiated by time and distance are theoretically suitable for increasing the welfare of public transport system users, equity issues mean that their application should be carefully considered. In addition, this type of pricing scheme may have very low political acceptability in developing countries. However, for BRT systems – especially new ones – the theory needs to be considered as a starting point. Setting fares is a complex activity, and it needs to be understood how the government's wish for related objectives to be met by the public transport system (such as social or economic inclusion, environmental aspirations) can impact on the structure, collection strategy and fare levels implemented. New BRT systems which replace unregulated and unsubsidised public transport services have a unique opportunity to charge a fare which is related to the cost of provision (and thus meet the second-best criteria of optimal fare derivation) and only create market distortions in favour of encouraging travel by public transport. This is clearly an issue to be considered in contract specification (see Chapter Seven).

References

Batarce, M. and Galilea, P. (2013) 'Cost and fare estimation for the urban bus transit system of Santiago', paper presented at *Transport Research Board Meeting*, Washington, DC.

Batarce, M. and Ivaldi, M. (2014) 'Urban travel demand model with endogenous congestion', *Transportation Research Part A: Policy and Practice*, 59: 331–345.

Baumol, W.J. and Bradford, D.F. (1970) 'Optimal departures from marginal cost pricing', *American Economic Review, Papers and Proceedings*, 60(3): 265–283.

Carbajo, J.C. (1988) 'The economics of travel passes: non-uniform pricing in transport', *Journal of Transport Economics and Policy*, 22(2): 153–173.

Fernández, J.E. and Muñoz, J.C. (2007) 'Privatisation and deregulation of urban bus services: an analysis of fare evolution mechanisms', *Journal of Transport Economics and Policy*, 41(1): 25–49.

Gómez-Lobo, A. (2007) 'Why competition does not work in urban bus markets: some new wheels for some old ideas', *Journal of Transport Economics and Policy*, 41(2): 283–308.

Gschwender, A. (2007) *Towards an Optimal Pricing System in the Urban Public Transport: What Can We Learn from the European Experience?*, Santiago, Chile: Actas XII Congreso Chileno de Ingeniería de Transporte.

Jara-Díaz, S. (2007) *Transport Economic Theory*, Oxford: Elsevier.

ITDP (Institute for Transportation and Development Policies) (2007) *Bus Rapid Transit, Planning Guide*, New York: Institute for Transportation and Development Policies.

Knight, F.H. (1924) 'Some fallacies in the interpretation of social cost', *Quarterly Journal of Economics*, 38: 582–606.

Laffont, J. and Tirole J. (1993) *A Theory of Incentives in Procurement and Regulation*, Cambridge, MA: MIT Press.

Lipsey, R.G. and Lancaster, K.J. (1956) 'The general theory of second best', *Review of Economic Studies*, 24(1): 11–32.

Mohring, H. (1972) 'Optimization and scale economies in urban bus transportation', *American Economic Review*, 62(4): 591–604.

Pigou, A.C. (1920) *The Economics of Welfare*, Reprinted by Macmillan in the Palgrave Classics in Economics Series, 2013.

Section 2
BRT and the City

NINE

Conflict over public space

Laurel Paget-Seekins

Introduction

Bus Rapid Transit's (BRT) promise for sustainability is more than improving public transit accessibility, it is also that by design BRT dedicates public space for bus and, in some cases, non-motorised users. Shifting space away from personal cars is a radical act that can have impacts beyond benefits for bus operations. It has the potential to reshape urban development away from car-centred cities. However, achieving this potential will result in conflict.

The reality is that transportation requires physical space and in urban areas the amount of space is limited. Decisions have to be made about whose mobility needs or what type of mobility (non-motorised, public transport, personal vehicles) is prioritised in the design, management, and enforcement of street space.

The competition for space generates conflicts, which are both physical and political (Vasconcellos 2001). The conflicts are not always explicit, but there are no neutral decisions. As Vasconcellos (2001, p. 71) notes, 'Every circulatory space is physically marked by past politics, revealing the dominate interests that shaped them'. The political conflicts can be just as challenging for BRT implementation as the institutional challenges discussed in Section 1 and operational challenges discussed in Section 3 of this book.

How governments and BRT implementers respond to conflicts has substantial impacts on the success of BRT projects and the ability of BRT to significantly reshape cities and contribute to sustainability. This chapter uses four transport projects with dedicated busway components, in cities with a high proportion of non-motorised and/ or public transit users, in order to examine how governments respond to conflicts over space and the impact on the outcome of the project.

Theoretical framework

Conflicts over transportation take place within the context of automobility. Automobility is the reliance on private motorised vehicles for mobility, but also a theoretical concept to describe how private car trips have been prioritised and have shaped not only the urban fabric of cities, but people's relationship to time and space (Sheller and Urry 2000). The reliance on cars did not just happen, but is the result of specific political decisions. Mobility is both created by and creates the production and distribution of power; there are struggles over which transport modes are prioritised in terms of resources and space (Cresswell 2010; Henderson 2004). Henderson (2009, p. 70) points out that 'the politics of mobility should also be understood in the context of how space is configured and organized to facilitate movement, and this in turn is determined by political power'.

All decisions over the design, management, and enforcement of mobility space are inherently shaped by political power, but the power dynamics are revealed only when those decisions are contested. An analysis of conflicts over space for transportation projects can illuminate the decision making and which groups have the ability to generate conflicts that can change the outcome of a project. Conflicts can be framed as between user types, but also between travellers and residents (or other types of user) of a space (Vasconcellos 2001).

In order to examine how conflicts over mobility spaces play out, this chapter looks at four examples of recent transport projects with a significant planned dedicated busway component. Two of the projects come from Latin America, where BRT first gained prominence, and two come from India, where BRT was a key component of the previous national government's urban transportation plan. The examples are Line 4 of the BRT network in Mexico City, the bus corridor component of Transantiago in Santiago, the BRT pilot project in Delhi, and the BRT network in Ahmedabad, India. These cases provide a range of types of dedicated busway projects from single corridors to a network to part of an integrated transit system.

Table 9.1 contains basic descriptive figures for each city. Each region includes a medium sized city (5–6 million) and a large city (15–20 million). Three of the four are national capitals and the fourth, Ahmedabad, is the former capital and largest city in the Indian state of Gujarat. Capital cities often face more institutional problems with implementing transportation projects due to competing interests and bureaucracies between different levels of government.

Table 9.1: Population and mode share of case study cities

City	Population (millions)	Percentage public transport	Percentage non-motorised	Percentage private motor vehicles
Mexico City, Mexico	8.8 (city), 20.1 (metro)	64% (2007)	10% (2006)	25% (2007) (includes taxis)
Santiago, Chile	5.1 (city), 6.3 (metro)	28%, (2011)	42%	30%
Delhi, India	11 (city), 16.3 (metro)	42% (2011)	33%	19%
Ahmedabad, India	5.6 (city), 6.4 (metro)	16% (2011)	36%	42% (includes 2 wheelers)

Sources: Delhi and Ahmedabad (Journeys References 2011), Santiago (personal communication from SECTRA 2011), Mexico City (Montgomery 2006; Rivera Islas et al 2011)

Comparing cities, especially between those of very different cultural and historical development contexts like Latin America and India, is always fraught with potential for oversimplification and false comparisons. For example, space is conceptualised differently (what is public, what is private) and this plays out on the streets. This research attempts to focus on variables that can be compared. It focuses on what types of users (private motorised vehicle users, public transport users, non-motorised mode users) have their mobility needs addressed by the project, how conflicts changed the project, and how governments responded to conflict over the project. The goal is to illuminate the way conflicts can have an impact on projects and not to provide generalisable results about the sources or results of conflicts over projects.

Researchers interviewed decision makers, nongovernmental organisations, and involved citizens in each city. In addition, we analysed press reports, documents from the planning process, and public transport user surveys and demographics from each city. This information was used to create short descriptions of the background of each project and the conflicts over them. We draw lessons from the similarities and the differences between the cities.

Project conflict descriptions

Delhi

The Indian national capital region of Delhi started planning a BRT network in 2004 with support for the plan coming from an

Environmental Pollution Authority appointed by the Supreme Court in 2005. The Delhi Integrated Multi-Modal Transit System (DIMTS), a public–private venture, was created in 2006 in part to oversee the BRT corridors. The plan for 98 kilometres of corridors called for a 14.5 kilometre pilot corridor (overall plans called for over 400 kilometres). This corridor was chosen in part because this roadway was owned entirely by a single agency, which was thought to simplify implementation (Personal interviews). It connects middle class South Delhi neighbourhoods to the centre of the city.

The first section of 5.8 kilometres on the southern end of the corridor opened in April 2008. The project has two central bus lanes (with overpassing lanes at intersections) with nine median bus platforms for each direction, general purpose traffic lanes in each direction, and sidewalks and cycle tracks on both sides of the corridor. Of the 50 metre road width, 13 metres (26%) is used for buses, 23 metres (46%) for other vehicles, and 11 metres (22%) for pedestrians and cycles (Delhi High Court 2012). It is an open corridor that allows all buses to use the bus lanes and does not have pre-board ticketing. The corridor designers stated their strong dedication to equity and serving the needs of the transport disadvantaged. They consulted with advocates for people with disabilities and included elements like tracks for the blind. Space for street vendors was designed into the project (Personal interviews).

The project initially received high satisfaction in surveys of corridor users (over 80% of bus, pedestrian, and cycle users were satisfied and about 50% of motorised vehicle users) (Hidalgo and Pai 2009). However, the operational design, especially at one critical intersection, did increase delays and cause vocal car drivers to complain that the BRT lanes significantly worsened traffic conditions. In addition, bus operations at stations were initially not properly managed. Since this was an open corridor, special attention was needed to prevent long bus queues. The capacity of almost all bus corridors is given by its critical station, so this had a significant impact on operations.

Project supporters blame the English language press for their particularly harsh criticism of the project and unbalanced reporting – in a study of 115 articles, 107 had negative headlines and of 52 interviews only 5 were bus or cycle users (Hazard Centre 2012). This created a general perception that the project was a failure amongst the elite classes (the audience of the English language media) even if they never used the corridor (Personal interviews).

The government almost immediately agreed to change the design of the rest of the initial corridor, dropping the dedicated centre lanes.

BRT supporters responded by holding marches and organising in support of the concept (Staff Reporter 2008, 2009, 2010). But they were unable to generate sustained political pressure, in part because bus riders, cyclists, and pedestrians are not organised in user groups and lacked political power (Personal interviews).

Using a feature of Indian law, a nongovernmental organisation filed a public interest lawsuit asking the Delhi High Court to force the government to remove the bus-only lanes. The petitioners argued that since motorised vehicles outnumber buses in Delhi by a ratio 1:214 the amount of space allocated to buses was 'arbitrary and unreasonable', was wasted since it was often empty, and caused an increase in travel time of 23 minutes for other vehicles. They claimed that car users have a higher value of time than bus users since they are 'wealth creators' (Delhi High Court 2012).

In March 2012 the court asked the government to commission a study on the impacts of the bus lanes on travel time and fuel consumption on the corridor. The government hired the Central Road Research Institute (CRRI) to perform the study. CRRI did a series of studies including reconfiguring the corridor to allow all vehicles in the bus-only lanes for eight days. Project supporters contend this was not part of the court order and significantly weakened enforcement on the corridor after the study finished (Personal interviews).

After receiving the report from the CRRI the High Court ruled that it is within the role of government to implement BRT and in the public interest. They particularly rejected the argument of allocating space by number of vehicles instead of number of people and the argument that car drivers have a higher value of time. In addition, the court pointed out that a vast majority of investment in transport infrastructure in Delhi was going to serve motorised vehicle users and the city, where 21% of its area is already roads, lacks the space to continue expanding them (Delhi High Court 2012).

Even though the government won the final round of the High Court case restoring the pilot corridor, plans for future expansion remain on hold. Enforcement of the lanes has suffered, with car drivers routinely driving in the bus-only lanes and auto rickshaws and motorised two wheelers driving on the cycle track and sidewalks and the Delhi Traffic Police abdicating enforcement to private marshals. Supporters say the short project length (5.8 kilometres of dedicated lanes) is too limited to show the benefits of the concept (Personal interviews). However, in 2012 the corridor was carrying 12,000 peak-hour passengers per direction, an average of 120,000 passengers per day on 3,000 buses, and 4,000–6,000 cyclists per day (Central Road Research Institute

2012). The average operating speed is 17 kilometres per hour (BRT Centre et al 2014).

Ahmedabad

The Indian city of Ahmedabad implemented its BRT plan rather quickly. Planning started in 2005, was approved in 2006, work began in 2007, and service started in October 2009. Since 2009 75 kilometres have been completed out of an original plan of 88 kilometres (which has since been expanded). The system uses a very different design than Delhi. It is a closed BRT network with special BRT buses in median lanes with central stations, off-board ticketing, and an operating speed of 24 kilometres per hour. In 2013 the system carried an average of 130,000 passengers per day. It is still not operating at the planned peak-hour capacity of 15,000–20,000 passengers per direction, but has increased from an estimate of 2,350–2,600 in 2012 (Central Road Research Institute 2012).

The project designers from CEPT University and the city government adopted a pragmatic approach to the design and implementation of the system. They use the phrase 'connect busy places, but avoid busy roads' to describe their approach. The initial corridors were on roads with lower traffic flows and room for right of way expansion ringing the dense old city. Space was not taken from general purpose vehicle lanes and, in some places, improvements were made for personal vehicle infrastructure as part of the BRT. Project designers accepted that they would have to make constant changes to the original design and route (Personal interviews). They negotiated about obstacles, like temples and holy sites, and moved the route if necessary (Rizvi and Sclar 2013).

Ahmedabad's philosophy of avoiding busy roads became a much bigger challenge as it attempted to connect the network through the denser old part of the city. Originally the designers from CEPT proposed an elevated busway on the southern edge of the old city, but this proposal was rejected by the city government due to interference with the historic nature of the area. This meant more changes to the original route and project delays (Personal interviews).

While the Ahmedabad BRT network has garnered significant international and national praise, it was not entirely without local conflict. Along with the initial scepticism and operational challenges that have to be overcome with any new technology, there were conflicts over space allocation. The project was designed not to take space from private motorised vehicles, but from the sides of roads instead, which, as in most Indian cities, is often occupied. In January 2012, 500 vendors and residents held a protest against a BRT expansion because the widening of the road would destroy 300 shops (DNA Correspondent 2012). There have also been complaints from informal vendors (hawkers) who were displaced and not accommodated in the corridor design, and along one corridor 7500 households faced displacement due to road widening for BRT and only 1050 were resettled (Mahadevia et al 2013; Our Inclusive Ahmedabad 2010).

Initially there was a commitment to include cycle tracks and sidewalks (which is a condition of the funding from the Indian national government) along the entire corridor. But in the first phase the sidewalk and cycle tracks were often incomplete, obstructed, and in places opposed by business owners who say they block access to parking (TNN 2009). In an assessment of both sides of 39 kilometres of the corridor only 26% had cycle tracks and 84% had footpaths and both were at least 40% obstructed (Mahadevia et al 2013). In later phases of the network, cycle tracks were dropped (or not segregated) from the design on narrower right of ways and the project designers downplayed their importance, pointing to their lack of use (TNN 2011; Personal interviews). But cyclists have criticised the design of the cycle tracks and lack of connectivity as a reason for their unpopularity (Mahadevia et al 2013).

Since the Ahmedabad BRT is a closed system, meaning only special BRT buses can use the lanes, it created a two-tier system. The BRT fares are higher than the pre-existing Ahmedabad Municipal Transport Services (AMTS) bus service and there is no fare integration between the systems. A parallel AMTS service is being discontinued to avoid competing with the BRT service. Even though the BRT network goes through low income neighbourhoods its ridership is mostly middle income workers in the formal economy. A survey of users done in 2011 when 44 kilometres were in operation found that only 13.7% of users were from low income households with an income under 5000 rupees (US$84) a month (about 30% of households are in this income category) (Mahadevia et al 2013).

The development of the BRT network comes as changes to Ahmedabad's urban structure (growth in population and area, the poor being displaced to the periphery) are increasing trip distances, which decreases walking and cycling trips and increases the need for affordable public transport. While the BRT project designers managed to largely avoid conflicts caused by displacing space for private motorised vehicles, they did this partially by displacing slums, vendors, and abandoning the commitment to cycle tracks. However, by using a pragmatic approach they developed the largest BRT network in India that is continuing to expand, unlike the system in Delhi, and the closed network limited their operational problems.

Mexico City

Mexico City opened its first BRT line in June 2005 on a busy corridor. The project faced some opposition from residents, but most of the government's negotiations were with existing bus operators to set up a new BRT operating company. In fact the corridor was chosen to minimise conflicts with bus operators (Flores and Zegras 2012). After its success, the BRT network was expanded to include an extension of the first line and four more lines. In 2014 it had 105 kilometres in operation and carried over 800,000 passengers daily.

The first three lines were on major corridors with a daily demand ranging from 140,000 passengers to 440,000 and were closed networks with segregated bus lanes. The fourth line deviated from the normal BRT operating model and connected the historical downtown of Mexico City to the airport. It has a much lower passenger demand (50,000 passengers daily) and runs on narrow streets in an area already served by the city's subway system. The narrow streets necessitated a different design: the stations are on the curbside, payment is onboard, and smaller, low floor buses are used. Some of the streets are exclusively for buses and pedestrians. (Until Line 5, the cycle infrastructure in Mexico City was designed and implemented separately from BRT.) Line 4 presented a series of conflicts for the government of Mexico City as the project faced opposition from local business owners and residents.

Residents, business owners, and street vendors objected to the cutting down of trees; the taking of space from parking, loading and unloading, street vendors, and pedestrians; impacts of the project construction on business; and impacts of the construction and buses on the historic buildings. One of the main issues was which streets would be bus and pedestrian only. Many of those who were opposed did not object to BRT in principle, but questioned the logic of the Line 4 route. They claimed it was mostly designed for tourists, would not solve the congestion problems in the historic centre, and the government should be investing in improvements to the ageing subway system. Some even saw the BRT as part of a larger scheme to push the poor and street vendors out of the downtown to make the city more cosmopolitan and able to attract global capital (Personal interviews).

Opponents claiming they had not been consulted beforehand took to the street in protest. They blockaded the cutting of trees, hung banners protesting against the project, organised marches and meetings of residents. The government responded by bringing in the police, but also started a series of meetings and negotiations in part due to the power the neighbourhood leaders claimed was derived through the clientelistic nature of Mexico City's political system (Personal interviews). The route of the project was significantly changed; it was moved further from the central square, off narrower streets, and in places into one way loops.

The opposition was not monolithic, especially amongst business owners. The Chamber of Commerce supported the project and tried to mediate, but one of its reasons for supporting the project was that it helped to get rid of the street vendors. Some business owners worked with the street vendors and opposed the Chamber of Commerce, saying it does not support small family businesses. In the end opponents felt they won some concessions with the route changes, but still think the project had negative consequences and is underused (personal interviews).

In a survey done on behalf of the city oversight agency, the users of Line 4 overwhelmingly consider it better than their previous mode of transport and say that it has cut their costs and travel times. A third switched from using the metro, a third switched from a combination of buses, and 9% switched from cars. Only 1.8% reported they did not previously travel in the area, which discounts the contention that the line is mostly for tourists (CTS EMBARQ Mexico 2013). However, the line remains underused compared to the other BRT lines and its capacity.

Santiago

In February 2007 the government of Chile implemented Transantiago, a massive reorganisation of public transport in Santiago that created a feeder and truck network with fare integration between the bus and metro. For various reasons, extensively documented (Muñoz and Gschwender 2008; Muñoz et al 2009; and Chapter Three), the project faced serious problems as implemented. This resulted in widespread protests and public outrage at the project. The government was forced to make significant changes, including adding additional buses and creating government subsidies to fund bus operations.

The original planning for what would become Transantiago, detailed in the 2000 master plan for transport in greater Santiago between 2000 and 2010, called for a network of exclusive bus lanes. The plan called for 12 corridors and a ring route to be built in 2004 and 2005, but by 2004 the investment plan for Transantiago only programmed the construction of two corridors. These two corridors of 14.4 kilometres were added to the previously built corridors for a total of 25 kilometres (Gobierno de Chile 2004; Sectra 2000a, 2000b). However, the project design for Transantiago was predicated on the existence of the bus corridors (and their associated high bus speed and productivity) and multimodal infrastructure in order to carry the increased capacity on the trunk lines. When asked after the failure of the implementation of Transantiago, Chile's Treasury minister claimed an ignorance of transportation for the decision to cut funding for the busways. Instead the funding went to the metro and freeway projects.

The fixes to make Transantiago functional after the initial problems did not involve constructing all the originally planned dedicated busways. Instead Transantiago includes a mix of three types of bus lanes. The first are streets that are reserved exclusively for buses only during peak hours. In 2013 there were 13 segments for a total of just over 30 kilometres; many are short stretches in the centre of the city. The second type is curbside lanes without any physical barrier and marked by paint and bus-only signs. Currently there are 90 kilometres of these lanes, but they are also used by taxis, vehicles turning right, bicycles, and often vehicles ignoring the restrictions. The authorities are still working on enforcing these two types of lanes by installing cameras and fining violators. Finally Santiago did build a total of 50 kilometres of centre segregated bus-only lanes (as of 2014), but they do not form a connected network and none enter the city centre (Muñoz et al 2014).

The segregated busways that have been implemented mostly added capacity and were chosen based on the corridors where this was possible. Space was taken from the sides of the street to create very wide streets. One of the implemented corridors is on a major arterial road named Santa Rosa. The residents dislike the 4.6 kilometre double lane, double direction corridor because it took space, is difficult to cross, and mostly does not serve their travel needs as a high speed bus service is most beneficial to people on the periphery. However, the benefit is limited since the segregated corridor does not extend all the way into downtown Santiago. The last 3.8 kilometres, as the street reaches the denser city centre where expanding the street is not possible, are unsegregated bus-only lanes that, lacking enforcement, are routinely used by other vehicles. This lowers the operating speed of buses significantly from over 30 kilometres per hour in the corridor to around 5 kilometres per hour. (The government has undertaken steps to address this in 2015.)

The current master plan for transport in Santiago calls for a more than doubling of the segregated corridors by 2025. Plans have been made to implement several of the corridors, but they are facing opposition from communities that do not want a 'Santa Rosa'. Residents on the San Pablo corridor are organising against a proposed 7.8 kilometre project that would expand the road from 14 metres to 35 metres and add two additional lanes, cycle tracks, and green areas. They object to the cutting down of trees, taking of land from houses and family businesses, the increased distance to cross the street, and reduced access to schools (Barriga 2013). Similar objections are raised by residents on two other corridors.

Due to low satisfaction with the informal bus system in place before Transantiago, the government of Chile had significant public support to address the issue. However, the problems created by the poor implementation of Transantiago destroyed that support and lost the government credibility. Afterwards the government had to pick its battles and implementing bus corridors that could generate conflicts was not made a top priority, in particular taking space from cars has been avoided and this has created conflicts with residents near potential bus corridors. Instead space for cars has increased as the number of buses decreased.

Discussion

These four cases provide very different examples of the form and outcome of a conflict over a transport project. In all of the cases people protested when they perceived space was being taken from them, but not all space users had equal ability to generate conflicts that resulted in changes to project plans or their needs being met. The minority of upset private motor vehicle users on the Delhi corridor lost their lawsuit to remove the BRT pilot corridor, but they created enough political cost to the government that plans for expansion of the system were put on hold. Changes were made to the Ahmedabad, India BRT network, but not everyone's protests were heard. Some slum residents, business owners, and street vendors were displaced. The business owners and residents in the historic district of Mexico City did manage to get the route changed on Metrobus Line 4, but the efforts to remove street vendors from the historic centre continue. The general conflict over Transantiago resulted in changes to improve transit service, but diminished the government's political capacity to implement bus corridors, especially as communities oppose expansion.

All of the governments chose their corridors with the goal of minimising a type of conflict, but given the complicated nature of implementing urban transport projects there were many to choose from. In Mexico City the corridors were initially chosen to minimise conflict with the existing minibus operators, but Line 4 was selected for urban redevelopment instead of transportation purposes. In Delhi the corridor was chosen in part to minimise interagency conflict. In Ahmedabad and Santiago corridors were chosen in part by the ability to add road capacity.

Regardless of the success of their initial conflict avoidance methods, the cases demonstrate that governments react in different ways to conflict. The authorities in Ahmedabad and Mexico City adopted a pragmatic approach to addressing conflicts over their BRT corridors; they picked routes and designs to limit conflicts and changed the routes when faced with powerful opposition.

The governments of Delhi and Santiago retreated from conflict over their projects. In Delhi the designers were steadfast in their commitment to serving the lowest income users of the corridor, but with government putting future expansion on hold the benefits are limited. The initial problems with the management of the bus lane also contributed to the conflict. The goal of Transantiago was to improve transit service and help retain transit mode share, but its lack of dedicated bus corridors continues to slow down bus users. In both Delhi and Santiago the hesitancy translated into a lack of strong initial enforcement of the bus (and in Delhi cycle) lanes. Not only does this render the lanes less effective, it also allows vehicle drivers to use their physical advantage to take space they feel should be available to them, reinforcing the existing hierarchy.

There is a sense of entitlement for street space for car users, even in cities where they make up the minority of the population. In Delhi the conflict could not be separated from issues of class; the documents from the lawsuit clearly show the plaintiffs see car drivers as the wealth creators. Policy makers' fear of taking space from car users can limit their ability to create rational public policy. A study on Santiago and London by Basso and Silva (2014) showed that segregated bus-only lanes can create higher social welfare than the optimal level of transit subsidisation. In fact, governments often turn to more expensive metro projects as an alternative to creating a more equitable distribution of surface street space for public transit users. Delhi, Santiago, and Mexico City are expanding their metro lines and the Ahmedabad BRT network was designed to not compete with a future proposed metro line.

One interesting distinction between the projects is whether they involved redistributing the existing street space between users, repurposing the existing space, or expanding the amount of space available. Repurposing streets to be bus and pedestrian only in Mexico City created complaints from business owners expecting easy car access. Redistributing the existing space, as in the case of Delhi, is always likely to generate resistance from the previously privileged users. Ahmedabad avoided this conflict by expanding the street space; this space was not previously unused, but the existing users (vendors, slum dwellers, business owners) lacked the political power of the car users in Delhi. This highlights the conflicts between the traveller and the resident often present over transport projects. While the residents mostly lost in Ahmedabad, they were able to win changes in Mexico City and are continuing to organise in Santiago. The relative power of the residents and travellers can determine whether governments seek to expand street space, setting up conflicts with residents, or to redistribute space, setting up conflicts with car users. A typology of the conflicts is given in Table 9.2.

A key finding of this limited comparison is that it is impossible to examine conflicts over space for mobility without considering space for livelihoods, like street vendors and corridor business owners. In

Table 9.2: Typology of conflicts and response

	Conflict type	Users benefiting	Changes	Government response	Type of space change
Delhi	Private motorised vehicles vs other modes	Bus riders, pedestrians, and bicyclists on corridor	Project not completed, lack of enforcement	Retreat	Redistribution
Ahmedabad	Travellers vs residents, vendors, businesses	Higher income bus riders	Route changed in some places, cycle tracks not completed	Pragmatic	Expansion
Mexico City	Travellers vs residents, vendors, businesses	Transit users in downtown area	Route changed	Pragmatic	Redistribution and repurposing
Santiago	Travellers vs residents	Bus riders	Bus corridors not completed, lack of enforcement	Retreat	Expansion

developing cities where a significant part of the population relies on income from the informal economy, public spaces, like streets and buses, act as marketplaces. Often by design bus corridor projects have displaced street vendors; in Mexico City and Ahmedabad opponents of the BRT projects see them as part of a larger attempt to displace street vendors and the informal economy from the city as a whole. Santiago displaced vendors from the buses when Transantiago was implemented, but they are coming back as enforcement of this rule is not consistent. Only in the case of Delhi were street vendors considered a part of the street ecosystem and space for them consistently designed into the project.

Conclusion

How public space is allocated has equity and sustainability implications. BRT projects start to address the inequity by prioritising space for bus riders and, in some cases, non-motorised mode users; but where that space comes from has implications.

In order to successfully implement BRT governments need to avoid or manage political conflicts that derail projects. One method, as was done in Ahmedabad and Santiago, is to add capacity to streets instead of taking lanes from the existing vehicle users. However, this can create conflicts with residents and other corridor users, especially if very wide corridors are created. As these cases illustrate, public streets and surrounding space is used for more than mobility, including livelihoods and dwellings. These users might lack the political power of private vehicle owners. In order to gain public support, project implementers need to consider how to design corridors that are appealing to residents as well as travellers.

Beyond the equity implications of whose space is taken, the question remains how successfully BRT can challenge automobility and improve the sustainability of cities. Taking space from cars not only makes a political statement of prioritising buses. It also improves the ability of BRT and bus services to compete with private vehicles in terms of trip time. One argument for how to improve transit mode share is that, in addition to transit services getting faster and more convenient, private vehicles need to be slower and less convenient. Reallocating space from cars to buses can 'level the playing field' to allow buses a chance to compete with cars.

This argument also applies to building metros (Mohan 2008). Building metros is often more popular with politicians in part because it takes away the conflict over street space. But another way to view the often debated BRT vs metro issue is that building metros is giving up the fight for the surface space of cities to cars.

The examples of Delhi and Ahmedabad illustrate the potential trade-off between principles and pragmatism. In Delhi the designers held true to their principles of reallocating space to be more equitable, but when the inevitable political backlash occurred BRT lacked the political support it needed to expand. This has significantly limited the benefits of BRT in the city. Ahmedabad was able to build a successful network, but its approach of adding capacity and jettisoning bicycle and pedestrian infrastructure limited the challenge to automobility.

Government can pragmatically address conflict or retreat from it. This is true not just for the design of street space, but the management and enforcement of the design. A lack of enforcement can reinforce the entitlement of privileged users and undermine the challenge to automobility. Errors in management of the physical space can generate political conflicts.

How space is allocated is critical to the future development patterns of growing cities, especially as incomes and private vehicle ownership rise. There is a great opportunity in cities still building their main transportation infrastructure to follow a different path that breaks the power of car users, but this will generate conflict.

References

Barriga, P. (2013) 'Enorme proyecto para ensanchar calle San Pablo tiene saltones a los vecinos', *El Dia*, 23 February 2013.

Basso, L.J. and Silva, H.E. (2014) 'Efficiency and substitutability of transit subsidies and other urban transport policies', *American Economic Journal: Economic Policy*, 6(4): 1–33.

BRT (Bus Rapid Transit) Centre of Excellence, EMBARQ, IEA (International Energy Agency) and SIBRT (Sistemas Integrados de Transporte y BRT) (2014) Global BRT Data: version 3.0, www.brtdata.org

Central Road Research Institute (2012) 'Evaluating bus rapid transit corridor performance from Ambedkar Nagar to Moolchand, Delhi', Transport Department, GNCTD Delhi, India.

Cresswell, T. (2010) 'Towards a politics of mobility', *Environment and Planning D: Society and Space*, 28: 17–31.

CTS (Centro de Transporte Sustentable) EMBARQ Mexico (2013) Presentación de Resultados Metrobús 2013 Satisfacción de Usuarios, Metrobús, Mexico City.

Delhi High Court (2012) Judgment Nyaya Bhoomi versus GNCT of Delhi and ANR, New Delhi, 18 October 2012.

DNA Correspondent (2012) 'Residents hold dharna to protest BRTS track in Ahmedabad', *Diligent Media Corporation*, 17 January 2012.

Flores, O. and Zegras, C. (2012) 'The costs of inclusion: Incorporating existing bus and paratransit operators into Mexico City's BRT', paper presented to Conference on Advanced Systems for Public Transport, Santiago, Chile.

Gobierno de Chile (2004) Prospecto de Inversión, Transantiago Súbete, MOPTT, Santiago, Chile.

Hazard Centre (2012) 'The BRT system in Delhi, an independent evaluation', Hazard Centre, Delhi, India.

Henderson, J. (2004) 'The politics of mobility and business elites in Atlanta, Georgia', *Urban Geography*, 25(3): 193–216.

Henderson, J. (2009) 'The spaces of parking: mapping the politics of mobility in San Francisco', *Antipode*, 41(1): 70–91.

Hidalgo, D. and Pai, M. (2009) 'The Delhi bus corridor', EMBARQ – The WRI Center for Sustainable Transport, Delhi, India.

Journeys References (2011) 'Passenger transport mode shares in world cities', *Journeys*, 7: 54–64.

Mahadevia, D., Joshi, R. and Datey, A. (2013) 'Low-carbon mobility in India and the challenges of social inclusion: BRT case studies in India', UN Environment Programme, Technical University of Denmark.

Mohan, D. (2008) 'Mythologies, metros and future urban transport', India Institute of Technology Delhi, New Delhi, India.

Montgomery, B. (2006) 'Micro-scale indicators for the urban pedestrian environment', *Urban Walk*, www.gtkp.com/assets/uploads/20091126-005015-9737-WalkabilityJuly3106.pdf.

Munoz, J.C. and Gschwender, A. (2008) 'Transantiago: a tale of two cities', *Research in Transportation Economics*, 22: 45–53.

Muñoz, J.C., Ortúzar, J. de D. and Gschwender, A. (2009) 'Transantiago: the fall and rise of a radical public transport intervention', in W. Saleh and G. Sammer (eds), *Travel Demand Management and Road User Pricing: Success, Failure and Feasibility,* Farnham: Ashgate, 151–172.

Muñoz, J.C., Batarce, M. and Hidalgo, D. (2014) 'Transantiago, five years after its launch', *Research in Transportation Economics*, 48: 184–193.

Our Inclusive Ahmedabad (2010) 'A public hearing on habitat and livelihood displacements in Ahmedabad', Our Inclusive Ahmedabad, Ahmedabad, http://cept.ac.in/UserFiles/File/CUE/Advocacy/Public%20Hearing%20on%20Displacements.pdf.

Rivera Islas, V., Hernández, S., Arroyo Osorno, J., Lelis Zaragoza, M. and Ignacio Ruvalcaba, J. (2011) 'Implementing sustainable urban travel policies in Mexico', International Transport Forum, Paris, France.

Rizvi, A. and Sclar, E. (2013) 'Implementing bus rapid transit: a tale of two Indian cities', paper presented to Thredbo (International Conference Series on Competition and Ownership in Land Passenger Transport) 13, Oxford, UK.

Sectra (2000a) Plan de Transporte Urbano Del Gran Santiago 2000–2010, Sectra, Santiago, Chile.

Sectra (2000b) Resumen Ejecutivo Plan de Transporte Urbano, Santiago 2000–2006, Gobierno de Chile, Santiago, Chile.

Sheller, M. and Urry, J. (2000) 'The city and the car', *International Journal of Urban and Regional Research*, 24(4): 737–757.

Staff Reporter (2008) 'March in support of BRT', *The Hindu*, 1 June 2008.

Staff Reporter (2009) 'Government urged not to budge from original BRT plan', *The Hindu*, 9 January 2009.

Staff Reporter (2010) 'Pedestrians march for BRT corridor', *The Hindu*, 29 December 2010.

TNN (Times News Network) (2009) 'Business groups want BRTS cycle tracks out', *The Times of India*, 28 September 2009.

TNN (2011) 'BRTS cycle-track discarded over space, security concerns', *The Times of India*, 23 July 2011.

Vasconcellos, E. (2001) *Urban Transport, Environment and Equity: The Case for Developing Countries*, London: Earthscan.

TEN

Designing BRT-oriented development

*Chris Zegras, Anson Stewart, Rosanna Forray, Rocío Hidalgo,
Cristhian Figueroa, Fábio Duarte and Jan Wampler*

Introduction

Bus Rapid Transit (BRT) signifies a concrete commitment to bus transit, encompassing coordinated institutional, financial, physical, and operational interventions. This commitment can catalyse wider urban development by improving local and metropolitan accessibility and urban spaces and streetscapes. This chapter explores prospects for such BRT-oriented development (BRTOD).

Transit-oriented development (TOD) aims to leverage the interactions between urban land use, mobility, and socioeconomic systems. This chapter examines how BRT corridors might spur TOD, structuring the city and its spaces towards more equitable and transit-conducive urban forms. Specifically, it uses results from a graduate level planning and design workshop in two regions, Boston, Massachusetts and Santiago de Chile,[1] to explore how BRT corridors might catalyse cross-disciplinary approaches to urban development. Adopting an integrated approach to the design of transit routes and infrastructures, surrounding public spaces, real estate projects, public policy and governance, the students' proposals for these two corridors highlight BRT's transformative potential across diverse urban settings.

The next section provides a brief theoretical and empirical background. The third section summarises the workshop's approach and contexts; the fourth presents workshop results, illustrating various possible design and planning innovations for realising BRTOD. The conclusion synthesises lessons learned.

Theoretical perspectives and empirical precedents

Basic economic theory suggests that households and firms make trade-offs between travel costs, land area, and other relevant attributes in their location decisions. These interactions essentially occur between two urban subsystems: land use and mobility. Land uses determine the locations of potential trip origins and destinations and influence the relative attractiveness of different travel modes. Mobility, in turn, influences the relative desirability of different locations, improving 'connectivity', but sometimes with negative consequences such as pollution. The interaction of these subsystems defines urban accessibility: the degree to which people and firms can reach activities, services, and goods (Geurs and van Wee 2004).

A major transportation investment will change accessibility across a metropolitan area, impacting the relative attractiveness of locations. System users and residents may benefit from lower travel costs, higher quality of life/wellbeing (see, for example, Cao 2013) and possibly increased social capital (Kamruzzaman et al 2014). These effects should be capitalised in land values (Zegras et al 2013). The accessibility benefits of mass transit, which enables relatively high concentrations of persons and firms in specific areas, include potential agglomeration economies, in the form of expanded labour markets, reduced costs of inputs, and enhanced knowledge spillovers (Chatman and Noland 2014), which may also influence land values.

Capitalising on these interactions has a long history in urban development. In the USA, for example, real estate interests in the early 1900s developed urban rail projects to increase the value of their land holdings, forming 'streetcar suburbs' (Warner 1962). Baum-Snow and Kahn (2000) find that land prices, development, and users respond modestly to new rail transit investments in five metropolitan areas in the USA, with ridership increases attributable to existing residents and new residents attracted to the transit accessible areas. Numerous reviews (including Martínez and Viegas 2009) of the now large body of empirical research on rail transit and land value effects suggest that – despite variations in contexts, types of properties analysed, types of infrastructures considered, and so on – property values around transit stations are typically higher, presumably reflecting benefits of proximity to the station, which are valued by users, landowners, and developers.

TOD aims to maximise land use–transit synergies, using transit investments and services to guide land development and, in turn, using urban form and design to boost transit ridership. Successful TOD includes attractive pedestrian access to quality transit service, compact, mixed land uses, and safe environmental conditions (Suzuki et al 2013). For maximum impact, TOD typically requires coordinated policies and regulations (such as parking restrictions and appropriate zoning), correct corridor alignment and station placement, a climate of economic growth, and some demand for density (Handy 2005).

TOD should also fulfil social development objectives, ensuring, for example, that lower income residents are not displaced by increased property values and by higher income residents more likely to use cars (Suzuki et al 2013).

Numerous detailed case studies and guidelines on effective TOD have been published. Rather than duplicating these efforts, this chapter highlights promises and challenges for TOD specifically related to BRT projects.

BRTOD promise

In theory, BRT's ridership, development, property value, and land use impacts can equal those of any other high quality public transport. Ben-Akiva and Morikawa (2002) find evidence supporting the idea that users care about service characteristics, not necessarily the transit mode itself. Chatman's (2013) analysis of light rail in New Jersey suggests that the form of urban development, not the transit mode, impacts on ridership and that, in fact, a regular bus service has stronger behavioural effects than light rail, after controlling for urban form characteristics. Nelson et al's (2013) examination of Eugene's (Oregon) BRT inaugurated in 2007 reveals that areas within 400 metres of a station attracted more jobs relative to the rest of the metropolitan area. These studies support the premise that BRT has similar TOD potential to rail based transit.

Emerging support for BRTOD also comes from property value studies. Rodríguez and Targa (2004) studied apartment rental asking prices about one year after Bogotá inaugurated its TransMilenio BRT system and estimate a 7–9% increase in rental asking prices attributable to station proximity; interestingly they find no significant effect due to the system's regional accessibility. This result suggests that the market does not value the initial BRT line's relative regional accessibility gains; rather, the value comes from proximity to the station area, which might be associated with public space improvements. In a later analysis, Rodríguez and Mojica (2009) find that subsequent TransMilenio extensions were associated with a 13–14% increase in property asking prices along the original line, suggesting regional accessibility gains may accrue with network growth.

More recently, for the Seoul case, Cervero and Kang (2011) find a 5–10% premium for residential property values within 300 metres of a BRT stop and a 3–26% premium for non-residential property within 150 metres of a BRT stop. Finally, Perk et al (2013) examine Boston's Washington Street corridor, where Silver Line stops were associated with a residential property value premium of up to 7.6%.

In terms of land use changes induced by BRT, Bocarejo et al (2013) find evidence that from 2001 to 2008, TransMilenio station areas increased in density relative to areas in the city without BRT; they suggest this happened without any supportive regulatory changes. Jun (2012), using a simulation model for Seoul, finds the BRT will probably increase firm location in the city centre at the expense of the suburbs (with concomitant relative changes in land values), but with no effects on residential redistribution.

Finally, evidence is emerging that the physical characteristics of BRT station areas influence ridership. Cervero et al (2010) find population density, distance to nearest stop, and parking capacity significantly explain ridership at Los Angeles' (CA) BRT stations. Estupiñán and Rodríguez (2008) find that characteristics favouring walking and cycling (for example, quality of sidewalks, amenities, and bicycle facilities) and disfavouring car use (for example, land use mix and density) were related to higher TransMilenio boardings. In Jinan, China, Jiang et al (2012) find support for the argument that BRT station type (for example, terminal), density, and corridor design influence the distances users will walk to access the system.

BRTOD challenges

Despite increasing empirical support for BRTOD potential, numerous challenges exist, from the streetscapes to the stations, station areas, corridors, and up to the citywide level. Without mitigation, these challenges undermine BRTOD possibilities.

BRT's at-grade operation, with higher speed and higher capacity vehicles, requires special attention to corridor design (see Chapters Nine and Sixteen). Often implemented on wide rights of way with ample motor vehicle space, BRT needs careful design of civic spaces that do not pose barriers for pedestrians and cyclists. For example, Lee et al (2013) find that 'walkable' neighbourhoods in Boston, particularly those with good accessibility to retail, are correlated with more crashes and higher pedestrian risks. In this sense, BRTOD must include urban design interventions that foster safer mobility, especially for schoolchildren, older adults, and other vulnerable users.

In the study of the initial TransMilenio system discussed above, for example, Rodríguez and Targa (2004) find that residential rental asking prices increase with distance away from the BRT corridor, by a magnitude greatly exceeding the value gained from proximity to the station area.[2] This result may simply reflect the negative effects of adjacency to the arterial, with or without BRT on it; Rodríguez and

Mojica (2009) find no evidence of negative effects due to corridor adjacency in the expanded TransMilenio network. BRT corridors may bring perceived and real negative effects, from the rights of way, air and noise pollution, and safety concerns regarding the vehicles themselves. In areas with diverse urban fabrics and multiple activities, BRT implementation requires a strategic approach to improving station area surroundings and the entire corridor, with special care to mitigate possible negative externalities that could compromise projects.

Social inclusion poses another important challenge for BRTOD. In general, TOD may induce 'gentrification', a neighbourhood's change towards higher income residents and/or higher property values. The latter can particularly impact on renters, who may be displaced by landlords raising rents in affected neighbourhoods (Freeman 2005). When TOD produces such outcomes, it might be particularly inequitable if lower income households, the most transit dependent, suffer decreased accessibility by being displaced from the areas improved by access to transport. Kahn (2007) examines 14 US cities with rail transit investments between 1970 and 2000 and finds mixed gentrification evidence, as measured by home price dynamics and share of college graduates in the affected areas.

In her assessment of BRTOD in North America and Australia, Judy (2007) identifies regional and local institutional challenges to realising BRTOD. Typically, BRT initiatives come from a metropolitan–scale agency, while land development is governed at the neighbourhood scale. In other words, land regulations, transportation planning, transit operations, and relevant financial instruments tend to reside in separate entities, often at different levels of government, requiring horizontal and vertical policy integration. BRTOD ultimately requires careful and unconventional considerations of real estate, governance, planning, and policy forces. Chapter Five discusses these institutional relationships in greater detail.

In sum

Just like TOD more generally, BRTOD aims to capitalise on the benefits that mass transit can bring to cities, including the possibilities to leverage improved accessibility, enhance agglomeration economies, address regional equity, and structure urban growth towards lower automobile dependency. As a road and tyre based transit mode, BRT has particular characteristics, which both enhance and impair its TOD potentials (see Table 10.1).

Table 10.1: BRT's theoretical TOD strengths and weaknesses relative to rail-based transit

Attributes	Potential strengths	Potential weakness
Implementation		
Speed	Shorter planning and construction timeline brings accessibility benefits more quickly for TOD potentials	Lower cost may encourage less detailed and comprehensive environmental and social assessments
Institutionality	Lower capital cost may allow for more local or less complicated financing	Greater need for cooperation between transit, traffic, public works, and development authorities
Cost	Cover a broader area with 'mass' transit, expanding TOD potential	Bus viewed as mode for the 'poor'; negative image
Flexibility	Infrastructure can be upgraded according to demand	Potential impermanence or under-delivery of services and infrastructure
Design		
Rights of way	Using existing roadways can reduce space dedicated to private vehicles	Large dedicated infrastructures can pose surface level barriers
Stations and environs	Enhance street level public space	Take space from and produce negative externalities for public amenities, real estate projects
Streetscapes	Innovatively integrate pedestrian, bicycle and motor vehicle infrastructures	Engineering, technical, design barriers to multi-modal infrastructures
Operations		
Flexibility	Services can be 'demand-responsive', modified/enhanced/expanded	Perceived and/or real concerns of service quality, service impermanence
Air/noise pollution, safety	May stimulate innovative mitigation designs	Negative impacts on quality of life, attractiveness, property values
Multi-modalism	Innovatively integrate pedestrian, bicycle and motor vehicle flows	Vehicular and transit congestion, risks of multiple users and conflicting movements

Method and contexts: international BRT corridor design workshop

The workshop

To explore the potentials for realising BRTOD, two distinct contexts – Boston, MA (USA) and Santiago de Chile – were examined through a graduate level urban planning and design workshop, co-taught in 2013 at the Massachusetts Institute of Technology (MIT) and the Pontificia Universidad Católica de Chile (PUC). The workshop's two fundamental questions were 'How can BRT corridor projects drive new *integrated* approaches to urban development?' and 'What urban design and policy measures might leverage these transit investments into wider urban change?' These research questions were identified by the workshop instructors, in consultation with stakeholders in both cities. In this academic exercise, students were tasked with exploring imaginative design proposals that could extend practitioners' thinking beyond traditional practical constraints.

The workshop involved 29 students with backgrounds in transportation planning and engineering, urban planning and urban design. This mixed composition aimed to encourage participants to consider the complex interactions among relevant dimensions and disciplines. Students from 10 countries brought a wide range of international perspectives on BRTOD challenges and opportunities.

Workshop leaders selected one potential BRT corridor in both cities, focusing on each for one-half of the 15-week semester. Both corridors cut across a reasonably wide range of their respective urban contexts; for each, discrete segments were identified to vary contextual conditions and expand the range of planning and design innovations discovered and the generalisability of the results. Fieldwork in both cities started with a weeklong charrette and site visit by all students and faculty, followed by five weeks of working in interuniversity groups assigned to the corridor segments identified. Although the workshop included discussions with, and final presentations to, stakeholders (representatives from transit agencies, municipalities, and citizen advocacy groups), time constraints impeded deeper stakeholder engagement.

Comparative contexts

Representing different socioeconomic, political-institutional, transportation, and urban contexts, the two settings provide some opportunity to discern the various factors that might influence corridor and station area planning and design. The comparison that follows offers an abbreviated, non-exhaustive, overview of pertinent characteristics.

Politically, Chile represents a younger and more centralised democracy, with a lower share of total government revenues raised and expended at the non-central level relative to the USA's federal democracy (Inman 2007). As a result, authority for land use and transportation regulation tends to be more local in the United States (see Table 10.2).

Table 10.3 compares the two metropolitan settings. In Boston, Massachusetts' state capital, public transportation services are operated almost entirely by a state agency, the Massachusetts Bay Transportation Authority (MBTA). In Santiago, Chile's capital and economic and population centre, the national government plays a prominent role in investing in and regulating transportation services. Transit services are operated by public (metro) and private (bus) companies, and planned and regulated by a relatively new authority, the Directorate for Metropolitan Public Transport (DTPM), which depends directly upon the national Ministry of Transport. The two places have roughly

Table 10.2: Transportation and land use regulatory authority

	Chile	USA
Transportation capital investment	Transit system: national and municipal general budget Highways: private concessions: user fees (such as tolls) No earmarking of motor fuel taxes	Transit system : dedicated federal and state motor fuel taxes with some local and metropolitan scale contributions (such as sales taxes) Highways: dedicated federal and state motor fuel taxes, some toll roads
Transportation operations	User fees (fares, tolls) and national budget subsidies	User fees (fares, tolls) and state and local government subsidies
Land use regulation	Approval from national Ministry of Housing and Urbanism (MINVU) required	Highly local municipal control

the same public transport fares, meaning that, relative to average incomes, Santiago's public transport system is less affordable. Housing affordability is a concern in both places, although comparable data are not readily available; in Boston median housing prices were 5.4 times greater than median household income in 2013 (Demographia 2014). In gross metropolitan-wide terms, Santiago is three times as dense as Boston.

The cities have different histories of public involvement and civic engagement in transportation, land use, environmental, and equity

Table 10.3: The BRT corridors' metropolitan contexts

Category	Characteristics	Santiago	Boston
Region	Area (sq. km)	4,215	8,632
	Population (million residents)	6.0	4.1
	Gross Density (residents/hectare)	1,423	475
	Percentage of national population	35%	1.5%
	GDP per capita (2010 US$ at PPP)	20,000	68,000
	Percentage of national economic output	40%	2%
	Auto ownership (cars per capita)	0.34	0.60
Transit service area	(sq km)*	955	2000
	(municipalities)	36	65
Mode share (Santiago, 2006; Boston, 2010–2011)	Walk/bike	40	12
	Private transport	22	76
	Public transport (%)	33	13
	Bus	25	3
	Metro	7	5
Transit demand and finance	Unlinked daily boardings (millions)	5.4	1.2
	Unlinked daily boardings (per capita)	0.9	0.3
	Average fare (2013 US$ at PPP)	1.75	1.75
	Farebox recovery ratio	60%	44%
Urban rail network	Total length (km)	104	102
	Stations	112	125
Bus network and service	Total length (km)	2,766	1,220
	Physically separated bus lanes	62	2
	Bus priority lanes	150	4
	Major transfer stops	40	17
	Stops with fare prepayment during peak	130	6
	Number of buses	6,300	1,100
	Total bus kilometres travelled	1,422,900	144,760

Notes and sources: Santiago's GDP and transit fare in PPP exchange values. DTPM (2013); MBTA (2011); SECTRA (2006); MassDOT (2012); Santiago 2006 travel and household related data come from 2006 household travel survey which may have been biased towards upper income households.

concerns. Boston was at the forefront of the USA's citizen led 'highway revolt' in the late 1960s, culminating in a state-declared moratorium on highway building within most of the urban area. Transportation controversies remain today, as some jurisdictions and communities suffer from relatively poor service and accessibility, plus exposure to transportation related negative externalities, like air pollution (see Bullard 2003). Boston has a large number of transportation focused citizen advocacy organisations.

In Chile, engaged citizen advocacy organisations emerged in the wake of the relatively recent return to democracy after the Pinochet dictatorship (1973–1990). The role of public participation in formal decision making remains somewhat weak, characterised by residual antagonisms and a lack of formal institutional structures, leading to a protest-oriented dynamic (Fernández and Ordóñez 2007). Many organisations mobilised and subsequently formalised after the city's own nascent highway revolt against the *Costanera Norte* urban highway proposal in the mid-1990s (Silva 2013). Efforts to improve bus based public transportation through corridor widening have met with large scale protests against expropriations and tree removal.

The corridors

The 21-kilometre Santiago corridor, Gran Avenida, a principal north–south radial axis of the city, runs from the downtown area through older commercial areas, middle and lower income neighbourhoods, toward older industrial areas and the rapidly suburbanising south. Comprised of a couplet of one-way streets in downtown that merge into a wide arterial, and branching again into two streets in the south, the corridor requires upgrades to improve reliability for the existing 25 bus routes and 200,000 average weekday passengers and to better integrate with existing and planned rail services nearby. Gran Avenida exemplifies Santiago's traditional pattern of urban segregation, with middle and higher income residents near the historic centre and groups of lower income residents concentrated in dense peripheral areas. Alleviating this segregation, and the associated lack of services and opportunities in the outlying areas, is a key challenge.

At the same time, the avenue connects important amenities and government facilities, including 43 educational institutions, three regional shopping centres, two major hospitals, and a military base. Gran Avenida presents an opportunity to demonstrate integrated design of a metropolitan scale multimodal corridor, renew existing urban fabric and public spaces, and integrate suburban expansion areas.

Key challenges include narrow rights of way along certain segments, intermodal integration, and community opposition to bus based transit enhancements in favour of a metro extension.

The 12-kilometre Boston corridor is a prospective, partially circumferential, route, connecting older de-industrialising areas in the north with high technology, higher education and health centres, and lower income communities of colour in the city's south. The corridor would entail the inauguration of new bus routes. Concepts for such circumferential transit through the dense communities surrounding Boston date back at least to the 1960s. Plans for a so-called Urban Ring project were put on hold in 2008, in part due to the cost of a tunnel segment demanded by stakeholders, but recent planning efforts have revived the possibility of new BRT corridors in the city.

The selected corridor, representing about one-third of the original Urban Ring, would help alleviate growing congestion in the transit network's downtown core by improving connections between existing radial rail lines and two major employment centres, the Longwood Medical Area (LMA) and Kendall Square, while also increasing transit access for surrounding residential communities and potentially serving to spur redevelopment of urban brownfields. Key implementation challenges along the corridor somewhat echo the Gran Avenida case: limited right of way along certain segments, intermodal integration (including proposed use of an existing rail corridor), and community opposition to bus based transit. The corridor also lacks infrastructure connections at key points.

Traversing diverse urban contexts, both corridors have considerable potential for BRTOD while exemplifying some of the challenges BRTOD might face. Communities' past rejection of bus projects in both settings stems from many of the potential liabilities of BRT identified in Table 10.1; integrated design of urban space and policies could use BRT's strengths to overcome these liabilities.

Figure 10.1 situates each corridor in its respective metropolitan context and Figure 10.2 provides a schematic representation of the corridors and the neighbourhood typologies (namely commercial core, central residential, marginal residential, neighbourhood subcentre, and brownfield/greenfield) they cross, divided into the segments analysed by the workshop teams.

Figure 10.1: The corridor metropolitan settings: Santiago (left) and Boston (right)

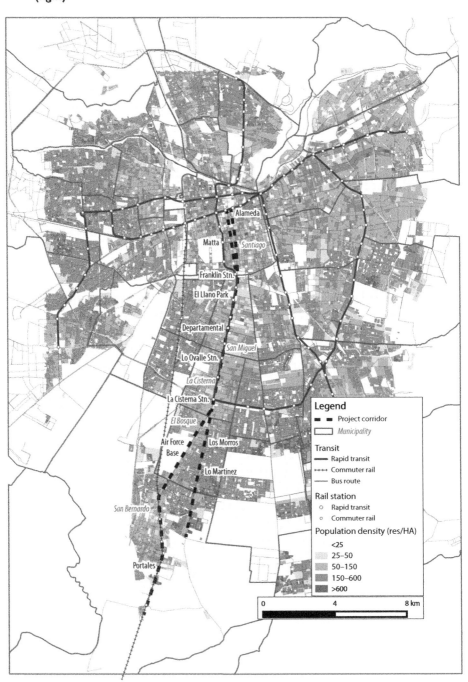

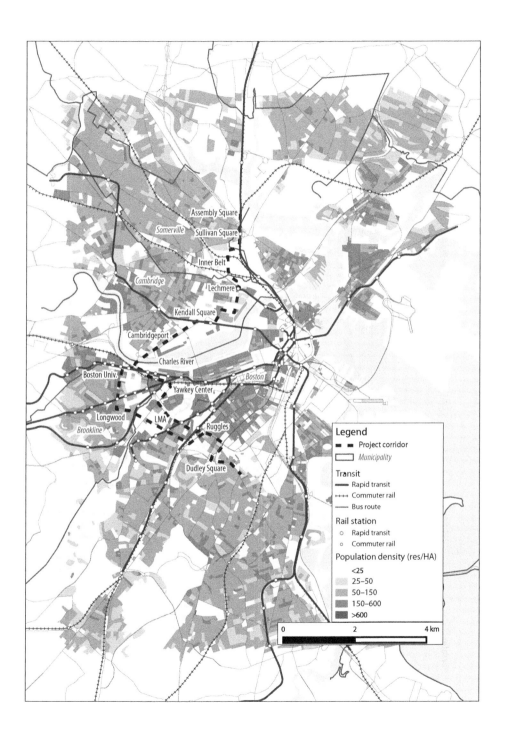

Figure 10.2: Corridor 'transects' – schematic representations of the selected Santiago (left) and Boston (right) BRT corridors, by segment

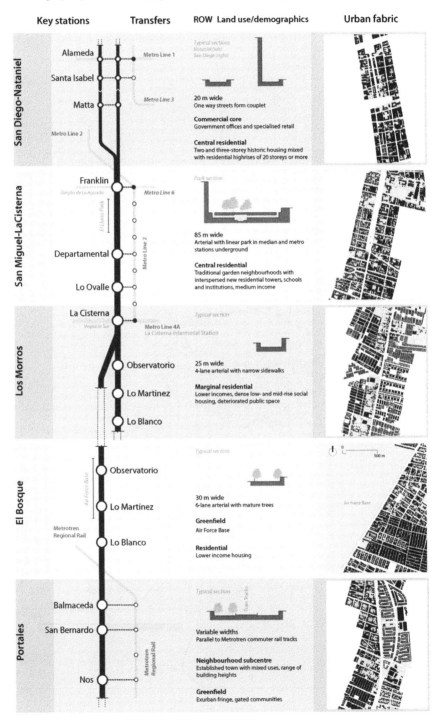

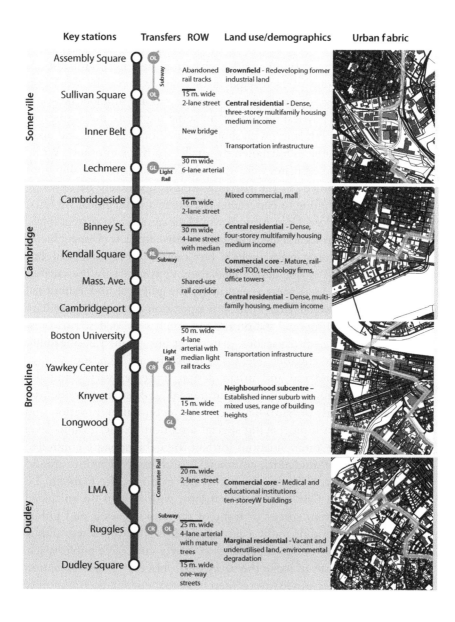

Key stations	Transfers	ROW	Land use/demographics	Urban fabric

Somerville

Assembly Square — OL Subway — Abandoned rail tracks — **Brownfield** - Redeveloping former industrial land

Sullivan Square — OL — 15 m. wide 2-lane street — **Central residential** - Dense, three-storey multifamily housing medium income

Inner Belt — New bridge — Transportation infrastructure

Lechmere — GL Light Rail — 30 m wide 6-lane arterial

Cambridge

Cambridgeside — 16 m wide 2-lane street — Mixed commercial, mall

Binney St. — 30 m wide 4-lane street with median — **Central residential** - Dense, four-storey multifamily housing medium income

Kendall Square — RL Subway — **Commercial core** - Mature, rail-based TOD, technology firms, office towers

Mass. Ave. — Shared-use rail corridor — **Central residential** - Dense, multi-family housing, medium income

Cambridgeport

Brookline

Boston University — 50 m. wide 4-lane arterial with median light rail tracks — Transportation infrastructure

Yawkey Center — CR GL Light Rail

Knyvet — 15 m. wide 2-lane street — **Neighbourhood subcentre** – Established inner suburb with mixed uses, range of building heights

Longwood — GL

Dudley

LMA — Commuter Rail — 20 m. wide 2-lane street — **Commercial core** - Medical and educational institutions ten-storeyW buildings

Ruggles — CR OL Subway — 25 m. wide 4-lane arterial with mature trees — **Marginal residential** - Vacant and underutilised land, environmental degradation

Dudley Square — 15 m. wide one-way streets

Workshop proposals[4]

Santiago's Gran Avenida corridor

Considering the varying widths, changing land uses, and distinct transport demands of each segment of Gran Avenida, the workshop proposed a range of transit priority configurations: shoulder bus-only lanes (without physical separation) in some segments and segregated centre-running bus lanes, with shoulder lanes for use by cars and bikes and through traffic redistributed to parallel roadways in others. While detailed demand estimates were not compiled, increased ridership from denser development in the corridor would most likely be offset by regional trips shifting to better integrated metro and regional rail lines; bus boardings along Gran Avenida would remain close to current totals, but with shorter local trips and related positive impacts on street life.

Major transfer stations include bus–metro and regional rail–bus interchanges. A major design challenge, epitomised by the current design of the La Cisterna station, is the physical and functional separation between large scale bus operations and the immediate surroundings. Proposed station designs emphasised pedestrian access and an opening up of facades, generating fine-grained permeability with immediate environs (see, for example, Figure 10.3, top).

Proposed land use and urban design strategies vary along the transect. Strategies for the commercial and central residential neighbourhoods of San Diego focus on economic renovation and historic preservation, paying special attention to the ground-level streetscape. Recommendations for San Miguel emphasise controlled densification of residential, commercial, and service activities around the major intermodal transfer points (for example, the Franklin, Lo Ovalle, and La Cisterna Metro stations), with a focus on enhanced quality pedestrian spaces in front of the area's schools and public institutions through traffic calming. In Los Morros, where public housing suffers from personal safety concerns and scarce public space, the proposal aims to make the street into a place of social interaction and to introduce productive garden plots that encourage community activity. Along El Bosque, where the abutting air force base poses a short term challenge and longer term opportunity, the flexibility of phasing BRT was applied to transform the base into an integrated urban fabric and economic development hub, with station areas serving as interfaces with existing residential areas (Figure 10.3, bottom). BRT flexibility also played a role in the proposed phased suburban consolidation strategies identified for the Portales segment.

Figure 10.3: Illustrative examples of proposed interventions, including new public space around La Cisterna Intermodal Station (top); regional rail–BRT intermodal station at San Bernardo (middle); intermediate stations and new neighbourhood at El Bosque (bottom)

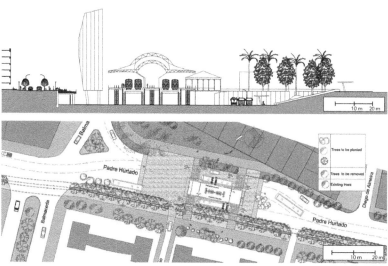

The range of urban contexts along the corridor requires consistent landscape and public space treatments, implying unified objectives (human scale, multimodality), but varying built forms. Achieving these results along a single structuring corridor, integrating socioeconomic and demographic groups, and financing the associated public works projects all require new governance that can coordinate across existing jurisdictional and regulatory boundaries.

Boston's 'Diamond Ring'

The workshop sought to produce innovative designs for circumferential transit that would inspire renewed attention for this corridor while building transit ridership. A sketch analysis using a travel survey and a four-step model run estimated 35,000 to 55,000 average weekday boardings along this new corridor in the short run, increasing to 80,000 after two decades of operation. The proposal rebranded this western portion of the Urban Ring as the Diamond Ring (DR), a nod to the famous Emerald Necklace park system the corridor intersects.

The proposed corridor occupies varied existing right of way configurations, from lightly used railroad tracks to wide avenues to narrow neighbourhood streets. The design proposals respond to heavy congestion at critical points, as well as to diverse surrounding urban contexts. In Somerville (see Figure 10.2), in concert with post-industrial brownfield redevelopment, initial services could operate on existing rights of way, but a new bridge would most likely be required eventually to achieve full BRTOD potential. Strategies in the Cambridge segment include use of existing roads through a dense commercial core, before turning onto a segment utilising an existing rail right of way (and proposed to share with the rail). A major upgrade to a river crossing would then bring the corridor to the neighbourhood subcentre of Brookline, and the branches of a light rail line (the Green Line) running along the Emerald Necklace parks, requiring special design sensitivity. The final segment serves the LMA, a congested employment cluster, and the historically marginalised neighbourhood of Dudley Square in Roxbury.

Similar to the Gran Avenida case, while the project aims for a coherent whole – unified by multimodal transfer points, bus priority, and the use of information technology at bus stops – the proposals reflect the heterogeneous settings and phased implementation. Major intermodal transfer stations would be linked to new mixed use developments, including public facilities, residences, and offices. For transfer points adjacent to heavy rail and elevated highway infrastructure, such as at the Charles River Crossing and Sullivan Square, proposals included new public spaces that transform such infrastructure. In the case of Brookline, access to narrow existing streets would be restricted to public transit and abutters.

Corridor implementation would entail phasing, with the first phase of the project, DR1, providing 3–5-minute peak headways and requiring 37 additional buses. Some existing services would be upgraded and rebranded to complement DR1 service. The workshop estimated US$360 million in upfront costs and US$18 million in annual operating costs, to be funded by a range of sources including tax-increment financing, joint development, transportation management agency contributions, and employer transportation fees.

The project opens new opportunities to improve housing, the environment, and equitable economic development in the region, but the current institutional structure inhibits the potential to maximise the DR's viability and positive impact. In response, the workshop proposed a state sponsored authority to implement the Diamond Ring, based on successful precedents in other places. This convening body would facilitate collaboration on housing and anti-displacement policies, environmental standards for transit-oriented (re)development, and economic development opportunities such as workforce training.

Synthesis

Table 10.4 synthesises the challenges and planning/design responses derived from the workshop, categorised in five general urban contexts the workshop identified as typical of BRT projects.

These five prototypical urban contexts, across two corridors with distinct characteristics, reveal common challenges and potential strategies that seek to harness the strengths and mitigate the weaknesses identified in Table 10.1. At the core, the themes revolve around congestion, intermodal connectivity, non-motorised transport, historic preservation, and the creation of new street landscapes. These themes reflect BRT's potential for transforming urban development in ways that urban rail may be less suited to do.

In central residential areas, key challenges are the inclusion of new residents, lack of available land and public space in densely developed areas, and transfers between modes. Strategies in these areas include affordable housing provision, workforce training programmes, traffic diversion, and station area development. In outlying areas, where social and economic isolation prevail, the strategies centre around optimising the performance of the transportation system, better connectivity between local communities and the metropolis, the creation of value generating spaces for residents to gather, and the articulation of new economic dynamics that reincorporate traditionally marginalised residents into the city. In subcentres, a flexible design that can change across time and complex urban surroundings is key. Finally, in greenfield and brownfield areas with available land, the emphasis should be on new mixed use development offering socially and mixed age housing opportunities, linked to the corridor by high quality public space, that is permeable, coherent, and connected with the existing urban fabric.

Connecting to existing anchor institutions and programmes may be an important way to advance BRT corridor projects. In both settings, proposed partnerships with existing educational and industrial anchor institutions drew on salient links to BRT corridor infrastructures and

Table 10.4: Synthesis of urban contexts, sites, and proposed strategies from the workshop

Urban context typologies	Santiago	Boston
Commercial core		
Challenges	• Vehicular and transit congestion • Deteriorating building stock	• Vehicular and transit congestion
Opportunities	• Build on commercial reputation • Construction of new metro lines • Proximity to national monuments	• Reinforce existing rail-based TOD • Restricted parking • Anchor institutions
Proposed strategies	• New intermodal districts • Historic preservation, art and culture • Mixed-income housing • Stronger priority for transit and non-motorised modes	• New multimodal stations, emphasising ground level • Strengthened parking limits and employer transportation programmes
Central residential		
Challenges	• Height and scale of new development • Limited commercial services, abundance of automobile-focused land uses	• Displacement and gentrification • Marginal access to rapid transit • Limited land availability and right of way
Opportunities	• Densification, mixed-use, socio-economic diversity • Existing rapid transit options	• Proximity to employment centres • Receptive local government
Proposed strategies	• Affordable housing requirements, medium-height densification • Diversion of through traffic to regional highways • Targeting of higher density, mixed-use development around transit stations	• Workforce development linked to corridor infrastructure and maintenance • Enhancing green space connectivity • Shared use of available rail corridor
Marginal residential		
Challenges	• Geographic and social isolation • Low accessibility to job and services • Personal security and safety • Scepticism of planning process and bus projects • Overcrowded transit services • Fare evasion	• Barriers between adjacent neighbourhoods • Low accessibility to jobs • Scepticism of planning process and bus projects • Potential gentrification due to relatively central location

(continued)

Table 10.4: Synthesis of urban contexts, sites, and proposed strategies from the workshop

Urban context typologies	Santiago	Boston
Marginal residential (continued)		
Opportunities	• Extensive walkability and public transit use	• Local government attention • Examples of successful community-led TOD
Proposed strategies	• Economic development and urban agriculture linked to streetscape improvements • Street as shared front yard and gathering space • Route restructuring to reduce crowding, congestion delays, and access times to regional rail	• Integration with existing community-led planning and economic development • Underground bus circulation to allow for better headway regulation and improved pedestrian areas • Extend routes to reduce transfers and travel times
Neighbourhood subcentres		
Challenges	• Integration with surrounding leapfrog development, through transit, especially regional rail	• Jurisdictional boundaries and political differences
Opportunities	• Build on existing mix of uses • Community advocacy for streetscape improvements	• Build on existing mix of uses
Proposed strategies	• Intermodal districts • Pedestrian connections to open space • Flexibility for eventual upgrade of bus corridor	• Enhanced vehicle technology for transit priority and quiet operation
Greenfield/brownfield		
Challenges	• Phasing and scale of new development • Air Force Base walls create barrier	• Phasing and scale of new development • Infrastructural barriers
Opportunities	• Master planning • Space for expansive development	• Master planning • Expand commercial tax base
Proposed strategies	• Pedestrian connections to open space • Innovation clusters • Phased development inward from existing urban fabric	• Phased development inward from existing urban fabric • Reconceptualise rail and highway infrastructure as attraction • Local and regional connections

services, whether through garden plots adjacent to the right of way linked to an existing university urban agriculture training programme, an electric propulsion facility linked to an existing technology research centre, or a cluster of maintenance facilities linked to a vocational training programme. In short, the workshop suggested how strategic BRTOD planning extends beyond pure mobility provision to examine ways to connect educational and economic clusters, improving their competitiveness, and imaginatively involving these anchor institutions with the needs of the corridor itself.

Lessons and challenges

A number of challenges and lessons for the BRT planning process emerged from the workshop.

Institutional structure

In both Boston and Santiago, design, funding, and policy proposals cut across existing jurisdictional boundaries. In particular, land value capture, employer levies, and affordable housing policies would be especially difficult to implement within current institutional structures. If the inertia of these institutional structures can be overcome, the potential economies of scope that these proposals identified could help maximise the benefits of BRTOD.

Service planning

Planning BRT corridor service in relation to other transit service was a key part of the proposals. Students proposed a range of complementary services, from station area circulators to freeway express routes, not necessarily constrained by a rigid trunk/feeder distinction. Phasing the implementation of these 'families' of transit services with changes in other parts of the network, such as the inauguration of metro Lines 3 and 6 and the upgrading of Metrotren regional rail service in Santiago or the inauguration of a diesel multiple unit service and the Green Line Extension in Boston, is critical.

Urban design

A number of urban design priorities, common to both contexts, emerged from the workshop. Intermodal transfer stations, where the BRT corridors intersect existing or proposed rail lines, were focal points for interventions. Instead of insular buildings, these nodes were conceptualised as cores of a permeable, walkable urban fabric.

The importance of thinking about streetscape transversely – not just along the corridor, but also across it – was clear in the designs. Active retail, street furniture, and public space along intersecting streets were important parts of the proposals. Unlike subway systems that have surface impacts limited primarily to station areas, BRT corridors impact on the street level public realm along their entire length.

The designs of corridors and surrounding streets reflect fundamental shifts in urban mobility. Proposals for Santiago argued that the Central Highway now provides regional automobile access previously served by Gran Avenida, so the latter no longer needs to be so automobile-centric. Similarly, highway projects in Boston like the Big Dig call into question the need for the automobile-centric designs of the antiquated McGrath Highway and the Charles River waterfront parkways. The need for such extensive capacity for automobile traffic deserves to be questioned given recent tendencies towards removal of urban freeways in the United States (Napolitan and Zegras 2008).

BRT projects offer the opportunity to rethink and reallocate urban street space, a theme considered in Chapter Nine. The proposals for these corridors emphasise the importance of prioritising connectivity for human powered modes. Whether in the historic urban fabric of downtown Santiago or the post-industrial redevelopment of Somerville's Inner Belt, improved pedestrian and bicycle amenities and connectivity were deemed key to fostering TOD. These proposals highlight BRT's potential not only as transportation infrastructure, but also as a tool to catalyse change in a city's development.

Limitations

The results presented here are entirely prospective, derived primarily from a semester-long graduate level pedagogical workshop. The format and approach posed numerous logistics, communication, and other challenges. In this sense the workshop might be viewed as a mirror of the challenges, potentials, and risks that decision makers face when confronted with interdisciplinary and inter-institutional collaboration increasingly at the heart of this kind of urban enterprise. Both proposals, despite being preliminary, comprise a base of work illustrating new ways of thinking for both cities.

Conclusions

Planning for both corridors remains underway. In the case of Gran Avenida, the nonprofit *Ciudad Viva* (Living City) and its Network of Active Neighbourhoods project has begun introducing approaches highlighted in the workshop to civil society and local governments and developing urban design criteria, which can serve as guides and tools for future streetscape projects. In the Boston case, a private foundation has convened a BRT Study Group which, among other corridors, is assessing the workshop corridor.

Even for cities with existing formalised transit systems, BRT further solidifies bus services, typically within consolidated built environments. Beyond merely improving bus performance and assuming the improvements will attract new riders, BRTOD's necessarily integrated approach can achieve additional synergistic benefits for both ridership and the surrounding urban context through land use, public space design, and policy strategies.

The workshop participants were a relatively well informed, multidisciplinary group of graduate students that generated a range of solutions for diverse corridor contexts. While the timeframe did not allow full feasibility analysis and evaluation, the proposals strongly suggest that economies of scope exist for BRT corridor planning; that is, including more uses and diverse means of connecting with the city in the design of a corridor can have multiplicative benefits for urban development. Bridging disciplinary and institutional barriers can be a challenge, but the integrated design facilitated by such collaboration may be a promising pathway to achieving public acceptance and maximising the benefits of BRT.

Notes

[1] Throughout this chapter, unless otherwise noted, Santiago and Boston refer to the metropolitan areas, not the specific jurisdictions (that is, city centres) from which both metropolitan areas take their names.

[2] Asking rents decrease by US$15 per 5 minutes walking distance from BRT stations, or US$4 per 100 metres (assuming 5 km/hr walk speed); at the same time, asking rents increase by an estimated US$77 per 100 metres straightline distance to the BRT corridor. Such apparent 'barrier/nuisance effects' are not exclusive to roadways; Zegras et al (2013), for example, find that residential property values in Chicago are negatively associated with proximity to at-grade urban heavy rail lines, regional rail lines, and highways.

[3] The approximate service coverage areas for Boston and Santiago do not include areas covered by suburban rail services.

[4] Details of the proposed designs and policies can be found at http://brtod.net

References

Baum-Snow, N. and Kahn M.E. (2000) 'The effects of new public projects to expand urban rail transit', *Journal of Public Economics*, 77: 241–263.

Ben-Akiva, M. and Morikawa, T. (2002) 'Comparing ridership attraction of rail and bus', *Transport Policy*, 9(2): 107–116.

Bocarejo, J.P., Portilla, I. and Pérez, M.A. (2013) 'Impact of TransMilenio on density, land use, and land value in Bogotá', *Research in Transportation Economics*, 40: 78–86.

Bullard, R.D. (2003) 'Addressing urban transportation equity in the United States', *Fordham Urban Law Journal*, 31(5): 1183–1209.

Cao, J. (2013). 'The association between light rail transit and satisfactions with travel and life: evidence from Twin Cities', *Transportation*, 40: 921–933.

Cervero, R. and Kang, C.D. (2011) 'Bus rapid transit impacts on land uses and land values in Seoul, Korea', *Transport Policy*, 18(1): 102–116.

Cervero, R., Murakami, J., and Miller, M. (2010) 'Direct ridership model of bus rapid transit in Los Angeles County, California', *Transportation Research Record: Journal of the Transportation Research Record*, 2145: 1–7.

Chatman, D. (2013) 'Does TOD need the T? On the importance of factors other than rail access', *Journal of the American Planning Association*, 79(1): 17–31.

Chatman, D. and Noland, R. (2014) 'Transit service, physical agglomeration and productivity in US metropolitan areas', *Urban Studies*, 51(5): 917–937.

Demographia (2014) '10th annual Demographia international housing affordability survey: 2014', www.demographia.com/dhi.pdf

DTPM (Directorio de Transporte Público Metropolitano) (2013) 'Informe de gestión 2012', Santiago: Directorio de Transporte Público Metropolitano, www.dtpm.cl/archivos/Informe_de_gestión_2012_4_de_Septiembre.pdf

Estupiñán, N. and Rodríguez, D. A. (2008) 'The relationship between urban form and station boardings for Bogotá's BRT', *Transportation Research Part A: Policy and Practice*, 42(2): 296–306.

Fernández, M. and Ordóñez, M. (2007) 'Participación ciudadana en la agenda gubernamental de 2007', Santiago: Ponticia Universidad Católica de Chile, www.innovacionciudadana.cl/portal/imagen/File/barometro/Informe%20final%20S.E..pdf

Freeman, L. (2005) 'Displacement or succession? Residential mobility in gentrifying neighbourhoods', *Urban Affairs Review*, 40(4): 463–491.

Geurs, K.T. and van Wee, B. (2004) 'Accessibility evaluation of land-use and transport strategies: review and research directions', *Journal of Transport Geography*, 12(2): 127–140.

Handy, S. (2005) 'Smart growth and the transportation–land use connection: what does the research tell us?', *International Regional Science Review*, 28: 146–167.

Inman, R.P. (2007) 'Federalism's values and the values of federalism', *CESifo Economic Studies*, 53(4): 522–560.

Jiang, Y., Zegras, P.C. and Mehndiratta, S. (2012) 'Walk the line: station context, corridor type and bus rapid transit walk access in Jinan, China', *Journal of Transport Geography*, 20(1): 1–14.

Judy, M. (2007) 'The potential for bus rapid transit to promote transit oriented development: an analysis of BRTOD in Ottawa, Brisbane, and Pittsburgh', Master of City Planning Thesis, MIT.

Jun, M.J. (2012) 'Redistributive effects of bus rapid transit (BRT) on development patterns and property values in Seoul, Korea', *Transport Policy*, 19: 85–92.

Kahn, M. (2007) 'Gentrification trends in new transit-oriented communities: evidence from 14 cities that expanded and built rail transit systems', *Real Estate Economics*, 35(2): 155–182.

Kamruzzaman, Md., Wood, L., Hine, J., Currie, G., Giles-Corti, B. and Turrell, G. (2014) 'Patterns of social capital associated with transit oriented development', *Journal of Transport Geography*, 35: 144–155.

Lee, J.S., Zegras, C. and Ben-Joseph, E. (2013) 'Safely active mobility for urban baby boomers: the role of neighborhood design', *Accident Analysis and Prevention*, 61: 153–166.

Martínez, L.M. and Viegas, J.M. (2009) 'Effects of transportation accessibility on residential property values: a hedonic price model in the Lisbon Metropolitan Area', *Transportation Research Record: Journal of the Transportation Research Record*, 2115: 127–137.

MassDOT (2012) *Massachusetts Travel Survey*. Boston: Massachusetts Department of Transportation.

MBTA (Massachusetts Bay Transportation Agency) (2011) 'Statistics presentation', Boston: Massachusetts Bay Transportation Agency, www.mbta.com/uploadedfiles/About_the_T/Financials/Stats%20Presentation%209-7-11.pdf

Napolitan, F. and Zegras, C. (2008) 'Shifting urban priorities: the removal of inner city freeways in the United States', *Transportation Research Record: Journal of the Transportation Research Record*, 2046: 68–75.

Nelson, A.C., Appleyard, B., Kannan, S., Ewing, R., Miller, M. and Eskic, D. (2013) 'Bus rapid transit and economic development: case study of the Eugene-Springfield BRT system', *Journal of Public Transportation*, 16(3): 41–56.

Perk, V., Bovino, S., Catalá, M., Reader, S. and Ulloa, S. (2013) 'Silver Line bus rapid transit in Boston, Massachusetts: impacts on sale prices of condominiums along Washington Street', *Transportation Research Record: Journal of the Transportation Research Record*, 2350: 72–79.

Rodríguez, D. and Mojica, C. (2009) 'Capitalization of BRT network expansions effects into prices of non-expansion areas', *Transportation Research Part A*, 43: 560–571.

Rodríguez, D. and Targa, F. (2004) Value of accessibility to Bogotá's bus rapid transit system', *Transport Reviews*, 24(5): 587–610.

SECTRA (2006) *Greater Santiago Origin-Destination Survey*, Santiago: Secretaría de Planifiación de Transporte.

Silva, E.R. (2013) 'Managing the citizen: privatized public works and the bureaucratic management of citizenship in post-authoritarian Chile, 1990–2005', *Citizenship Studies*, 17(5): 611–626.

Suzuki, H., Cervero, R. and Iuchi, K. (2013) *Transforming Cities with Transit: Transit and Land-Use Integration for Sustainable Urban Development*, Washington, DC: World Bank, www.wds.worldbank. org/external/default/WDSContentServer/IW3P/IB/2013/01/09/0 00425962_20130109153314/Rendered/PDF/NonAsciiFileName0. pdf

Warner, S.B. (1962) *Streetcar Suburbs*, Cambridge, MA: Harvard University Press and MIT Press.

Zegras, C., Jiang, S. and Grillo, C. (2013) 'Sustaining mass transit through land value taxation? Prospects for Chicago', Working paper for the Lincoln Institute of Land Policy, Cambridge, MA.

ELEVEN

Preferences for BRT and light rail

David Hensher, Corinne Mulley and John Rose

Introduction

In many developed countries there is a debate, usually 'won' by the implementation of light rail transit (LRT), on the potential role of bus rapid transit (BRT) in comparison with LRT and heavy rail. Despite the arguments promoting the advantages of BRT, there exists a lot of resistance to BRT as an alternative to rail options. Part of the problem may be the perception that any public transport (PT) option associated with the word 'bus'[1] conjures up images of noisy, polluting buses in mixed traffic congestion. Yet BRT can, if designed appropriately, deliver a service that is equivalent to or better than LRT and/or heavy rail with built in growth prospects, which competes very favourably with the equivalent cost outlays of rail options.

Although the predominant focus of traveller behaviour research has been on studying the choice of mode for specific trips, a growing challenge is to understand why stakeholders (that is, the community at large) in specific geographical jurisdictions, prefer one PT mode over another. When asked, stakeholders frequently and overwhelmingly support LRT, regardless of whether they themselves use a specific mode, and irrespective of cost considerations. There may be a strong sense of imagery conditioning modal preferences for LRT without a full appreciation of the equivalent or better benefits than can flow from the less favoured BRT. Hensher (1999) has referred to the debate as one of 'choice vs. blind commitment'.

The purpose of understanding community perceptions is to assist in the development of a strategy to promote BRT and to break through the barriers that have created the modal misperceptions so common in many geographical jurisdictions. In this chapter a survey of residents of six capital cities in Australia provides the empirical context, but ongoing research is extending the study to other locations (cultures and languages) throughout the world. Overall this chapter suggests that there are often good rational reasons to implement BRT over LRT;

however, this often does not happen, so there must be some other factors (emotional/ideological) that impact on the decision making. This study is designed to identify those factors and how one might overcome them.

The chapter is organised as follows. The essence of the debate between BRT and LRT is outlined next before turning to the methodology underpinning the study designed to shed light on potential modal bias between LRT and BRT. The literature suggests factors that influence stakeholders' views on the appeal (or otherwise) of LRT and BRT, distinguishing between those factors associated with design of a PT system, and those associated with service delivery. In addition, there are dimensions of PT that are not explicitly associated with a particular mode that matter to stakeholders and which would have impact if stakeholders were to vote on PT priorities. Against this background, an experiment is designed to seek the preferences of the wider communities and this is described, before turning to the results and conclusions as to the policy implications of to the study.

The role of perceptions

The previous section highlights a number of issues that point to the implementation of BRT as a 'sensible' option for cities in the twenty-first century. And yet LRT is consistently implemented, particularly in developed countries, in preference to BRT – for example, LRTs in Dijon and LeHavre (France, 2012); Murcia and Zaragoza (Spain, 2011); Salt Lake City (US, 2013) and Tucson Arizona (US, 2014). This chapter reports how stakeholders or citizens in the capital cities of Australia have revealed their views of BRT versus LRT, thus allowing the identification of barriers that mitigate against support for BRT in the presence of LRT options, a common context in many metropolitan areas. Whilst this chapter is specifically about the evidence from a developed world context, as it includes the surveying of participants from Australian capital cities, the preference for rail over bus exists in developing countries too, even where the bus solution is adopted on a value for money basis.

The chapter focuses on the informed or uninformed perceptions of the wider population of stakeholders, regardless of whether they are actually a user (frequent or infrequent) of various available forms of public transport. We reviewed the published literature, selecting studies that are representative of a much larger literature. We drew in particular on the contributions by Hensher (1991), Swanson et al (1997), Chinnock et al (2013), Cain et al (2009), Cirillo et al (2011), dell'Olio et al (2010a, 2010b), Eboli and Mazzulla (2008a, 2008b, 2010), and Gatta and Marcucci (2007), which provide a framework within which to identify attributes that are important to the wider community. We also drew on papers that have presented the merits of BRT and LRT, providing more strategic overviews of the debate, in contrast to systematic inquiries of a more formal survey and modelling sense. Examples of such studies are Hass-Klau and Crampton (2002), Hensher and Waters (1994), Hensher (1999), Mackett and Edward (1996a, 1996b), Canadian Urban Transit Association (2004), Cornwell and Cracknell (1990), Kain (1988), Pickrell (1992), and Sislak (2000).

This review of the very wide and varied literature on PT design and service provision allowed the development of a list of statements that formed the basis of engagement with the wider community. This list captured the main features of PT mentioned as either an influence on views about PT in general and/or on views of specific modes of transport. A short pilot survey refined the final set of statements. This final set of questions relating to public transport design and service in the context of buses (including BRT) and LRT are shown in Tables 11.1 and 11.2 and the statements relating to stakeholder support in a voting context are shown in Table 11.3. Tables 11.1 and 11.2 present the statements favouring BRT and there is a similar set of statements which are the reverse of this, favouring LRT as required by

Table 11.1: The set of statements related to public transport design

ID	Design statements on bus/BRT relative to light rail in best–worst experiment
1	There are fewer bus stops than light rail (tram) stations so people have to walk further to catch a bus
2	Bus systems provide better network coverage than light rail (tram) systems
3	A new bus route in a bus lane or dedicated corridor can bring more life to the city than a new light rail (tram) line
4	A bus service in a bus lane or dedicated corridor looks faster than a light rail (tram) service
5	Bus routes are fixed, so bus stops provide more opportunity for new housing than a light rail (tram) line which can be changed very easily
6	New bus stops or a new bus route in a bus lane or dedicated corridor will improve surrounding properties more than new light rail (tram) stops
7	Buses in a bus lane or dedicated corridor are more environmentally friendly than light rail (trams)
8	More jobs will be created surrounding a bus route in a bus lane or dedicated corridor than a light rail (tram) route
9	A bus service in a bus lane or dedicated corridor is more likely than a light rail (tram) to still be in use in 30 years' time
10	Bus services stop nearer to more people than light rail (trams) services

(continued)

Table 11.1: The set of statements related to public transport design (continued)

ID	Design statements on bus/BRT relative to light rail in best–worst experiment
11	Bus services are less polluting than light rail (trams)
12	Bus services are more likely to have level boarding (no steps up or down to get on the vehicle) than light rail (trams)
13	Buses are quieter than light rail (trams)
14	Bus services in a bus lane or dedicated corridor services have been more successful for cities than light rail (trams)
15	Buses in a bus lane or dedicated corridor are more permanent than light rail (trams)
16	Buses in a bus lane or dedicated corridor provide more opportunities for land redevelopment than light rail (trams)
17	Buses in a bus lane or dedicated corridor provide more focussed development opportunities than light rail (trams)
18	Buses in a bus lane or dedicated corridor are more likely to be funded with private investment than light rail (trams)
19	Buses in a bus lane or dedicated corridor support higher population and employment growth than light rail (trams)
20	Building a bus lane or a dedicated roads and buying buses makes a bus system cheaper than putting down rails and buying light rail (trams)
21	Bus services provided in a bus lane or dedicated corridor have lower operating costs than light rail (tram) systems
22	Bus services provided in a bus lane or dedicated corridor have lower operating costs per person carried than light rail (tram) systems
23	Building a new bus route in a bus lane or dedicated corridor will cause less disruption to roads in the area than a new light rail (tram) line
24	Overall, buses in a bus lane or dedicated corridor have lower maintenance costs than light rail (trams) and light rail (tram) track
25	Bus stops have greater visibility for passengers than light rail (tram) stops
26	Buses in a bus lane or dedicated corridor have lower accident rates than light rail (trams)
27	Buses in a bus lane or dedicated corridor provide a more liveable environment than light rail (trams)
28	Buses in a bus lane or dedicated corridor have greater long term sustainability than light rail (trams)
29	Buses provide more comfort for travellers than light rail (trams)
30	Bus systems are quicker to build and put in operation than light rail (tram) services in a light rail (tram) lane or dedicated corridor
31	The long term benefits of a new bus route in a bus lane or dedicated corridor are greater than a new light rail (tram) line
32	House prices will rise faster around new bus stops associated with a bus lane or dedicated corridor than light rail (tram) stops
32	House prices will rise faster around new light rail (tram) stops than bus stops associated with a bus lane or dedicated corridor
33	Buses in a bus lane or dedicated corridor provide better value for money to taxpayers than light rail (trams)

Table 11.2: The set of statements related to public transport service levels

ID	Service statements favouring buses/BRT in best–worst experiment
1	Travelling by bus is safer than travelling by light rail (tram)
2	Bus travel times in a bus lane or dedicated corridor are faster than light rail (tram)
3	Crowded buses are less horrible to travel in than crowded light rail (trams)
4	Buses in a bus lane or dedicated corridor are more reliable than light rail (trams)
5	Buses look cleaner than light rail (trams)
6	Buses are cleaner than light rail (trams)
7	A bus journey in a bus lane or dedicated corridor is more comfortable for passengers than a light rail (tram) journey
8	Buses are more modern looking than light rail (trams) and hence have more appeal in urban settings
9	Bus journeys require fewer transfers than light rail (tram) journeys
10	Buses have cleaner seats than light rail (trams)
11	Buses are cleaner on the outside than light rail (trams)
12	Bus stops are cleaner than light rail (tram) stops
13	Bus services in a bus lane or dedicated corridor are more frequent than light rail (tram) services
14	Bus stops are safer than light rail (tram) stops
15	Bus services in a bus lane or dedicated corridor do not get delayed like light rail (tram) services
16	Buses provide a better comfort level than light rail (tram) services
17	Buses provide easier boarding than light rail (trams)
18	Car drivers are more likely to transfer to bus services in a bus lane or dedicated corridor than to light rail (tram) services
19	Buses in a bus lane or dedicated corridor provide a better quality of service than light rail (trams)
20	Buses provide better personal security for travellers than light rail (trams)
21	Buses are sexy and light rail (trams) are boring
22	A public transport network with bus rapid transit (BRT) will provide a greater network coverage than one with light rail (trams)

the methodology of the best–worst survey design which is discussed in the next section.

The next section describes how we designed the best–worst preference experiments to identify the role of each statement in revealing the preferences of stakeholders for specific PT initiatives. The evidence from these experiments, presented in the following sections, provides an important source of information on the barriers that exist in the population as a whole that mitigate against a particular mode and more general PT initiatives.

Table 11.3: The set of statements related to public transport voting preferences

ID	Voting statements in best–worst experiment
1	Systems with comfortable vehicles
2	Smart vehicles
3	Quick journey times
4	Some corridors with good service levels, even if other corridors had less good service levels
5	New rail links, even if these are shorter than a package of investments with good bus-based services
6	Value for money for the taxpayer
7	The greatest length of high quality corridors, irrespective of whether train, tram or bus
8	A network that is cost effective to operate
9	Low fares
10	Higher fares to pay for higher quality services
11	Frequent services
12	Fast overall journey time to destination, including getting to and from the station or stop
13	A network with few interchanges
14	Interchanges between services and modes (bus, train, ferry) if this makes overall journey times quicker
15	The package that is quickest to implement
16	Slow implementation is not a problem if the package delivers the right public transport system
17	High quality bus routes on dedicated roads (so that they do not suffer from delays due to cars)
18	Systems that give wide network coverage
19	Packages which offer good safety for the passenger
20	Packages which give an outcome that will last for many years
21	Bus-based systems of public transport
22	Easy to use fare system
23	The package of investments most likely to benefit your city
24	The package of investments most likely to benefit you
25	The package of investments most likely to get car drivers out of their car and onto public transport
26	The package of investments least likely to increase taxes
27	The package of investments giving the highest capacity for travellers
28	The package of investments which allows the city to grow sustainably
29	The package of investments which allows housing to be built around stations.

The approach

The list of statements shown in Tables 11.1 and 11.2 are the framework used in this paper to identify stakeholder preferences and identify barriers to the implementation of BRT. Although there are a number of methods available to elicit preferences (for example, Likert scales, discrete choice methods), this chapter uses the methodology of best–worst choices. In recent years there has been growing interest within the discrete choice framework on seeking responses to scenarios where stakeholders select both the best option and worst option (or attribute) from a set of alternatives (which may be a list of attributes, statements or alternatives), and this literature recognises the additional behavioural information in the best and worst response mechanism (for example, Marley and Louviere 2005; Marley and Pihlens 2012). The best–worst scaling is gaining popularity as a way to narrow down a large set of possible attributes for a choice experiment. Frequently we find that there are many possible attributes that might influence stakeholder preferences, and best–worst scaling is an attractive method to begin to narrow down the large number of statements in Tables 11.1 to 11.3 to make, in the future, a sensible choice experiment with the number of attributes that allow a comprehensive, but comprehensible choice based on already expressed importance of attributes.

The process of best–worst allows, in addition to the standard choice response (the most preferred option), a response mechanism to reveal the respondents' perceived worst alternative. This method can be implemented at the attribute or statement level (as in the current study) or at a choice alternative level. As is common practice with best–worst choice data, the observation for the worst choice is assumed to be the negative of the best choice data. Under this assumption, preferences for the least preferred choice are assumed to be the negative inflection of preferences for the most preferred choice (Marley and Pihlens 2012).

For each set of questions (design attributes, service attributes and voting influences) experimental designs were created that allowed for all main effects. In generating these designs, the alternative chosen as best was deleted when constructing the pseudo worst choice task. The final designs had 22, 34 and 15 choice tasks for the design barriers, service barriers and voting influences experiments respectively.

The best–worst preference survey was given to respondents, as described in the next section. Each respondent was given choice screens covering the service attributes and design attributes of BRT and LRT and features of BRT and LRT that would influence their vote for implementation. Figure 11.1 illustrates the format of a choice

Figure 11.1: Example best–worst scenario for design statements

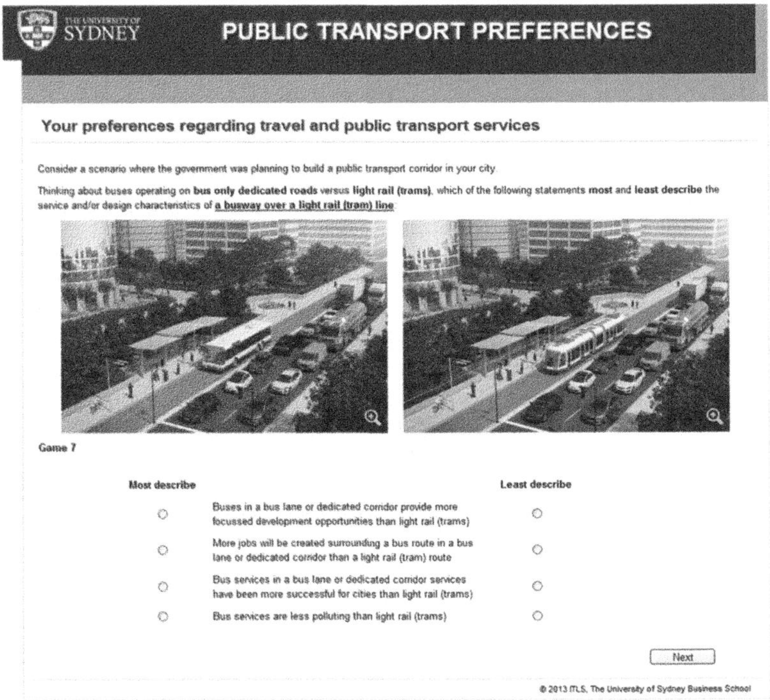

screen. Respondents were also shown pictures of the specially designed images of BRT and LRT (shown in Figure 11.2) and asked for a ranked preference as part of the design of the preference experiment. The underlying experimental designs are available on request from the authors.

Sampling, data collection and data profile

To obtain a broad assessment of the interest in the role of BRT and LRT in the provision of metropolitan public transport, the residents of six Australian cities (Sydney, Melbourne, Canberra, Adelaide, Brisbane and Perth) were surveyed. The choice of cities was motivated by the way in which their residents have been exposed to real BRT and/or LRT systems as well as, to varying degrees, the debate on proposals to promote LRT or BRT.

We used the Pureprofile consumer panel (www.pureprofile.com) for Australia as a sampling frame. Pureprofile has over 350,000 individuals on the Australian panel, and will not undertake a project if it believes

Figure 11.2: BRT and LRT images

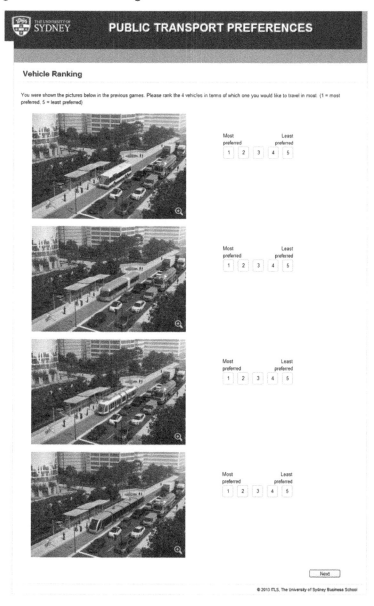

that the target sample is not achievable. Pureprofile paid each respondent $10 for a completed survey. There is growing evidence that a consumer panel can be representative if relevant quota criteria are applied (see Hatton McDonald et al 2010; Lindhjem and Navrud 2011).

In addition to the best–worst preference screens, additional information was obtained on recent public transport usage, and socioeconomic descriptors (summarised in Table 11.4). Interviews were undertaken over the period May to June 2013. The effective number of interviews by city is provided in Table 11.4.

The socioeconomic profile of the sample shows a similar mix of respondents in terms of mean age and occupational status. The incidence of males varies from 31.7% in Perth to 50% in Canberra, and average personal income per annum is at its lowest in Adelaide ($51,112), increasing to the highest level in Canberra ($76,582), which is in line with the Australian Bureau of Statistics (ABS) 2011 Census. The evidence of preferences for each of the four public transport images shows an overriding preference for modern LRT, consistent with our expectations, given what has been said in the media, and the strong confusion with any form of bus-based system that is typically understood as 'buses in mixed traffic'. Mulley et al (2014) discuss the data is more detail.

Table 11.4: Descriptive overview of total sample and six capital cities

	All cities	Sydney	Melbourne	Canberra	Adelaide	Brisbane	Perth
Sample size	2052	476	450	99	342	343	341
Used PT in last month (% yes)	55.6	65.5	61.1	37.8	49.1	52.9	49.6
Male (%)	39.9	40.9	45.1	50.0	39.5	38.1	31.7
Annual personal income ($)	58,221	63,267	58,400	76,582	51,112	53,678	57,346
Age (years)	43.1	42.8	42.7	44.5	44.5	43.1	42.5
Full time employed (%)	47.1	51.9	50.7	58.2	40.1	42.7	43.9
Part time employed (%)	21.2	22.1	21.1	18.4	21.1	20.6	21.7
Retired (%)	13.3	11.7	10.7	13.3	16.4	15.1	14.1
Student (%)	4.7	4.8	3.6	1.02	4.4	6.4	5.9
Most preferred Image (Figure 11.2):							
BRT standard vehicle (%)	9.6	12.6	10.2	8.2	9.1	10.2	4.7
BRT modern vehicle (%)	15.3	17.4	13.6	10.2	15.8	15.1	15.8
LRT standard vehicle (%)	15.4	14.9	14.9	18.4	15.8	15.2	15.2
LRT modern vehicle (%)	53.1	48.1	52.4	55.1	55.6	50.9	60.7

Source: Mulley *et al* (2014)

Findings: the barriers to BRT implementation

This section identifies clues as to where a campaign to inform the public of the appeal of both BRT and LRT is required. This is especially true of the LRT features where BRT is identified as being able to deliver as good an outcome. If BRT is to be given serious consideration, evidence is needed to create an accurate perception of BRT's level of service compared to LRT.

A standout result of Table 11.4 is the very high percentage of respondents in each city ranking the LRT modern vehicle as their top choice. To explore the extent to which there could be a preference bias for each of the BRT and LRT images, regression models were estimated to investigate the possible link between modal image preferences and the socioeconomic profile of stakeholders in each city as well as their status as a user or nonuser of public transport. The results are summarised in Table 11.5. The dependent variable is the first rank preference with responses from the question shown in Figure 11.4 being transformed with 1 = rank 1 and 0 = ranks 2–5. The overall explanatory fit of each model is very low (adjusted R^2); however, the statistical significance of many of the parameters is informative. In particular, males have a statistically significant positive first rank preference in favour of standard BRT and standard LRT compared to a negative first rank preference for the modern versions of BRT and LRT. Whilst this might seem a perverse outcome, we speculate that the majority of male travellers on public transport are often simply commuters and see their journey in a different light to the higher proportion of women who use public transport as their everyday and all day travel mode. As personal income increases, we see a statistically significant first rank preference for each of the images decreasing except for the modern LRT, which may suggest a general lack of support for BRT, but good support for modern LRT.

Dummy variables, which allow interpretation of these results relative to Perth, tell an intriguing story about relative support for each BRT and LRT proposition. Sydney has the greatest first rank preference for standard BRT out of the six cities, including preservation of a positive first rank preference when modern BRT is considered compared to the other cities. The negative support relative to Perth for LRT is consistent across both standard and modern LRT with the exception of Canberra for standard LRT. The result for respondents from Canberra showing greater support for standard LRT as well as standard BRT, compared to Perth, may well be the result of the continuing

Table 11.5: Relationship between preference for images of BRT and LRT and socioeconomic status (t-values in brackets)

	BRT standard	BRT modern	LRT standard	LRT modern
Constant	0.0085 (1.42)	0.1617 (20.3)	0.0299 (4.06)	0.5859 (53.7)
Used PT in last month (1,0)	0.03283 (12.9)	0.0031 (0.98)	0.0290 (9.55)	−0.0184 (−4.29)
Male (1,0)	0.0091 (3.37)	−0.0090 (−2.78)	0.0208 (6.27)	−0.0226 (−5.01)
Annual personal income ($)	−0.0002 (−5.47)	−0.0003 (−7.17)	−0.0006 (−14.1)	0.0003 (4.34)
Age (years)	0.0013 (11.3)	0.0005 (3.27)	0.0027 (18.6)	−0.0006 (−3.21)
Full time employed (1,0)	−0.0399 (−9.30)	−0.0037 (−0.69)	0.0361 (7.24)	0.0448 (6.09)
Part time employed (1,0)	−0.0192 (−4.26)	−0.0083 (−1.56)	0.0223 (4.44)	0.0770 (10.7)
Retired (1,0)	−0.0042 (−0.71)	0.0325 (4.74)	0.0294 (4.32)	0.0422 (4.79)
Student (1,0)	−0.0528 (−8.81)	−0.0498 (−6.48)	−0.0209 (−2.99)	0.0301 (2.62)
Sydney specific effect (1,0)	0.0764 (21.0)	0.0165 (3.31)	−0.0122 (−2.54)	−0.1213 (−18.3)
Melbourne specific effect (1,0)	0.0516 (14.8)	−0.0236 (−4.88)	−0.0137 (−2.81)	−0.0745 (−11.1)
Canberra specific effect (1,0)	0.0404 (7.13)	−0.0534 (−7.71)	0.0289 (3.50)	−0.0565 (−5.23)
Adelaide specific effect (1,0)	0.0371 (10.3)	−0.0062 (−1.19)	−0.0068 (−1.31)	−0.0416 (−5.81)
Brisbane specific effect (1,0)	0.0514 (13.7)	−0.0104 (−1.98)	−0.0092 (−1.79)	−0.0906 (−12.7)
Perth specific effect (1,0)	–	–	–	–
Adjusted R^2	0.020	0.072	0.017	0.010

contemporary debate there on the merits of LRT compared to bus-based options solutions.

Although differences in first preference ranking for each city are interesting, it cannot be the main basis of establishing why LRT or BRT is preferred by stakeholders. This is better informed by estimating the multinomial logit models on the best–worst data and establishing relative weights that represent the substantive contribution of each statement to the utility of a package of public transport initiatives. scaled multinomial logit (SMNL) choice models are estimated for the entire sample using a methodology explained in detail in Greene and Hensher (2010).[2]

Since the statements in the service and design experiments are written out as comparators of LRT and BRT (being described as LRT compared to BRT or BRT compared to LRT), statements that result in positive parameter estimates work in favour of an initiative associated with BRT or LRT, and statements with negative parameter estimates work against the initiative. After estimation, the parameter estimates are converted to a range that is positive to ease interpretation and these are shown in Figures 11.3–11.5. In these figures, the statements have been shortened to make the figures easier to understand (the full text is in Tables 11.1 to 11.3) and statements with a statistically insignificant parameter estimate are identified by (*).

Design barriers

Figure 11.3 shows the top 15 statements in terms of relative level of utility or preference support. All statements could be plotted, but Figure 11.5 illustrates the point that, of the top 15 statements (which is approximately half of all the statements in total), 11 of the statements relate to the benefits of LRT over BRT. The four statements favouring bus-based and BRT services (shown in italics) relate to the speed with which BRT systems can be constructed and opened for operations, the greater network coverage of bus systems, the improved access as a result of bus services stopping closer to where people get on and off, and the view that there is less disruption on the roads than associated with LRT (presumably many stakeholders are familiar with LRT systems that conflict with car traffic such as much of the Ultimo-Pyrmont light rail in Sydney).

The perceived relative strengths of LRT relate to (i) environmental friendliness and polluting impacts including quietness, (ii) permanence, (iii) level boarding, (iv) personal security, (v) greater long term sustainability and the liveability of the city, (vi) perceived speed advantage, and (vii) supports higher population and employment growth. If we drill down in these top 15 statements, there are clear opportunities where the perceptions favouring LRT offer opportunities to educate the public on the validity of the LRT claims that have become the basis of perceived preferences. For example,

Figure 11.3: Top 15 design barriers (normalised and ranked)

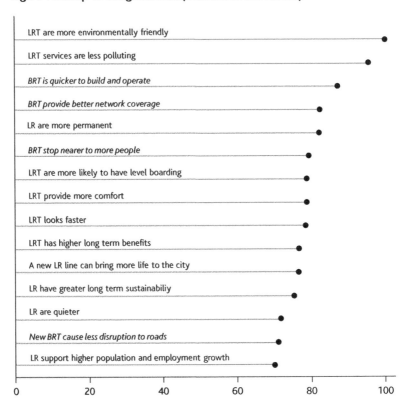

on environmental friendliness and pollution, the full life cycle effects associated with the source of the electricity (for example, coal fired power stations) through to the operations of LRT need to be compared with full life cycle costs of clean diesel or compressed natural gas (CNG) or electric buses, including energy used in maintenance of buses compared to LRT.[3] Level boarding and personal security can be achieved equally well for BRT, and indeed personal security is often enhanced in a bus given the relative closeness to the driver. Against this, there are some features that are not able to be designed out of a LRT or BRT system, such as the economic status of the area through which the service runs, which has been identified as creating poor perceptions of a system (Cain et al 2009).

Service barriers

Moving to service barriers, we see in Figure 11.4 that all of the top 15 statements support the benefits of LRT over BRT. Cleanliness, speed,

Figure 11.4: Service barriers (normalised and ranked)

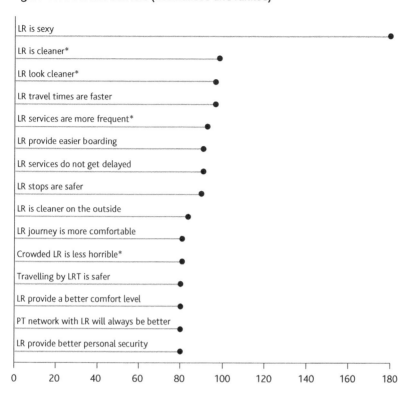

frequency, ease of boarding, delay minimised, safety at stops, comfort, crowding, ride quality and personal security favour LRT over BRT. The only statement favouring bus-based and BRT modes that appears in the top half of ranked statements, at number 16, is the way in which the bus-based mode provides higher network coverage. Indeed, when it is the LRT which provides the higher network coverage, it is LRT which achieves the preference vote (Chinnock et al 2013). What is noteworthy from the survey in Australia is that many of these attributes are associated with the particular design of the system, and can work in favour of either mode if designed appropriately. There is nothing in these LRT biases that cannot be delivered equally well by BRT, as shown in a number of systems.

Some of the results show preferences contrary to the evidence and suggest that the public in general are poorly informed about the real situation. Whilst this is discussed in more detail below, there is a clear link from design barriers to the preferences displayed in voting.

Voting preferences

Successful BRT systems have been largely led by high profile politicians. Informing politicians as to the preferences of voters is therefore an important policy direction in creating some balance in the LRT/BRT debate. This underpins the importance of seeking the wider community's perceptions in relation to what attributes of a public transport system are important to their voting behaviour. The voting preferences put to the respondents of this survey are positioned in a neutral way, as shown by Table 11.3, where the voting statements were not linked to any particular mode

Asking respondents about their voting preferences is putting questions about service and design elements in a different way. Moreover, it is often the case that citizens are asked to vote on 'packages' of outcomes. So as to capture this, some of the attributes were characterised as 'packages' combining elements of design and service so that we can see how the service and design attributes impact specifically on a respondent's preferences without relating it to a specific mode (either BRT or LRT). This means that the results, for the voting choices, are mode free both in terms of utility for use (for example, fare, time, security, crowding, comfort) and the equally relevant considerations of the costs and benefits to society overall (what it costs to construct, to operate, obstructions during construction, value for money to taxpayers, contribution to sustainable and liveable urban environments and so on). Figure 11.5 shows many of the top ranked preferences are those which could easily be associated with BRT – fast overall journey time, frequent services, low fares, value for money to the taxpayer, and a network that is cost effective to operate. What is noteworthy here is that respondents appear to be 'voting' for characteristics of service and design easily provided by BRT, and yet when asked about their preferences in relation to BRT or LRT they choose LRT. Taken together with the results on design and service attributes, these voting preferences may in fact be the best guide to the priorities to ensure stakeholders are better informed about the relative merits of BRT and LRT. This provides a starting point as to the attributes which should form part of an educational or marketing campaign to provide information to correct what we can see as a ('emotional ideological') modal bias in favour of LRT.

Figure 11.5: Voting preferences (normalised and ranked)

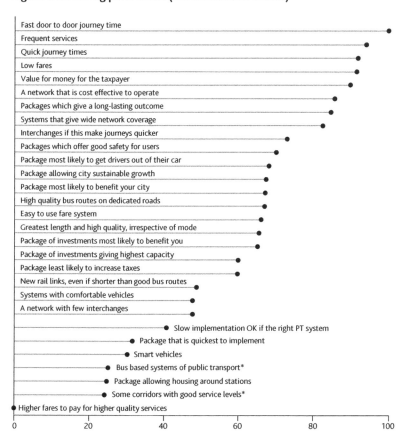

Conclusions

Although in many cases it is generally accepted that emotional ideology and perceptions, based on a lack of adequate information, underlie the strong biases in favour of LRT systems, there has been no systematic investigation of this proposition. This chapter provides some evidence.

For many cities there is a case to be made for considering BRT in the candidate set of PT solutions when cities are seeking ways to reduce car use and to make cities more sustainable and liveable in a cost effective way. In these environments, this chapter offers new information to assist in developing a promotional strategy to break down the barriers that deny BRT a fair hearing when the facts would support it in terms of (perceived or real) benefits to users and to society.

Policy moving forward needs to be informed by the evidence presented here, which shows very real barriers driving the perceptions that result in supporting LRT over BRT. In combination with the understanding about what drives voting behaviour, it would seem key to concentrate on the following attributes in marketing and informing citizens about the potential of BRT as a mode in its own right.

In summary, for attributes related to use, information and marketing needs to concentrate on:

- travel times (including getting to and from the station or stop);
- service frequency (peak and off-peak);
- fares, ease of boarding; and
- ease of transfer.

For societal related attributes, campaigning to provide information on the way in which BRT can contribute to goals of:

- value for money for the taxpayer;
- taxpayer outlays per passenger kilometre (or per in-service kilometre);
- capital cost per passenger;
- environmental friendliness (fuel type, noise);
- the liveability of a city/neighbourhood;
- the time taken to construct and open for operation;
- the life of investment (permanence over time, greater long term sustainability);
- network coverage (including fewer stops, and access to stops/ stations (stop spacing), routes and route kilometres); and
- the way in which BRT can provide a network that is cost effective to operate (operating costs per passenger).

One future direction, in addition to designing a choice experiment related to scenarios under which BRT and LRT might be delivered, includes investigating differences between users and nonusers of PT. This should allow more specific targeting of information in the developed world in cities contemplating infrastructure investment. In addition, future research will extend the preference survey to developing world contexts where a point of interest will be the extent to which differences in attitude between developing and developed world citizens prevail.

Notes

[1] Hensher in various public addresses has suggested that BRT be renamed Dedicated Corridor Rapid Transit (DCRT).

[2] The standard multinomial logit model incorporates both scale and preference weights associated with each attribute; but normalises the scale to unity as a result of the independence of irrelevant alternatives which condition when the error component is independently and identically distributed (IID). The validity of this assumption is testable through allowing the scale parameter to be estimated, as in the SMNL model. If it is found to be statistically significant (that is, not equal to one), as in our model, then we can reject the IID assumption and allow the scale effect to be separated out from the preference parameter. We also investigated including error components in the model, but they did not change the parameter estimates and all error component parameter estimates investigated were statistically insignificant.

[3] Unpublished research by David Hensher for Australia shows that when we account for the full lifecycle of energy involved in bus and rail, the CO_2-e per passenger kilometre in gigajolues in 2013 is approximately 10.6% greater for rail than bus (that is, 0.1052 compared to 0.0941).

References

Canadian Urban Transit Association (2004) 'Bus rapid transit: a Canadian perspective', Issues paper #10, CUTA, Toronto.

Cain, A., Flynn, J., McCourt, M. and Reyes, T. (2009) 'Quantifying the importance of image and perception to bus rapid transit', Report for US Department of Transportation, Federal Transit Administration, Project No. FTA-FL-26-7109.2009.3, www.nbrti.org

Chinnock, D., Routaboul, C. and Swanson, J. (2013) 'Do passengers prefer BRT or LRT?', Association for European Conference, 2013, Frankfurt, Germany.

Cirillo, C., Eboli, L. and Mazzulla, G. (2011) 'On the asymmetric user perception of transit service quality', *International Journal of Sustainable Transportation,* 5(4): 216–232.

Cornwell, P. and Cracknell, J. (1990) 'The case for busway transit', *PTRC 18th Summer Annual Meeting*, 1990, Reading, UK. (This paper is a summary of TRL Research Report 329 and Overseas Road Note 12 of the Transport Research Laboratory, Berkshire, UK.)

Dell'Olio, L., Ibeas, A. and Cecìn, P. (2010a) 'The quality of service desired by public transport users', *Transport Policy*, 18(1): 217–227. doi:10.1016/j.tranpol.2010.08.005.

Dell'Olio, L., Ibeas, A. and Cecìn, P. (2010b) 'Modelling user perception of bus transit quality', *Transport Policy*, 17: 388–397.

Eboli, L. and Mazzulla, G. (2008a) 'An SP experiment for measuring service quality in public transport', *Transportation Planning and Technology*, 31(5): 509–523.

Eboli, L. and Mazzulla, G. (2008b) 'Willingness-to-pay of public transport users for improvement in service quality', *European Transport*, 38: 107–118.

Eboli, L. and Mazzulla, G., (2010) 'How to capture the passengers' point of view on a transit service through rating and choice options', *Transport Reviews*, 30(4): 435–450.

Gatta, V. and Marcucci, E. (2007) 'Quality and public transport service contracts', *European Transport (Trasporti Europei)*, 36(1): 92–106.

Greene, W.H. and Hensher, D.A. (2010) 'Does scale heterogeneity across individuals matter? A comparative assessment of logit models', *Transportation*, 37(3): 413–428.

Hass-Klau, C. and Crampton, G. (2002) *Future of Urban Transport: Learning from Success and Weaknesses*, Brighton: Light Rail, Environment and Transport Planning Consultants.

Hatton MacDonald, D., Morrison, M., Rose, J.M. and Boyle, K. (2010) 'Untangling differences in values from internet and mail stated preference studies', *Fourth World Congress of Environmental and Resource Economists*, Montreal, Canada, 28 June–2 July.

Hensher, D.A. (1991) 'Hierarchical stated response designs and estimation in the context of bus use preferences', *Logistics and Transportation Reviews*, 26(4): 299–323.

Hensher, D.A. (1999) 'Bus-based transitway or light rail? Continuing the saga on choice versus blind commitment', *Roads and Transport Research*, 8(3): 3–21.

Hensher, D.A. and Waters, W.G. II (1994) 'Light rail and bus priority systems: choice or blind commitment?', in B. Starr Macmullen (ed), *Research in Transportation Economics*, Vol. III, Greenwich, CT: JAI Press.

Kain, J.F. (1988) 'Choosing the wrong technology: or how to spend billions and reduce transit use', *Journal of Advanced Transportation*, 21: 197–213.

Lindhjem, H. and Navrud, S. (2011) 'Using internet in stated preference surveys: a review and comparison of survey modes', *International Review of Environmental and Resource Economics*, 5: 309–351.

Mackett, R.L. and Edwards, M. (1996a) 'Guidelines for planning a new urban public transport system', *Proceedings of the Institution of Civil Engineers: Transport*, 117: 193–201.

Mackett, R.L. and Edwards, M. (1996b) 'An expert system to advise on urban public transport technologies', *Computers, Environment and Urban Systems*, 20: 261–273.

Marley, A. and Louviere, J.J. (2005) 'Some probabilistic models of best, worst, and best–worst choices', *Journal of Mathematical Psychology*, 49: 464–480.

Marley, A.A.J. and Pihlens, D. (2012) 'Models of best–worst choice and ranking among multi-attribute options (profiles)', *Journal of Mathematical Psychology*, 56: 24–34.

Mulley, C.M., Hensher, D.A. and Rose, J.M. (2014) 'Do preferences for BRT and LRT vary across geographical jurisdictions? A comparative assessment of six Australian capital cities', BRT Centre Perceptions Study Paper #4, *Case Studies on Transport Policy*, 2: 1–9.

Pickrell, D.H. (1992) 'A desire named streetcar: fantasy and fact in rail transit planning', *Journal of the American Planning Association*, 58: 158–176.

Sislak, K.G. (2000) 'Bus rapid transport as a substitute for light rail: a tale of two cities', 8th Joint Conference on Light Rail Transit sponsored by Transportation Research Board and American Public Transportation Association, 11th–15th November 2000, Dallas, Texas.

Swanson, J., Ampt, L. and Jones, P. (1997) 'Measuring bus passenger preferences', *Traffic Engineering and Control*, 38(6): 330–336.

TWELVE

User preferences and route choice

Sebastián Raveau, Juan Carlos Munoz
and Juan de Dios Ortúzar

Introduction

To efficiently design and operate public transport (PT) systems it is important to understand the decision making process of users as well as their preferences and perceptions. The introduction of BRT corridors in a city, as any major PT system modification, can have significant impacts on the decision making processes of the travellers. Let us consider the case of Santiago, Chile, where there are two main public transport modes: buses and metro. In February 2007, the entire PT system of Santiago was changed from a non-integrated 'door to door' bus system to a 'trunk and feeder' integrated system. Two main behavioural changes occurred: many travellers (who previously had a direct service) were forced to transfer, and many travellers (who previously used only buses) could access the metro system without having to pay a new fare. When designing the new system, and forecasting what would happen, it was essential to understand how travellers would perceive transfers and what they would choose under a single fare.

Decisions can be considered at two levels: (i) choice of a PT mode within the system (bus, metro, combined modes, and so on) and (ii) choice of travel route (selection of PT lines and transfer points along the way). These decisions are interrelated, and their order might depend on a particular PT system's characteristics. Traditional mode and route choice models tend to consider only tangible attributes (that are easily measured/understood, such as fare, travel time, and number of transfers) to analyse and explain the travellers' decisions (Ortúzar and Willumsen 2011). Nevertheless, we know that *intangible* attributes, such as safety and comfort, are also considered by individuals (Koppelman and Pas 1980; Ben-Akiva et al 2002; Raveau et al 2010). These attributes tend to be highly subjective and cannot generally be quantified directly; therefore, we need to study them to understand how they affect individuals' decisions.

The general objective of this chapter is to understand how travellers choose their modes and routes when travelling in a PT system, identify the relevant factors taken into account and quantify the impact that different characteristics of the system (such as station infrastructure, available information and schematic maps) may have on the preferences of the travellers. This allows the PT system to be evaluated and analysed at a tactical level and allows future scenarios to be forecast, which is necessary for selecting the ideal design and operation of the PT system. An incomplete specification of the travellers' preferences could seriously bias the analysis and results when forecasting their decisions in a given context.

Although route choice models have been explored and developed for private transport networks, not much work has been done for PT networks (Hunt 1990; Bovy and Hoogendoorn-Lanser 2005). Our scope is to answer one fundamental question: what are the relevant factors that affect the mode and route choices within a PT system? The answer to that question determines the levels and structure of PT demand. To achieve this objective, our study has two main tasks: data collection and mathematical modelling.

This chapter focuses on analysing the travel decisions of PT users, without considering the decisions of travellers by other modes (most significantly, car users). Although the decision of choosing PT modes over other alternatives is a significant choice to be analysed (as has been done extensively in the literature), we only analyse the subsequent decisions, once travellers have decided to use the PT system. Two study cases from Latin America are considered: the case of Santiago, Chile, where PT users can travel in bus and/or metro (which are fare integrated); and the case of Bogotá, Colombia, where PT users can choose between traditional buses and BRT (which are not fare integrated).

The traditional and most direct approach for analysing travellers' decisions is based on surveys, either from actual choices (revealed preferences) or for choices in hypothetical situations (stated preferences). Focus groups, where PT users discuss the factors considered when deciding how to travel, can also be used to identify relevant variables for choosing mode and route. In these focus groups it is also possible to focus on the wider set of factors related to mode and route choices (such as comfort, safety, and network topology). At the same time, is also necessary to identify how users perceive such attributes, as these tend to be subjective. A more detailed analysis of these factors can enhance significantly the mathematical models used for forecasting and evaluation.

Factors that influence mode and route choice

The most common and important variables used to explain mode and route choice behaviour are travel times and fares (Ortúzar and Willumsen 2011). Users tend to look for the fastest and least expensive way of getting from their origins to their destinations, and these two variables are the main criteria to discard unattractive (that is, slow or expensive) alternatives. Regarding travel times, many components can be considered: time in vehicle, waiting time at the origin station and all subsequent transfer stations, walking time when accessing or egressing the network, and walking time when transferring. These different time components should be considered separately to address their different perception and importance in the traveller's decision making process.

In addition to the time components, which apply to all public transport modes, BRT corridors have some particular characteristics that must be taken into account. BRT corridors tend to be located in the centre of the streets. In terms of access times, this might produce a difference with other systems in which the buses operate on the sides of the streets. If the BRT corridor is located on a highway (such as in Istanbul or Lima), the additional access time to the BRT stations could be even higher.

Regarding the transfer experience, the traditional approach is to consider the total number of transfers for each alternative route; as the walking and waiting time variables capture the actual transfer time, the number of transfers solely captures the displeasure of having to transfer. To further understand the value of transferring, we can differentiate between possible types of transfers (Guo and Wilson 2011; Raveau et al 2011; Navarrete and Ortúzar 2013). They can depend on stations layout: transfers can either be made between ascending levels (that is, going up), even levels (usually walking across the platform) or descending levels (that is, going down). Another important element is station infrastructure: transfers can be assisted (made completely by escalator and/or lift), semi-assisted (made partially by escalator and/or lift and partially on foot), and non-assisted (made completely on foot). Available travel information and additional services (such as toilets, ATMs or shopping stores) can also influence decisions when choosing amongst PT options.

In terms of station design, BRT stations share many characteristics with rail-based modes (such as metro or trams) that differentiate them from traditional bus-based alternatives. BRT stations provide level access from the platform to the vehicles, usually by multiple doors (when the ticketing is done off-board). At the same time, BRT stations (which almost always provide transfers between services) tend to have a single street level layout, which differs from traditional metro transfer stations. This single level layout can result in long stations, increasing the transfer times.

The level of comfort and crowding experienced by PT users during their trips is also an important factor (Tirachini et al 2013). Capturing the comfort perception is not easy, as there is no clear measurement scale for comfort. One alternative is to use proxy variables, such as the mean occupancy along the route or the availability of air conditioning in the vehicles. Additional variables related to vehicle usage, such as the possibility of getting a seat or the possibility of not boarding the first train, can be also considered (Raveau et al 2011, 2014). In terms of the latter, when that happens there is an excess waiting time that can be added to the time components mentioned above. Crowding at the stations is also relevant, particularly in closed systems such as BRT or metro, where the waiting space is limited.

Other qualitative factors mentioned in the literature are the routes' topology and geometry, and measurements of safety and reliability (traditionally in terms of the different time components, but it can be extended to other attributes with uncertainty). Finally, socioeconomic characteristics that can influence individual decisions are: trip purpose, income level (especially when related to fare), gender and age of the traveller, fare type (full fare or discount pass), time of day and journey frequency (for example, daily, weekly, monthly, first time ever). The level of familiarity with the system is relevant, especially on systems with different service structures, such as BRT corridors with different limited stop services.

Traditional route choice and trip assignment models, applied on either private or PT networks, assume rational travellers maximising the utility (or alternatively minimising the cost) associated with their different travel alternatives. In PT networks, where the time the next vehicle arrives at the station is uncertain (especially in frequency-based systems without timetables), travellers can reduce their expected total travel time by following different choice strategies.

The choice strategies that can be applied by travellers differ in complexity and require different levels of information from the system. In the literature, it is usual to assume that all travellers are capable of considering highly complex strategies, which might require developed analytical capacities (Spiess and Florian 1989; Nguyen and Pallottino 1988). Similarly, it is also assumed that all travellers have information regarding the levels of service of all available alternatives, and therefore can make a rational decision. As expected, these assumptions might not be true for a considerable proportion of the travellers. Information availability is therefore a key element when understanding the travellers' decisions. In terms of users' information, BRT outperforms traditional bus-based services; this issue is further discussed in Chapter Thirteen.

Discrete choice modelling

We propose a random utility approach to model PT travellers' behaviour, where each individual q chooses an alternative i from a choice set $A(q)$, to seek the maximum utility level U_{iq}. The modeller, who is only an observer without perfect information regarding the decision making process, is only capable of observing a limited representative systematic utility level V_{iq}; this way, the modeller needs to considerer error terms e_{iq} on each alternative typically defined as (McFadden 1974):

$$U_{iq} = V_{iq} + \varepsilon_{iq} \tag{1}$$

The systematic utility V_{iq} is a function of different attributes X_{ikq} related to the alternatives and individuals (such as travel time, transfers, and socioeconomic characteristics). Typically, it is assumed that V_{iq} is a linear function of the attributes where θ_{ik} are parameters that must be estimated:

$$V_{iq} = \sum_{k} \theta_{ik} \cdot X_{ikq} \tag{2}$$

To characterise the travellers' decisions it is necessary to define binary variables d_{iq} as follows:

$$d_{iq} = \begin{cases} 1 & \text{if} \quad U_{iq} \geq U_{jq} \quad , \quad \forall j \in A\left(q\right) \\ 0 & \text{in other case} \end{cases} \tag{3}$$

If we assume that the error components ε_{iq} are distributed identically and independently (iid) Gumbel, a multinomial logit (MNL) model is obtained, for which it is possible to derive an analytical expression of the choice probabilities P_{iq}, according to equation (4):

$$P_{iq} = \frac{\exp\left(\lambda \cdot V_{iq}\right)}{\displaystyle\sum_{j \in A(q)} \exp\left(\lambda \cdot V_{jq}\right)} \tag{4}$$

where λ is a scale factor (inversely related to the unknown variance of the Gumbel errors) which usually needs to be normalised to one and the parameters θ_{ik} can be estimated using maximum likelihood based on the attributes X_{ikq} and choices d_{iq} (Train 2009).

The assumption of independence among alternatives of the MNL model can be unrealistic, as in PT networks the different lines can have overlapping links or the routes can have overlapping legs. This topological overlapping generates spatial correlation among the alternatives. To address this issue, different models (mainly extensions of the MNL model) have been proposed in the literature (Prato 2009).

When studying individual preferences, it is of interest to analyse the marginal rates of substitution between the various attributes in the utility function. The marginal rates of substitution correspond to the ratio between the marginal utilities of each attribute. Although marginal rates of substitution can be obtained for any pair of attributes, in practice the most important one is the value of travel time savings (marginal rate of substitution between travel time and monetary cost). For a MNL model with a linear representative utility, the marginal rate of substitution between attributes X_{ik1q} and X_{ik2q} is given by:

$$ MRS_{k1,k2} = \frac{\partial V_{iq}/\partial X_{ik1q}}{\partial V_{iq}/\partial X_{ik2q}} = \frac{\theta_{ik1}}{\theta_{ik2}} \tag{5} $$

While the marginal rates of substitution are an indicator of trade-offs between attributes, the model elasticities are an indicator of trade-offs between an attribute and the probability of choosing (demand) a given alternative (they are defined as the ratio of the percentage change in demand to the percentage change in an attribute). Direct elasticities (effect on the demand for an alternative when one of its attributes changes) and cross-elasticities (effect on the demand for an alternative when an attribute from another alternative changes) for a MNL model, are given by equations (6) and (7) respectively.

$$ E\left(P_{iq}, X_{ikq}\right) = \frac{\partial P_{iq}}{\partial X_{ikq}} \cdot \frac{X_{ikq}}{P_{iq}} = \theta_{ik} \cdot X_{ikq} \cdot \left(1 - P_{iq}\right) \tag{6} $$

$$ E\left(P_{iq}, X_{jkq}\right) = \frac{\partial P_{iq}}{\partial X_{jkq}} \cdot \frac{X_{jkq}}{P_{iq}} = -\theta_{jk} \cdot X_{jkq} \cdot P_{jq} \tag{7} $$

Case study 1: Santiago, Chile

To identify and analyse the route choice strategies of PT travellers in Santiago, we conducted a travel survey on Plaza de Maipú, Santiago's most visited PT hub (located in the southwest of the city) in June 2011. The data gathered (demand information) was complemented with data regarding levels of service (supply information) provided by the PT authorities. The destinations considered in the survey included the central and eastern parts of the city, where most of the travellers from Plaza de Maipú are headed.

The main objective of the survey was to gather a large amount of information regarding mode and route choices within Santiago's PT system, Transantiago. It is important to consider that Transantiago is an integrated system where both decisions (mode and route) can be made simultaneously; this way, multimodal routes arise. Additionally, the survey included information regarding the socioeconomic characteristics of the travellers.

The selected origin, Plaza de Maipú, is an interesting node of Santiago's PT network, as 1% of all PT trips made in the morning (approximately 30,000 trips between 7:00am and 12:00pm) start, transfer or end at this point. Plaza de Maipú is also an attractive study node in terms of available services, as it provides access to the Santiago metro, two feeder (local) lines, eight trunk lines and two express lines. The survey gathered information from 1,892 individuals of diverse socioeconomic characteristics about all modal choices within the PT network of Santiago, from 7:00am to 12:00pm.

Travel strategies

When conducting the survey, additional emphasis was placed on obtaining information regarding the route choice strategies of the respondents. Two different strategies were observed: travellers either waited for a particular line, or boarded the first arriving line among a set of 'attractive or common lines'. The set of common lines is comprised by different services that can be taken for a particular trip leg (although not necessarily all existing services, as some of them might be considerably slower, which the traveller will not consider). As expected, the PT travellers reported fairly different strategies. Although 51% of individuals had only one travel alternative on each travel leg (mainly, for those using metro, where no lines overlap), the remaining 49% had the possibility of choosing a strategy. Among these, 67% of travellers waited for a specific line (even though they could board other lines to make the trip leg), and the remaining 33% boarded the first common line arriving at the bus stop. It is clear that assuming that all individuals follow the same strategy (as is usually done in the literature) could lead to biased predictions in this case.

Given the (unexpectedly) low proportion of PT travellers considering common lines, we centred our analysis on understanding the differences between the 67% of individuals that did not consider common lines and the 33% of individuals that did. Note that the different travel alternatives between the origin–destination pairs in the survey tend to share the infrastructure and follow the same stopping outline, so the in-vehicle times of the different alternatives tend to be similar. This means all the available lines would be attractive and would belong to the set of common lines. Therefore, it is difficult to understand why 67% of the individuals did not consider common lines, as they are overlooking a way of reducing their waiting times (and therefore their total travel times).

Among the 67% of individuals that did not consider common lines were the travellers that were not familiar with the PT system or with the particular trip they were making (either made the trip occasionally, or had not made the trip before) and therefore did not know other PT lines apart from the chosen one. In general, the remaining 33% tended to make the trip on a weekly basis. The level of knowledge of the PT system and its alternatives is very relevant.

Age is also a relevant factor: the 67% that did not consider common lines tended to be older than the reminding 33%. Among the latter we found people younger than 30 years of age, possibly because they are more familiar with Santiago's current PT system (which was completely redesigned in 2007, see Muñoz et al 2009), while those older than 30 were more likely to try and replicate the paths they followed before the system was redesigned, instead of making proper use of the current PT lines.

The trip purpose is also a relevant factor. Among the 33% of the individuals considering common lines we tended to find those travelling to work or study. Aside from familiarity with the alternatives (as work and study trips are usually made daily), these individuals have temporal restrictions (they have to be at the destination at a specific time) and therefore probably analysed and optimised their travel choices; the reduction of waiting times associated with considering common lines is valuable for them. Of the remaining 67%, the presence of leisure travellers without temporal restrictions is higher; for them, the waiting time reductions are usually less valuable.

Finally, income appears to be a key stratification variable in this case. The 33% that considered common lines had a higher average income than the rest. Although it is possible to identify individuals of different income levels in both groups, those with a monthly income below US$600 tend to be in the 67% that did not consider common lines; those with a monthly income between US$ 600 and US$1,200 distribute themselves homogeneously in both groups, and those with a monthly income above US$1,200 tend to be in the 33% that considered common lines. This can be seen as an indirect effect of the level of education of individuals: as income increases, higher education levels are achieved, and therefore people´s analytical capacity (that is, identifying a set of common lines to reduce total travel time) also increases. Access to additional information through smartphones and other technologies is also higher in higher income groups. This is an important issue in developing countries with BRT corridors, where among the PT users tend to be the lower income and less educated population (which are captive PT users).

Modelling travellers' behaviour

Based on the previous analysis and on the relation between individuals' socioeconomic characteristics and route choice strategies followed, we propose treating route choice strategies as an additional socioeconomic characteristic of the individuals (which can be modelled based on their characteristics) to model the decisions of PT travellers in Santiago. Once the strategy is modelled, we can analyse and study the factors that travellers take into account when choosing travel routes within the PT system.

Modelling travellers' strategies

To model the route choice strategy (reduced in this case to considering common lines or not) we formulated a binary MNL model, using as explanatory variables the socioeconomic characteristics of the individuals. Table 12.1 presents the estimated results for modelling the probability of considering common lines. All the socioeconomic characteristics considered are statistically significant. The signs of the parameters are consistent with the previous analysis. The probability of considering common lines is greater for those PT travellers that: (i) make the particular trip more frequently, (ii) have a higher income level, and (iii) are younger.

Table 12.1: Results of the probability of considering common lines for Santiago

Variable	Parameter	t-test
At least weekly travel	1.322	4.98
At least monthly travel	0.766	3.71
Occasional/first travel	0.000	Base category
High income (over US$1,200)	0.940	3.22
Medium income (US$1,200 to US$600)	0.327	3.45
Low income (less than US$600)	0.000	Base category
Young (under 30 years old)	0.399	2.90
Adult (over 30 years old)	0.000	Base category
Constant	−2.051	−5.76

The trip purpose is not considered in the model as it is highly correlated with the frequency of the trip. With the estimated parameters it is possible to compute the probabilities of considering common lines for each socioeconomic category. These probabilities are shown in Table 12.2. There is a wide range of probability values, varying from 11% to 65% depending on the socioeconomic characteristics of the individuals.

Table 12.2: Percentages of considering common lines in Santiago

Socioeconomic category		Young (%)	Adult (%)
At least weekly travel	High income	65	55
At least weekly travel	Medium income	50	40
At least weekly travel	Low income	42	33
At least monthly travel	High income	51	41
At least monthly travel	Medium income	36	28
At least monthly travel	Low income	29	22
Occasional/first travel	High income	33	25
Occasional/first travel	Medium income	21	15
Occasional/first travel	Low income	16	11

Modelling travellers' route choice

With the route choice data gathered in the survey, we were able to estimate mode and route choice models within the PT system. The in-vehicle times and waiting times for each alternative (both considering and not considering common lines) come from global positioning system (GPS) data provided by the Santiago PT authorities. Additionally, the fare, walking time (when transferring) and number of transfers are also explanatory variables. Given the fare scheme in Santiago's PT network, the fare of each mode/route alternative depends exclusively on the usage of the metro in any of the trip legs (using the metro adds an additional cost of US$0.16 in the peak period and US$0.04 at off-peak times). The waiting time considers the initial wait at Plaza de Maipú and all subsequent waits at transfer stations.

The modelling approach was sequential: each individual in our database had a probability of considering common lines and then a conditional probability of choosing a given alternative depending on the particular strategy followed. We consider a linear systematic utility V_{iq} for each alternative i, composed of the attributes mentioned above. The parameters of the model distinguish two different classes of individuals: those who consider common lines, and those who do not. Although some other factors may influence the decisions of PT travellers (Raveau et al 2011), the specification considered is a robust approximation of the general behaviour of Santiago's PT users.

Table 12.3 presents the result of the estimation of a MNL model for mode/route choice, considering the five explanatory variables mentioned above. All variables have the expected sign (negative, as they represent a disutility) and are statistically significant at the 95% confidence level. Differences arise between the parameters for individuals that consider common lines and the rest. These differences support the fact that there are different behavioural patterns among PT travellers, and that it is necessary to distinguish them.

Based on the estimated parameters, it is possible to calculate monetary valuations and marginal rates of substitution for the time and transfers variables (Table 12.4).

It can be seen that individuals considering common lines show a higher monetary valuation than individuals that do not consider common lines (this is possibly because they tend to have a higher income, and therefore a higher value of time). In particular, for

Table 12.3: Results of the mode/route choice model for Santiago

Variable	Individuals that consider common lines		Individuals that do not consider common lines	
	Parameter	t-test	Parameter	t-test
Fare (US$)	−21.04	−2.33	−25.05	−2.45
In-vehicle time (min)	−0.623	−2.17	−0.479	−2.39
Waiting time (min)	−1.598	−4.35	−1.217	−3.77
Walking time (min)	−1.849	−2.11	−1.349	−2.43
Number of transfers	−2.585	−2.45	−1.569	−1.98

* At the time of the survey 1 US$ ≈ 470 CLP$.

Table 12.4: Subjective monetary valuations and marginal rates of substitution for Santiago

	Individuals that consider common lines	Individuals that do not consider common lines
Variable	Subjective monetary valuations (US$)	
In-vehicle time	1.78 per hour	1.15 per hour
Waiting time	4.56 per hour	2.92 per hour
Walking time	5.28 per hour	3.24 per hour
Transfers	0.12 per transfer	0.06 per transfer
Variable	Marginal rates of substitution regarding in-vehicle time	
1 min of waiting time	2.56 min of in-vehicle time	2.54 min of in-vehicle time
1 min of walking time	2.97 min of in-vehicle time	2.82 min of in-vehicle time
1 transfer	4.15 min of in-vehicle time	3.28 min of in-vehicle time

individuals that consider common lines, transfers appear to be twice as valuable.

Regarding the temporal marginal rates of substitution, they do not vary much between both types of individual. This way, although the monetary valuations are significantly different, the ratio between them remains relatively constant. However, there are differences between the marginal rates of substitution of the transfers regarding in-vehicle time between both types of individuals.

Case study 2: Bogotá, Colombia

To analyse the decisions in Bogotá's public transport system, we designed and conducted a revealed preferences survey in the TransMilenio BRT system. In this case, special emphasis is placed on understanding the public transport users' perceptions towards crowdedness, one of the main problems of the system. The alternatives are the potential routes to be taken between the travellers' origin and destination, which differ mainly in terms of in-vehicle travel time and waiting time (due to the different all-stop and express services of the system). This database consists of 1,113 choices from a survey conducted in April 2014. Different origin–destination patterns were considered (covering both the suburbs and centre of the city), between 7:00am and 12:00pm, in order to capture different crowdedness levels in the network.

The utility function is composed of four main attributes: in-vehicle time, waiting time, walking time and number of transfers. The crowding in the vehicles (which was reported by the respondents, based on schematic representations of different crowdedness levels) is directly related to the in-vehicle travel time, and measured in passengers per square metre (pax/m²). This way, the travellers' perception of travel time (that is, their subjective value) depends on how crowded the vehicle is. The utility function does not include the cost of the alternative (and therefore no monetary valuations can be obtained), as the data correspond to individuals making route choices inside the BRT network without having to pay extra for changing between the lines.

Table 12.5 presents the results of the route choice model estimation, where all explanatory variables are significant (with the exception of walking time, which is kept in the model as its sign and magnitude are as expected). The marginal disutility of in-vehicle travel time increases as the crowdedness levels increase.

To further analyse the individuals' perceptions, Table 12.6 presents the marginal rates of substitution between variables. As the perception

Table 12.5: Results of the route choice model for Bogotá

Variable	Parameter	t-test
In-vehicle time (min) at 1 pax/m²	−0.0180	−3.12
In-vehicle time (min) at 2 pax/m²	−0.0410	−4.82
In-vehicle time (min) at 3 pax/m²	−0.0640	−5.69
In-vehicle time (min) at 4 pax/m²	−0.0871	−6.23
In-vehicle time (min) at 5 pax/m²	−0.1101	−6.58
In-vehicle time (min) at 6 pax/m²	−0.1331	−6.84
Waiting time (min)	−0.1112	−6.20
Walking time (min)	−0.1030	−1.32
Number of transfers	−0.1641	−6.25

Table 12.6: Marginal rates of substitution for Bogotá

	Marginal rates of substitution regarding in-vehicle time
Variable	**Crowdedness at 1 pax/m²**
1 min of waiting time	6.18 min of in-vehicle time
1 min of walking time	5.72 min of in-vehicle time
1 transfer	9.12 min of in-vehicle time
Variable	**Crowdedness at 3 pax/m²**
1 min of waiting time	1.74 min of in-vehicle time
1 min of walking time	1.61 min of in-vehicle time
1 transfer	2.56 min of in-vehicle time
Variable	**Crowdedness at 6 pax/m²**
1 min of waiting time	0.84 min of in-vehicle time
1 min of walking time	0.77 min of in-vehicle time
1 transfer	1.23 min of in-vehicle time

of in-vehicle time depends on the level of crowdedness, three cases are presented: good comfort level (1 pax/m²), medium comfort level (3 pax/m²) and poor comfort level (6 pax/m²). As the crowdedness level increases, the disutility of travelling in such conditions also increases; this way, the relative importance of the remaining variables depends on the crowdedness of the routes taken.

Conclusions

Understanding public transport users' preferences and decision making processes is essential in transportation planning to correctly predict travel decisions and the resulting flows on public transport networks. The purpose of this study is to understand public transport travellers' behaviour, identify the relevant factors that are considered, quantify the impact that different characteristics of the system have on their decisions, and enhance the mathematical models used for transportation planning.

The Santiago study case provides an empirical analysis of the various route choice strategies that travellers might follow: either board the first line (within a previously selected set of lines) that arrives at the stop, or wait for a specific line. Although the traditional modelling approach assumes that all travellers behave in the same way, the empirical data for Santiago shows that different travellers follow different strategies. Our analysis shows a strong relationship between the travellers' socioeconomic characteristics and the route choice strategies they tend to follow. Based on these results, the route choice strategy is treated as an endogenous socioeconomic characteristic of the travellers, which depends of other socioeconomic characteristics (in particular, the frequency of the trip, age and income). The resulting mode/route choice models are capable of reproducing the travel decisions and resulting flow patterns in a better way.

Explicitly distinguishing between different types of public transport travellers (based on whether they consider a set of attractive lines or not), allows significant differences in their preferences and decision-making processes to be identified. In particular, there are differences in the subjective monetary valuations and marginal rates of substitution derived for the different strategy-followers. Ignoring the behavioural differences in terms of route choice strategies can also lead to bias results. At the same time, the importance of providing information is made clear; travellers need the necessary tools for making appropriate decisions, in order to experience the best possible level of service (in accordance with their preferences and travel needs).

The Bogotá study case provides insights regarding the importance of travel conditions (particularly vehicle crowding) in the travellers' decisions. Traditionally, the value of time is considered to be a unique value, independent of other attributes of the travel options. Nevertheless, it has been shown that the value of time can depend on the comfort experienced; and therefore this effect (and others) should be considered. This can have significant impact on the valuation of transport projects and plans.

References

Ben-Akiva, M.E., Walker, J.L., Bernardino, A.T., Gopinath, D.A., Morikawa, T. and Polydoropoulou, A. (2002) 'Integration of choice and latent variable models', in H.S. Mahmassani (ed), *In Perpetual Motion: Travel Behaviour Research Opportunities and Challenges*, Amsterdam: Pergamon, 431–470.

Bovy, P.H.L. and Hoogendoorn-Lanser, S. (2005) 'Modelling route choice behaviour in multi-modal transport networks', *Transportation*, 32(4): 341–368.

Guo, Z. and Wilson, N.H.M. (2011) 'Assessing the cost of transfer inconvenience in public transport systems: a case study of the London Underground', *Transportation Research Part A*, 45(2): 91–104.

Hunt, J.D. (1990) 'A logit model of public transport route choice', *ITE Journal*, 60(12): 26–30.

Koppelman, F.S. and Pas, E.I. (1980) 'Travel-choice behaviour: models of perceptions, feelings, preference, and choice', *Transportation Research Record*, 765: 26–33.

McFadden, D. (1974) 'Conditional logit analysis of qualitative choice behavior', in P. Zarembka (ed), *Frontiers of Econometrics*, New York: Academic Press, 105–142.

Muñoz, J.C., Ortúzar, J. de D. and Gschwender, A. (2009) 'Transantiago: the fall and rise of a radical public transport intervention', in W. Saleh and G. Sammer (eds), *Travel Demand Management and Road User Pricing: Success, Failure and Feasibility*, Farnham: Ashgate, 151–172.

Navarrete, F. and Ortúzar, J. de D. (2013) 'Subjective valuation of the transit transfer experience: the case of Santiago de Chile', *Transport Policy*, 25(1): 138–147.

Nguyen, S. and Pallottino, S. (1988) 'Equilibrium traffic assignment for large scale transit networks', *European Journal of Operational Research*, 37(2): 176–186.

Ortúzar, J. de D. and Willumsen, L.G. (2011) *Modelling Transport*, Chichester: John Wiley and Sons.

Prato, C.G. (2009) 'Route choice modelling: past, present and future research directions', *Journal of Choice Modelling*, 2(1): 65–100.

Raveau, S., Alvarez-Daziano, R., Yáñez, M.F., Bolduc, D. and Ortúzar, J. de D. (2010) 'Sequential and simultaneous estimation of hybrid discrete choice models: some new findings', *Transportation Research Record: Journal of the Transportation Research Record*, 2156: 131–139.

Raveau, S., Muñoz, J.C. and de Grange, L. (2011) 'A topological route choice model for metro', *Transportation Research Part A*, 45(2): 138–147.

Raveau, S., Guo, Z., Muñoz, J.C. and Wilson, N.H.M. (2014) 'A behavioural comparison of route choice on metro networks: time, transfers, crowding, topology and socio-demographics', *Transportation Research Part A*, 66(1): 185–195.

Spiess, H. and Florian, M. (1989) 'Optimal strategies: a new assignment model for transit networks', *Transportation Research Part B*, 23(2): 83–102.

Tirachini, A., Hensher, D.A. and Rose, J.M. (2013) 'Crowding in public transport systems: effects on users, operation and implications for the estimation of demand', *Transportation Research Part A*, 53(1): 36–52.

Train, K.E. (2009) *Discrete Choice Methods with Simulation* (2nd edn), Cambridge: Cambridge University Press.

THIRTEEN

Passenger information systems

Carola Zurob, José Manuel Allard, Rosário Macário,
Bernardo Garcia and Camila Garcia

Introduction

Passenger information systems play a key role in the experience of users of public transport. The main role of passenger information systems is to inform users about travel options and modes. As noted in Chapter Twelve, there are many different aspects involved in a user's decision to use specific or combined transport modes. Travel time, fare and number of transfers are some of the main related issues taken into account by users. However, users also take into account factors that relate to more personal perceptions, such as the safety of the route, perceived waiting times, vertical movements (going up or down staircases and lifts), availability of services at bus stops and interchange points, among others. Through the planning and decision process, users are ultimately reducing the uncertainty of the trip that will be undertaken. The anxiety and insecurity caused by an unknown journey can have serious impacts on users (Mijksenaar 1998). Passenger information systems can serve as an important tool to reduce these feelings of anxiety.

The implementation of Bus Rapid Transit (BRT) systems opens great possibilities for passenger information in public transport. Because BRT provides increased certainty about routes and waiting times compared to regular buses, this information can complement information systems and constitute an important improvement in the user's experience of public transport. The incorporation of time schedules and/or estimated wait times, as well as more detailed information about the route and bus stops (for example, connections with other transport services, commerce or the availability of car or bike parking) can help users to understand what to expect from the service and therefore allow for a trip to be planned with more certainty, reducing the discomfort or anxiety associated with travelling.

In addition, if the implementation of a BRT project involves a major reorganisation of the public transport network in a city, passenger information is critical. For example, in a switch from a direct service model (where buses serve point to point with limited need for transfers) to a trunk feeder model (where local buses feed into main BRT corridors), users have to get used to a new logic of navigating the city that requires more passenger decisions. This necessitates a new approach to passenger information, sometimes in cases where no formal system previously existed, and very clear marketing to explain to users the benefits of the new system.

This chapter outlines some of the needs for a passenger information system and how to manage it. Then we present lessons learned from the implementation of the first centralised and universal passenger information system for Santiago, Chile.

A user centred approach to public transport information

A key issue for the success of public transportation systems is the provision of user information about the services offered; ill-informed travellers may not be able to identify services which best suit their needs, leading to a poor perception and low use of public transport (Balcombe 2004).

Informing the public about service availability is considered a basic action needed for the proper functioning of a system and to maintain ridership. User information also reduces uncertainty and gives transit operators a means to inform passengers in the event of irregularities in the service.

Such information can be provided in many different forms, ranging from printed media, such as timetables and maps, to verbal media like instructions or messages delivered by transit staff, to electronic media such as real-time display panels and online trip planners (Cain 2007). It is important to provide a coherent and consistent system according to the information needs of the user throughout the trip.

Information needs and media preferences vary tremendously among users, depending on the type of trip being undertaken and the personal characteristics and experience of each traveller. Studies on the information needs of public transport users generally consider travel as a dynamic process where the user has to carry out different tasks in order to reach their destination successfully (Infopolis 2 1999). This process consists of a sequence of stages that can be summarised as follows.

Pre-trip (prior to the beginning of the trip)

Pre-trip essentially refers to the travel planning context and is usually carried out before the trip is undertaken. Traditionally, this planning stage referred mainly to the home or the workplace, but the ubiquity of mobile phones, laptops and tablets has expanded this step to other places and facilitated en route planning as well. When the user prepares his/her future travel, the planning stage defines the way in which the tasks must be performed to reach the end of the journey. Every user has a different set of criteria for choosing the most convenient route, by virtue of his/her personal context and reason for travelling, or due to the situations they are trying to avoid (such as interchange between different modes). Journey planners, service guides and maps are among common materials used at this stage. However, especially among users of informal systems, word of mouth – asking friends, bus drivers or strangers at a bus stop how to get to a certain location – is common.

The pre-trip stage is extremely important for users travelling for the first time to a certain destination, but is almost nonexistent among experienced users. In this last case, the pre-trip stage could be solely oriented to gather information about the current state of roads or services in order to reach the destination in the expected time.

On-trip (during the trip)

The on-trip stage starts at the first point of the journey (the bus stop) and the main task for the traveller at this point is to track the different situations or places that are involved in the trip. The tracking task involves verifying that their understanding of the information and therefore their actions are correct, that the planned events are working out as expected and that their behaviour is appropriate to the information that is being collected. The on-trip stage is therefore concerned with the execution of accurate movements at the correct time. Moreover, the disruption/adjustment process requires that the user anticipates future problems from current conditions. At this stage, confirmation and real-time information are crucial to allow passengers to adjust to current conditions.

End-trip (from the last vehicle to the final destination)

The end-trip considers the results of the journey. The user acquires new experience and applies this knowledge to future trips. Thus, the information provided at this stage creates a feedback loop that influences future planning and tracking tasks.

In the case of the implementation of BRT, delivery of information is an important part of a successful operation. Compared to regular bus systems, BRT systems increase speed and certainty of journeys, but can also increase interchange points or transfers. Users commonly want to avoid interchange points since they are an important source of uncertainty. For this reason, BRT passenger information should deliver specific information about these places, service availability, walking distances between stops, and so on, in order to reduce the uncertainty caused by these points.

BRT's characteristics can also be considered advantageous in terms of user information when compared with regular bus systems. For instance, closed BRT systems offer the advantage of increased certainty of arrival/departure times and route options, which makes possible the use of more precise graphic display information such as route diagrams, timetables and dynamic information. Also BRT signage usually is implemented in protected stations, which reduces its exposure to vandalism when compared with street signage.

Management of passenger information systems

A passenger information system has the purpose of providing the user of public transport with information about the nature and state of the service offered. The kind of information available and the way it is delivered are important factors in managing a passenger information system. Generally, a distinction can be drawn between static information and dynamic or real-time information. The former is previously planned, changes slowly, and refers to routes, schedules, fares, and so on. The latter is dynamic information that changes continuously, such as delays, arrival/departure times, and information about incidents that affect service operations.

In BRT systems, the use of intelligent transportation systems (ITS) technologies makes possible the provision of real-time information, which represents leverage for the system's image and ultimately for its passengers. Such technologies allow BRT systems to emulate rail services and consequently be able to implement similar automated passenger information features. By monitoring bus operations through automatic vehicle location, a rigorous and consistent collection and updating of information is achieved. This improves both quality and quantity of information available to the passengers, decreasing uncertainty and increasing flexibility and travel choices, and consequently their satisfaction.

Additionally, passenger information systems can also be a source of revenue through advertisements. A common practice in public transportation is the sale of space and time within the system for commercial messages. Stations may offer specific spaces for printed and electronic advertising, while vehicles can carry advertisements on their sides and/or inside. Shelters can be provided by interested companies in exchange for advertising. Printed materials may have a part reserved to include advertisements, as in the case of pocket maps or printed timetables.

However, although advertisements may secure income for the system, this must be explored carefully in order to avoid conflicts with the delivery of the information. An excess of signage or commercial messages can distract passengers and prevent them from getting crucial information. For instance, an advertisement on the side of a bus may reduce the visibility for those inside or even jeopardise the image of the system that is easily sold through an identifiable vehicle (ITDP 2007). Commercial advertisements can work together with passenger information, but in a discreet and non-prominent fashion.

Advertisements can also be explored as a marketing strategy to publicise the BRT system itself. The image of the system presented through its name, logo and slogan in vehicles, stations and printed materials exposes riders and non-riders to the system's identity so that it can be easily recalled and identifiable. Campaigns should focus on communicating the benefits BRT introduces to the public transport system, appealing to potential new users. This is the most important marketing action in BRT systems, since a well-developed brand and identity is not actually able to reach and convince non-passengers without an appropriate publicity campaign.

The image of the system

In addition to providing users with basic information, public transportation systems should communicate the benefits to the community resulting from its operation. Publicising those benefits helps to enhance the image of the system and may increase the willingness of nonusers to consider it as a transportation option (Giuliano and Hayden 2005). This can be done through a variety of means, such as educational programmes, advertising, branding, development of a system identity and other marketing or information strategies.

For BRT systems specifically, the communication of their benefits has a strategic value. In order to attract new users and also maintain regular ones, they need to present an image/identity to differentiate the service from regular bus systems. Frequently, potential users have a negative image of buses regarding issues such as noise, pollution, reliability, convenience, accessibility and safety. Therefore, the development of this image/identity is an opportunity to differentiate BRT from users' negative perceptions of buses and increase ridership by attracting new users to the system.

An identity programme for a BRT system should seek to establish an image that distinguishes it from regular bus services and allows people to remember the unique qualities (Hess and Bitterman 2008). It may include not only visual design elements such as signs, but also feature information related to service quality, like comfort and reliability (Díaz and Hinebaugh 2009). Additional to graphic elements, features from BRT systems that have a direct impact on its quality of service must be accounted for in the identity programme. Intrinsic characteristics of the systems, such as signal priority and exclusive running ways, as well as advanced technology like automated guidance and fare collection systems, are features that improve the performance of the BRT system, impacting on its reliability, comfort and convenience. Moreover, well-trained customer contact personnel and employee appearance contribute to a positive assessment of the quality of service, having a direct influence on the image of the system (Díaz and Hinebaugh 2009).

An identity programme can also be explored through marketing strategies that go beyond the use of graphic elements and include a variety of campaigns and education plans with the objective to promote the system (ITDP 2007). In this way, BRT communication campaigns must be developed in order to promote a good image of the system and persuade different passenger segments, including nonusers, to use it. It explores not only the use of advertising material through different media channels such as radio, television and social networks, but also events like car-free days, as well as social marketing to promote and induce changes in travel behaviour. Small presentations of the system at schools or other community organisations are also ways in which the system can be promoted.

Another form of communication of BRT benefits is the implementation of education plans before the system is implemented. Actions such as the construction of prototype stations and display of vehicles allow the public to see how the services will function and may contribute to a successful launch of the system. Long-term goals of targeting different market segments such as women, business professionals, commuters, students and disabled persons, and to attract specific groups like car drivers, are also important parts of a complete marketing strategy.

Development and maintenance of BRT identity programmes may be very challenging. Usually, the agencies responsible for planning and operation of BRT systems are not familiar with the process behind the development and maintenance of identity programmes. It also implies collaboration among urban and transportation planners, designers, marketers and stakeholders (users, nonusers and providers) which is a highly complex task, but can be even more difficult if adequate channels of communication are not established. Differences in work procedures of design and transportation professionals generate obstacles that may hamper the creation and maintenance of identity programmes (Hess and Bitterman 2008).

The identity programme should coordinate with passenger information; however, it is important to differentiate the approaches. While a marketing strategy may focus on communicating the benefits of the system and its advantages compared to other transportation modes, passenger information is concerned specifically with delivering the information that users require to perform the tasks mentioned earlier associated with the different stages of the trip.

General considerations in the design of an information system, based on the case of Transantiago

Transantiago, a new integrated public transport system for Santiago, was implemented in February 2007 and projected to replace overnight the previous Micros amarillas (yellow buses) system. The new system was considered the most ambitious transport reform ever implemented by a developing country (Hidalgo cited in *The Economist*, 2007).

Transantiago was developed combining local bus lines (feeder routes), main bus lines (trunk routes) and the metro network (subway). It has an integrated fare system, which allows passengers to make bus to bus or bus to metro transfers for the price of a single ride, using a prepaid contactless smart card.

Transantiago's original objectives were to enhance the quality of public transport and encourage its use, eliminate on-street competition of buses and modernise the existing bus fleet, palliate the city's elevated air and sound pollution levels by reducing the number of buses and their emissions, and be socially, environmentally and financially sustainable (Allard 2008; or see Chapter Three).

For decades, bus transportation in Santiago had been the worst evaluated of public services. Atomisation of the system, with over 3,000 micro-businesses with an average of two buses each in 2000 (Minteguiaga 2006) and scarce regulation was considered an endemic problem of the old Micros network. The absence of a formal information system beyond a designated typeface and a standard yellow colour for buses, made it almost impossible for users to access information about the available services. Bus drivers and locals of the system were the main sources of information before Transantiago was launched. Buses had displays on their windows with printed information about the main routes and city highlights served. But the arbitrariness of the information displayed and the absence of information available in other formats and on platforms made it almost impossible for new users to access the system. Due to the unintelligibility of the bus system, tourists and visitors to the city were pretty much relegated to the subway as far as public transport was concerned.

With Transantiago, for the first time in the history of Santiago's public transport a passenger information system was developed. This development faced important challenges, such as a limited graphic information culture among users and the lack of experience of the authorities. The information on the subway system and reduced impact initiatives like Metrobus (an information system based on coloured pairs that identified the origin and destination points of bus routes) were part of the limited experience of Santiago's citizens with printed transport information.

In 2009, an assessment of Transantiago's passenger information was performed in order to observe the use of the system and the strategies that citizens employed to access information about routes and services (Informe de Avance 1, Estudio de Actualización del Manual de Normas Gráficas, enero 2010). As a result of this experience, there are several lessons that could be extrapolated to the development of an information system for BRT or other new integrated systems.

Multiple and diverse users (internal and external/stakeholders)

Passenger information systems usually involve a variety of actors or stakeholders in the process of delivering information: transport authorities, operators, municipalities, ministries, designers, producers and users all have different requirements and expectations for the information system. In integrated public transport systems, there are multiple content generators and entities in charge of producing, implementing and managing the system. Each of these actors has a different set of requirements for carrying out the assigned job. Even though passenger information is generally focused on passenger needs, it is necessary to identify all of these actors or intermediate 'users' and their specific processes and needs in order to design an information system that suits their requirements and therefore has a better chance of being implemented correctly. These processes include things such as the software they use to handle the digital files of signage, or the way they identify the streets or highlights of the city. In Santiago, for instance, one street could be named in as many as five different ways, which resulted in different spelling for different applications.

A detailed and profound understanding of the process of producing and delivering information, identifying the actors and processes involved, can make a big difference in the consistency of the information system being implemented and the pertinence and feasibility of the proposed elements.

Expectations of the system

Public transport's success in providing mobility depends on people knowing that services exist and understanding how to use them. While transit marketing focuses on making people aware of available services, transport information systems should focus on providing people with the information they need to use the network effectively.

The launch of Transantiago was preceded by a major marketing campaign that raised high expectations among Santiago's citizens. The political authorities at the time promised a 'world class' transport system with the latest technology, buses and infrastructure. These expectations crashed with an erratic implementation of the system, causing great disappointment among users and citizens (Allard 2008).

Despite the progress of Transantiago in terms of its technical standards, the disaffection of users towards the system persists until today. The initial disappointment and sense of deception experienced by citizens at the launch of the system has not been easily overcome during the last seven years that Transantiago has been operating (DTPM 2013). Managing expectations is crucial for its success and can greatly affect the perception and predisposition of users towards the system.

Local practices and getting to know your user

When information systems are planned, there is a general tendency to look to developed countries where maps and written information are the main components of passenger information. However, local research carried out in Santiago during the evaluation of the system showed the importance of local practices, such as the role of oral information. Many people's first source of information is to ask another passenger at the bus stop, street vendors, bus drivers or to call a friend or relative for instructions when dealing with an unknown destination (Informe Transantiago 2010). This practice could be attributed to the lack of a written or graphic information tradition in public transport in Santiago, or to the inaccuracy of the information displayed on the street.

Another particularity of Transantiago is the importance of the bus stop as the main source of initial information. As opposed to the different phases of the trip proposed by Infopolis, in Santiago many people will start their information collecting process when they are already en route, at the first bus stop. Finding required information at bus stops gains special relevance in the information system, concentrating authorities' efforts on delivering complete and up to date information in this context.

International experience and guidelines are a valuable source of information for the development of a passenger information system. However, Transantiago's experience exemplifies how this research must be contrasted with local culture and user practices in order to create more pertinent and useful solutions to inform users.

Keeping information up to date

One of the main challenges for information systems is to gain credibility among users. This credibility is due in large part to the accuracy of the information displayed and the capability of keeping the system up to date. In order to design a system that is capable of constantly updating itself, it is necessary to consider the process of producing the information.

In Transantiago's case, the change in the transport system was faster than the capacity to update street signs and other information. A graphical display of the workflow, from when information was generated by the transport engineers until the sign was installed on the street, allowed authorities and technicians to visualise the complexity of the system and identify where bottlenecks were located. This

Figure 13.1: Passenger information in Santiago, Chile: (a) different types of printed bus stop signs, (b) passengers reading the Transantiago map

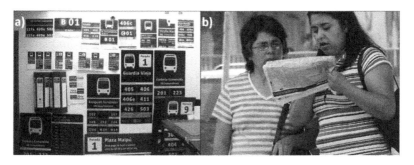

influenced important changes in the production and implementation process, such as the design of digital templates that could be filled with data directly from the spreadsheets used by those generating the information. Another important measure was to give new powers to the transport authority allowing it to have a direct relationship with providers of the infrastructure, a process that until then depended on other government services. These important changes increased the speed and control of what was implemented on the street.

Planning vs. practice: need for constant monitoring

Needs and practices around public transport evolve at the same time the system adapts to changes in cities. It is necessary to consider the monitoring of people's needs as a regular task in the implementation of the system. Passenger information is not something you can update every three or four years and expect it to remain relevant for users. The system, but also people's understanding of it, is constantly evolving, which is something that authorities should monitor constantly.

After the first assessment of Transantiago's passenger information system, the authority acknowledged the need and decided to form a team composed mainly of anthropologists and social scientists constantly monitoring and observing what happens on the street. The information on current practices around public transport supplied by this team is of great value for improvement, not only of passenger information, but of service standards in general.

Regulatory framework and normative overlap

Another important finding of the research carried out for Transantiago's passenger information system was that many buses did not comply with the information that was specified in the Graphic Standards Manual. This Manual is an official document detailing all the norms and standards that operators have to comply with in order to convey passenger information and graphic guidelines of the system correctly.

During the research, the team realised that one of the main reasons why operators did not comply with the information they were supposed to display was the existence of different norms that were still valid at the time, despite the creation of a new graphic and information standard for buses. The need to comply with different norms and regulations caused a conflict of (frequently contradictory) information. These norms were enforced at the mandatory review that buses had to go through in order to receive their permit. This resulted in companies complying with all current norms in order to avoid fines and gain permission to travel through the city, even though this meant repeating information or displaying contradictory messages.

Lessons from the Transantiago experience and future challenges in passenger information for BRT systems

The development and management of a passenger information system is undoubtedly a key action for a successful BRT system. It should be developed based on the specific needs of its passengers and have in consideration the local practices, especially when a new system is to be implemented, as in the case of Transantiago. Guidelines derived from the experience of consolidated public transport system can be a starting point, but passenger habits must also be taken into account in order to provide adequate information. Moreover, knowing and managing the expectations that potential passengers have for the system constitutes a powerful tool to improve its image and consequently the confidence and willingness of passengers to use the services.

The process of generating and implementing a passenger information system involves a variety of actors dealing in distinct ways with the information they are responsible for. Therefore, a comprehensive identification and understanding of these actors and their processes represents a crucial issue for the success of an information system. Besides, the normative context in which the system works has a significant impact on its performance. A reduced number of norms and regulations for implementing and managing the information system helps the operators to observe them, hence contributing to improvement in the quality of the information delivered.

The reliability of the information provided is also a fundamental issue for a successful passenger information system. An accurate and updated system, where timely information is delivered according to passengers' needs and preferences, helps to improve the credibility of the services offered. Supervision and control of the information implemented in the city, as well as monitoring of users' needs and expectations, is necessary to create and maintain a reliable and quality passenger information system.

An important barrier that needs to be overcome in order to achieve an efficient information system for BRT is the integration with other transport systems in the city. Fragmented information of available services delivered to passengers through different systems makes it difficult for them to fully comprehend their travel possibilities, reducing their use of public transport. Therefore, coordination and consistency between BRT system and other available transport modes such as regular buses, metro, bike sharing or car sharing, are essential. Coordination of these systems enables a better management of the information provided to passengers, leading to improved navigation through the network and eventually attracting new passengers to public transport due to the new opportunities that BRT contributes to the system.

Additionally, new ways of delivering basic information about the system must be explored. Personalised information according to the specific needs of social groups (the elderly, disabled, students, and so on) can be one form of improvement in their travel experience. For example, the elderly may prefer to receive information orally instead of in a printed or electronic form.

References

Allard, J. (2008) 'Coping with complexity; reconfiguring the navigation system for Santiago's new transportation plan', *Information Design Journal*, 16(3): 163–177.

Balcombe, R. (2004) 'The demand for public transport: a practical guide', *TRL Report*, TRL 593.

Cain, A. (2007) 'Developing a printed transit information material design manual', *Designing Printed Transit Information Materials – A Guidebook for Transit Service Providers*, Tampa: National Center for Transit Research (NCTR).

Díaz, R.B. and Hinebaugh, D. (2009) 'Characteristics of bus rapid transit for decision-making', *National Bus Rapid Transit Institute – Center for Urban Transportation Research*, www.nbrti.org/CBRT.html

DTPM (Directorio de Transporte Público Metropolitano) (2013) 'Satisfacción con Operadores Transantiago ICCOM, Informe de Resultados 2013', www.dtpm.cl/archivos/Satisfacci%C3%B3n%20 Operadores.pdf (accessed 5 August 2015).

Giuliano, G. and Hayden, S. (2005) 'Marketing public transport', in K.J. Button and D.A. Hensher (eds), *Handbooks in Transport: Handbook of Transport Strategy, Policy and Institutions*, Vol 6: 635–649. Brighton: Elsevier Science.

Hess, D.B. and Bitterman, A. (2008) 'Bus rapid transit identity: an overview of current branding practice', *Journal of Public Transportation*, 11(2): 19–42.

Infopolis 2 (1999) 'Needs of travellers: an analysis based on the study of their tasks and activities', *Advanced Passenger Information for European Citizens of 2000* – TR 4016, Commission of the European Communities – DG XIII.

ITDP (Institute for Transportation and Development Policy) (2007) 'Bus rapid transit – planning guide', *Institute for Transportation and Development Policy*, www.itdp.org/the-brt-planning-guide/

Mijksenaar, P. (1998) 'Maps as public graphics: about science and craft, curiosity and passion', in H.J.G. Zwaga, T. Boersema and H. Hoonhout (eds), *Visual Information for Everyday Use: Design and Research Perspectives,* London: Taylor & Francis, 211–224.

Minteguiaga, J. (2006) 'Transantiago: Redesigning Public Transport in Santiago, Chile', *Public Transport International* 55(6): 16–19.

The Economist (2008) 'The slow lane', February.

Section 3
Operations and Design

FOURTEEN

Opportunities provided by automated data collection systems

Nigel Wilson

Introduction

In much of the developed world public transport operators and authorities are beginning to take advantage of the opportunities presented by the increasing deployment of automated data collection systems (ADCS). For example, the use of automatic vehicle monitoring systems to measure on-time performance for bus service and to provide accurate real-time information to customers on when a bus will arrive at a particular stop. Similarly, automatic fare collection systems such as contactless smart cards can give a clear picture of system usage at the individual customer level, information previously available only through quite expensive and unreliable customer surveys. However, even in the most advanced organisations the full potential of these systems is far beyond current uses.

In urban areas of the developing world the opportunities presented by the introduction of ADCS are even greater because of the typical paucity of data, especially in the case of informal public transport markets. Some level of formalisation will be required to take advantage of the benefits of ADCS. A fragmented service delivery model, where each bus owner may own one or two buses, provides neither the financial incentive nor the operational capacity to allow the effective deployment of ADCS technology.

Bus Rapid Transit (BRT) requires a significant increase in information if it is to be run efficiently and provide a high level of service. Customers rightly expect accurate information on how long they must wait for a bus serving their destination to arrive at their station and how long it will be before they get there. Operators need to be able to estimate the productivity and reliability of individual vehicles and drivers, as well as the productivity and reliability of each route operated. Automated data collection systems are fundamental to this type of performance monitoring. Even in developing cities, with current high public transport modal shares, for BRT to be successful in the long term as incomes increase, it will need to offer a service quality providing high customer satisfaction. These systems can also provide rich information for route and network planning.

In this chapter we describe the roles that ADCS can play in improving public transport performance and illustrate several of them through case studies from recent research. While the cases presented here are based on MIT research, similar research has been conducted elsewhere with similar results, including extensive work at PUC (see for example Munizaga and Palma 2012; Larrain et al 2012; Muñoz et al 2013). These examples illustrate the types of initiatives which are likely to improve performance monitoring, operational efficiency and customer information in many urban areas over the coming decade.

The perspective taken throughout this chapter is that for public transport to be most effective all services must comprise an integrated public transport system. ADCS can be of value to the operator of a single mode – the general framework as well as the examples presented in this chapter certainly apply at this level; however, customers need to understand the operation of the complete system if they are to take full advantage of the accessibility it can provide. This authority-level view of the entire system, encompassing network planning, is a vital element in fully capitalising on the potential contributions of ADCS to public transport. Chapters Fifteen to Eighteen of this book discuss the key functions of network design, corridor performance, control, operations and scheduling, all of which can benefit significantly from ADCS. This is a basic driver of the move to formalise currently informal public transport services so that they can play a critical role in the total urban transport system.

Automated data collection systems

This chapter focuses on three types of ADCS: automatic fare collection systems, automatic vehicle location systems and automatic passenger counting systems, each of which is described briefly below.

Automatic fare collection systems (AFC) are typically based on contactless smart cards which are tapped at a reader to register the transaction. To date most of these smart cards have been issued by the operator or authority, for example Oyster cards in the case of London or Bip cards in the case of Santiago. However, there is increasing interest in using media issued by other organisations, such as contactless bank cards, which have recently been introduced in London, and mobile phones equipped with near-field communication, which are now being introduced in cities such as Salt Lake City and London, and which many people expect to become the electronic wallets of the future. Whatever the technology, the key characteristic is recording individual fare transactions which can be linked to a specific card. In some systems, notably those which have fares differentiated by trip distance or zone, the smart card is tapped both on entry to and exit from the system, whereas in many systems with flat fares the card is tapped only upon entry. AFC data have not typically been available in real time, but this may become possible in the future.

Automatic vehicle location systems (AVL) are typically based on global positioning systems (GPS) for bus systems and track circuit occupancy for rail systems and provide vehicle location information in real-time off the vehicle. These systems support real-time operations control and management, and provide customer information including next stop announcements. An example of this is the iBus system used for buses in London, which supports all the key authority functions discussed below. It is critical that AVL systems have a real-time capability.

Automatic passenger counting systems (APC) are typically based on sensors mounted in doors for buses which have channelled passenger movements, and counters at gates for systems which have fare barriers. This data is typically not available off the vehicle in real time.

Of these types of systems arguably AFC and AVL are the essential elements to obtain most of the benefits achievable from the use of ADCS. In particular, as will be clearer in later sections of this chapter, AFC can serve as a limited form of APC when combined with AVL data, since inference methods can provide a comprehensive picture of system operation and usage.

Key agency/operator functions

ADCS have the potential to affect several key functions which any public transport organisation must provide, including both offline and real-time processes. The distinction between offline and real-time functions is important both because of the difference in data that is typically available off the vehicle in real time, and because of the difference in computational requirements for real-time applications. The key offline functions which can be enhanced by ADCS are *service and operations planning*, and *performance measurement*. The key real-time functions are *service and operations control and management*, and *customer information*.

Service and operations planning include the specification of services to be offered as well as basic determinants of efficiency in providing these services, here referred to as *operations planning*. Fundamental decisions affecting the service offered to the public involve network and route planning, frequency setting and timetable development. Given the underlying modal technology, these decisions largely specify the service characteristics as perceived by the public, which will determine their interest in using the system. The operations planning process is focused on vehicle and crew scheduling, which are key determinants of the cost of operations given the service plan, and labour constraints and pay provisions (see Chapter Eighteen).

ADCS have significant impact on all aspects of service and operations planning, first and foremost through the provision of large amounts of data with measurable accuracy. ADCS data is replacing largely manually collected data with its typical connotations of small sample sizes, uncertain and hard to measure accuracy and bias. For example, estimation of origin–destination travel patterns previously relied on passenger surveys and used manual passenger counts to expand the resulting seed matrix to the full system ridership. With ADCS systems, as will be illustrated later in the chapter in the case of the London public transport network, a seed origin–destination matrix reflecting well over half of all passenger journeys can be inferred from ADCS data and then expanded to full system ridership using the same ADCS data. This should result in more effective service plans and more efficient operations plans, directly as a result of ADCS systems.

Performance measurement is fundamental in assessing all aspects of service delivery and has two particularly important parts: assessing the performance of operators providing service under contract to a public authority, and measuring service quality in a manner which reflects customer satisfaction as well as operator performance. Increasingly public transport systems are expected to deliver service within specified quality ranges (for example, no one waiting for more than X minutes, nobody making more than Y transfers). ADCS allow us to determine if the promised level of service is being delivered. It also enables the operator to identify the customers who receive the worst level of service. With the increasing use of models of service delivery relying on private companies to operate services under a contractual relationship with a public authority, the ability to measure performance against financial incentive and penalty terms included in the contract is critical (see Chapter Seven). Since one goal of high quality public transport is to attract choice riders to the system, thus increasing ridership and moving toward more sustainable urban accessibility, it is also important to measure performance in ways which reflect the customers' real perceptions of service quality.

ADCS make it possible to fulfil both these performance measurement roles more effectively. For example, for many years customer surveys have revealed that service reliability is one of the most important service attributes for many customers, but it has been virtually impossible to assess service reliability using manually collected data because of the inevitably small sample sizes practical with such labour intensive data collection methods. Now, with AVL systems, it is practical to amass large numbers of observations, even of a single scheduled vehicle trip, which can be used to support a range of reliability metrics of a traditional operator-oriented nature – for example, percentage of trips 'on time'. Even better, by combining AFC and AVL data it is now possible to measure service reliability for an individual customer, which is presumably much closer to how reliability is perceived. Clearly there are limits to how close ADCS systems can come to true perceptions, so there will remain important roles for other customer satisfaction assessment methods including surveys of attitudes and perceptions and mystery shopper observations, but it is certainly possible with ADCS to measure reliability in a way not previously feasible.

Service and operations control and management deals with day-to-day operations management, in particular responding to unexpected events such as incidents which disrupt normal operations, or significant changes in demand. Depending on the magnitude of the event it may not be feasible to continue to operate the service as planned, at least for a period of time, and so an alternative plan must be developed and deployed immediately (see Chapter Seventeen).

ADCS systems make it possible to respond more effectively to unexpected events, principally through AVL, which provides current locations of all vehicles in the system, making it possible to choose a better recovery strategy than without this information. AFC data has the potential to further enhance the response to unexpected events by providing the decision maker with information on the typical travel patterns in the vicinity of the disruption at this time of day so that a better strategy can be developed.

Customer information allows the individual customer to be informed of the state of the system, which is particularly important in the case of disruptions, and assists them in their travel planning, given deviations from the operations plan. Customers expect current and accurate real-time information at all stages of their journeys through a variety of media, and if public transport is to be perceived as a high quality alternative to driving it must meet these ever-increasing expectations (see Chapter Thirteen).

ADCS allows dynamic customer information to be targeted to the individual through a combination of real-time AVL data and detailed profiles of the travel patterns and preferences of the individual developed through analysis of their historical travel behaviour as revealed through AFC data. Pre-trip information can be based both on the operations plan for advanced trip planning, as is the norm for existing journey planners, or based on the current state of the system for immediate and en route trip planning, and re-planning when unexpected events occur. The value of the AFC data should not be underestimated because a successful customer information system must mean that only information of value to the individual, given their current or anticipated trip making, should be communicated. A danger which must be avoided is providing too much information, given the vast amount of data which is now becoming available. The customer must be assured that only important information will be communicated, otherwise the system will quickly become discredited and marginalised.

Analytic framework

The interrelationships between the different public transport operator/ authority functions and the roles which can be played by ADCS are illustrated in Figure 14.1. This figure shows the heart of the system which is responsible for the integration of the data coming from the ADCS to form a comprehensive picture of the current state of the system, the analysis of this data to support the real-time functions and the offline functions, and the prediction of the implications of different strategies on future system performance.

Figure 14.1: Key functions of ADCS

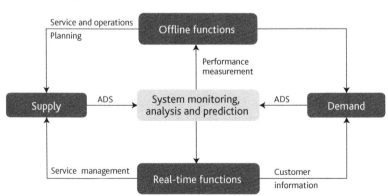

From this figure it is clear that the ADCS, while essential for effective public transport, are just the first steps toward optimising system performance. Analysis methods are required to develop a deep understanding of the factors which determine performance, and prediction methods are essential if the outcomes of particular actions are to be anticipated and used to select the preferred strategies. Ultimately the goal is to develop analysis and prediction methods which can function effectively in real time to support the supply management and dynamic customer information functions. In the short term, if the computational burden is too high for real-time application, significant value should be achievable through the planning and performance monitoring functions.

Given the complexity of predicting the performance of public transport systems, which involves understanding customer behaviour as well as developing both short term and longer term service and operations plans, the analysis methods required will inevitably be complicated. They will certainly include simulation-based performance models, which are the only credible way to incorporate both customer response to information and decision support for operations controllers and managers. Their development will be a demanding research activity which will require a deep understanding of both the demand for transport services and their performance.

While we are not close to having a comprehensive model which encompasses all these desirable features, researchers have made significant progress on some of the key modules that are required for such a model. In the following three sections we present examples of several of these sub-problems and their solution based on MIT research in collaboration with Transport for London over the past decade. It should be noted that similar applications have been conducted by other researchers in other cities, including Munizaga and Palma (2012) in Santiago.

Inference of full journey origin-destination matrix

One basic building block for understanding system performance is knowledge of the origin–destination matrix for existing customers. While for public transport systems which require exit (as well as entry) transactions – generally referred to as 'closed systems' – it is straightforward to create an origin–destination matrix; this will not generally capture the full journey on public transport which often includes multiple lines or modes. Yet it is the full journey origin–destination matrix which is of greatest value for a range of functions from network planning to customer information. In these systems you may know the stations at which a passenger entered and left the system, but not the transferring stations and the route taken. In the more common, and more difficult, case in which fare transactions are required only upon system entry – generally referred to as 'open systems' – the process requires inference of the alighting location for each entry and then linking consecutive journey segments if they satisfy various criteria that define the components of a single complete journey (Gordon et al 2013).

The inference process starts by sorting all AFC records chronologically by card ID for a specific day. A single AFC record includes a unique ID, a transaction type (for example, fare payment on entry), transaction time and location. All of these are straightforward to obtain, although for fare payment when boarding a bus, the boarding stop may have to be inferred through the transaction time tied to location through AVL records. Analysis of several bus routes in London has shown that the correct boarding stop can be inferred with high reliability (Wang et al 2011), even when customers complete their fare transaction after the bus has left the stop.

Destination inference is based on the observation that generally the alighting stop for a customer on a bus will be the stop on that route closest to the next boarding location for that customer. This trip linking principle is illustrated in Figure 14.2, which shows three consecutive transactions on the same card and day. The first transaction defines the origin (A) of the first trip segment (TS1). The destination of TS1 is inferred to be the stop on the route boarded at A which is closest to the location of the next fare transaction on this card (B), as long as it is within a reasonable walking distance. This assumption underlies the trip linking process no matter what the elapsed time is between the (inferred) alighting close to B and the time of the transaction at B: it could be just a few minutes, indicating that TS1 and TS2 are most likely part of the same full journey, or it could be a matter of hours, indicating that an activity took place between TS1 and TS2 and they should not be connected as a single journey.

Figure 14.2: Trip linking

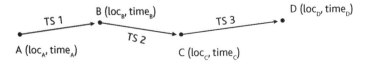

The key assumptions underlying this inference process are the following:

• No private transport segment occurs between two consecutive public transport trip segments.
• Public transport customers will not walk long distances between consecutive public transport trip segments.
• The last trip segment of the day returns close to the origin of the first trip segment of the day for that customer.

Clearly not all these assumptions will hold in all cases; however, the goal of this inference process is not to determine correctly the full journeys for every individual using the system, but to estimate the general journey patterns of all customers. Individual errors are not important for this goal. Evidence from several bus routes in London shows that this destination inference process represents true alighting patterns well, with errors typically being by no more than one stop in the alighting location (Wang et al 2011).

The next stage of the inference process is to connect consecutive trip segments together to form full journeys based on applying various spatial and temporal tests (for more detail on these tests see Gordon et al 2013).

The full journeys are then aggregated to form a seed origin–destination matrix which includes all journeys that could be inferred. Inevitably some journeys cannot be inferred using the methods described above, including those by customers who make only a single journey in a day, and those for whom some trip segments cannot be inferred. However, in the case of the Transport for London public transport network, full journeys could be inferred for approximately 76% of all bus AFC transactions, providing a seed matrix representing well over half of all public transport journeys made. Note that this is consistent with findings of researchers in other cities, including Munizaga and Palma (2012) in the case of Santiago. Nonetheless, there will always be a need for a final stage in the process which expands the seed matrix to a full origin-destination matrix for all public transport customers using the system. This expansion makes use of available control totals such as passenger entries and exits by station and boardings by bus line and by time period (for details on the expansion process used in London see Gordon et al 2013).

This inference and expansion process has been applied to the complete London public transport network, including approximately 12 million Oyster card transactions per day on a prototype basis, and takes about 30 minutes of computation time on a 2.8GHz Intel 7 machine with 8GB of RAM. The resulting origin–destination matrix is shown as a time-lapsed video as 'London in Motion' which can be viewed at http://jaygordon.net/londonviz.html

Measuring service reliability

Measuring service reliability is a critical step toward improving public transport given the importance that customers place on highly reliable service. ADCS provide the ability to assess service reliability in ways which were previously impossible. The approach taken to this problem is built upon the concept of reliability buffer time (RBT) first introduced by Furth (Furth and Muller 2007). It is defined as follows:

$$RBT(od) = JT(n\%) - JT(median)$$

where:
RBT(od) is the reliability buffer time for journeys between an origin–destination pair (od)
JT(n%) is the nth percentile of the journey time between o and d
JT(median) is the median journey time between o and d.

Figure 14.3 shows a typical distribution of journey times observed between an origin–destination pair with the RBT for the 95% illustrated. The RBT indicates the extra time which should be allowed for the journey above the median time if the customer wants to be confident at a level of 95% of arriving by a specified time. The RBT reflects the typical variability of the journey time for this trip.

The full journey time includes access time, wait time, transfer time, in-vehicle time and egress time, but from the public transport operator perspective only the components of the journey times which are under

Figure 14.3: Reliability buffer time

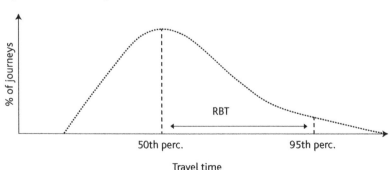

their control should be included, for example the walk to (from) the stop (station) used to start (end) the public transport portion of the journey should not be included if the public transport operator is being held to account.

There is an important distinction to be made here between reliability for high frequency service and low frequency service: with a high frequency service customers are generally assumed to arrive at stops (stations) randomly without consulting a schedule, whereas with a low frequency service many customers time their journeys to catch a specific scheduled vehicle trip (see Frumin and Zhao 2012). In the latter case on-time performance is critical to service reliability, whereas in the former case customer waiting time is minimised by maintaining even headways (see Chapter Seventeen). Typically the boundary between high frequency and low frequency service is a headway of about 10 minutes. The methods proposed here are designed primarily for high frequency services (which is the goal of BRT services), although the RBT concept can also be applied to low frequency services (see Zhao et al 2013).

The most direct way of measuring journey time through ADCS is the difference between exit time and entry time as recorded through the AFC system in closed systems, or through the inferred alighting location and time in open systems. Where the fare transaction occurs upon entering a station, which is common in many urban rail systems as well as BRT systems, the journey time includes in-station access as well as waiting times. However, in systems with fare payment as the customer boards the vehicle, which is typical of most conventional bus service, wait time occurs before the fare transaction and must be estimated separately if it is to be included in the journey time, as it should be. This can be approximated as in Ehrlich (2010) under the assumption of random customer arrivals.

One concern with using RBTs calculated for a set of customers, the easiest approach, is that they will reflect differences among customers as well as differences due to system performance. Clearly differences among customers have nothing to do with the operator's performance and should not be used to assess, and potentially reward (or punish), an operator based on performance. One way to deal with this concern is to measure RBT for individual customers so that differences among customers are eliminated. Of course this approach is possible only for customers who make repeated journeys between the same origin and destination at much the same time of day over many days.

The results of one recent attempt to explore this approach are summarized in Figure 14.4, which shows individual and overall

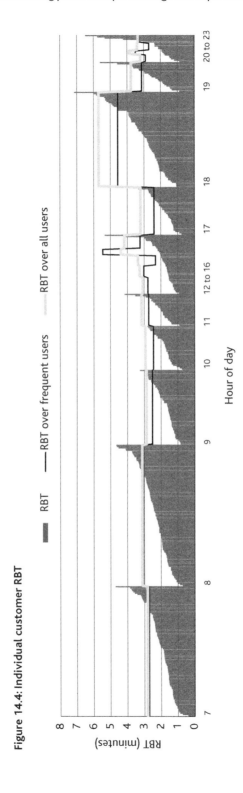

Figure 14.4: Individual customer RBT

RBTs for one origin–destination pair for a two-month period in a large urban rail system. In this case individual RBTs were calculated only for customers who made at least 20 journeys between this origin–destination pair within a one-hour time window over a two-month period. The figure shows that the individual customer RBTs are almost always lower than the aggregate RBTs for all frequent customers, which are themselves lower than for all customers, particularly in the afternoon and evening when many travellers are non-commuters.

There are several important findings from this research. First, RBT is an effective way to capture service reliability in a manner which is understandable and meaningful to many customers – that is, the amount of extra time to allow over the average to arrive at a specified time with very high probability. Hence it should be included, in some form, in performance measures for public transport systems. Second, reliability measures should generally not be used in isolation from other measures reflecting the overall journey times on the system: typically strategies to improve reliability also exact some price in terms of average journey times, and the operator (or authority) needs to be aware of these tradeoffs as changes in the operating plan, control strategies, or performance regime are considered. Finally, care should be taken to exclude differences among customers, particularly when RBT-based measures are included in contractual incentive and penalty terms.

Customer classification

ADCS allow the analysis of behaviour at the level of the individual customer, which can be vital in providing targeted customer information to those who are likely to be affected by changes in operations, for example. However, there is also great potential value in classifying customers into homogeneous groups. This allows the operator (or authority) to communicate with groups of customers sharing similar traits and to more carefully target and (eventually) evaluate strategies for travel demand management.

Critical input into any form of customer classification is the full journey records of individual customers over a period of months. These records can be used to estimate key travel characteristics for each individual which can then be used for clustering individuals into groups. At the outset, however, certain issues which make this process difficult must be recognised. First and foremost, the travel records are associated with specific smart cards whereas the classification of interest is for the individual customer, not the card. While there will often be a one to one relationship between a card and a customer, this will not always be the case. Two common exceptions may occur: a customer may make use of multiple cards over a period of time, or a single card may be shared among multiple customers. A customer may use multiple cards at various points in time because of the high cost of travelling with a card that lacks sufficient funds, or in the interests of convenience, and over time a card may be lost and replaced with a different card, and it may not be possible to link both cards to the same customer. In the case where several cards are shared among members of a single household, it may be hard to associate specific journeys with a specific customer. Notwithstanding these challenges it should be possible to form coherent classes of customers based on analysis of records associated with individual cards.

Frequency, intensity, and regularity have been the initial characteristics used to summarise travel associated with an individual card. Frequency could be measured by number of days of public transport travel over some period. Intensity relates both to how much travel occurs on days with public transport use and how concentrated public transport travel is on these days. Regularity captures both spatial and temporal aspects in the single day and day to day contexts.

Table 14.1 (Ortega-Tong 2013) presents an initial attempt to form customer clusters in the case of London. The suggested classification distinguishes between regular and occasional travellers, and forms eight groups which can be further aggregated into four classes: nonexclusive commuters, exclusive commuters, noncommuter residents and leisure travellers.

This research is still at an early stage but appears to have potential for improving understanding of customer behaviour as well as the effectiveness of customer communication and travel demand management strategies.

Conclusion

Automated data collection systems have the clear potential to affect the four critical operator/authority functions addressed in this chapter. The combination of smart card-based automatic fare collection systems and automatic vehicle location systems can reveal the way individual customers use the system, and how their use changes over time in response to changes in the public transport system and in the environment. This presents the opportunity to more effectively evaluate existing services and to improve planning and analysis methods

Table 14.1: Passenger travel profiles

Cluster	Frequency	Start times	Activity duration	Mode	Type of card	
Regular users						
1. Everyday regular users	7 days (2–4 journeys/ day)	w: 8:30– 19:30 we: 9:30– 18:15	w: 5.4 hrs we: 4.1 hrs	Mix	Travelcard	Non-exclusive commuters
2. All week regular users	6 days (1–2 journeys/ day)	w: 10:30– 16:30 we: 13:30– 17:00	w: 5.3 hrs we: 2.7 hrs	Mix	Mix PAYG/ travelcard	
3. Weekday rail regular users	5 weekdays (2 journeys/ day)	7:30– 15:30	7.4 hrs	Rail	Travelcard	Exclusive commuters
4. Weekday bus regular users	5 weekdays (2 journeys/ day)	9:30– 16:00	7.2 hrs	Bus	Child bus pass	
Occasional users						
5. All week occasional users	3 days (1–2 journeys/day)	15:30– 18:00	4 hrs	Mix	PAYG	Non-commuter residents
6. Weekday bus occasional users	2 weekdays (1 journey/ day)	13:00– 15:30	–	Bus	PAYG	
7. Weekend occasional users	2 weekend days (1–2 journeys/day)	17:30– 20:30	1.8 hrs	Mix	PAYG	Leisure travellers
8. Weekday rail occasional users	1 weekday (1 journey/ day)	13:00– 14:00	–	Rail	PAYG	

by comparing forecast and actual change in demand after significant changes in service.

Both types of ADCS also support a range of performance metrics which can be better proxies for customer satisfaction than traditional measures with their reliance on manual data collection. Service reliability can be assessed in a serious way for the first time, and this forms the basis for much more effective customer information based on actual performance, not just on the operating plan.

However, it must be acknowledged that we are only at the start of this line of exploration and are far short of the sort of real-time, prediction-based appraisal of current performance and assessment of strategies affecting both customer information and system control illustrated in Figure 14.1, which is the 'holy grail' for truly intelligent public transport systems.

BRT systems are a vital element in integrated high quality public transport systems, and ADCS systems can play a significant role in fulfilling their potential, but for these systems to be fully effective substantial movement toward formalisation of the informal sector in many developing cities will be required. While Part 1 of this book explores all aspects of the formalisation process, several points need to be made here about the implications of ADCS specifically. ADCS systems will generally be more costly and less flexible than the equivalent systems currently used in the informal sector. The benefits described in this chapter do come at some cost, albeit small compared with the overall cost of these public transport systems, but will require formalisation for implementation. For example, AFC systems will prevent the driver negotiating fares with individual customers based on their circumstances, but they will allow the driver to focus on driving rather than collecting money from customers and dealing with fare evasion, which should result in a safer system (see Chapter Nineteen). There are many challenges to overcome along the way, ranging from institutional resistance to change to privacy concerns around accessing the large amounts of data becoming available about the travel of individuals. Work to date in London and elsewhere suggests that these obstacles can indeed be overcome, but it will require a serious commitment from authorities to achieve the potential.

It should also be noted that ADCS systems can provide significant benefits through better operations control (see Chapter Seventeen) and understanding of user behaviour (see Chapter Twelve).

References

Ehrlich, J.E. (2010) 'Applications of automatic vehicle location systems towards improving service reliability and operations planning in London', Master's thesis, Massachusetts Institute of Technology.

Frumin, M. and Zhao, J. (2012) 'Analyzing passenger incidence behavior in heterogeneous transit services using smartcard data and schedule-based assignment', *Transportation Research Record: Journal of the Transportation Research Board*, 2274: 52-60.

Furth, P.G. and Muller, T.H.J. (2007) 'Service reliability and optimal running time schedules', *Transportation Research Record: Journal of the Transportation Research Board*, 2034: 55–61.

Gordon, J. (2011) *London in Motion*, http://jaygordon.net/londonviz. html

Gordon, J., Koutsopoulos, H.N., Wilson, N.H.M. and Attanucci, J. (2013) 'Automated inference of linked transit journeys in London using fare-transaction and vehicle', *Transportation Research Record: Journal of the Transportation Research Board*, 2343: 17–24.

Larrain, H., Muñoz, J.C. and Giesen, R. (2012) 'Express services for a bus corridor: a case study and some analytical insights', paper presented at the 12th Conference on Advanced Systems for Public Transport, Santiago, Chile.

Munizaga, M. and Palma, C. (2012) 'Estimation of disaggregate multimodal public transport origin–destination matrix from passive smartcard data from Santiago, Chile', *Transportation Research Part C*, 24: 9–18.

Muñoz, J.C., Cortes, C., Giesen, R., Saiz, D., Delgado, F., Valencia, F. and Cipriano, A. (2013) 'Comparison of dynamic control strategies for transit operations', *Transport Research Part C*, 28: 101–113.

Ortega-Tong, M. (2013) 'Classification of London's public transport users using smart card data', Master's thesis, Massachusetts Institute of Technology.

Wang, W., Attanucci, J.P. and Wilson, N.H.M. (2011) 'Bus passenger origin–destination estimation and related analyses using automated data collection systems', *Journal of Public Transportation*, 14(4): 131–150.

Zhao, J., Frumin, M., Wilson, N. and Zhao, Z. (2013) 'Unified estimator for excess journey time under heterogeneous passenger incidence behaviour using smart card data', *Transport Research Part C*, 34: 70–88.

FIFTEEN

Designing a BRT-based network under integrated operations

Homero Larrain, Omar Ibarra, Juan Carlos Munoz and Corinne Mulley

Introduction

Network design usually refers to the stage in public transport planning where the routes and frequencies are defined for the services in a public transport system. However, network design can also consider more strategic decisions, such as which transport modes will be involved, and how they will interact in the system. Designing a network is a very complex problem which spans economic, environmental and social aspects, involving a great variety of actors with conflicting interests. Passengers, for instance, are interested in a transit system with low fares, high frequency and direct, fast journeys; private car users may prefer a system that reduces traffic congestion without taking up car space; driver unions will care about the drivers' working conditions; and operators may be interested in providing highly productive operations at low costs. All these trade-offs must be faced at the design stage, and good coordination of the involved bodies will play a decisive role in the successful outcome of the projected system. In addition, there are no blank slates and cities have to build on existing transit networks, operators, and travel and land use patterns. Chapter Three discusses some of the challenges in implementing a new integrated system.

Whether Bus Rapid Transit (BRT) is introduced in an existing formalised transit system or used as a tool to formalise an informal bus sector, the service network will be questioned. In the case of a city already operating under formalised services, the integration between those services and the new BRT corridor should be discussed. Will previous services running parallel to the corridor be cut, changed by shorter feeder services or allowed to enter the corridor? How will the interchanging infrastructure between feeder buses and other modes be built? The implementation of a BRT corridor presents an opportunity to re-evaluate not just the routes, but also the network configuration. For example, if a system is being operated using point-to-point services, some of these services could be rerouted to use the capacity and improved speed of the BRT corridor. In some cases even a switch to something closer to a trunk and feeder network configuration could be justified in the presence of new BRT corridors and fare integration. This type of decision is further discussed in the next section of this chapter.

Network design involves decisions both on a strategic level, involving long term processes, and on a tactical level, with medium term impact and which can be revised periodically to adapt to changing conditions. In this chapter we discuss several stages of the BRT network design process. Section two presents the strategic decisions involved in this process: mode choice, network configuration, and the degree of openness of the system. In section three we discuss how to design the BRT network and its service routes and frequencies. In section four we present a case study illustrating the importance of correct service design on a BRT system. Finally, in section five we summarise the main ideas presented in this chapter.

Network modes and configurations

Designing a public network means dealing with a variety of factors that go beyond quality of service. A successful solution that balances all of these aspects of the problem usually involves a multimodal system, which can include city buses, taxis, bicycles, heavy rail (such as metro), light rail transit (LRT), and BRT. The different modes can be seen as building blocks for an integrated, sustainable urban transport system. In order to choose the right combination of modes for a city, it is fundamental to know their different strengths and shortcomings. Some modes can play the same role within a network, for example BRT or LRT, and some modes have a distinct role. For the purpose of this book we focus on the role of BRT.

Direct trips versus trunk and feeder

A key strategic decision involved in the planning of any public transport network is what type of service configuration to provide. The two main types of configurations of services using a corridor are 'point to point' or 'direct trip' systems, and 'trunk and feeder' systems. These network configurations are shown in Figure 15.1.

As shown in Figure 15.1, under a direct trip configuration point to point services offer a direct ride between two points outside of

Figure 15.1: Network configurations based on (a) direct trip services and (b) trunk and feeder systems which satisfy demand for four origin points/zones

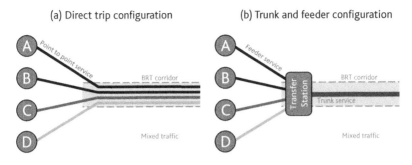

the BRT corridor. Under a trunk and feeder configuration, trunk services operate inside the BRT corridor, and feeder services connect the corridor to the rest of the destinations. Note that in both cases the corridor can be connected to the rest of the network not only in its extreme terminals, but also in intermediate points. In what follows we discuss the benefits of both configurations, but it is important to keep in mind that in practice the best solution can often be a combination of both types of configuration.

The main benefit of a direct trip system is that it reduces the number of transfers per trip. Transfers are a very important cost in users' travel experience: not only do they take time, they also usually mean walking, going up and down stairs, crossing streets, and in addition they add uncertainty to the trip. Raveau et al (2011) show that even in a protected environment such as a subway, users would be willing to use a route taking 15 additional minutes to avoid specific transfers. Avoiding these transfers also reduces the need to provide the infrastructure necessary to handle high volumes of passenger transfers. The concentration of this passenger interaction at certain stations creates friction among them that not only damages the level of service as perceived by a user, but also the actual service provided since boarding and alighting take longer.

One drawback of direct trip systems is that they need more different services and, usually, each of them is significantly longer. This also leads to vehicle underutilisation. Due to the length of these bidirectional routes, the capacity offered in each of them will be given by its critical link, while in the rest of the route the load factor may be significantly lower. Thus, vehicles will usually have spare capacity on long spans of their routes. This inefficient use of the vehicle capacity significantly increases operational costs. It also affects the level of service since multiple routes operating in the same corridor without a proper coordination may lead to congestion and slower travel times.

By running shorter routes, trunk and feeder systems adapt the capacity of each route to better fit local demand. This is achieved by providing high frequency trunk lines in high demand zones, which are accessible by feeder lines that cover the lower demand zones. Thus, trunk and feeder systems have the flexibility to adapt to the characteristics of each zone, taking advantage of the different modal options available and their different attributes.

The main concern with trunk and feeder systems is the number of transfers per trip users are forced to make. Thus, transfers should be designed to be as seamless and smooth as possible. The location of the stops should be carefully planned and ideally a transfer should not require changing stations or platforms. In case some walking is needed, the transfer should happen at the same level whenever possible and with attention to safety conditions. User information should be clearly provided. For medium to low frequency periods, timetables should be coordinated at these transfer stations. This is particularly relevant during the night, when frequencies are the lowest and waiting conditions are the most uncomfortable. Also, during the night travel times are less variable, which makes timetable coordination easier to achieve. Since in this system many passengers are forced to transfer to reach their destinations, fare integration is usually implemented, in which passengers pay a minor amount (if any) for their transfers.

Due to all of the above, trunk and feeder systems involve greater planning and implementation effort than direct trip schemes. This explains why the direct trip configuration is usually the one that arises spontaneously when no attention is given to public transport planning.

The above discussion of the differences between trunk-feeder and direct trips can be summarised in the following guidelines, taken from Wright and Hook (2007). A trunk feeder system will potentially work better when: (i) the demand on the system is high; (ii) demand is not homogeneously distributed along the corridor, and (iii) the distance traversed by the services is greater. Direct services are more likely to be attractive in the opposite case.

It is possible to merge the two approaches in a mixed system with some feeder services, some trunk-only services and some direct services coming from local neighbourhoods into the trunk corridor and then visiting another neighbourhood. Several of these services could run express within the corridor. Such a system is preferable in many circumstances, although its complexity could make it more difficult for users to navigate, and more challenging to design.

Open versus closed systems

BRT systems are usually associated with corridors where special buses operate in exclusive lanes. However, the use of these lanes can vary, defining how closed or open a BRT system is.

The use of exclusive lanes might be a privilege allowed for just part of the bus services, leaving some non-BRT buses to operate outside of the infrastructure. This is the case when a new BRT system is implemented on top of an existing public transport system, usually an informal one. The planner has to decide, in these cases, if the non-BRT buses will be allowed to use the exclusive lanes.

A closed BRT system is one where only BRT buses are allowed to make use of the exclusive lanes and these buses do not operate outside of the lanes. Open BRT systems allow buses to operate on regular streets and then turn into a BRT corridor for part of their trip.

The main advantage of closed systems is that they ensure a lower level of congestion and more controlled operations for BRT buses, allowing higher speeds and shorter cycle times. A shorter cycle time allows a higher frequency and therefore a higher capacity to be offered with a given fleet.

Openness can reduce transfers and add flexibility to service design, allowing the network to adapt to better fit the demand patterns of the city, as discussed in the next section. However, this must be carefully designed to allow smooth interactions affecting operational speeds and safety as little as possible.

Designing a BRT network

Once the transportation modes and the network configuration type have been defined, the next step involves where to build the BRT infrastructure and which specific routes and services to provide. Thus, the BRT network design problem can be separated into two different levels: (i) location of BRT corridors and stops, and (ii) service design within the BRT system and in its surroundings.

We refer to the *corridor design problem* as the problem of defining where the BRT corridors will be built and where their terminals and stations will be located. A by-product of this problem is the origin–destination matrix of trips within stations on the BRT corridors. This matrix feeds the *service design problem* that determines the services that will operate inside the BRT corridors and their frequencies. Besides the regular service that stops at every stop along every route, there are many types of service that could be provided to improve the performance of the system. Furth and Day (1985) suggest three types of special services or strategies for high demand corridors that can be especially attractive for BRT corridors: short turning services, deadheading, and express services.

It is worth mentioning before detailing the design stages that network design is an iterative process that involves trying many alternatives and comparing different scenarios to orient the decision making process. In order to determine, for instance, whether to work with direct services or trunk and feeders (or a combination of both), it is advisable to define different preliminary scenarios and build solutions for each of them. At this stage it is not necessary to invest great effort in the optimisation process; an order of magnitude of the costs involved should be enough to make a decision. Even when strategic decisions are already made, it is likely that the design process will receive feedback from the lower level problem which will suggest new updates to the upper level solution, and new scenarios to be tested.

Corridor design

The first stage of the network design problem for BRTs involves deciding where to build corridors and where to locate the bus stops. We can assume that the other strategic design decisions mentioned in section two are already settled: intermodality, openness of the corridor, and service configuration (direct or trunk and feeder). We will also assume that there is knowledge about the public transport demand matrix (or, more likely, a series of demand scenarios), and about the current transport system in the city.

In some cases, the BRT network design problem can be tackled using a continuous approach. In this kind of approach, proposed by Daganzo (2010), demand is modelled as a continuous function over a geographical space, and the optimal spacing between services arranged in a lattice, or a trunk and feeder system is determined. This offers idealised representation of the city, which can be used as a starting point to design the network. In this approach the authors obtain analytical expressions for the optimal distance between corridors, which rise with the operational cost and access speed, and fall with the value of time and the demand level. Through this approach, Daganzo (2010) also shows that the optimal distance between stations should rise with the square root of the access speed, the dwell time and the load profile. Finally, an expression for the optimal frequency of the regular service stopping in every station is obtained. In Medina-Tapia et al (2013) this methodology is extended to consider a multi-period case. An application of an extension of the methodology proposed by Daganzo (2010) for the city of Barcelona can be found in Estrada et al (2011).

The two level approach with a continuous formulation makes special sense when designing a trunk and feeder structured network, where the trunk service network and the feeder service networks can be seen as two interacting subsystems that can be designed and optimised separately. However, when designing point to point services, a different approach should be considered, where the whole network is designed at once.

Some public transport network design models available in the literature can deal with the problem described above. Ceder and Wilson (1986) and then Ceder and Isreali (1989) solve the problem by dividing it into two stages, namely route design and frequency optimisation. In the frequency optimisation stage, service frequencies and passenger assignment are solved iteratively. Baaj and Mahmassani (1995) propose another design methodology divided into three stages: route generation, where initial possible routes are designed connecting the most demanded pairs by the shortest paths; analysis of procedure, where an array of descriptors is generated for a given set of routes and frequencies; and route improvement, where routes are modified and combined in different ways to look for improvements.

These models will yield a public transport network that has to be analysed to decide where to locate the BRT corridors. The natural approach to this is to locate the BRT corridors in the route segments with a higher total frequency of services. Factors that impact on corridor performance are discussed in Chapter Sixteen.

The location of the stations have to be decided based on the activities of the city, but can also be oriented by the optimal densities estimated by the continuous approaches mentioned earlier. Note that the frequencies from this stage are only used as a guide to design the corridors, but the definitive frequencies must be designed in conjunction with different types of services (for example, express services), as shown in the following section.

Service design

After the previous stage, we should have a network of BRT corridors, their station locations, and possibly some point to point services that partially use the BRT network. Combining this information with the trip demand for the whole public transport network it is possible to obtain an origin–destination matrix for trips inside the BRT network, assuming that a trip accessing (or exiting) the corridor on a point to point service originates in the station where it enters (or exits) the corridor.

For the services on the BRT network, a single regular service in each corridor is straightforward to operate: it is easy to design, it ensures a direct trip for every passenger travelling in the corridor, it distributes waiting times evenly along the corridor and it is very simple to communicate to users. Most metro lines operate in this way. However, buses can be much more flexible than trains and this flexibility should be exploited.

Under high demand volumes, significant improvements in the quality of service and system capacity can be achieved by the use of special services and strategies such as short turning, deadheading, express and intercorridor services. These strategies, although simple to implement in most cases, might require some special care during the corridor design phase. For instance, short turning services need space to manoeuvre to turn around, and express services can only work when overtaking is possible.

Short turning services, first studied by Ceder (1989) and Furth (1987), are defined as services that cover only a section of the whole corridor. These services are attractive when the demand is concentrated in a section of the corridor. Short turning services allow the capacity being offered to adapt to the load profile of the corridor better by providing a higher frequency where it is mostly needed. This provides a more efficient use of the resources and a more even load factor across the corridor.

Deadheading is an operating strategy for bidirectional corridors that is attractive when the demand presents a significant imbalance between both directions. The strategy consists of returning some of the buses empty (nonstop and therefore faster) on the less used direction of the corridor, reducing cycle time and consequently increasing capacity on the more used direction. This strategy has been studied by Ceder and Stern (1981) and Furth (1985). In the work of Cortés et al (2011), deadheading strategies are analysed in joint operation with short services under different scenarios. The authors conclude that while significant benefits can be achieved by the use of short turning services when demand is unbalanced both between directions and within directions, deadheading strategies yield smaller benefits, due to the inefficiency involved in running empty buses on the corridor.

The last type of service proposed by Furth and Day (1985) is the express service, in which some of the stops along the corridor are skipped in order to provide a faster service. These services not only provide a faster ride to some passengers, they also reduce cycle time, increasing the aggregated frequency and its associated capacity that can be offered in the critical link. They also reduce the friction in crowded stations since they stop only in a fraction of them. These types of service have proven to be very attractive in diverse contexts: according to our Global BRT Database there are 186 cities around the world where this type of service is implemented in some way.

Jordan and Turnquist (1979) is the first work that addresses the express service design problem. This work reports a dynamic programming model to solve a zoning problem for a corridor where every trip shares its destination. Later Ercolano (1984) and Silverman (1998) report case studies of the express service problem for New York City. The latter work concludes that express services not only generated operating cost savings, they were also very well perceived by users, who often even overestimated their travel time savings.

Different mathematical formulations and algorithms for the express service design problem for general demand matrices are proposed by Sun et al (2008), Chiraphadhanakul and Barnhart (2013), and Leiva et al (2010). Using this last formulation, Larrain et al (2010) studied various scenarios in order to determine what factors make a given corridor a good candidate for express services, concluding that high demand corridors (and therefore high frequency) with long trips (measured in number of stops) and unbalanced demand (both between directions of the corridor, and within the corridor) are the most promising scenarios for express services to operate. It is also clear that express services are more beneficial if stations are close to one another.

Express services are crucial to provide a fast trip to the passengers and increase the productivity of the fleet. They are probably the only tool for a high demand system to provide a capacity exceeding 20,000 passengers per hour per direction. The most successful high demand BRT corridors around the world are equipped with overpassing facilities at stations for express services. Under this high frequency operation, station capacity becomes an active bottleneck. The design methodology must be adapted to handle station capacity constraints. In the final section of this chapter an example of this situation is presented.

When the services operating inside the BRT network are defined, it is necessary to attend to the rest of the services. In the case of a trunk and feeder system, the problem can be divided into zones connecting each station, and the feeders for each zone can be designed using the public transport network design models described in the previous section. When designing point to point services, it is necessary to decide at each station how to combine the services inside of the corridor with those outside of it.

Case study

Express services are a key element in the successful design of a BRT corridor. They make efficient use of bus and infrastructure and benefit passengers by reducing travel times.

We illustrate the impact of express services with a design problem that came up during the planning stages of the Transbrasil BRT corridor in Rio de Janeiro, Brazil. This is a very ambitious project, still in development, which aspires to carry more than 60,000 passengers per hour in its critical segment, which exceeds by more than 20% the maximum demand faced by TransMilenio in Avenida Caracas, Bogotá.

During one of its stages, the design of the Transbrasil corridor had 28 stations and 6 terminals, as shown in Figure 15.2 (its final design is somewhat different to this diagram). Each one of the terminals connected the corridor with the rest of the transit network. Two of them, labelled 14 and 16, connected this corridor with Transcarioca, an existing BRT corridor. As shown in the diagram, these terminals were located outside of the corridor and their connections to the corridor were designed to allow buses to enter only towards downtown (and vice versa).

Transbrasil is, by design, an open BRT corridor which allows point to point services connecting different parts of the city to enter or exit the corridor at the terminals. The corridor also allows a returning manoeuvre in three specific stations, as shown in Figure 15.2.

The demand for this corridor is exceptionally high. Figure 15.3 shows its demand profile, and the total trips that originate or end at every terminal and station in the corridor, for both directions during the morning peak. Note that in both graphs the load profile shown for every node corresponds to the segment $(i, i + 1)$. This information is

Figure 15.2: Transbrasil corridor configuration

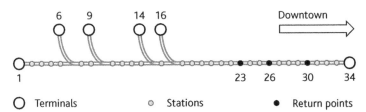

Figure 15.3: Demand profile of the Transbrasil corridor, during the morning peak

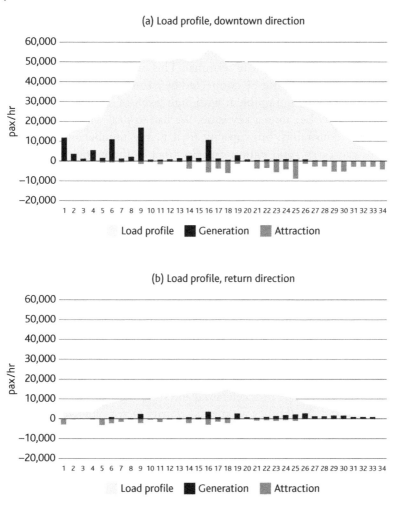

(a) Load profile, downtown direction

Load profile ■ Generation ■ Attraction

(b) Load profile, return direction

Load profile ■ Generation ■ Attraction

obtained from an estimated demand matrix. The trips in terminals do not necessarily originate or end there: in most cases, these travellers are using the terminal to access or egress the BRT corridor.

Identifying a feasible set of services that could meet the demand in the corridor and satisfy infrastructure capacity constraints is not straightforward. To illustrate this we decided to ask some experts in the field to suggest a set of services with their respective frequencies that could provide such a solution. We then used the methodology introduced in the previous section to predict how these services would be loaded along their routes to detect possible oversaturation. Also, we looked for an alternative solution based on the methodology and compared the results. We constrained the problem to only symmetric services starting and ending at terminals or return points. Additionally, services coming from a terminal could only serve the downtown direction, and when going in that direction they could not exit the corridor in an intermediate terminal. This meant that terminals 1, 6, 9, 14 and 16 could not be connected by a single service.

In a service design problem with high levels of demand such as this one, capacity becomes a key issue. We had to deal with two types of capacity constraints: bus capacity (that is, the number of passengers a bus can carry), and station capacity (that is, the number of buses a station or terminal can accommodate). Regarding bus capacity, it was decided that the corridor was going to be operated by a homogeneous fleet of 200-passenger biarticulated buses, and using a safety factor of 90% bus capacity was adjusted to 180 passengers per bus. For station capacity, the number of buses that can operate at the same time (number of bays) is predefined as two, four or six, depending on the station. Terminals were assumed to have infinite capacity.

To determine the required number of bays, it is necessary to determine the total time buses need to be in the station every hour. This can be obtained as $bays_i = \sum_{l \in L_i}$ (frequency$_l$ dwell time$_l$), where L_i is the set of services using station $_i$. The dwell time of service l on station i will depend on how many passengers are using the station. Dwell time was computed as the sum of boarding and alighting times, and a fixed time due to accelerating and stopping. For both the station capacity and dwell times we used a security factor of 80%.

To obtain a solution we needed to assign passengers to routes on the corridor. We assumed that passengers minimised the inconvenience of their routes, as defined in Sheffi (1984). The waiting times were evaluated assuming that buses followed a Poisson process. The parameters involved in this model are presented in Table 15.1.

The methodology was used to test three different sets of services. The first one is the case where only all-stop services are provided, one each for terminals 1, 6, 9, 14 and 16 going to terminal 34. The second scenario corresponded to the design provided by our set of experts, and the third to an improved solution designed by the full methodology. Services, frequencies, bus capacity and critical arcs for the three scenarios are illustrated in Figure 15.4.

In this figure an 'o' is used to denote the stations or terminals visited by each service. As stated before, the first network consists of operating regular services only. Since it is not possible to connect terminals 1, 6, 9, 14 and 16, a specific service is provided for each of them. In

Table 15.1: Parameters used in the evaluation

Parameter	Value
Value of time (in vehicle)	2 US$/hr
Value of time (waiting)	4 US$/hr
Transfer cost	0.16 US$/transfer
Bus capacity	200 pax/bus
Boarding rate	4 pax/sec
Alighting rate	3 pax/sec
Fixed dwell time	0.50 min
Bus capacity safety factor	90%
Station capacity safety factor	80%

the second scenario the logic is to connect the zones between the terminals before 14 to the second half of the corridor, and to provide fast services in this second half, alternating the stops. This scenario does not use any regular services. The services in scenario 3 were designed grouping neighbouring stops into clusters, which allowed us to better adjust the frequencies to match the capacity requirements, and to simplify the solution.

Figure 15.4: Scenarios under evaluation

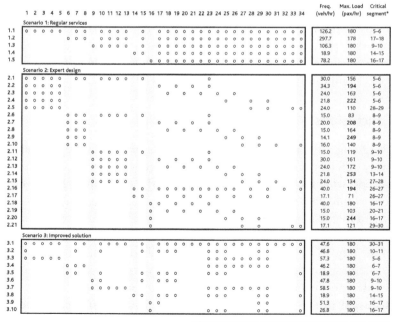

*All the critical segments occur on the downtown direction of the services.

In scenarios 1 and 3, the frequencies were calculated in order to satisfy bus capacity restrictions. In scenario 2 the frequencies were predefined by the experts. As highlighted in bold in Figure 15.4, in this case our model predicted that some services would become overcrowded, while others underutilised.

Figure 15.5 shows each station in the downtown direction, its capacity and its utilisation in each of the three scenarios, measured in number of bays. Note that we do not allow a station to be used over 80% of its capacity as a safety factor. As the figure shows, in the first scenario, with no express services, capacity is exceeded in many stations. Since the frequencies were the minimum that satisfied bus capacity, there is no way these frequencies can be reduced to relieve this problem. This shows that in corridors with a high level of utilisation, express services are sometimes the only feasible way to carry the passenger load given the available infrastructure capacity.

Figure 15.6 shows the total user costs experienced by passengers for each of the three scenarios as travel time, waiting time and transfers. The size of fleet needed is also displayed. The figure shows that the scenarios using express services (2 and 3) reduce travel times, but at the expense of increasing waiting times and transfers. It can also be observed that the number of buses used in the solution is very similar between scenarios 2 and 3, but rather lower than in the first. This was done on purpose when designing the services for the third scenario: we restricted the search to identify the minimum user cost solution for the same fleet size. This makes the solution in scenario 3 quite remarkable, since it solves all capacity issues and improves the level of service. It is also easier to navigate for the user than scenario 2 because it has significantly fewer services (10 versus 21).

Conclusions

Designing a BRT system is a very complex problem which involves many different agents and levels of detail; a good design should be part of a citywide multimodal transport network, and could be used as a tool to integrate bus operations in some contexts. The type of BRT system to implement depends on the circumstances: the correct mix of direct, trunk and feeder services will depend largely on particularities of the city, its demand patterns and political constraints.

Mathematical modelling can be a very useful tool to support the decision making process for the design of a BRT network. As discussed in this chapter, there are many models in the literature that can help in deciding where to locate the corridors and their

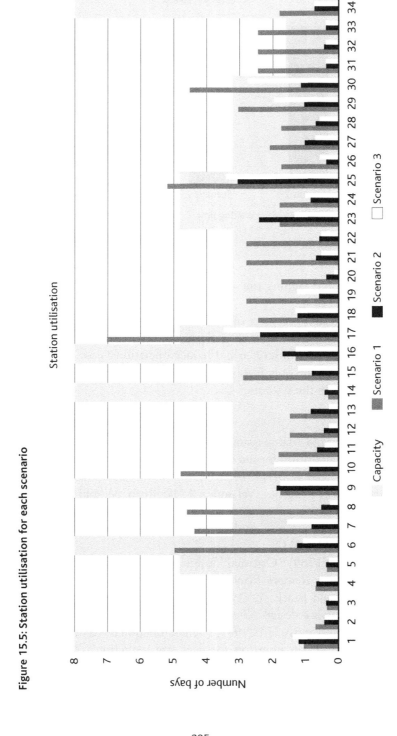

Figure 15.5: Station utilisation for each scenario

Figure 15.6: Breakdown of social costs for each scenario

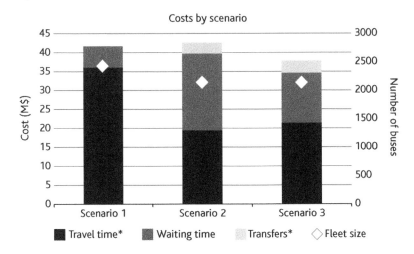

*Measured against a lower bound

stations, and designing the services to operate in the BRT network and outside of it.

One crucial aspect of a successful BRT network design is service design. As shown in the case study, good service design can not only improve the level of service and reduce operational costs, it may also sometimes be the only feasible way to operate within the capacity of the stations in the system.

References

Baaj, M.H. and Mahmassani, H.S. (1995) 'Hybrid route generation heuristic algorithm for the design of transit networks', *Transportation Research – Part C*, 3(1): 31–50.

Carrigan, A., King, R., Velasquez, J., Raifman, M. and Duduta, N. (2013) 'Social, environmental and economic impacts of BRT systems: bus rapid transit case studies from around the world', Technical Report, EMBARQ.

Ceder, A. (1989) 'Optimal design of transit short-turn trips', *Transportation Research Record*, 1221: 8–22.

Ceder, A. and Israeli, Y. (1998) 'User and operator perspectives in transit network design', *Transportation Research Record*, 1623: 3–7.

Ceder, A. and Stern, H.I. (1981) 'Deficit function bus scheduling with deadheading trip insertion for fleet size reduction', *Transportation Science*, 15(4): 338–363.

Ceder, A. and Wilson, N.H.M. (1986) 'Bus network design', *Transportation Research – Part B*, 20(4): 331–344.

Chiraphadhanakul, V. and Barnhart C. (2013) 'Incremental bus service design: combining limited-stop and local bus services', *Public Transport*, 5(1–2): 53–78.

Cortés, C.E., Jara-Díaz, S.R. and Tirachini, A. (2011) 'Integrating short turning and deadheading in the optimization of transit services', *Transportation Research – Part A*, 45(5): 419–434.

Daganzo, C. (2010) 'Structure of competitive transit networks', *Transportation Research – Part B*, 44(4): 434–446.

Ercolano, J.M. (1984) 'Limited-stop bus operations: an evaluation', *Transportation Research Record*, 994: 24–29.

Estrada, M., Roca-Riu, M., Badia, H., Robusté, F. and Daganzo, C.F. (2011) 'Design and implementation of efficient transit networks: procedure, case study and validity test', *Transportation Research – Part A*, 45(9): 935–950.

Furth, P.G. (1985) 'Alternating deadheading in bus route operations', *Transportation Science*, 19(1): 13–28.

Furth, P.G. (1987) 'Short turning on transit routes', *Transportation Research Record*, 1108: 42–52.

Furth, P.G. and Day, F.B. (1985) 'Transit routing and scheduling strategies for heavy demand corridors', *Transportation Research Record*, 1011: 23–26.

Jordan, W.C. and Turnquist, M.A. (1979) 'Zone scheduling of bus routes to improve service reliability', *Transportation Science*, 13(3): 242–268.

Leiva, C., Muñoz, J.C., Giesen, R. and Larrain, H. (2010) 'Design of limited-stop services for an urban bus corridor with capacity constraints', *Transportation Research – Part B*, 44(10): 1186–1201.

Larrain, H., Giesen, R. and Muñoz, J.C. (2010) 'Choosing the right express services for a bus corridor with capacity restrictions', *Transportation Research Record: Journal of the Transportation Research Board*, 2197: 63–70.

Medina-Tapia, M., Giesen, R. and Muñoz, J.C. (2013) 'Model for the optimal location of bus stops and its application to a public transport corridor in Santiago, Chile', *Transportation Research Record: Journal of the Transportation Research Board*, 2352: 84–93.

Raveau, S., Muñoz, J.C. and de Grange, L. (2011) 'A topological route choice model for metro', *Transportation Research – Part A*, 45(2): 138–147.

Sheffi, Y. (1984) *Urban Transportation Networks*, Englewood Cliffs, NJ: Prentice-Hall.

Silverman, N.C. (1998) 'Limited-stop bus service at New York City transit', *Journal of Transportation Engineering*, 124: 503–509.

Sun, C., Zhou, W. and Wang, Y. (2008) 'Scheduling combination and headway optimization of Bus Rapid Transit', *Journal of Transportation Systems Engineering and Information Technology*, 8(5): 61–67.

Wright, L. and Hook, W., (2007) *Bus Rapid Transit Planning Guide*, Technical report, Institution for Transportation and Development Policy.

SIXTEEN

Assessing corridor performance

Juan Carlos Herrera, Juan Carlos Munoz, David Hensher,
Corinne Mulley, Zheng Li and Luis Antonio Lindau

Introduction

Public transport systems are increasingly aiming at providing an integrated service for the user. In these systems, BRT is a key component since it can provide a fast trip to users in congested urban setting. The promise of BRT is not just that it can be delivered at a fraction of the cost of a rail-based system and considerably faster, but also that it can provide an equivalent level of service and capacity. This combination of cost and performance leads to the growing global interest in BRT as an urban passenger transport solution in situations typified by maximum peak hour ridership often in the range 7,000 to 45,000 passengers per hour per direction.

As discussed in Chapter Fifteen, public transit should be designed, implemented, and evaluated as a system. BRT can either play the role of a main structural spine of the system or of a high capacity feeder from the periphery into a rail network. In cities without an integrated system BRT can also be implemented on its own, but as a building block toward a full system. In any of these cases, the basic unit of BRT is a corridor; its potential to attract demand and to offer a high level of service depends on the characteristics of the corridor.

Using the corridor as a unit of analysis is limiting since it does not address overall system performance. But corridor performance measures can provide valuable insight into how to improve operations on existing BRT corridors and act as inputs into the decisions around new corridors. Understanding the relationship between the operational performance of a corridor and its design characteristics is crucial when planning, designing and implementing a BRT corridor.

In this chapter we identify key performance measures and focus our analysis on ridership and operational performance. For the latter, we discuss how to improve speed, frequency, vehicle load, and reliability.

The results are based on studies with samples from BRT systems around the world.

Of course, the urban context of any BRT corridor affects its performance. In some contexts some of the high productivity opportunities could be much harder to implement than in others. Thus, corridor planners need to consider their local conditions in addition to these results.

Recognising that every city has a different set of circumstances, the goal of this research is to inform decision makers on the relationship between possible performance measures and design and operations characteristics. Thus if a city identifies high ridership as a goal, they can learn what features have been shown to impact on ridership in existing BRTs around the world.

Key BRT design characteristics

When planning and designing a BRT corridor, the project leaders have to make multiple decisions regarding the infrastructure and operation. These decisions will greatly affect the performance of the corridor. The list of characteristics or decisions to make is long but key decisions include:

- Closed versus open system. Whether the system is designed as an open or closed corridor has a fundamental impact on operations. In a closed system only BRT buses use the corridor and they stay on the corridor. In an open system different bus services can enter and leave the corridor. An open corridor operation exploits one of the main attributes of BRT over metro: bus flexibility. This can reduce transfers, which significantly affects the level of service perceived by users. However, in an open BRT corridor bus interaction at several intersections where buses enter and leave the corridor grow significantly. This reduces the capacity and the operating speed of the corridor. Also, the number of different lines operating in the corridor grows, demanding longer platforms and a much more complicated information system. Thus, deciding over a closed or an open system usually depends on users' characteristics, land use, and travel demand patterns. Examples of closed systems can be found in Curitiba (Brazil), Quito (Ecuador), and Bogotá (Colombia). Examples of open systems can be found in Guangzhou (China), Taipei (Taiwan), São Paulo and Porto Alegre (Brazil), and Kunming (China) (Hook 2005).

- Corridor type: segregated busway versus exclusive lanes, curb lanes or median lanes, number of lanes (one lane, one lane with overtaking at stations, or two lanes), and so on. Segregation from the rest of the traffic is critical for buses to bypass congestion and to maintain a desired speed, while overtaking is crucial for express service operation. As explained in Chapter Fifteen, express or semi-express services are more relevant for long corridors, far apart stations, long trips, and concentrated demand in a few origin–destination pairs.

- Stations type: station layout (island vs staggered[1]), difference between platform levels (bus and station), station location (mid-block or right before/after traffic light), number of berths per station, spacing between consecutive stations, and so on. Most of the time, the capacity of a corridor is given neither by the width of the road nor the number of passengers that can fit inside the buses, but instead by how many buses can visit a critical stop. The internal station capacity may also become a bottleneck in handling the boarding and alighting passengers. Finally, the distance between consecutive stations affects the speed of the non-express services.

- Operation: pre-boarding fare collection, express services, contra-flow operation, and so on. These elements directly affect speed, which is the main feature of BRT since it affects travel time, frequency, and capacity.

- Vehicle technology: size of buses, propulsion system (diesel, hybrid, gas, electric), buses with doors on both sides or only on one, low floor versus high floor buses, driver assistance for precise docking at stations, and so on.

- Intersections type: grade separated, priority or signal junctions. Grade separated junctions eliminate the conflict between the corridor and cross streets, but it is expensive. At-grade junctions solve the conflict by giving priority to one street over the other (priority intersection) or by alternating in time the use of the junction (signal intersection). In the latter case, the length of the cycle and the fraction of the time that traffic signals give a green light to the corridor directly influence the corridor's performance. To increase the corridor's speed, dynamic bus priority systems and short cycle lengths (since they reduce the average time spent by each bus at signals) could be implemented.

- Control systems: most BRT services offer medium to high frequencies so no timetables are offered. Under these circumstances the control mechanism is relevant to keep a reliable service. Chapter Seventeen provides deeper insights on this topic.

Ridership on a BRT corridor

The goal of a BRT corridor is to move high volumes of passengers with good levels of service; this requires both passenger demand and a high enough capacity to handle them. Passenger demand is determined by trip origins and destinations in the corridor's area of influence, by interconnected multimodal feeding services and facilities, and by the attractiveness of the service offered. In this section we first present some figures of BRT's ridership worldwide. This is followed by an analysis performed to identify ridership drivers of BRT systems and to quantify their impact.

Considering all different types of bus priority systems that may coexist in a city, the total daily passenger ridership differs significantly from city to city. The top 15 cities with highest demand in bus priority systems as of 2014 are shown in Figure 16.1. Notice that cities like Bogotá (Colombia) and Curitiba (Brazil) only have fully segregated BRT corridors, while other cities like São Paulo and Rio de Janeiro (Brazil) also have busways and bus corridors.

Figure 16.1: Top 15 cities for daily demand as of 2014 (in thousands of passengers per day)

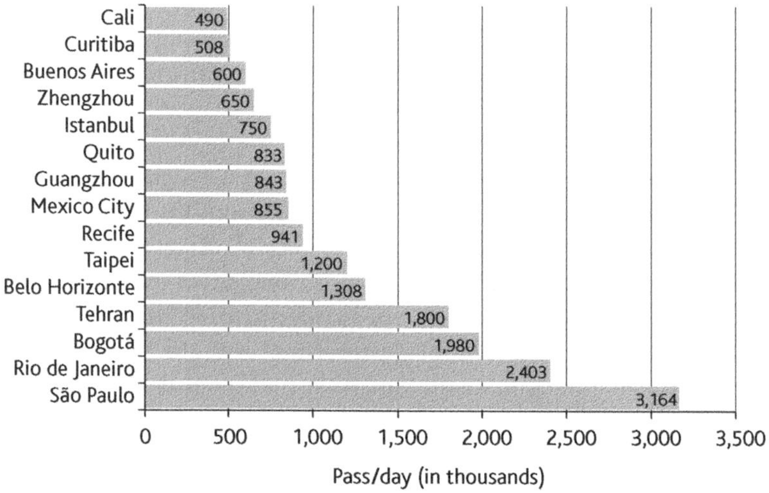

City	Pass/day (in thousands)
Cali	490
Curitiba	508
Buenos Aires	600
Zhengzhou	650
Istanbul	750
Quito	833
Guangzhou	843
Mexico City	855
Recife	941
Taipei	1,200
Belo Horizonte	1,308
Tehran	1,800
Bogotá	1,980
Rio de Janeiro	2,403
São Paulo	3,164

Source: EMBARQ Brazil based on data from www.brtdata.org

302

A number of studies have conducted reviews of BRT systems (see for example Hidalgo and Graftieaux 2008; Hensher and Golob 2008; Deng and Nelson 2011; Hensher and Li 2012). Among these existing BRT review studies, only Hensher and Golob (2008) and Hensher and Li (2012) conducted formal statistical analyses to comparatively assess BRT systems (their infrastructure costs and ridership). Hensher and Li (2012) collected information on 46 BRT systems from 15 countries to investigate the potential ridership drivers. They identified a number of sources of systematic variation which have a statistically significant impact on daily passenger numbers. These sources include fare, headway, the length of the BRT network, the number of corridors, the average distance between stations, whether there is an integrated network of routes and corridors, modal integration at BRT stations, pre-board fare collection and fare verification, and quality control oversight from an independent agency, as well as the location of BRT.

Hensher et al (2014) did a follow-up empirical study focusing on ridership drivers to deliver greater comparative and analytical power relative to traditional literature reviews, to determine which BRT system factors systematically affect BRT ridership. This study used a sample of 121 BRT systems[2] from different countries, which had started operation between 1974 and 2011.

Table 16.1 contains the descriptive profile of the key variables. In addition to a number of continuous explanatory variables such as fares and frequency, the study also included categorical variables such as whether the BRT system has pre-boarding fare collection, at-level boarding and alighting, segregated busways, modal integration at stations, and signal priority or grade separation at intersections, among others. All categorical variables are coded as dummy variables (yes or no) in the regression model.

The best ridership model from Hensher et al (2014) is presented in Table 16.2. This model explains 87.5% of the variation in daily passengers of the 46 BRT systems without missing data items. All parameter estimates are statistically significantly different from zero at or over the 95% confidence level.

The estimated fare elasticity of −0.366 is close to common estimates of fare elasticity associated with conventional bus and rail systems, and suggests a drop of 36.6% in ridership if the fare is doubled. The elasticity of the length of the headway is −0.243. That is, a 100% increase in frequency (inverse of headway) would increase ridership by nearly 24.3%. The analysis in both cases assumes that others factors remain constant.

Table 16.1: Profile of candidates variables to be included in the model

Variable			
Quantitative variables	*Unit*	*Mean*	*Standard deviation*
Fare	US$2006*	1.04	1.30
Total length of BRT network	Kilometres	27.38	22.90
Number of existing trunk corridors	Number	2.30	2.27
Number of stations	Number	38.33	43.96
Average distance between stations/ population density	Metres/(persons/ square kilometre)	0.69	0.95
Average commercial speed	Kilometres per hour	25.68	12.40
Average peak headway	Minutes	3.35	2.80
Trunk vehicle length	Metre	16.69	3.85

Qualitative variables: whether the BRT system has	*Percentage of 'Yes'*
Segregated busways	78.3
An integrated network of routes and corridors	52.2
Enhanced station environment	71.7
Pre-boarding fare collection and fare verification	47.8
At-level boarding and alighting	54.3
Competitively-bid and transparent contracts and concessions	26.1
Signal priority or grade separation at intersections	47.8
Distinctive marketing identity for system	71.7
Quality control oversight from an independent entity/agency	41.3
High-quality customer information	76.1
Modal integration at stations	23.9

Location of BRT systems	*Percentage of 'Yes'*	*Location of BRT systems*	*Percentage of 'Yes'*
Latin America	*26.0*	India	2.2
Brazil	8.7	Thailand	2.2
Colombia	4.3	*North America*	*17.4*
Ecuador	8.7	USA	15.2
Mexico	4.3	Canada	2.2
Asia	*34.9*	*Europe*	*15.2*
China	23.9	France	10.9
Indonesia	2.2	The Netherlands	4.3
Japan	2.2	*Oceania*	*6.5*
Taiwan	2.2	Australia	6.5

* All fares are converted into a common currency (US$) and period (2006).

Table 16.2: Ridership model (dependent variable: natural logarithm of daily passenger trips)

Explanatory variable	Parameter	t-ratio
Continuous variables		
Natural logarithm of fare (US$2006)	−0.366	−2.11
Natural logarithm of headway (minutes)	−0.243	−2.57
Number of existing trunk corridors	0.223	4.18
Total length of BRT network (kilometres)	0.558	3.40
Average distance between stations/population density (metres/ (persons/square kilometre))	−0.174	−2.08
Years difference relative to 2011	0.167	2.22
Dummy variables		
Existence of an integrated network of routes and corridors (Yes)	0.414	2.22
Modal integration at stations (Yes)	0.453	2.04
Pre-boarding fare collection and fare verification (Yes)	0.628	2.89
Doorways located on median and kerbside (Yes)	2.098	4.03
Quality control oversight from an independent entity/agency (Yes)	0.761	4.45
Latin America (location of BRT)	0.625	2.09
Constant	7.244	11.69
Disturbance term effects		
Country-specific disturbance (u_i)	0.133	
Random error term (ε_{it})	0.156	
Sample size	46	
Adjusted R^2	0.875	

In addition to *fare* and *headway* (or *frequency*), Hensher et al (2014) identified other systematic sources significantly influencing ridership. The *length of the BRT network* is a dimension of the *capacity* of a BRT system, and it has a positive parameter estimate, which suggests that the increased length would lead to an increase in ridership. This result is expected, given that increased capacity would stimulate demand. The *number of existing trunk corridors* represents the catchment coverage of a BRT system, which also has a positive impact on ridership. The *average distance between stations, normalised by population density*, has a negative parameter estimate, which in turn suggests that ridership would be increased by reducing distance between stations. The distance between stations is also influenced by other considerations such as station costs and urban impact; thus it should be expected that the right balance between all these costs should leave users requesting more stations.

A number of categorical variables are found to have a statistically significant influence on ridership, providing further insights into the design and planning of BRT systems. The statistical model suggests that two levels of *integration* are crucial to ridership, namely between systems (*existence of an integrated network of routes and corridors*), and at stations (*modal integration at stations*). A BRT system needs to be integrated with other public transport routes to allow for more convenient transit (for example, door to door service) so as to attract more users to public transport. Integration at stations is also important, such as bicycle parking, taxi stations, and easy transfers between public transport systems. At the planning stage, these two levels of integration have to be carefully considered.

All other things being equal, a BRT system equipped with *pre-boarding fare collection and fare verification* would attract more ridership. Pre-boarding fare collection and fare verification would significantly reduce the boarding time, and hence contribute to the reduction in total journey time and time variability, as well as less crowding at stations and reduced congestion amongst buses. These features would substantially improve user benefits and consequently increase public transport ridership.

If there is *quality control oversight from an independent entity/agency*, the ridership numbers would be higher, holding other influences constant. This finding highlights how important it is to ensure the service quality of BRT. The model also finds that the BRT systems operating in Latin America have significantly higher ridership than BRT in other locations, all other factors remaining unchanged.

Operational performance measures

Performance measures are often used to describe operational characteristics of a service. These characteristics are most relevant if they affect the experience of the users, which in turn define the level of service (LOS) they perceive. If users perceive a low LOS, cars become more attractive for transit users and ridership goes down, causing a deterioration in the system's performance as predicted by the so-called car/public transport vicious circle (Ortúzar and Willumsen 2011). On the other hand, if the LOS is improved, the vicious circle may become virtuous, as more passengers are attracted to the system and the revenue can be increased (which can be invested in new equipment and infrastructure).

To improve the LOS it is critical to know first what attributes users consider relevant. Among other things, users expect the system to be fast, with low waiting times at stations, comfortable, and reliable (for a more detailed discussion about user preferences, see Chapter Twelve). Each of these attributes is strongly related to an operational feature of the system, and, hence, can be quantified to determine the corridor performance:

- Whether a system is fast or not can be answered by observing the average operating speed in the corridor. This speed includes dwell times and should average regular and express services.
- The waiting time at stations is related to bus frequency and headway variability. High frequencies are attractive to users since they imply low waiting times, while high variability increases waiting times (as is discussed in depth in Chapter Seventeen).
- To measure how comfortable the system is, the vehicle load profile compared to the capacity being offered can provide an idea of the passenger density inside the buses. Higher passenger density is associated with low levels of comfort.
- A reliable system exhibits regular bus headway at stations and low variability in travel times. Therefore, the variability of these quantities provides a measure of reliability.

Therefore, understanding the impact of the system's characteristics on these performance indicators is critical when planning and designing a corridor. We are interested in how the corridor type, station type, and land use – to name a few – affect the speed, frequency, vehicle load profile and regularity of the service in the corridor.

Notice that these corridor performance measures are interrelated. For instance, higher operating speeds allow buses to reduce their cycle time, increasing frequency for a given fleet. A higher frequency also increases capacity. Therefore, improving speed reduces travel time, waiting time and discomfort. Also, operating services with low headway variability improves not only reliability and reduces waiting time, but also improves comfort inside the buses, since buses become more homogeneously loaded. The rest of this subsection analyses how the performance measures are affected by different design options or operational decisions.

Operating speed

The speed of the buses is highly related to the travel time that the passengers experience in the corridor. The R in BRT stands for rapid and a primary goal of BRT is to provide lower travel times than conventional bus services.

Figure 2.6 in Chapter Two shows a distribution of operating speeds considering 202 corridors worldwide. The predominant speed in the graph is between 17.6 and 20 kilometres per hour. In fact, 53% of all corridors have an operating speed under 20 kilometres per hour.

As of 2014, the 10 corridors with the highest operating speeds are shown in Figure 16.2.[3] Some of the corridors are not strictly BRT systems, but most of them have signal priority at intersections and other features to increase speeds.

Lindau et al (2013) and Gandhi et al (2013) study the relationship between the operating speed and several BRT operational and design options. While Lindau et al (2013) use a simulation tool for BRT operation developed by EMBARQ (Pereira et al 2010), Gandhi et al (2013) rely on motion equations to conduct a comparative analysis of the impact on the performance of the options studied.

As expected, both studies find that operating speed increases with the spacing between stations. Gandhi et al (2013) show that the benefit of having fewer stops and longer distances travelling at cruise speed overcomes the cost of stopping longer at each stop (since more passengers are boarding and alighting at each one). However, we should notice that longer spacing between consecutive stations implies longer walking distances for passengers accessing the BRT corridor.

Both studies also agree that increasing passenger demand reduces the operating speed, since buses need to stay longer at stations. The boarding and alighting passenger rate and the number of berths can be increased to reduce this time and, thus, improve speed. The best way to improve the rate of passenger boarding and alighting is implementing off-board payment stations so users can board buses through all doors simultaneously.

Figure 16.2: Top 10 in operating speed (km/h)

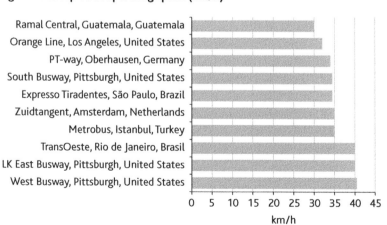

Source: EMBARQ Brazil based on data from www.brtdata.org

In general, closed systems achieve higher operating speeds than open systems, but this does not necessarily mean that the passengers' travel time will be higher in an open system than in a closed one. Closed systems force passengers to transfer when reaching the corridor in a feeder bus, increasing their journey time and inconvenience. In the open systems considered by Gandhi et al (2013), only 30% of feeder bus users entering the corridor must transfer to reach their destination. Thus, passengers in a closed system not only have to transfer more often than in an open system, but their transfer from and to a feeder service is longer; therefore their access time and walking distance are higher. However, in open systems buses are trying to get in and out of the corridor more frequently, disrupting through traffic. Moreover, more buses stop at each station, requiring longer stations and more berths. Therefore, overtaking lanes, which allow buses to avoid other buses stopped at stations and buses waiting to turn, are much more relevant in open systems.

Whether the station is located right next to the junction or midblock has an impact on the operating speed. If the station is just upstream the junction (*nearside* station), the queue at the traffic signal could block access to the station. If the station is just downstream the junction (*far side* station), the queue at the station could block the intersection. If the station is located midblock then blockages are less likely to occur. In fact, stations with several berths are usually located midblock. The best location depends on the features of the corridor, such as the spacing between stations, the length of the blocks, and the presence of transit priority systems at traffic lights, among others. However, in any case, having an overtaking lane at least at the station is always recommended to increase buses' operating speed.

Increasing the length of the cycle at traffic lights reduces bus operating speed since a long cycle length imposes excessive delays on vehicles. Long cycles imply long waits at red lights as well, and the total delay experienced by those waiting for the green light increases proportionally to the square of the length of the red light. That is, if the length of the red light is doubled, total delay is increased by a factor of four. Since delay is related to speed, longer cycles are expected to reduce buses' operating speed. Moreover, buses running on a corridor do not need long green lights since private vehicles do not obstruct their circulation.

While higher operating speeds decrease trip times, they may be problematic since they could affect safety performance. Buses travelling at higher speeds can put pedestrians and bicyclists along the corridor in danger. As discussed in Chapter Nineteen, safety considerations must be central in BRT corridor design. It is quite possible that the fastest possible speed on a corridor (especially of express services overpassing stations where pedestrians usually cross the streets) may be considered unsafe and speed limits should be imposed.

Frequency

The frequency refers to the number of buses per unit of time passing through a given point in the corridor. High frequencies are likely to increase ridership, but they are also more demanding in terms of the infrastructure required (number of berths at the station, number of lanes). If these demands are not met, bus congestion will probably arise at stations or at the corridor.

As explained in Chapter Fifteen, when there are no capacity constraints, the frequency should grow proportionally to the square root of the demand and to the square root of the ratio between the waiting time cost and the operating cost. However, when demand grows, higher frequencies may trigger capacity constraints. In most developing countries, the size of the fleet is chosen to satisfy the peak demand (critical link at peak period), with every bus operating at its maximum capacity. In this case the frequency of the service is determined by the ratio between the demand of the critical link of the corridor and the capacity of the buses (increased by a safety margin to allow for variability across bus loads and unavoidable uncertainties). Notice that the capacity of a bus is a policy decision determined by the maximum average density that the authority expects to observe across all buses at the critical link and peak period. This in turn determines the size of fleet (for more details about fleet size requirements refer to Chapter Eighteen).

The maximum frequency can also be determined by infrastructure constraints. In most high demand corridors, the maximum frequency (and therefore the maximum number of passengers that can be transported) is given by bus stations' capacity to serve buses. If no overtaking facility is provided, a single berth at a station will serve two buses per minute at the most (considering an off-board payment system). This means that if all buses must visit this station, the corridor will serve 120 buses per hour which at 150 passengers per bus yields an optimistic upper bound of 18,000 passengers per hour. All corridors serving a higher demand have solved this problem by adding berths to stations to allow simultaneous boarding and alighting of several buses (the most interesting examples are Istanbul, Turkey, and Guangzhou, China) and installing overtaking facilities that allow express service operation that can skip stations (as nearly 90% of TransMilenio buses do in Bogotá, Colombia). If bus stations are the active capacity constraint limiting the maximum frequency in the corridor, extremely crowded stations will reduce this maximum capacity even more since boarding and alighting will take longer, increasing dwell times. In this case dwell times directly influence maximum frequency since the frequency is given by the time it takes a bus to visit the station. If this time doubles, the maximum frequency drops by half.

Crowding

One measure of the comfort experienced by passengers is the level of crowding (that is, the number of passenger per square metre) on the bus and/or at the stations. In this subsection we focus on the crowding experienced on the bus, but it is worth noting that highly crowded BRT stations is an issue in multiple systems.

The most direct design feature that affects the level of crowding on buses is the capacity of the buses. Obviously, a big bus is able to accommodate a given number of passengers with a lower level of crowding as compared to a smaller bus. However, big buses are more expensive and their operation is usually associated with longer headways, increasing passengers waiting times. As mentioned before, the capacity of a bus is a policy decision determined by the maximum average level of crowding that the authority expects to observe across all buses at the critical link and peak period. The level of passenger density which is acceptable in some places may not be acceptable in others. That is, crowded conditions (and hence comfort levels) are defined differently depending on the city/country. This implies that even for the same bus, the maximum number of passengers that can be on the bus at the same time is not a fixed number since the maximum passenger density on the bus differs among cities/countries. In addition to the bus frequency, this maximum density explains the capacity of the corridor, defined as the number of passengers per hour that can be transported in the most critical section of the corridor in one direction.

Headway variability directly affects the variability of load profiles[4] across vehicles on the same route since a bus preceded by a long headway is more likely to be full than a bus preceded by a short one. Notice that this variability of maximum crowding over several buses increases the average density experienced by users since the crowded bus is experienced by many more passengers than the empty bus. So if bus A and B operate at full capacity and half capacity respectively, then the average load may be 75%: twice as many passengers experience the full bus than the half-full bus. Thus, the average density experienced by a user would be $(100 \cdot 100\% + 50 \cdot 50\%)/150 = 83.3\%$. This phenomenon, known as the *inspection paradox*, is very relevant on services experiencing high headway variability since it distorts passenger experience related to average operating figures.

Figure 16.3 presents the number of passengers transported during peak hours on the top 10 corridors worldwide. The highest peak loads are on corridors in Brazil and Colombia. With a corridor in Rio de Janeiro (Brazil) carrying approximately 65,400 per direction per hour at its peak load. This is a significant increase from the previous top corridor Av. Caracas (Bogotá, Colombia), which carries 48,000 passengers per direction per hour at the peak. One corridor from China in Guangzhou makes the top 10. This is an open BRT corridor using a direct service model.

Via simulation, Lindau et al (2013) found that a single lane per direction, no overtaking BRT corridor can achieve a capacity of

Figure 16.3: Number of passenger transported during peak hour on top 10 corridors (passengers per hour per direction)

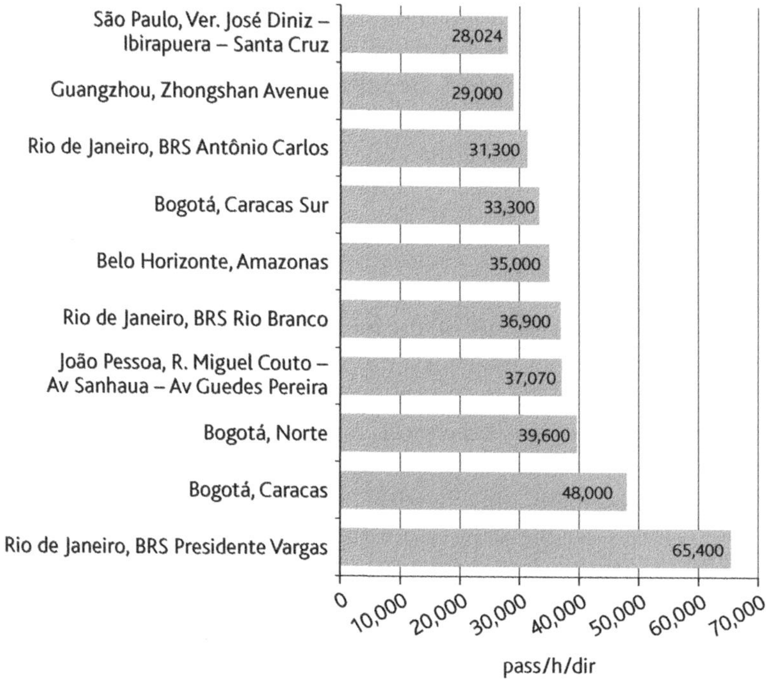

Source: EMBARQ Brazil based on data from www.brtdata.org

15,000 passengers per hour per direction along its critical section, using vehicles with a capacity of 170 passengers.

Overcrowding is not a hypothetical constraint. Many BRT corridors around the world offer overcrowded conditions that impact on passenger comfort and travel times since riders have to wait for multiple vehicles to pass before boarding. As was mentioned before, overcrowding also affects frequency and capacity since dwell times grow. Finally, nothing is more damaging to the image of a successful BRT project than overcrowded buses and stations. Bogotá (Colombia) and Santiago (Chile) have faced a series of passenger protests due to station overcrowding.

Reliability

On their daily travelling experience, passengers expect their waiting time and travel time to exhibit low variability. This feature is related to the reliability of the system's performance. Traffic congestion (especially high when cars and buses share the infrastructure) and the randomness in passenger arrival times at stations are daily contributors to the variability of waiting and travel times. As a result of these unavoidable circumstances, buses tend to bunch, affecting waiting times, bus loads, and reliability. This is an extremely relevant issue on which BRT compares negatively to metros and is discussed in depth in Chapter Seventeen.

Conclusions

Identifying the impact of different features on the performance of a BRT corridor is relevant when planning and designing new BRT systems. In this chapter we discussed the relationship between some of these features and the BRT corridor performance in terms of ridership and operational measures. The goal is to provide useful information to guide decision makers regarding the impact of their infrastructure and operating decisions when designing a BRT corridor.

Although some features are identified as always beneficial for the corridor performance (for example, segregated busways and off-board payment stations), the effect of some others depends on the way in which different features are combined and/or the context in which the corridor is to be deployed (for example, closed or open system, distance between stations, the location of a station relative to its closest junction). Some of these trade-offs were discussed in this chapter.

As a consequence, a good BRT corridor cannot be defined by the presence or absence of a given feature since there is no silver bullet. That is, no feature by itself is enough to explain a good BRT corridor. The interaction between features makes the issue of designing a good BRT corridor highly challenging.

In that sense, efforts in developing a metric to classify BRT corridors according to their performance may be worthwhile. However, this metric should also include the way in which the corridor solves or mitigates mobility problems since this is central to the purpose of developing a BRT corridor. This chapter uses the corridor as a unit of analysis, but the role a corridor plays in the overall network is also central to ensure that corridor performance translates to overall urban accessibility and mobility and so the corridor needs to provide accessibility through its connections to the rest of the network. The topic of a BRT corridor as part of an overall network is discussed in Chapter Fifteen.

Notes

[1] Island stations are those stations located between the two bus lanes serving both directions, while staggered stations are located on each side of the corridor and serve only one direction.

[2] Given that some variables have missing data (see Table 16.1), the final models reported have fewer than 121 observations, with the final sample size determined by the dependent or explanatory variable that has most missing observations.

[3] Three corridors achieve very high average operating speeds (Adelaide and Brisbane, Australia; Cambridge, UK), benefiting from features like shuttle services, fully exclusive lanes, guided buses and traffic signal priorities. These three corridors are not included in Figure 16.2.

[4] The load profile corresponds to the number of passengers on the bus as the bus travels its route.

References

Deng, T. and Nelson, J.D. (2011) 'Recent developments in Bus Rapid Transit: a review of the Literature', *Transport Reviews*, 31(1): 69–96.

Gandhi, S., Tiwari, G. and Fazio, J. (2013) 'Comparative evaluation of alternate Bus Rapid Transit System (BRTS) planning, operation and design options', *Journal of the Eastern Asian Society for Transportation Studies*, 10: 1292–1310.

Hensher, D.A. and Golob, T.F. (2008) 'Bus rapid transit systems – a comparative assessment', *Transportation*, 35(4): 501–518.

Hensher, D.A. and Li, Z. (2012) 'Ridership drivers of bus rapid transit systems', *Transportation*, 39(6): 1209–1221.

Hensher, D.A., Mulley, C. and Li, Z. (2014) 'Drivers of bus rapid transit systems – influences on ridership and service frequency', *Research in Transportation Economics*, 48: 159–165.

Hidalgo, D. and Graftieaux, P. (2008) 'BRT systems in Latin America and Asia: results and difficulties in 11 Cities', *Transportation Research Record: Journal of the Transportation Research Board*, 2072: 77–88.

Hook, W. (2005) *Institutional and Regulatory Options for Bus Rapid Transit in Developing Countries*, New York: Institute for Transportation and Development Policy.

Lindau, L.A., Pereira, B.M., Castilho, R.A., Diógenes, M.C., Herrera, J.C. (2013) 'Exploring the performance limit of a single lane per direction Bus Rapid Transit System (BRT)'. *92nd TRB Annual Meeting Compendium of Papers*. Washington, DC: Transportation Research Board.

Ortúzar, J. de D. and Willumsen, L.G. (2011) *Modelling Transport* (4th edn). Chichester: John Wiley & Sons.

Pereira, B.M., Lindau, L.A. and Castilho, R.A. (2010) 'A importância de simular sistemas Bus Rapid Transit', in *Proceedings of XVI CLATPU (Congreso Latinoamericano de Transporte Público y Urbano)*, Mexico City.

SEVENTEEN

BRRT: adding an R for reliability

Felipe Delgado, Juan Carlos Munoz and Ricardo Giesen

Introduction

To achieve high satisfaction indicators, a public transport system needs to provide a high level of service to its users. A high level of service not only requires that users experience low waiting times, fast travel times, and a minimum comfort standard, but also that this service is reliable – that is, it does not change significantly from day to day. These expectations explain some of the success of heavy rail systems around the world. However, heavy rail has a high infrastructure cost, ranging between US$70 and US$350 million per kilometre (Wright and Hook 2007). This cost makes rail an unattractive alternative for corridors with passenger demand under 20,000 passengers per direction per hour, and makes it very often too expensive for most developing countries. These are precisely the countries where demand for public transport is high.

To overcome these problems, Bus Rapid Transit (BRT) has arisen as an alternative to rail potentially offering the same level of service at a reduced cost. BRT bases most of its high level of service on rapidness. The Rapid in BRT stands for both the speed of the buses and their frequency. High frequencies create shorter trip times and higher capacity. This reduces waiting times and improves comfort, two critical elements of the level of service perceived by users. In the developed world, low frequency services (fewer than six buses per hour) are often operated with schedules. Under this scheme, passengers may experience not just a low wait time, but a reliable service. However, operating a medium or high frequency service on a timetable is not only challenging, but also inefficient since cycle times would be increased by extra travel times needed for buses to reach control points on schedule. Thus, most BRT services commit to an average frequency, not a schedule. Even though segregated lanes help isolate bus operations from general traffic, BRTs operation is still affected by traffic signals and demand fluctuations. It is well known that such perturbations affect the regularity of bus headways, inducing what is called bus bunching, where buses travel together. This phenomenon happens because buses trailing a longer than average headway get more loaded than usual, and therefore run more slowly than the average bus. On the other hand, buses trailing a shorter than average headway are less loaded and run faster than the average bus. Under these circumstances, a passenger waiting at a stop will very often experience a long headway with no service and then see two or three buses of the same line arriving together. Even though rail services also face demand uncertainty, centralised control systems in trains prevent trains from bunching for safety reasons (a train is forbidden from getting too close to the train in front). However, these systems are not very effective in preventing long train headways from happening.

So even if buses are dispatched at regular headways, they will tend to bunch. Keeping regular headways is difficult since it becomes a textbook example of an unstable equilibrium in which any disturbance will affect the desired constant headways. Bus bunching has been widely studied in the literature (Newell and Potts 1964; Potts and Tamlin 1964; Chapman and Michel 1978).

This phenomenon substantially worsens the level of service, generating problems for the users, the operators and the authority. Users wait longer and their waiting time has more variability. Also, most users suffer from crowded buses while only a few enjoy empty ones. For users, bunching negatively affects waiting time, service reliability and comfort, creating an incentive for a shift away from the transit mode. At the same time operators experience high cycle time variability, since some buses run faster than others, increasing the number of buses and drivers needed to keep a smooth operation. Finally, it puts pressure on the authority for more buses due to the negative frequency and comfort as perceived by users.

This reveals that rapidness is not enough to provide a rail-like level of service. BRT must also be reliable. Hence, version 2.0 of this industry must come with an extra 'R': Bus Rapid and Reliable Transit (BRRT). Otherwise it will still be considered a second best alternative to rail by most public transport users.

Informal bus operations, existing in many developing cities, created their own methods to avoid bunching. Since in these systems bus drivers are paid based on the number of passengers boarding their bus, getting too close to the bus ahead reduces the demand captured and therefore their earnings. But decelerating too much risks the bus being overtaken by the one behind, triggering a competition between the drivers. This conflict is the main reason why travelling by bus under informal operations is usually considered a traumatic experience and why these cities have a very high accident rate involving buses. Since this conflict also affects drivers, they have designed some mechanisms to avoid it.

In Santiago, Chile for decades bus operations were assisted by a group of people called '*sapos*'. They stood on key street corners and provided information to bus drivers regarding the headways of the buses ahead. The goal of the '*sapos*' was to help drivers to choose where to position their buses to avoid direct competition with other drivers and keep their buses as full as possible. Since drivers benefited from this information, *sapos* were financed by drivers, not by bus owners. As Johnson et al (2015) show, *sapos* were quite effective in keeping headways more regular. This is common in the developing world. In Bogotá and Lima groups called '*calibradores*' and '*dateros*' respectively play the same role and establish a very similar relationship with bus drivers.

Under formalised bus operations drivers are no longer paid depending on the passengers they carry, therefore they no longer have the financial incentive for regularity. But a formalised system often brings technological devices, such as a global positioning system (GPS), onto every bus. A centralised control system taking advantage of this information can be designed to address this problem.

The most common way to address reliability is to hold buses at certain critical stops, aiming at keeping similar headways ahead and behind every bus. However, as shown by Delgado et al (2012), if holding is implemented in a myopic way (as *sapos* did in Santiago), the system will end up over-holding buses and therefore damaging travel and cycle times. Many other control strategies have been proposed in the literature: station skipping, boarding limits, overpassing-and-expressing, transit signal priority, and so on. Some of them have been implemented in practice, but always based on strictly local conditions (such as skipping a stop or running express if two vehicles have already bunched).

In this chapter we start by presenting a classification of control strategies according to two different criteria. Then we introduce the holding in real time optimisation model (HRT) presented in Delgado et al (2012). In this control strategy every action extensively considers its effects in time and space along the route. Thus, to decide when and for how long a bus will be held, the method estimates the complete status of the system. The data requirements and technology necessary for a complete implementation of the HRT are then discussed. Then, two case studies are presented in order to highlight the benefits of this strategy. The first case study is a simulation experiment where we compare the proposed strategy against two benchmarks. In the second case study, we present the results of a pilot programme run in one service of the Transantiago system in Santiago, Chile. Finally, we summarise the main achievements, for users and operators, of controlling headways with a centralised approach and discuss the main challenges in the implementation of such a strategy in real operations.

Classification of control strategies

In high frequency services, control strategies to avoid bus bunching have been widely studied over the last 50 years. These strategies can be classified according to two dimensions: (i) the location where the control strategy is implemented and (ii) the level of real-time information required to apply these strategies.

In the first dimension, Eberlein (1995) identified three categories: at station control strategies, interstation control strategies and other control mechanisms. The most commonly studied control strategies at stations are holding, station skipping, deadheading and short turning. At-station control strategies are the most widely used because they are easy for bus drivers to understand and implement. In the case of interstation control strategies, overtaking, speed control and transit signal priority (TSP) are the most common. Even though these strategies are more difficult to implement in practice, because they need the direct intervention of the driver, they are more easily accepted by passengers since they seem to be less directly affected. Finally, among the remaining control mechanisms, we find strategies such as vehicle injection at specific points on the route to overcome significant disruptions in bus service operation.

Depending on the level of information, strategies can be classified as locally driven or system wide. Locally driven strategies require less information than system wide strategies – generally just the headway of the preceding bus – and therefore are simpler to implement. Barnett (1974), Turnquist and Blume (1980) and Fu and Yang (2002) developed holding strategies based on local information.

The development and expansion of intelligent transportation systems (ITS) have enabled more advanced control strategies that overcome the limitations of local control strategies. Dessouky et al (1999) specified the basic technological components needed to implement these strategies: automated vehicle location systems (AVL), wireless communication systems, transit operations software and hardware and automatic passenger counter (APC). Some components like GPS have become a standard in most modern transit systems around the world, like the ibus system in London which provides data at 30 second intervals for control and real-time information for passengers with audio-visual announcements. For other components like APC, even though they have been implemented in many systems in the form of radio-frequency identification (RFID) smart cards (such as Oyster in London, Octopus in Hong Kong, Charlie Card in Boston, Bip in Santiago), the information is still not always available in real time for transit operators (see Chapter Fourteen for a more in-depth discussion on the advancement of data collection), and the data collected is still not very precise. Nevertheless, the information to be gathered by an APC device on a specific bus can be estimated roughly based on the headways trailed by the bus and an origin–destination matrix (static or dynamic) for the corridor.

Since 2000 control strategies using real-time information assuming a complete knowledge of the state of the system have been widely studied. Among at-station control strategies we find holding control (Ding and Chien 2001; Eberlein et al 2001; Puong and Wilson 2008; Sun and Hickman 2008; Daganzo 2009; Bartholdi and Eisenstein 2012; Delgado et al 2009, 2012). Real-time information has also allowed deployment of interstation control strategies such as transit signal priority, in which a bus approaching an intersection triggers a process that may affect the length of the phases in its traffic light cycle.

Despite the widely available new technologies, lack of incentives directly targeting bus bunching has prevented bus operators and agencies from implementing more advanced control strategies. Unlike under informal operations, the actors in a formal system very rarely have a clear direct financial incentive and the increased number of actors complicates implementation. Transantiago in Chile is a noteworthy exception to this trend. Chapter Seven discusses contract design, specifically addressing this issue. The next section provides a brief overview of the control strategy proposed by Delgado et al (2012).

Methodology: the HRT control strategy

In the HRT control strategy proposed by Delgado et al (2009, 2012) control actions are taken by a central control which has a complete knowledge (or estimation) of the state of system. The state of the system is defined by the location of all buses in the corridor and the number of passengers on each bus and waiting at all stops. This information when possible is obtained by dynamic data from GPS that is updated at predefined time intervals (every 30 seconds in the case of Transantiago). A complete description of the information flow around the control software is presented in the section describing the Transantiago pilot programme. The central control runs a deterministic rolling horizon mathematical programming model that minimises total waiting times by choosing where and for how long each bus should be held. By optimising over a rolling horizon, the model considers the impact of each decision on every other bus and over a long period of time. This process is repeated at certain time units, refreshing the model with the new information available and the control actions with the new output obtained.

The bus line is modelled as a closed circuit, in which the last stop on the bus route is also the beginning of the same line. Therefore, the outbound and inbound directions of a line are considered as part of a single cyclical line. This is somewhat consistent with the reality observed in bus systems, since very often buses arriving at the last stop of the outbound leg must quite soon depart on the inbound leg of the service. However, the line considers only one terminal. The planning horizon can be set to cover a full cycle for each bus (as in Delgado et al 2012) or to cover a fraction of the total number of stops (Ortiz et al 2013) in order to decrease the size of the optimisation model and make solving times compatible with a real-time application.

The model minimises the total waiting times experienced by users during the planning horizon, which is composed of three terms: (i) W_{first} – at-stop waiting time experienced by users as they wait for the first bus to arrive; (ii) $W_{in\text{-}veh}$ – in-vehicle waiting time for passengers aboard a bus that is being held; and (iii) W_{extra} – extra waiting time for passengers who could not board a bus because it is at capacity. All these terms are weighted according to the relative cost given by users, recognising, for example, that waiting for another bus because the first one was full is probably more annoying than waiting inside the bus while the bus is held at a stop.

The constraints of the model simply represent the correct evolution of the system (travel time between stops, dwell times, passenger demand) during the planning horizon. The model can handle a heterogeneous fleet of vehicles with different capacities without the need for binary variables, making the optimisation process compatible with real-time requirements.

The data required as an input for the optimisation model can be divided into two categories: static and dynamic data. Static data refers to information that will remain constant as the system evolves in time:

- Number of bus stops on the line and the en route distance between them.
- Time needed for a passenger to board and to alight from a bus.
- Origin–destination (OD) demand matrix: average number of trips that board at stop 'i' and alight at stop 'j' during the period of analysis.

Dynamic data is expected to vary on time, and therefore should be updated every time the optimisation model is run:

- Number of buses operating in the line, the location within the route (en route distance from the last bus stop visited) and capacity of each of them.
- Speed between consecutive bus stops.
- Passengers waiting at each bus stop.
- Passengers inside each bus.

The two main sources of uncertainty affecting the performance of this process are passenger arrivals at each stop and bus speeds. Notice that they are not just uncertain, but strongly time dependent. Depending on the operator's data collection and processing technologies, some of the above dynamic data can be converted into static data and vice versa. For example, if buses or stations have APC devices, real-time passenger arrivals can be obtained. Otherwise, the number of passengers arriving at a stop between consecutive buses can be estimated by multiplying a fixed arrival rate (determined from the OD matrix) by the (real-time) headway between those buses. Certainly, dynamic and real-time information about passenger arrivals and bus speeds should improve the performance of the control process. Nevertheless, it has shown a good performance when this advanced information is lacking and therefore must rely on static data.

The optimisation model yields a desired holding time, which could be null, for each bus visiting a stop during the rolling horizon. These holding instructions are sent to drivers, and updated once the output of a new optimisation process becomes available.

Results/case study

In this section we present two different case studies. The first is based on a simulation while the second is a real pilot programme on one line of the Transantiago system. The simulation study is used as a means to compare the HRT strategy and two benchmark strategies:

- *No control.* That is, the spontaneous evolution of the system, where buses are dispatched from the terminal at a previously designed headway, without taking any control action along the route – that is, the only place where holding can take place is at stop 1.
- *Threshold control.* This is based on a myopic rule of headway regularisation between buses, where at every stop a bus is held if the headway with the previous bus is less than the schedule headway or is dispatched immediately otherwise. This strategy mimics local street-controllers such as *sapos* in Santiago.

The simulation scenario allows a deep understanding of the effect that different control strategies have on both users and operators. While the pilot programme strengthens the potential of the tool and shows the challenges that need to be addressed in real-world applications.

Simulation scenario

To compare the performance of the HRT model against the benchmark strategies, we consider a high frequency service (two minute design headway) in which buses may reach capacity at certain stops.

The transit corridor is 10 kilometres long, with 30 bus stops evenly spaced, where the terminal is denoted by stops 1 and 31. Buses have a strict capacity of 100 passengers. Travel times between stops follow a lognormal distribution with mean 0.77 minutes and a coefficient of variation of 0.4. Boarding and alighting time per passenger are set at 2.5 and 1.5 seconds respectively.

For the proposed holding strategy and the two benchmark strategies, we carried out 30 simulation runs, each of them representing two hours of bus operations. We consider a warmup period of 15 minutes before any control strategy is applied to let the system freely evolve. This warmup period is long enough for some bus bunching to appear. This warmup period also allows us to distinguish the effect of the control strategies when facing stationary conditions and a more chaotic situation.

We present four performance indicators to compare these strategies:

- Average waiting times and standard deviations.
- Bus trajectories.
- Bus loads.
- Cycle time distribution.

Average waiting times and standard deviations

Average waiting times are calculated during the time period when the control strategies take place (minutes 15–120). To highlight the effect of the control strategies we will focus on the excess waiting time consisting of the part of the waiting time that is due to headway variability (in contrast to the part that cannot be avoided even if headways were perfectly even). Thus, in W_{first} we subtract half of the average headway (that is, the average waiting time if headways were all identical for a given frequency) from the average waiting times experienced by users until the first bus visits their stop.

Table 17.1 presents the results yielded by the three control strategies. In this table the average value for W_{first}, W_{in-veh}, W_{extra} and the total waiting time with their respective standard deviations are reported. In each case the percentage change with respect to the no control case are added. The table shows that the proposed HRT strategy reduces excess total waiting time due to bunching in around 63% when compared with no control. The table also shows that the proposed strategy presents a much more stable performance, with standard deviations significantly lower than with no control and threshold control. Table 17.1 also indicates that even though the threshold strategy reduces waiting time for the first bus significantly, this comes at the cost of very high holding times, resulting in a worse performance than no control. This situation, as was explained before, is due to the strictly local view of the control mechanism tending to overreact in some cases, as will be shown in the next subsection.

Table 17.1: Objective function value and standard deviation for the three strategies

	No control	Threshold control	HRT control
W_{first}	5349.06	1514.73	972.59
Std. Dev.	476.53	601.48	255.10
% reduction		−71.68	−81.82
W_{extra}	1535.20	2147.45	139.25
Std. Dev.	703.16	3180.44	147.14
% reduction		39.88	−90.93
W_{in-veh}	388.40	8127.44	1582.36
Std. Dev.	63.31	1320.70	115.46
% reduction		1992.53	307.40
Total	7272.66	11789.62	2694.20
Std. Dev.	877.59	4906.92	425.08
% reduction		62.11	−62.95

Bus trajectories

Figure 17.1 shows the bus trajectories for the three different control strategies for a typical simulation run. While in the no control strategy (1a) buses bunch up, which leads to long periods of time where no buses pass a stop, the threshold control strategy (1b) avoids this bunching, allowing buses to maintain more uniform headways. However, in the figure we can also see how some long holdings at a stop affect the next buses visiting it. This causes significant delay for passengers already on the buses, reducing the operational speed and the frequency of the line. The trajectories of the HRT control strategy (1c) produce a more uniform headway pattern between buses than the no control case, and avoid holding buses mainly because the previous bus was also held, as in the threshold case.

Bus loads

Figure 17.2 presents, for each control strategy, the load profile of each bus along the route. The horizontal line at the top of each figure represents the bus capacity. The figure shows that under no control bus loads at any stop present high variability, with many buses riding half empty while others reach capacity (2a). This affects the level of service experienced by most users since a very uncomfortable bus ride is experienced by many more users than a quite comfortable one. Also, discomfort is highly nonlinear, with the occupancy meaning that the impact of an extra passenger in the bus increases with the load of the bus. The HRT and the threshold strategies present a more stable bus load, while in HRT fewer buses reach capacity and at fewer stops along the route. These findings suggest that a real-time holding strategy can improve comfort compared to the other strategies, allowing passengers to travel in less crowded buses and providing a more reliable service.

Cycle time distribution

A common concern regarding controlling by holding buses is increasing cycle times which would delay passengers and reduce the maximum frequency to be offered by a given fleet. Figure 17.3 shows the distribution of cycle times across all buses for the three different control strategies. As can be observed, under the no control strategy cycle time varies substantially, with some buses completing their cycle in 25 minutes while others spend more than 40 minutes (3a). The use of local strategies reduces this variability but at the cost of increasing

Figure 17.1: Trajectories of buses for the three strategies

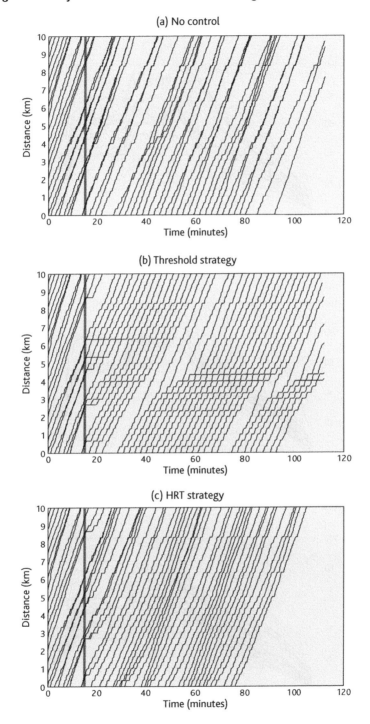

Figure 17.2: Bus load at different stops, for different strategies

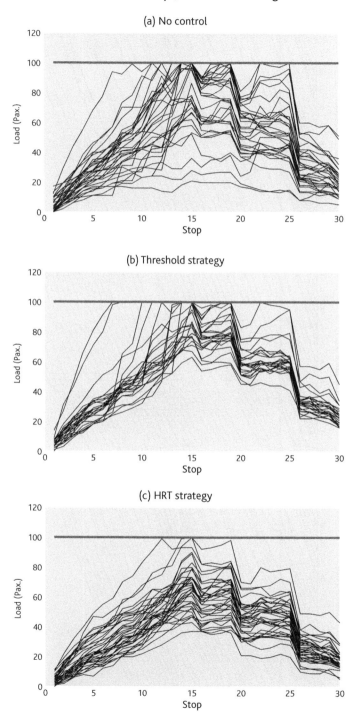

(a) No control

(b) Threshold strategy

(c) HRT strategy

Figure 17.3: Cycle time distribution, for three strategies

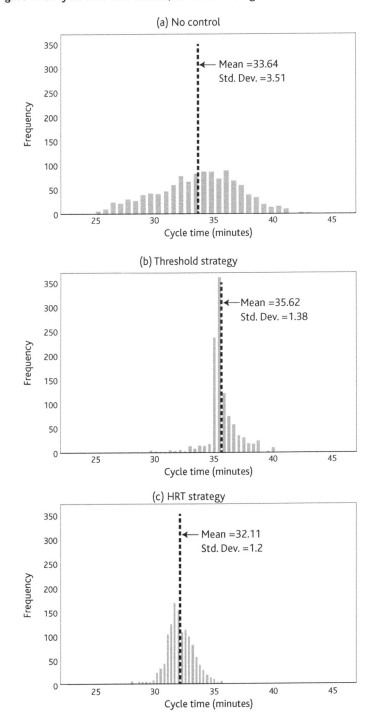

the average cycle time (3b). In contrast, the HRT strategy presents the smallest average cycle time and the lowest variability across the three strategies (3c). The reduction of the cycle time is due to the fact that in the no control case buses reach the terminal under a very chaotic pattern, resulting in holding times there that are longer than the sum of those implemented by HRT along the route. This data suggests that the proposed strategy is also the most beneficial strategy from the operator's perspective since the low variability allows a smoother and more robust operation and planning at the terminals. Furthermore, the reduction in cycle time also decreases the number of buses needed to provide a given frequency. Thus, regarding the concern of holding being detrimental to the capacity of the system, in our simulation experiments we have shown that when implemented myopically this is what happens. However, our simulation results have also shown that if holding is applied with a system-wide perspective, as the HRT strategy does, the capacity can be increased.

In summary, the proposed HRT strategy not only reduces passenger waiting times, it also improves comfort and reliability by allowing buses to travel with more similar loads and at regular intervals. For operators, this real-time holding strategy presents an opportunity to offer a better level of service at a reduced cost and also to reduce cycle time variability, which allows for a better and less costly shift planning process.

Transantiago pilot programme

In order to validate the results obtained by simulation, we executed a pilot study on one of the bus lines in Santiago from February to September 2014. This line runs through the city in a south–north direction (56 kilometres long), has a high frequency (one bus every 3–4 minutes during the morning peak period) and is one of the most used services in the city (48,000 passengers transported on an average weekday and 9,500 in the morning peak period).

The line examined in the experiment suffers severe problems of regularity that are amplified along the route because most of the time buses are not dispatched at regular intervals at the head of the service. Figure 17.4 displays the coefficient of variation (COV) of headways in this service, which is defined as the ratio of the standard deviation to the mean, measured at its initial point against the COV in a location in the middle of the route, approximately 13 kilometres apart. Every dot corresponds to a specific period of time during a specific day (for example, morning peak 6:30–8:30 on 11 March). As can be seen,

Figure 17.4: Correlation between COV of headways at the first and second control point

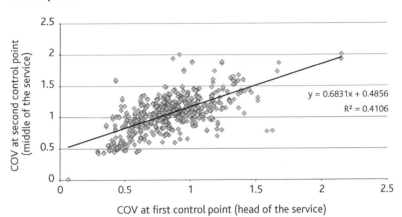

$$y = 0.6831x + 0.4856$$
$$R^2 = 0.4106$$

the COV is very rarely lower than 0.5 (it would be zero if buses were dispatched regularly) and most of the time it is higher than 1 (which is worse than a Poisson process in which buses are dispatched independently of one another without taking account of the previous departure). The figure also shows a clear correlation between the two measurements, indicating that if buses are dispatched regularly, then bus bunching will be less severe along the route and therefore easier to correct.

Figure 17.5 shows a diagram with the information flow implemented in the control software during this project. First the vehicle location data and passenger load data (if available) are sent from the bus to the operator, which sends the information to the server using a web service communication channel. Then the programme processes all this information and feeds the optimisation model, which is solved every minute.

As a way to incentivise high quality of service, Transantiago fines operators if the promised frequency is not achieved or if headway regularity does not reach certain standards. The regularity fines are calculated based on an index which accumulates the number of minutes that bus headways exceed a certain threshold (minutes of incidence). This calculation takes place at three points along the route – the beginning, a middle point and at the end of the route – and is computed for different periods of the day (morning peak, off-peak, and so on) in which the frequency to be offered changes.

The results from the pilot programme show a progressive drop in the rate at which threshold is exceeded from the start in March to September when the pilot programme ended (see Figure 17.6).

Figure 17.5: Schematic representation of information flow

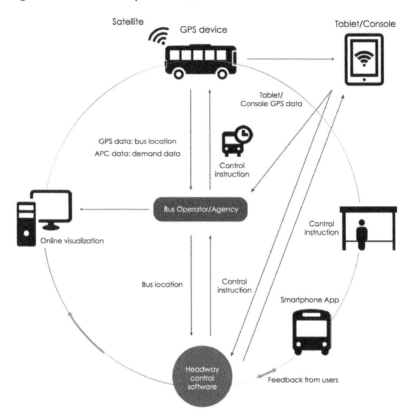

Figure 17.6: Minutes by which the threshold was exceeded during the pilot by month

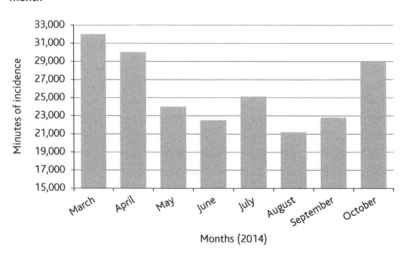

In September there was a 30% reduction compared to March. It is important to point out that when the pilot stopped in October the rate at which threshold is exceeded increased again to similar levels to when the pilot was starting. Even though this result is far from the impacts promised by the simulation study, it is still promising since it was achieved under very problematic circumstances: the dispatches at the head of the service were extremely irregular and only 15% of instructions sent to drivers were fully implemented by them. Getting bus drivers to follow holding instructions is one of the main challenges for successful implementation. Training sessions, focus groups and surveys should be used to understand their motivations and adapt communications to their requirements.

Discussion

To offer a rail-like level of service to passengers, high frequency bus services need real-time control strategies such as those described in this chapter. The performance of the holding in real-time strategy presented here shows that bus headway regularity can be improved significantly in comparison to a laissez-faire operation. For users, headway regularity reduces waiting, improves comfort and increases reliability. Since these three attributes significantly impact on the level of service, it also reduces the incentives for a shift away from the transit mode. For operators, headway regularity improves the adherence of fleet and crew operation to the programmed schedule, while not increasing cycle times. Our field study also suggests that under some circumstances (competition with other services or large incidence of fare evasion due to active capacity constraints), a service can even capture more passengers by improving its headway regularity, thus increasing its revenue.

If the implementation challenges of headway control tools are overcome and they become a standard in the industry, cities may start considering buses as a solution to providing a high level of service for urban mobility. In this scenario buses could become a stronger element of the transportation plans of cities around the globe, particularly those offering high frequency services. Planners and authorities would see BRRT as a very cost-effective option to provide a high level of public transport service and as an attractive and indispensable tool to halt the increasing market share of private cars, with their associated externalities such as congestion, accidents and pollution.

However, several challenges must be addressed for successful implementation of these real-time control strategies. First, bus drivers' behaviour must be considered, since they are the ones applying the control decisions. If not properly incorporated, a small fraction of indifferent or boycotting drivers can be enough to eliminate the promised benefits (Phillips et al 2015). The formalisation of the bus industry usually involves removing drivers' incentives to capture more demand and finish the fight for the passenger. For drivers to get involved in headway regularity efforts, new incentives need to be designed. Also, the success of these control systems relies on several technological components such as periodic GPS pulse, console platforms, communication systems. These elements must be adequately implemented, handled and maintained, and secured against vandalism or theft. Finally, users should be educated about these control mechanisms to avoid a negative perception when being held.

Demand and traffic patterns are nothing but stable in transit operations as the mathematical model in Delgado et al (2012) assumes. The demand and the speed can change significantly in short periods of time. Sanchez-Martinez et al (2014a, 2014b) tackle this issue based on the methodology of Delgado et al (2012). It is sometimes argued that these control mechanisms should be implemented only if buses operate on segregated corridors. Even though these corridors may have optimal facilities for holding buses, the benefits of these control strategies grow when the uncertainty of operating conditions grow.

Another concern regards who should be in charge of implementing these control mechanisms when several lines overlap. Hernández et al (2015) show that the performance improves if a centralised system controls all buses since it can keep headways between buses from different lines more regular. They also find that a decentralised control system (as in Santiago, Chile) performs well as long as bus operators do not know the position of their competitors' buses. Otherwise, if their revenues are linked to the number of passengers they transport, they may use the control strategy to strategically position their buses to capture more demand. This harms the level of service instead of improving it. If the transit authority is in charge of controlling the buses (as in the case of TransMilenio, Bogotá), incentive mechanisms must be designed to ensure that operators and drivers obey instructions. This is another example of how these new formalised bus systems require new institutional structures, as discussed in Chapter Three, and well designed contracts, as discussed in Chapter Seven.

References

Barnett, A. (1974) 'On controlling randomness in transit operations', *Transportation Science*, 8(2): 101–116.

Bartholdi, J.J. and Eisenstein, D.D. (2012) 'A self-coordinating bus route to resist bus bunching', *Transportation Research Part B*, 46(4): 481–491.

Chapman, R.A. and Michel, J.F. (1978) 'Modelling the tendency of buses to form pairs', *Transportation Science*, 12(2): 165–175.

Daganzo, C.F. (2009) 'A headway-based approach to eliminate bus bunching: systematic analysis and comparisons', *Transportation Research Part B*, 43(10): 913–921.

Delgado, F., Munoz, J.C., Giesen, R. and Cipriano, A. (2009) 'Real-time control of buses in a transit corridor based on vehicle holding and boarding limits', *Transportation Research Record: Journal of the Transportation Research Record*, 2090: 59–67.

Delgado, F., Munoz, J.C. and Giesen, R. (2012) 'How much can holding and/or limiting boarding improve transit performance?', *Transportation Research Part B*, 46(9): 1202–1217.

Dessouky, M., Hall, R., Nowroozi, A. and Mourikas, K. (1999) 'Bus dispatching at timed transfer transit stations using bus tracking technology', *Transportation Research Part C*, 7(4): 187–208.

Ding, Y. and Chien, S. (2001) 'Improving transit service quality and headway regularity with real-time control', *Transportation Research Record: Journal of the Transportation Research Record*, 1760: 161–170.

Eberlein, X.J. (1995) *Real-Time Control Strategies in Transit Operations: Models and Analysis*, Cambridge, MA: MIT Press.

Eberlein, X.J., Wilson, N.H.M. and Bernstein, D. (2001) 'The holding problem with real-time information available', *Transportation Science*, 35(1): 1–18.

Fu, L. and Yang, X. (2002) 'Design and implementation of bus-holding control strategies with real-time information', *Transportation Research Record: Journal of the Transportation Research Record*, 1791: 6–12.

Hernández, D., Muñoz, J.C., Giesen, R. and Delgado, F. (2015) 'Analysis of real-time control strategies in a corridor with multiple bus services', *Transportation Research Part B: Methodological*, 78: 83–105.

Johnson, R.J., Reiley, D.H. and Muñoz, J.C. (2015) '"The war for the fare": how driver compensation affects bus system performance', *Economic Inquiry*, 53(3): 1401–1419.

Newell, G F. and Potts, R.B. (1964) 'Maintaining a bus schedule'. *Proceedings of 2nd Australian Road Research Board (ARRB) Conference*, 2(1): 388–393, Melbourne: ARRB.

Ortiz, F., Giesen, R., Muñoz, J.C., Lindau, L. and Delgado, F. (2013) 'Analysis and evaluation of different headway control strategies for BRT: simulated with real data', 13th World Conference on Transport Research (WCTR), Rio de Janeiro.

Phillips, W., del Rio, A., Muñoz, J.C., Delgado, F. and Giesen, R. (2015) 'Quantifying the effects of driver non-compliance and communication system failure in the performance of real-time bus control strategies', *Transportation Research Part A*, 78: 463–472.

Potts, R.B. and Tamlin, E.A. (1964) 'Pairing of buses'. *Proceedings of 2nd Australian Road Research Board (ARRB) Conference*, 2(2): 3–9, Melbourne: ARRB.

Puong, A. and Wilson, N.H.M. (2008) 'A train holding model for urban rail transit systems', in M. Hickman, P. Mirchandani and S. Voß (eds), *Computer-Aided Systems in Public Transport*, Berlin and Heidelberg: Springer, 319–337.

Sanchez-Martinez, G.E., Koutsopoulos, H.N. and Wilson N.H.M. (2014a) 'Real-time holding control for high-frequency transit with dynamics', submitted to *Transportation Research Part B*.

Sanchez-Martinez, G.E., Koutsopoulos, H.N. and Wilson, N.H.M. (2014b) 'Real-time holding control for high-frequency transit under event-driven dynamics', submitted to *Transportation Research Record: Journal of the Transportation Research Record*.

Sun, A. and Hickman, M. (2008) 'The holding problem at multiple holding stations',In M. Hickman, P. Mirchandani and S. Voß (eds), *Computer-Aided Systems in Public Transport*, Berlin and Heidelberg: Springer, 339–359.

Turnquist, M. and Blume, S. (1980) 'Evaluating potential effectiveness of headway control strategies for transit systems', *Transportation Research Record*, 746: 25–29.

Wright, L. and Hook, W. (2007) *Bus Rapid Transit Planning Guide*, Technical Report, Institution for Transportation and Development Policy.

EIGHTEEN

Managing drivers and vehicles for cost-effective operations in regulated transit systems

Omar Ibarra, Ricardo Giesen and Juan Carlos Munoz

Introduction

In deregulated transport systems, operation is often based on multiple owners of a few vehicles each providing transport services. This usually leads to on-street competition between operators to attract demand, yielding severe traffic congestion and unsafe conditions for both passengers and drivers. Through the formalisation of the industry into a few firms operating larger fleets that are required to satisfy minimum standards, the system drastically reduces these externalities. In this process, to stay in the market, firms must manage their fleet and drivers efficiently and with fewer degrees of freedom than when a firm handled just a few buses. Public transport formalisation leads to policies to meet specific levels of service, vehicle regulations and contractual conditions for workers that should be satisfied by operators, whether they are public or private agencies. Thus, formalisation usually increases operational costs (see Chapters Three and Four), increasing the fare or the subsidies needed to finance the system. However, transit formalisation also opens the door to the implementation of operational research techniques in order to optimise planning and operation of transport systems to achieve a more cost-effective network. These techniques can also be applied in already formal public transport systems.

Under large operations, attractive and flexible solutions for these planning and operational problems are much less apparent, and their impact can be huge in contrast with decisions based on very simple rigid rules. Also, these big firms reach the economic scale at which they can invest in management support tools that could improve their performance. Cost savings usually amount to around 10% of operational costs while providing similar or better service to users.

The main aspects of transit operations that operational research tools can address are the vehicles and drivers. Their associated decisions can be structured into strategic (long term), tactic (medium term) and operational (short term) planning stages (see Ibarra-Rojas et al 2015). The cost involved in providing a BRT (Bus Rapid Transit) service can be structured similarly – that is, by respectively structuring (i) the infrastructure of the streets that the bus takes and the bus stations, (ii) buses and technology systems and (iii) daily bus operations and maintenance and drivers' wages.

Formalisation brings several operating constraints with which bus firms must comply. In some cases, the government agencies impose upper and/or lower bounds on the frequencies that must be offered in every time period, including at night. In others, the agency not only states the frequency, but also the specific dispatch time of each bus on each route. Additionally, formalised firms must adhere to various working conditions. For example, small firms under informal operations usually have their drivers work very long shifts. Formalisation limits not just the length of each shift, but also the maximum continuous time a driver can work, and the minimum rest time that each driver must take. All these considerations affect the efficiency of a firm when compared with informal operations. For instance, in Santiago, Chile, the average number of drivers per bus grew from around two system-wide to 2.7–3.2, depending on the firm, once the system was formalised. We must highlight that vehicle utilisation may increase under the formalised system by defining a proper planning stage where vehicles'/drivers' idle time is a common measure for optimisation.

An element that directly affects the performance of a system is its flexibility. For example, the number of drivers needed drops when some labour constraints are relaxed. Also if vehicles operate different routes, the number of vehicles needed to satisfy passenger demand would be lower than if every vehicle was to stay on a single route. Operational flexibility provides an opportunity for an improved level of service and cost savings, but taking full advantage of it requires sophisticated tools for good solutions.

In this chapter we present some decision support tools to improve the level of service to users and the operational effectiveness of the firms under different transit network conditions. We present two specific optimisation problems to minimise the fleet size and drivers' wages, respectively. These problems illustrate the potential benefits that may be obtained by implementing operational research techniques in regulated transit systems under flexible characteristics.

Optimisation affecting vehicles

At the strategic level, we must determine the type of bus (for example, capacity) to be used in each route and the fleet size, along with the public transport network. At the tactical level, the public transport network and the vehicle fleet is given and we must assign a frequency to each route. Finally, at the operational level we must schedule each bus to a sequence of trips.

Vehicles at strategic and tactical level

Transit formalisation and BRT play an important role in selecting the type of vehicle to be used since usually it must satisfy several regulations. As Hardy and Stevens (2001) explains, the vehicle chosen must not exceed pollutant and noise emissions standards, must match a certain size and door characteristics (steps, floor-level doors, width, quantity, location and so on), incorporate information technologies (AVL systems, traffic signal systems, in-vehicle fare validation and so on) and satisfy technical characteristics (acceleration, braking, suspension, air conditioning and so on) oriented to the specific characteristics of each route (pavement, slope of the land, weather and so on).

The network structure determines the alternative routes offered to each traveller (see Chapter Fifteen) and their characteristics (vehicle type, frequency, travel time, and so on). For example, trunk and feeder networks usually require a heterogeneous fleet, in which smaller vehicles are assigned to feeder routes covering the outskirts with different road characteristics (commonly operating in mixed traffic) while larger vehicles operate in trunk routes in high demand corridors (possibly exclusive or segregated). Direct trip-based systems could operate with large vehicles to cover certain concentrated origin–destination demand on trunk corridors, but this may lead to lower fleet size elsewhere in the corridor at the expense of increasing the average waiting times. Vehicles with fewer seats may be acceptable for short trips (for example, in feeder lines), but a larger number of seats may be recommended for trunk lines, where trips can be longer.

As it is highlighted by Wright and Hook (2010), another important element to determine the characteristics of the vehicles is the network infrastructure, especially the characteristics of bus stops or stations. If vehicles are to operate in mixed traffic as well as in exclusive corridors (open systems as described in Chapter Fifteen), doors on both sides of the vehicle may be needed. Station design may also require steps or floor-level doors, a certain door width and location and other features suited to the characteristics of the infrastructure. Finally, the number of seats in the vehicle plays a major role in the comfort experienced by passengers and the capacity of each bus.

Given a certain seat configuration, the capacity of a bus is determined by the maximum passenger density that the network design bears among standees. Notice that this is a policy decision. The same bus has a higher capacity in a developing city than in a developed city because in the former higher densities are tolerated by the authorities. We should realise that a system designed at capacity will very often violate it since the occupation varies significantly across buses and across different areas inside the bus. This is especially relevant under frequency-based operation since in these cases bus bunching becomes very hard to avoid (see Chapter Seventeen). Under these circumstances buses running behind a long headway will be overloaded, while buses running behind a short one will be underloaded. In this case the average load across buses is a biased estimation of the average comfort experienced by passengers. Consider a corridor where half of the buses reach 60% of their capacity in the critical segment of the route while the other half reaches 120%. The average load of 90% across buses not only hides that 50% of the buses are significantly overloaded, but also that if we ask the passengers, the average load they experience is really (60*60% + 120*120%)/180 = 100% since more passengers are experiencing the overcrowded buses than the emptier ones. In this example, two out of three passengers are experiencing overcrowded conditions.

The vehicle's capacity (passengers/bus) and the frequency of a route determine the capacity of the route to serve its demand. The authority must find the right balance between prioritising operational costs (leading to high capacity buses) and user costs (leading to high frequency service). In most high demand corridors, the active bottleneck affecting the maximum combined frequency offered by bus services is found in the stations. To overcome this, critical stations should be built with several bus bays allowing simultaneous boarding and alighting in multiple buses. A discussion on the trade-offs involved in determining the vehicle capacity for a service is presented in Chapter Nine of Ceder (2007).

Once the vehicle type is defined, the frequency of a route for different periods must be determined. In peak periods, the frequency is often set as the minimum needed to satisfy the demand, that is:

$$f = \frac{MaxDemand}{CapVeh \cdot LoadFactor} \qquad (1)$$

where *MaxDemand* is the demand on the critical segment of the route (passengers per hour), while *CapVeh* corresponds to the capacity of the bus and *LoadFactor* is a correction factor representing the fraction of the capacity of the average bus to be considered as full (for example, 90%). During off-peak periods the frequency should be given by the following expression (Welding 1964; Newell 1971):

$$f = \sqrt{\frac{kc_w q}{c_o}} \qquad (2)$$

where c_w is the value of wait time, q is the arrival rate of passengers to the service (across all stops), c_o is the operating cost per route cycle and k is a headway constant defined so that $k = \frac{1}{2}$ if headways are perfectly regular and grows as they become increasingly irregular. This *square root* relation is quite convenient not just because of its simplicity, but also because the social cost (involving users' waiting time and operational costs) is quite insensitive to changes in the optimal frequency (or in the parameters in the square root expression). For example, it can be shown that if instead of operating a route at its optimal frequency, a 20% higher or lower frequency is chosen, the total social costs will only grow by 1.6%. However, this aggregated analysis may hide that those benefiting and those suffering from a higher (or lower) frequency are different groups: users versus operators.

As can be inferred from this argument, a relevant decision is to determine periods in which a regular service will be provided. Travel pattern data is usually used to determine time intervals during which trip volumes and their space and time characteristics are relatively homogeneous. The fleet size, n, needed to satisfy the demand in a corridor is governed by the peak demand period since then the frequency and the cycle time, t_c, are the highest, and given by $n = ft_c$. This fleet should be increased around 5% as spare fleet is needed to address unexpected events and scheduled maintenance activities.

These calculations assume that each corridor is served by a single route visiting all stops. However, a more cost-effective operation with higher quality of service could be achieved if a combination of express, short turning and limited stop routes were provided. These routes reduce the travel times for passengers, increase bus productivity, concentrate operation where it is most needed and avoids critical stations if possible (see Chapter Fifteen).

Finally, bus schedules for each route based on the frequency for each period must be determined. This involves assigning departure times from each terminal for each route. As a general rule, if demand is relatively uniform over a given period the departures are scheduled to maintain equal headways. If demand varies significantly, on the other hand, departure times can be adjusted so that passenger load levels are equalised over the most heavily used segment of a route, yielding irregular headway timetables. The problem is considerably more complex if it is desired to synchronise transfers between different routes at transfer stations.

For low frequency routes (for example, fewer than six buses per hour) and low variance travel times (as is the case with BRT) schedules can be published for users to plan their arrival times at stops to minimise waiting. With high frequency routes, schedules are rarely published as the inevitable variations in actual service relative to the scheduled service intervals will be relatively large, rendering detailed timetables of little practical use to riders. They may still be used by the firm as a general guide for its operational programme.

The formulas in this section assume that transit service is provided regularly and where the right bus type is always ready to start a new run. However, at the daily operational level, timetables must be turned into a sequence of trips assigned to each bus to ensure that the available fleet is large enough to operate the programme. Timetables may also be adapted to better match the vehicle arrival sequence to the terminals. In the next section, we explain how a schedule for each vehicle can be defined for a given timetable, whether based on regular or irregular headways.

Vehicles at the operational level

At the operational level, in which it is assumed that departure times and cycle times for a set of trips previously planned are given, a critical problem is the vehicle scheduling problem (VS), which *assigns a vehicle to each planned trip such that all trips can be carried out as scheduled and costs based on vehicle usage are minimised.*

Important elements to be taken into account to define the vehicle scheduling problem are listed below (Daduna and Paixão 1995):

- Number of depots from which vehicles may depart. If there are multiple depots, it is important to define if a vehicle must return to the same depot from which it departed or if depots can share vehicles.
- Fleet size per vehicle type (small, normal, articulated and so on) and their operating costs.

- Resting points, where vehicles may remain until the start time of the next trip. A depot may be used as a resting point, but a resting point does not necessarily require infrastructure.
- Operating constraints such as the following: (i) inter-routing – that is, a vehicle could perform a trip of a route *r1*, and then perform another trip of a different route *r2*; (ii) deadheading – that is, a bus could travel empty along a route, increasing vehicle availability for the high demand direction.

The more flexible the system is, the greater the potential improvements. In addition, different timetables may be used to reduce operating costs through vehicle scheduling decisions. To illustrate the benefits of flexible timetables and different characteristics of the VS, 10 hypothetical cases (C1–C10) were randomly generated, considering the following assumptions: a subnetwork of five routes, a single depot, homogeneous fleets, three planning periods of 120 minutes each, cycle times between 60 and 120 minutes and an even headway between 2.5 and 6 minutes. The VS may include inter-routing operation and flexible departure of the first trip, which may be between the beginning of the planning period and the beginning of the planning period plus the headway. The problem is modelled using a network flow formulation as in Ibarra-Rojas (2013) and solved using the optimisation solver of CPLEX 12.5.[1] Numerical results are shown in Table 18.1, where 'VS/–/' represents the vehicle scheduling without flexible departure times and no inter-routing.

We can notice the significant reductions in the fleet size needed when inter-routing and flexibility of first trip are allowed – that is, the more flexible case. Individually, flexible departure of the first trip and inter-routing yield the lowest and larger improvements, respectively. Although flexible departure of the first trip seems to lead to the smallest benefits, larger improvements could be obtained by considering flexible departure times for all trips (deviating within a threshold from the timetable) and not only for the first one. We

Table 18.1: Fleet size obtained for 10 cases C1–C10 using different levels of flexibility for vehicle scheduling decisions

Characteristics of the VS problem	Fleet size									
	C1	C2	C3	C4	C5	C6	C7	C8	C9	C10
VS/–/	136	162	124	137	147	136	132	156	143	135
VS/first trip/	134	161	123	137	145	134	129	156	141	134
VS/inter-routing/	119	152	104	112	130	118	108	132	133	133
VS/first trip/inter-routing/	115	151	103	111	129	118	107	131	128	132

study the latter case later. Implementing inter-routing may lead to confusion for drivers assigned to different routes and a more complex operation of the transit system; thus, scheduling problems should probably balance cost reduction and system complexity. In general, flexible timetables can be used if passengers are not too sensitive to delays and inter-routing can be implemented for similar bus routes. To avoid confusion, information for passengers and drivers should be provided when needed. As is argued in Chapter Thirteen, information is a powerful tool to avoid uncertainties during the operation of the transit system. Another very important operational problem involving buses is headway control to prevent bus bunching. This problem is thoroughly addressed in Chapter Seventeen.

A case study: vehicle scheduling with flexible timetables

In this section, we present a problem in which the flexibility of the timetable can be exploited to improve passengers' experience. Consider a system operating low frequency routes in which vehicle travel times show little variability. In this case, not only can bus operations be scheduled through timetables, but they can also be coordinated to avoid transferring passengers experiencing long waits. This problem is particularly appealing for a night service where not only are the above conditions present, but also waiting times are the worst within the day. Of course, the more buses are added to the schedule, the less waiting there will be. In this case we want to know how many passengers could benefit from introducing an extra vehicle to the fleet. To achieve this, we develop an integrated approach for timetabling and vehicle scheduling problems. From the passenger perspective, there is a requirement for a fairly regular service (using minimum and maximum headway times) and low waiting time for transfers (we assume mid/low frequencies). However, operators are most interested in reducing the operating costs of vehicle usage. We do not present here the mathematical formulation of how this trade-off can be addressed (which can be seen in Ibarra-Rojas et al 2014). Instead, we tackle the key elements involved in the optimisation problem.

The transit network is represented by a set of routes and a set of stops where user transfers occur. To consider the behaviour of the system, the operational day is divided into shorter planning periods (morning peak/non-peak, afternoon peak/non-peak, night and so on) with a constant demand rate, a given number of trips to be planned and deterministic travel times from the first stop to each transfer stop. We assume that the number of passengers transferring from one route to another is proportional to the load of the bus in the former route. The flexibility of the system is given by a feasible departure time interval, D'_p, for each trip, p, of route r. Thus, instead of defining the departure of the p-th trip of route r as $(p - 1)h^r$ (h^r being the even headway), the departure time for the p-th trip must lie within the following interval:

$$D'_p = [(p - 1)h^r - \Delta^r, (p - 1)h^r + \Delta^r] \qquad (3)$$

Parameter Δ^r is a fraction of the average headway of route r, representing a small deviation from the regular service. Thus, dispatch times D'_p define an almost regular timetable that has taken advantage of available flexibility to reduce operating costs (see Ibarra-Rojas 2013).

On the basis of the above considerations, our timetabling–vehicle scheduling problem (called TTVS) *determines the departure time for all trips and assigns them to vehicles such that the number of well-timed passenger transfers is maximised and the fleet size is minimised.* In contrast to sequential approaches, our integrated TTVS problem jointly defines the timetable and vehicle schedule, considering the degrees of freedom of both problems; thus, it is possible to study the compromise between passenger transfers and the fleet size. The TTVS problem can be described as the bi-objective optimisation problem described in equation (4), where X, $\mathbf{X}$, $F_{TT}(X)$ and $F_{VS}(X)$ refer to the solution, the solution space, objective function of timetabling and objective function of vehicle scheduling, respectively:

$$[TTVS]: \{[\max F_{TT}(X), \min F_{VS}(X)]: X \in \mathbf{X}\} \qquad (4)$$

In this multiobjective optimisation problem we are not looking for an optimal solution. Instead, we search for a set of Pareto optimal solutions, called the Pareto front, which is the set of solutions where it is impossible to find a solution X' that improves one objective function without worsening another (see Ehrgott 2005).

We test our approach in randomly generated cases, considering six different network sizes (with different flexibility levels), 10 cases for each type, 60 cases in total. The instance sizes are defined in terms of the following elements: the number of routes, R; the set of synchronisation stops, S, where the number of pairs of lines to be synchronised at each stop is randomly generated between 1 and 7; and an interval, $[a,b]$, where the flexibility parameter, Δ^r, is randomly generated. The specific data involved in each of these cases can be found in Ibarra-Rojas et al (2014).

To obtain the Pareto front, we implement an ε-constraint algorithm (see Ehrgott and Ruzika 2008). Numerical results show that 40% of the cases have only one optimal solution. Therefore, we can guarantee that the maximum number of well-timed passenger transfers may be achieved with the minimal fleet size (ideal solution); both objectives can be achieved simultaneously. However, we identify cases where the compromise between well-timed passenger transfers and cost saving becomes more evident. Figure 18.1 shows the Pareto front for two representative cases in which we can see the improvement in the level of service from having an extra vehicle.

This trade-off between different goals is quite common in public transport design and operation. In this case we need to identify a balance between operational costs and user costs. As mentioned earlier, this conflict also happens when the frequency and the bus capacity for a route must be determined. Similarly, defining the distance between consecutive stops along a route triggers a conflict between the local

Figure 18.1: Pareto front: (a) instance 2 of type T2, (b) instance 1 of type T6

(a) Pareto front of instance 2 of type T2

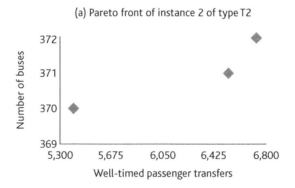

(b) Pareto front of instance 1 of type T6

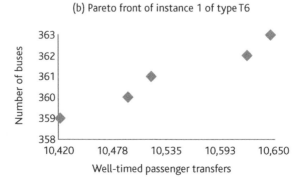

Source: Ibarra-Rojas et al (2014)

riders, who would rather have them close to reduce their walking time, and those already on the bus, who would prefer to have long spaces between stops in order to speed up their bus.

The regulatory authority plays a crucial role in solving these conflicts since passengers' satisfaction and operators' costs are expected to be balanced. This balance is not as straightforward as determining a value of time with which all these trade-offs could be solved. The authority should also determine the geographic and temporal boundaries of the service provided by the system and define minimum standards that the service must comply with (for example, minimum frequency or service density). Public transport agencies always have a budget (usually coming from fares and subsidies) to fund the service they provide. Too small a budget can be extremely damaging to the level of service provided, orienting most decisions towards cost-effective service. In this case the authority may be forced to operate fewer routes with low frequencies and large buses, forcing passengers to walk and wait longer than would be recommended if the tight budget constraint was relaxed.

Moreover, the public transport authority should play a key role in achieving a proper coordination of different agencies and companies participating in the system. We highlight that these improvements can only be achieved in regulated transit systems. Otherwise the competition to gain more demand and/or the lack of incentives to make the required efforts would be a handicap to coordinate routes belonging to different operators.

Vehicle scheduling problems, such as the one shown in this subsection, are needed to manage the vehicles and perform the planned trips. In this case travel times and demand rates were assumed constant. However, in many cases a more realistic approach should consider time varying conditions. Particularly during peak periods, conditions may change significantly within 15 minutes, and it is during these periods that the system is more stressed and fleet size is determined. The main drawback of most approaches to address vehicle scheduling is the assumption of a deterministic context – for example, cycle times and passenger demand. Even though BRT operations face less variability than mixed traffic routes due to their segregated operation and massive demand rates, this is still a strong assumption that should be considered in scheduling problems.

A very important problem which has captured little attention in the literature is how the system adapts to unforeseen uncertainties. Public transport operations continuously face different types of uncertainties that are impossible to foresee when the vehicle schedules are planned.

Drivers may not go to work, vehicles may be unavailable for operation, major network disruptions can occur, the demand volume or distribution may change significantly, and so on. In these cases, the vehicle scheduling decisions may need to be adapted dynamically once these uncertainties materialise. In this case, a new schedule – and thus workloads for drivers – would be known just a few hours before the daily operation, which also poses a challenge to the firm's management.

Managing drivers

Most of the decisions regarding drivers are handled at the operational level by two optimisation problems: (i) the driver scheduling problem (DSP) in which a set of daily tasks is assigned to each individual yet not personalised driver and (ii) the driver rostering problem (DRP) in which daily work assignments are assigned to specific drivers. However, characteristics of contracts, such as the limit on working time, homogeneity of workloads and incentives considered, have a great impact on decisions taken at the operational level. Below we present the decisions and considerations involved in these DSP and DRP. Then we present an optimisation approach to define flexible workloads considering the characteristics of contracts for drivers.

Driver scheduling and driver rostering

The daily workload assigned to a driver is called duty and the driver scheduling problem *determines the duties that cover a set of trips assigned to a vehicle with the objective of minimising operational costs related to drivers.* Due to contractual regulations and agency preferences, DSP considers several constraints, such as limits on the length of daily duty, meal breaks for drivers, limit on continuous working without a break, break duration, limit on idle time, and start and end times for duties. Then, it could be difficult to find high-quality – or even feasible – solutions; thus, a common objective is the minimisation of a weighted objective function which consist of driver wages and penalties for constraints violation. A common objective is the minimisation of a weighted objective function of driver wages and penalties for violation of regulations.

The set covering is a classical optimisation problem and the DSD can be modelled using the formulation of set covering (see Portugal et al 2009). In such a formulation, the set D of all possible duties for a general driver is defined (each duty having a specific start and end time); then a binary decision variable, taking the value of one if a duty, d, is included in the solution and 0 otherwise, is considered. The single family constraint of the problem is trip coverage, while the goal is to minimise driver wages and penalties for violation of regulations. Thus, the mathematical formulation can be represented as follows:

$$\{\min \textstyle\sum_{d \in D} c_d \cdot x_d ; \textstyle\sum_{d \in D(p)} x_d \geq 1 \text{ for all trip } p\} \qquad (5)$$

Set $D(p)$ represents all duties, including trip p, and c_d represents the cost of duty d (including eventual overtime). The previous formulations are commonly solved using a column generation approach (see a review in Desaulniers and Hickman 2007). The output of this process is the set of duties to be worked by generic drivers and the set of trips each of them will work.

Once the daily duties are defined, it is necessary to assign drivers to longer working periods. To achieve this, the driver rostering optimisation problem determines the assignment of drivers to the daily duties yielded by the DSP solution. This assignment, called roster, must comply with labour rules and the company's regulations. These regulations are not only important for the workers themselves, but also for the employer, since worker satisfaction lowers the incidence of illness, accidents and absenteeism. The constraints that are often considered are: days off for drivers, specific days off such as holy days and weekends, limited consecutive work days for drivers, not assigning a late night duty just before an early morning duty, limits for working hours within periods of specific length, equity in the drivers' rosters and rotation for each driver – that is, a driver should not always be assigned to the same period of the day. The mathematical formulation and solution approaches are similar to the DSP. However, the number of constraints may be greater due to different planning periods and contractual regulations.

This sequential approach usually assumes a deterministic system. However, uncertainties are present at all operational levels (for example, driver absenteeism, passenger demand, roundtrip durations, and vehicle failure) and should be considered in these decisions (for example, hiring extra drivers, called *extraboard*, may allow operation continuity in case of absenteeism).

As mentioned earlier, duty driver assignments are short term decisions. However, many transit agencies redefine their driver contracts periodically (for example, once every three months) and the contract structure influences the behaviour of drivers (see Chapter Seven) and also the operational decisions to be taken by the DSP and

DRP. Thus, in some sense the level of flexibility to be considered in driver contracts could be considered a tactical or even strategic decision. For example, labour contracts usually consider daily duties of identical length and additional costs are added for drivers working extra hours, but according to Miranda et al (2008), not every driver has the same preference regarding work shifts. While some drivers prefer standard duty of identical length every day, others prefer workload variability in which duties may change in duration from day to day. This heterogeneity of duty length benefits the firm since the workforce can be adapted better to peak/off-peak driver requirements. Montalva et al (2012) show that the benefits of this heterogeneity can be shared with all drivers, potentially improving conditions for everyone, including the firm. The next section presents the opportunities for the firm during the DSP and DRP of considering duties of different duration.

A case study: the potential of a flexible driver shift design

According to Muñoz (2002), very often public transport firms arrange their driver shifts so that the same number of hours are worked each day and the same number of days worked each week. The author shows that if these constraints were relaxed while keeping the total weekly work hours constant, considerably fewer driver hours would be needed to cover the schedule. This happens since, at peak periods, the number of drivers needed is significantly greater than during off-peak periods. In this scenario, having all drivers working equally long shifts leads to underutilisation of drivers during off-peak periods. To deal with this handicap, transit agencies have tried different alternatives: splitting shifts, overstaffing or hiring temporary staff to work particular trips, or even outsourcing the high demand periods to a third party. In this section, we illustrate the potential impact of considering work shifts of different lengths in the driver assignment problem.

Let us consider a transit network operating only Monday to Friday with a given timetable per route. The timetables for each day are identical. As is typical in this industry, the number of drivers needed through the day shows a double peaked shape: more drivers are needed early in the morning and late in the evening. The goal is to identify the minimum number of drivers and their respective work shifts that could work the planned schedule. We will compare two labour regulation contexts. In the first one, every driver has a rigid contract of eight continuous hours a day. In the second, more flexible one, drivers can be assigned to three different contracts: (i) the rigid eight hours per day, (ii) a flexible scheme of three days working ten hours and two days only five, and (iii) a split shift with a four-hour interval during the morning peak hour and another four-hour interval during the afternoon peak hour, five days a week. Note that every driver would work exactly 40 hours per week.

We assume a set of routes with timetables showing the typical double peaked shape from urban contexts. Figure 18.2a shows the number of active drivers needed at different times on a typical day of the week. Figure 18.2b shows the number of drivers assigned to work according to the optimal set of shifts in the rigid context. As can be seen, during the morning peak drivers start their shifts as soon as they are needed, but later in the day the number of working drivers exceeds the number of drivers strictly needed in several periods. In this solution almost 40% of the daily hours of work would be idle. Figure 18.2c shows that in the flexible context the assignment of work matches the number of drivers needed during the day almost perfectly.

These results show the potential of having some heterogeneity in the set of different contracts that a firm can offer to drivers. Interestingly, Miranda et al (2008) show that drivers are heterogeneous in their preferences since different drivers prefer different types of contract and many drivers prefer flexible contracts since they match their personal lifestyle better. This is a great opportunity for firms since it shows that by offering a diverse set of work structures cost effectiveness and labour conditions can be improved simultaneously. Montalva et al (2012) show that the potential savings obtained from this flexibility can be shared, with the firm and all drivers better off in comparison to all drivers working a standard rigid shift.

Conclusions

Transit formalisation and BRT projects open the door to implementing operational research techniques to improve not just cost effectiveness, which is critical to reducing subsidies or avoiding fare increments, but also the level of service offered to users and drivers' satisfaction with their work. In this chapter we focus on decisions regarding vehicles and driver management at the strategic, tactical and operational decision levels.

Each of these decisions is problematic because a trade-off between different impacts often experienced by different actors must be faced. Operational research tools suggest a decision after comparing a huge number of alternatives which would be impossible without them. Efficiency improvements, with significant cost savings, are a standard

Figure 18.2: Numerical results of implementing flexible driver shifts

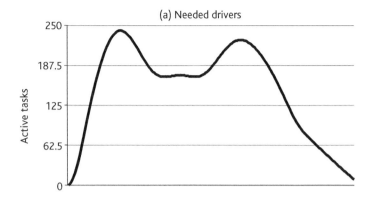

(a) Needed drivers

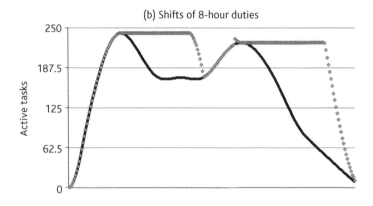

(b) Shifts of 8-hour duties

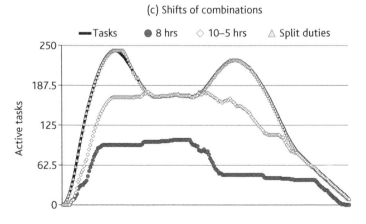

(c) Shifts of combinations

Source: Muñoz 2002

in this industry. However, most of these tools require formal systems in which different vehicles, drivers and services can be coordinated and managed. They also require firms to have a minimum size to make the savings worth investing in.

These analytical tools require a framework to search for a good solution and set a criterion to compare the attractiveness of different solutions. In the first case, the more flexible the system can be, the more solutions can be considered and therefore the better the optimal solution will be. However, flexibility comes with a cost since the solution will be more complex and therefore harder to understand and manage. Regarding how different solutions will be compared, the manager must determine a mechanism to balance the different trade-offs involved in public transport design and operation. Sometimes a monetary value for different impacts (such as travel time, accidents, pollution) will be needed, at other times a minimum standard may be set. These inputs into the model will determine the optimal solution. In cases where this balancing mechanism is unclear, a Pareto frontier of optimal solutions may be preferable as an input for the decision maker.

Note

[1] http://www-01.ibm.com/software/commerce/optimization/cplex-optimizer/

References

Ceder, A. (2007) *Public Transit Planning and Operation: Theory, Modeling and Practice*, Oxford: Elsevier, Butterworth-Heinemann.

Daduna, J. and Paixão, J. (1995) 'Vehicle scheduling for public mass transit – an overview', *Computer-Aided Transit Scheduling*, 430: 76–90.

Desaulniers, G. and Hickman, M. (2007) 'Public transit', in C. Barnhart and G. Laporte (eds), *Handbooks in Operations Research and Management Science: Transportation*, 14: 69–128.

Ehrgott, M. (2005) *Multicriteria Optimization* (2nd edn), New York: Springer.

Ehrgott, M. and Ruzika, S. (2008) 'Improved ε-constraint method for multiobjective programming', *Journal of Optimization Theory and Applications*, 138(3): 375–396.

Hardy, M.W. and Stevens, D.R. (2001) *Bus Rapid Transit Vehicle Characteristics*, Technical Report, Department of Transportation, Washington, DC, USA.

Ibarra-Rojas, O. (2013) 'Models and algorithms for transit network planning', PhD thesis, Graduate Programme of Systems Engineering, Universidad Autónoma de Nuevo León.

Ibarra-Rojas, O., Giesen, R. and Rios-Solis, Y. (2014) 'An integrated approach for timetabling and vehicle scheduling problems to analyze the trade-off between level of service and operating costs of transit networks', *Transportation Research B*, 70: 35–46.

Ibarra-Rojas, O., Delgado, F., Giesen, R. and Muñoz, J. (2015) 'Planning, operation, and control of bus transport system: a literature review', *Transportation Research B*, 77: 38–75.

Miranda, F., Muñoz, J. and Ortúzar, J. (2008) 'Identifying transit driver preferences for work shift structures: an econometric analysis', *Transportation Science*, 42(1): 70–86.

Montalva, S., Muñoz, J. and Paredes, R. (2012) 'Assignment of work shifts to public transit drivers based on stated preferences', *Public Transport*, 2(3): 199–218.

Muñoz, J. (2002) 'Crew-shift design for transportation systems with uncertain demand', PhD thesis, Institute of Transportation Studies, University of California at Berkeley.

Newell, G. (1971) 'Dispatching policies for a transportation route', *Transportation Science*, 5: 91-105.

Portugal, R., Lourenço, H. and Paixão, J. (2009) 'Driver scheduling problem modelling', *Public Transport*, 1(2): 103–120.

Welding, P. (1964) 'The instability of a close-interval service', *Operational Research Quarterly*, 8: 13-148.

Wright, L. and Hook, W. (2010) *Bus Rapid Transit Planning Guide*, Technical Report, Institute for Transportation and Development Policy, New York, USA.

NINETEEN

Road safety impacts of BRT and busway features

Nicolae Duduta and Luis Antonio Lindau

Introduction

Traffic accidents account for over 1.2 million annual deaths around the world, and this number is expected to increase, making road fatalities one of the leading causes of premature mortality worldwide by 2030 (World Health Organization 2013). The increase in traffic fatalities is expected to be concentrated in low and middle income countries, which are now experiencing a significant growth in motorisation. With the recent increase in the popularity of Bus Rapid Transit (BRT) systems worldwide – over 180 cities featured some type of BRT system by 2014 – there is an opportunity to jointly tackle the traffic safety and mobility issues faced by developing world cities.

BRTs are usually implemented on high demand corridors, particularly urban arterials, which are typically the most dangerous types of roads in urban areas. Research from New York City, for instance, has shown that arterials represent only 15% of the road network in a city, but concentrate over 65% of severe crashes (Viola et al 2010) and data from the developing world indicate similar trends (EMBARQ 2014). While there is a potential concern that implementing a BRT along a busy arterial road may attract pedestrians to areas of high risk, this is also an opportunity to improve the infrastructure and achieve significant safety benefits. Evidence from BRT implementation in Latin America and Asia supports this claim (Table 19.1), as BRT systems in these different regions have shown positive safety impacts. Our research shows that the safety improvements are due to the changes to the street geometry needed to accommodate the BRT infrastructure (for example, lane removals, medians, turn prohibitions).

In this chapter, we provide an overview of the results of BRT safety impact assessments, with a brief discussion of the methodology and its challenges. We then explore the infrastructure components of BRT that contribute to the safety impacts. We conclude by discussing how

355

safety countermeasures specific to BRT corridors can impact the system's operational performance.

Evidence on the safety impact of BRT

The traffic safety aspects of BRT systems are typically not as well understood as their better documented impacts on travel times, greenhouse gas and local pollutant emissions, or land values. However, our research shows that BRTs in Latin America and Asia have had significant positive impacts on traffic safety, reducing injuries and fatalities by upwards of 50% on the corridors where they were implemented (Duduta, Lindau and Adriazola-Steil 2013; Duduta et al 2014). In this section, we start by explaining the methodology we used to carry out safety impact assessments of BRT systems. Then we show results from assessments conducted in Mexico, Colombia and India.

Methodology for carrying out safety impact assessments on BRT systems

The main challenge in evaluating the safety impact of any transport infrastructure intervention is determining to what extent the change in the number of crashes is attributable to the intervention. It is important to distinguish the impact of the intervention from the general randomness of crash data (particularly the regression to the mean effect, or RTM) and from the impact of various other policies or trends at the citywide and national level. Simple comparisons of crash counts before and after project implementation does not take into account RTM and can lead to inaccurate results. For this reason, the preferred technique for evaluating the safety impacts of interventions such as BRT is the Empirical Bayes (EB) method (Hauer et al 2001).

The basic premise of the EB method is that there are more clues to the safety record of a street than the actual crash counts, and that additional information can be derived by studying the safety performance of 'similar and nearby streets' (Goh et al 2013). This is done through a safety performance function (SPF), which is a crash frequency model that seeks to predict crashes as a function of traffic volumes and infrastructure characteristics. The safety record of a street is estimated as a weighted average of actual crash counts and expected crash counts from the SPF, with the weight typically being a function of the variance of the crash data. A more detailed discussion of the EB method and its application to a BRT safety impact assessment can be found in Duduta, Lindau, and Adriazola-Steil (2013).

Another challenge to estimating safety impacts is that most developing world countries tend to underreport traffic injuries and fatalities. In part, this is due to different definitions as to what constitutes a traffic fatality or a traffic injury, but it is also due to reporting errors (Hijar et al 2011). The World Health Organization (WHO) has developed adjustment factors to standardise the data across the different countries (WHO 2013) and we apply these factors in our analysis.

Results of BRT safety impact assessments

The different safety impact assessments we were able to carry out on BRT systems in Latin America and India indicate that, in general, they have had a significant positive impact on safety, especially on severe and fatal crashes (Table 19.1). The definition of what constitutes a severe crash can vary significantly between countries, but it generally refers to serious injuries that typically require hospitalisation. Despite the differences in definitions, a trend emerges from the different safety assessments in Table 19.1: the different BRTs have reduced the incidence of severe crashes more than that of total crashes. The data in Table 19.1 represents safety impact assessments carried out for a period of three to nine years after implementation.

We also estimate that safety impacts are typically the third largest benefit of a BRT system and can account for 10–16% of the total economic benefits of such an intervention (Figure 19.1).[1] While measuring these impacts can be challenging, especially in the developing world context where the quality and availability of crash data are poor, it is important to capture these impacts and understand the infrastructure characteristics that contribute to safety improvements when BRTs are implemented.

Table 19.1: Results of safety impact assessment on bus priority systems in Latin America and India

City	Type of BRT system	Percentage change in crashes, by level of severity		
		Crashes	Injuries	Fatalities
Ahmedabad	Median-running BRT	−32%	−28%	−55%
Mexico City	Median-running BRT	+11%	−38%	−38%
Guadalajara	Median-running BRT with overtaking lanes at stations	−56%	−69%	−68%
Bogotá	Multi-lane median-running BRT	n/a	−39%	−48%

Source: Duduta et al 2014

Figure 19.1: Safety impacts as a percentage of the total economic benefits of a typical Latin American BRT

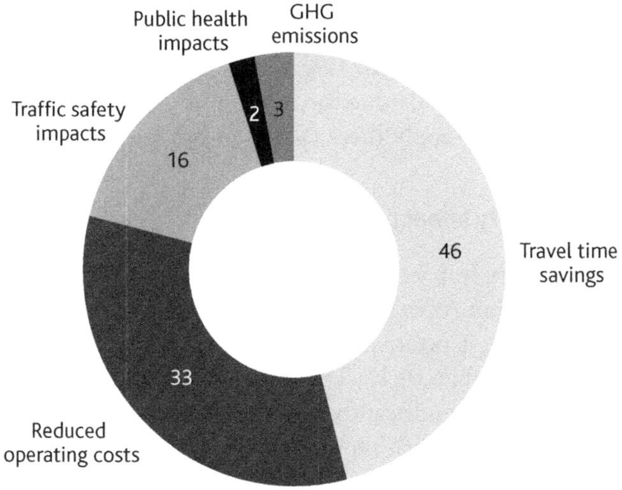

Source: Duduta et al. 2014

The evaluations in Table 19.1 refer exclusively to safety impacts on the streets where BRTs were implemented. However, it is important to also consider potential spillover effects. Indeed, the removal of traffic lanes when implementing bus priority reduces the capacity of the street for mixed traffic. This raises a potential concern that some traffic might be diverting to parallel routes and that some of the observed crash reductions on the transit corridor are offset by increases on these other streets. Our analysis of the crash data from Guadalajara suggests this was not the case. We selected a 3-kilometre buffer zone on both sides of the corridor, to include several major arterials that run parallel to the BRT corridor. We found that crashes in the buffer zone (excluding the BRT corridor) decreased by 8% over the same period of time – a trend consistent with the rest of the city. This indicates that the safety improvements observed on the corridor in Guadalajara were not offset by increases along parallel streets, after accounting for citywide trends.

At a smaller scale, however, there were several instances where the implementation of the BRT in Guadalajara may have shifted the risk of crashes to nearby streets. Left turns were prohibited at most intersections – a common feature on median-running BRT systems in countries where traffic drives on the right. The left turns were replaced with loops, redirecting traffic through the neighbourhood. Some of the better designed loops did not have any impact on crashes in the neighbourhood around the BRT corridor. But in at least one case, the creation of the loop resulted in an increase in crashes at the intersections along it. This suggests that the design and planning of the BRT should extend beyond the corridor itself, and should consider and mitigate potential spillover effects.

The safety impact of different BRT design features

Accommodating a BRT on a street involves creating or widening a central median, thus shortening pedestrian crosswalks and transforming some four-way intersections into T-junctions. It also typically involves eliminating at least two, and often up to four mixed traffic lanes in order to accommodate the transit infrastructure (lanes and stations). This is not always the case however, as some BRTs are implemented as part of larger infrastructure projects that can involve road widening, increasing the overall number of lanes.

Our analysis indicates that these infrastructure changes are associated with positive safety impacts. Fewer approaches per intersection, fewer lanes, shorter crosswalks, and central medians were all associated with lower crash frequencies and were statistically significant across all the models we developed.

We evaluated the detailed safety impact of these different design features using crash frequency models. Also known as accident prediction models or safety performance functions, these are cross-sectional models that seek to explain differences in crash rates at different locations using factors such as road and intersection geometry, after controlling for exposure (that is, the number of vehicles or pedestrians).

Crash data are count variables, which are usually best represented by a Poisson distribution (Ladrón de Guevara et al 2004). However, previous studies have noted that crash data are also overdispersed (that is, the variance is much greater than the mean) and therefore are better represented by a negative binomial distribution (also known as Poisson–Gamma), which, unlike Poisson, allows the variance to differ from the mean (Dumbaugh and Rae 2009). For this reason the negative binomial (NB) is the preferred probability distribution for modelling crash frequencies in most cases. The coefficients of NB and Poisson models can be expressed as incidence rate ratios (IRR), which are useful for practitioners, since they can easily be interpreted as the percentage change in crashes as a result of a one unit change in the independent variables.

Table 19.2 shows the weighted mean safety impact of various infrastructure changes typically associated with BRT implementation. The coefficients were estimated from a meta-analysis of crash frequency models on BRTs, busways, and other urban arterials in Mexico City, Guadalajara, Bogotá, and Porto Alegre. The percentage changes in Table 19.2 represent a weighted average impact across different models in different cities.

Table 19.2: Weighted mean safety impact of street design features associated with BRT

Type of infrastructure intervention	Crash type	Percentage change in crashes	
		Mean	95% confidence interval
Converting a four-way intersection into two T-junctions	Severe	−66	(−1, −88)
	All types	−57	(−37, −70)
Removing a traffic lane	Severe	−15	(−11, −17)
	Vehicle collisions	−12	(−9, −15)
Shortening crosswalks (each additional metre removed)	Severe	−2	(−0.04, −4)
	Pedestrian crashes	−6	(−2, −8)
Prohibiting left turns on main corridors (driving on right)	Severe	−22	(−12, −32)
	Vehicle collisions	−26	(−10, −43)
Introducing a central median	Severe	−35	(−8, −55)
	Vehicle collisions	−43	(−26, −56)
Introducing a counterflow bus priority lane	Severe	+83	(+23, +171)
	Vehicle collisions	+35	(+0.02, +86)
	Pedestrian crashes	+146	(+59, +296)
Reducing distance between traffic signals (for each 10m)	Severe	−3	(−1, −5)
	All types	+2	(+0.03, +4)
	Pedestrian crashes	−5	(−1, −7)
Introducing a pedestrian bridge on expressway	Pedestrian crashes	−84	(−55, −94)
Introducing a pedestrian bridge on arterial road	Pedestrian crashes	No statistically significant impact	(−23, +262)

Source: Duduta et al 2014

Impact of bus lane location and configuration on safety

Counterflow bus lanes are typically built in situations where a transport agency seeks to implement two-way bus service on a street that previously had a one-way configuration for mixed traffic. There are various street configurations that can be categorized as counterflow. They all have in common the fact that vehicle and pedestrian traffic crossing a street with counterflow will have difficulties understanding the traffic pattern.

Our research indicates that counterflow lanes are associated with an increase in crashes at all severity levels (+83% fatal or injury crashes, +146% pedestrian crashes, +35% vehicle collisions). The consistency of the results across the different models suggests that counterflow lanes are the most dangerous configuration for the bus systems included in our study. Observations from road safety audits and inspections carried out on urban roads across Latin America suggest that the main risk lies in the fact that counterflow is an unexpected configuration, and many road users may not anticipate vehicles arriving from a counterflow direction.

Curbside bus lanes did not have a statistically significant impact on crashes, and neither did median bus lanes, after controlling for street geometry. However, the changes introduced by a median BRT on a street are measured by several variables. Unlike curbside bus corridors, which usually only replace one traffic (or parking) lane with a bus lane, centre-lane systems imply a more significant reconfiguration of the street. Typically, this involves introducing a central median to replace a traffic lane, shortening the pedestrian crossing distance by creating a pedestrian refuge in the centre of the street, and creating more T-intersections and fewer four-way intersections along the corridor. While the dummy variable accounting for the presence of the median BRT was not significant, the variables accounting for number of lanes, central median, crossing distance, and number of legs were all correlated with lower crash rates and were significant across the different models.

Impact of street geometry on safety

The model results indicate that the size and complexity of intersections along a bus corridor are better predictors of crash frequencies than the configuration of the bus system. Only about 9% of all crashes occurred in the bus lanes; the vast majority occurred in the general traffic lanes and did not involve buses.

Key issues include the number of approaches per intersection, the number of lanes per approach, and the maximum pedestrian crossing distance. Intersections where traffic on the cross-streets is allowed to cross the bus corridor are more dangerous than intersections where only right (nearside) turns are allowed. In other words, turning a standard four-way intersection into two T-junctions by continuing the median on the main street should improve safety. However, this is only the case if the intersection remains signalised. Often on BRT corridors, traffic signals are eliminated at the intersection if the cross-street is blocked, and so are the pedestrian crossings. This can allow buses to continue through the intersection with no delays, but it puts pedestrians at higher risk.

The impact of block size and speed

Speed is recognised as one of the key risk factors in traffic safety. Our crash frequency models could not account directly for speed as an independent variable, since no speed measurements were available for the street sections included in our sample. However, we were able to test the impact of speed by using a proxy – distance between signalised intersections. Indeed, the spacing of traffic signals is a key predictor of travel speeds. The findings indicate that sections with longer distances between signalised intersections (and therefore higher speeds) have a lower incidence of crashes overall. This is explained by the fact that fewer intersections along the sections means that there are fewer conflict points. However, while there were fewer crashes overall, those crashes that did happen were more severe.

The impact of land uses around the corridor on safety

Similar streets in different land use contexts can have very different safety records. The presence of a major market near the corridor was one of the strongest predictors of pedestrian crashes. In Mexico City, for instance, street sections along the Merced market experienced 94% more pedestrian crashes than other streets, after controlling for street geometry (Duduta et al 2012). Increases in pedestrian crashes in these areas result not only from higher pedestrian volumes, but also from additional risks related to the configuration of the market. Near the Merced market in Mexico City, for example, vendors often take up all or most of the space on the sidewalks, leaving insufficient capacity for the existing pedestrian volumes, forcing some pedestrians to walk in the traffic lanes and reducing visibility for drivers. This underlines the importance of considering the urban context of a street in its design.

Understanding the trade-offs between safety and operational performance

The results in Table 19.2 suggest that traffic calming features, including lane removals, speed reductions, and more closely spaced signals, are some of the key interventions for improving safety performance on a BRT. However, there are potential trade-offs between safety and operational performance. The traffic calming measures just described are likely to have a negative impact on BRT operating speeds and passenger travel times. We cannot provide any general guidance on how to address the trade-offs, because the impacts on operations are highly context specific and will vary greatly depending on the operational design of the BRT and the overall layout of the street and the road network.

We can, however, suggest an appropriate methodology for addressing the issue, by first identifying the key safety countermeasures needed, and then using microscopic traffic simulation software to test the impact on BRT operations for a specific BRT corridor. We illustrate the methodology here by documenting its application to the case of the TransOeste BRT in Rio de Janeiro, using the EMBARQ BRT Simulator – a microscopic traffic simulation software specifically geared towards analysing operations on high capacity BRT systems (Duduta et al 2013). This software allows for the detailed modelling of BRT routes, including terminal layouts, terminal holding zones, signalised intersections, and complex station configurations with multiple sub-stops and a combination of local and express services. The description, calibration, and previous applications of the EMBARQ BRT Simulator can be found in Pereira, Lindau, and Castilho (2010).

For this application, we first developed a baseline scenario aimed at replicating current conditions on an existing BRT corridor, and validated that model with actual measurements of operating speeds, travel times, and dwell times at stations. Finally, we developed a series of project scenarios featuring different combinations of safety countermeasures. We then simulated the performance of the BRT during a weekday morning peak period with and without safety countermeasures. More details on the modelling approach, as well as the model specification and calibration for the case study of the TransOeste BRT in Rio de Janeiro, can be found in Duduta et al (2013).

In this case, we considered the following safety countermeasures: speed reductions along the entire route from 80 to 60 kilometres per hour (km/h), with further reductions to 30 kilometres per hour at the approach to stations; placing additional signalised mid-block crossings to lower the average distance between crossings; and reconfiguring signals to minimise pedestrian delays. We tested the impact of these countermeasures on operational performance of the BRT by looking at three main indicators:

- Commercial speed, by type of service: this is defined as the average operating speed of a specific type of bus by type of service (i.e. local or express) over the entire simulation period; this is considered a key performance indicator for BRT systems, and it is common to use a 25 kilometres per hour benchmark as the threshold for high quality operations (Wright and Hook 2007).
- In-vehicle travel time: this is defined as the total time between the moment a vehicle leaves the platform at one of the terminals until the moment it docks at the platform of the terminal at the opposite end of the route.
- Operating speed variance: this is an indicator of the reliability of service offered by the BRT, and we would prioritise solutions that minimise this variance. It is calculated from the standard deviation of operating speed by type of service reported by the model. We do not only report variance, but also the coefficient of speed variability, defined as the ratio of standard deviation to the mean, and which is a more effective measure for comparing scenarios (Moreno Gonzalez et al 2013).

Simulation results

We tested three different project scenarios. In the '60 km/h' scenario, the only change introduced is the reduction in overall speed limits to 60 kilometres per hour. The '60/30' scenario further restricts speeds for all buses approaching stations to 30 kilometres per hour (including buses not stopping at those stations). Finally, the 'complete' scenario also includes the additional signalised mid-block crossings as well as the speed reductions.

The columns from left to right in Table 19.3 show the impact of adding each safety countermeasure on the different performance indicators. The reduction in speed limits result in slightly lower commercial speeds for buses and higher travel times for passengers. However, they also reduce speed variability, meaning that the service

Table 19.3: Impact of safety countermeasures on BRT operational performance

Indicator	Type of service	Baseline	60km/h	60/30km/h	Complete	Difference
Commercial	Express	32	31.5	29.6	29.6	−2.4
speed (km/h)	Local	25.6	25.6	25.45	25.43	−0.17
Travel time (min)	Express	71	72	77	77	+6
	Local	89	89	89	89	0
Speed variance	Express	37	31.3	22.33	15.57	−21.43
(km/h)	Local	16	14.94	14.85	15.57	−0.43
Speed variability	Express	0.19	0.18	0.16	0.16	−0.03
coefficient	Local	0.16	0.15	0.15	0.16	−0

is more reliable and bus frequency is better maintained throughout the route. The traffic signals have a negative impact on commercial speed. Overall, the simulation results show that while the safety recommendations have a negative impact on some operational parameters (commercial speed and travel times), these impacts are relatively small, which indicates that BRTs could maintain high quality operations even when implementing the safety features presented here. It should also be noted that operating speeds are equal or higher than the 25 kilometres per hour benchmark across all scenarios.

Conclusion

The best way to design a high performance transit system is to have an integrated approach that considers the needs of all road users and the impact of each design or operational decision on a wide range of performance indicators, including safety, operational performance, and environmental impacts. Safety is often overlooked in the planning and design of new transport infrastructure, including BRT systems. While we have made the case here for including safety considerations, it is also important to avoid addressing safety as a separate issue.

By implementing an integrated approach to the planning and design of a BRT corridor, it is possible to help decision makers understand which design options to choose and what impact to expect on a range of performance indicators. Our evidence suggests that if safety countermeasures are designed as part of an integrated approach that also considers bus operations, a BRT system can have a positive safety impact and provide a high quality service to its passengers.

For practitioners involved in planning, designing or operating BRT and busway corridors, we recommend consulting *Traffic Safety on Bus*

Priority Systems (Duduta et al 2014). It is an illustrated report featuring design concepts for common BRT and busway design configurations, including recommendations for addressing common safety issues, based on crash data analysis from existing bus systems.

Note
[1] Estimated using the value of a statistical life based on cost–benefit analysis carried out for BRT systems in Mexico City and Bogotá (Carrigan et al 2013).

References

Carrigan, A., King, R., Velasquez, J.M., Raifman, M. and Duduta, N. (2013) *The Social, Environmental, and Economic Impacts of BRT Systems, EMBARQ Report*, Washington, DC: EMBARQ.

Duduta, N., Adriazola-Steil, C., Hidalgo, D., Lindau, L.A. and Dos Santos da Rocha, P. (2013) 'The relationship between safety, capacity, and operating speed on Bus Rapid Transit', Paper presented at the 13th World Conference on Transport Research (WCTR), Rio de Janeiro.

Duduta, N., Adriazola-Steil, C., Hidalgo, D., Lindau, L.A. and Jaffe, R. (2012) 'Understanding the road safety impact of high performance BRT and busway design characteristics', *Transportation Research Record: Journal of the Transportation Research Record*, 2317: 8–16.

Duduta, N., Lindau, L.A. and Adriazola-Steil, C. (2013) 'Using empirical Bayes to estimate the safety impacts of transit improvements in Latin America', Paper presented at the International Conference in Road Safety and Simulation, RSS 2013, Rome.

Duduta, N., Adriazola-Steil, C., Wass, C. Hidalgo, D. and Lindau, L.A. (2014) *Traffic Safety on Bus Priority Systems*, Washington, DC: World Resources Institute Report.

Dumbaugh, E. and Rae, R. (2009) 'Safe urban form: revisiting the relationship between community design and traffic safety', *Journal of the American Planning Association*, 75(3): 309–329.

EMBARQ (2014) *Saving Lives. Status Report – Data Collection, Methodologies, and Impact*, Washington, DC: EMBARQ.

Goh, K., Currie, G., Sarvi, M. and Logan, D. (2013) 'Investigating the road safety impacts of Bus Rapid Transit priority measures', Paper presented at the Transportation Research Board 92nd Annual Meeting, Washington, DC.

Hauer, E., Harwood, D., Council, F.M. and Griffith, M.S. (2001) 'Estimating safety by the empirical Bayes method: a tutorial', Paper presented at the Transportation Research Board 80th Annual Meeting, Washington, DC.

Híjar, M., Chandran, A., Pérez-Núñez, R., Lunnen, J.C., Rodríguez-Hernández, J.M. and Hyder, A. (2011) 'Quantifying the underestimated burden of road traffic mortality in Mexico: a comparison of three approaches', *Traffic Injury Prevention*, 13(suppl 1): 5–10.

Ladrón de Guevara, F., Washington, S.P. and Oh, J. (2004) 'Forecasting crashes at the planning level. Simultaneous negative binomial crash model applied in Tucson, Arizona', *Transportation Research Record: Journal of the Transportation Research Record*, 1987: 191–199.

Moreno Gonzalez, E.G., Romana, M.G. and Alvaro, O.M. (2013) 'Effectiveness of reserved bus lanes in arterials', Paper presented at the 92nd Transportation Research Board Annual Meeting, Washington, DC.

Pereira, B.M., Lindau, L.A. and Castilho, R.A. (2010) 'A importância de simular sistemas Bus Rapid Transit', in *Proceedings of XVI CLATPU (Congreso Latinoamericano de Transporte Público y Urbano)*, Mexico City.

Viola, R., Roe, M. and Shin, H. (2010) *The New York City Pedestrian Safety Study and Action Plan*, New York City: Department of Transportation.

Wright, L. and Hook, W. (2007) *Bus Rapid Transit Planning Guide*, New York: Institute for Transportation and Development Policy.

World Health Organization (2013) *Global Status Report on Road Safety: Supporting a Decade of Action*, Geneva: WHO.

TWENTY

Looking forward

Juan Carlos Munoz and Laurel Paget-Seekins

Introduction

Our goal for this book is to present the wider context of BRT and show its potential role to restructure transportation and urban space to improve sustainability. These chapters have highlighted the opportunities and challenges of fulfilling this potential. Our wider vision is created by the interconnections between multiple research projects, disciplines, and methodologies. It is also formed by the collaboration of academics and practitioners working to solve real-world problems. From that experience we offer this assessment of the role of BRT and propose steps for moving forward.

Institutional relationships

Before a bus ever runs along a corridor, a BRT system requires appropriate institutional structures. This includes a governance framework to regulate bus operators, the alignment of urban policies (Chapter Five), and the situating of the public and local community in the process (Chapter Six). Since BRT is often used as a tool to formalise informal bus services in developing cities, it can provide a mechanism to strengthen institutions and the regulatory capacity of authorities (Chapter Four). This process can provide a catalyst to discuss policy issues such as fares, operating subsidies (Chapter Eight) and the need for a metropolitan authority. However, one of the greatest challenges in addressing urban transport problems and BRT implementation comes from the weakness and fragmentation of existing institutions.

Public transport policy should be aligned with urban, land use and wider transportation policy to ensure the proper incentives and cohesive decision making. Failure to align land use and transport policy with the broader goals of liveable cities constrains the planning process and may increase transport costs and exacerbate urban inequities.

This is a challenge for developed and developing cities alike. But it is particularly difficult in developing cities where organisations lack institutional capacity and a tradition of working together. This difficulty is highlighted in a project as challenging as the integration of a citywide transport system (Chapter Three). The issue of who operates the system further strains the public sector capacity. Private operators add another set of actors, which requires careful contract design to align public and private interests (Chapter Seven).

As we see in the multiple case studies throughout the book, BRT projects add an additional layer of complexity since their success requires different organisations working together (local authorities, different central government divisions, private operators, technology providers) and with a lack of coordination triggering problems. Too often the connections between different components of a BRT system (like the lanes, stations, operations, user information and control, surrounding land uses, traffic management, and so on) are not correctly designed, or even some components are simply not considered as part of the system at all.

This is a major difference from rail systems, which are usually conceived and designed as a robust, complete system in which each piece is fundamental. For example, a metro would never be built without a signalling system, but BRT projects are often constructed without key components such as priority at intersections or headway control mechanisms. Too often, BRT is conceived as the inexpensive alternative in which some of the essential features can be deferred.

One of the main challenges faced by the BRT industry is defining benchmarks which guarantee that BRT is a coherent and sensible solution that achieves a high level of service at a low cost. Since BRT is a surface mode, it has to fit into the existing urban context and adhere to cultural norms; any standards must be flexible enough to adapt to local circumstances. Still, the BRT basics, like exclusive bus lanes, preferably in the median, off-board ticket validation, level boarding, lower emission buses, centralised control and adequate user information systems should be present to achieve the best results.

Since BRT is just one element of an urban transport system, which should be designed to provide intermodal solutions, the challenge of institutional cooperation and service coordination becomes even greater. Integrated BRT-based systems must include convenient connections with bicycles, passenger drop-offs, metro, paratransit, rickshaws, and so on. This requires more effective metropolitan level governance, capable of coordinating and regulating all transport modes, together with land use. Most cities in the developing and developed world implementing BRT would benefit from more effective regional governance and greater partnerships.

Most public transport systems worldwide face very tight financial conditions and increasing costs hamper efforts to improve the levels of service. There is a consensus that subsidising public transport is not just equitable, but also efficient. However, a deeper understanding is necessary for defining optimal fares, the optimal level of service from a social perspective, and how subsidies can be most effectively targeted to the users who need them.

BRT in the city

As with any surface mode, BRT cannot be considered separately from its urban context. This provides a positive opportunity for its implementation to improve more than just transit level of service. In both developing and developed cities, BRT offers the possibility for coordinated land use planning and transit-oriented development (Chapter Ten). It can be a tool for reallocating how public space is used (Chapter Nine).

Since BRT penetrates into local neighbourhoods, it must do more than just increase accessibility. To win the necessary public support it must enrich the quality of the neighbourhoods it touches. Otherwise it will be fiercely resisted. The corridors should be designed to minimise widths on the streets it uses, while still providing the necessary speed and capacity. These interventions may not involve just the corridor in which BRT is being built, but also the streets that will provide multimodal access to its users. A BRT intervention can offer the opportunity to enhance neighbourhoods with bike paths, improved sidewalks, recreational areas, and other amenities. This implies BRT is as much an urban design and revitalisation project as an engineering one.

In many cities, public transport stations serve as central areas where people meet every day. This concentration provides an opportunity to offer the traveller not just mobility, but a place to access public services, commerce, entertainment or cultural opportunities, and have social encounters. A public transport user could access many more services and experiences if the system is also designed to fulfil this purpose. In this case, public transport would play a much more substantial role in the city and provide extra justification as a public service meriting public funding.

But BRT's potential to reshape urban space is also a key reason why implementation is so difficult. Strong public support is critical to overcome the conflicts presented in Chapter Nine over the allocation of public space for BRT. We should acknowledge that very often those benefiting from a BRT corridor do not live along the corridor and do not suffer the negative externalities, but instead come from the periphery of the city. It is this spatial mismatch of beneficiaries that challenges the design and implementation and underpins the importance of achieving public buy-in.

Chapter Six suggests that more than marketing, community members working as collaborators with transport planners at all stages of BRT design and implementation is fundamental to building support. But this requires a robust civic society, which is not always the case in developing cities. In previous decades we have seen strong lobbies advocating for investments in freeways or rail-based solutions while in the last decade a strong lobby for bike facilities has emerged. Even though protests due to fare increases, overcrowding or lack of service are not uncommon and can have massive support, public transport users very rarely organise into representative groups that could advocate for their interests. This is unfortunate since BRT solutions would be significantly easier to implement if those benefiting were more vocal and empowered. In addition, local champions have been essential to the success of BRT in cities such as Curitiba, Brisbane and Bogotá.

The lack of community support for BRT is also intertwined with the ongoing emotionally laden debate on BRT versus LRT. In both developed and developing cities, the positive perception of bus alternatives lags behind rail regardless of the ability of BRT to provide the necessary level of service for a given corridor at a significantly lower cost. Chapter Eleven identifies some of these perception problems and the need for clearer communication of the BRT alternative. But BRT will not earn the respect it deserves if it is marketed as a less expensive and lower quality solution than rail.

As illustrated by the example of Transantiago in Chile, the initial experience of passengers is critical to acceptance of the new service, especially if more transfers are required. Not only can poor implementation impact on lasting perceptions of service quality, but passenger information is necessary to help riders adapt to a new network design or efficiently use a new corridor. This is illustrated in the interplay between Chapters Twelve and Thirteen. Information systems are critical, especially for users with little formal education.

Operations and design

BRT offers significant opportunities for improving service to passengers and making public transport a competitive alternative to private motorised modes. As discussed in Chapter Fifteen, BRT offers the potential to improve the efficiency of a public transport network by providing room for flexible service options such as express services and direct service BRT corridors which can reduce the travel time experienced by passengers. In addition, the formalisation of BRT services creates internal efficiencies in how a bus service is operated (Chapter Eighteen).

New technologies and increasingly available data provide opportunities at the design, operation and control levels to improve service and passenger information (Chapter Fourteen). In this process, agencies should open this information to the general public to harness their creativity towards new and previously unthought-of products and services, particularly comprehensive passenger information systems (Chapter Thirteen).

There are many factors influencing corridor performance (Chapter Sixteen) and there are tradeoffs to ensuring trip reliability, speed, capacity and safety. Most BRT implementations worldwide are far from flawless; a high frequency surface bus network presents a host of design and operation challenges. Nevertheless, some existing systems do demonstrate best practices that serve as examples of what other BRTs could achieve. As shown in Chapter Nineteen, BRT projects can also improve safety for all street users.

To really achieve its promise of providing metro-like services, even the most sophisticated BRT systems with excellent reputations must improve in three critical dimensions: reliability, comfort and, as previously discussed, local urban impact. The bus industry must fight a systematic battle against bus bunching which harms not just reliability, but also waiting, comfort, operational costs and, ultimately, user opinions on service quality. Public transport agencies must provide strong incentives (both sticks and carrots) for operators to resolve these concerns. Too often operators do not even care how the buses are being dispatched from terminals. As shown in Chapter Seventeen, there are tools to overcome this problem.

Comfort is important because it is one of the main reasons that nonusers dismiss public transport as a second class alternative. This particularly affects buses since rail queues are always underground and therefore harder for nonusers to see. The long term urban sustainability battle cannot be won with buses (or trains) filled with people packed beyond the limit of dignity. Unfortunately, too many BRTs are designed to provide little comfort at the designed capacity. Investing in increasing a corridor's capacity to provide an attractive level of service would still keep BRT as a very cost effective alternative.

There are ways to expand the current service that BRT systems provide to meet new challenges, for example, for very long trips in large cities with urban freeways, buses can provide a high speed service at a very low investment cost. With integrated fare systems, these express bus services could provide the long distance portion of the trips connecting to feeder services for the first and last kilometres of the trip. In such a scheme, a new type of bus must be designed in which these long trips can be delivered not only fast, but comfortably, with high productivity and safety standards.

Putting research into practice

All of these challenges require continuing research, but also movement from research to implementation. A fundamental goal of the BRT Centre is to make the knowledge we have developed available to create more successful BRT implementation and operations. In part this is done by identifying elements which are transferable between existing and prospective BRT systems and elements that are project specific. We see our BRT Centre as an active agent of change in cities worldwide, searching for positive transformation opportunities for public transport systems. In addition to research, we are constructing tools to share data and build connections between academics and practitioners around the world.

Building these relationships is often difficult. There is a gap between academic research and the needs of public transport stakeholders (agencies, operators, authorities and users). We believe a good way to start the connection between academics and practitioners is to actively consider practitioners' inputs to research agendas so that the outcomes provide an evidence base. In addition, involving the public transport stakeholders and urban communities in the production of knowledge and solutions provides an opportunity to embed the views of providers and users.

The relationship between academia and practitioners is also relevant because pilot projects often are needed as part of the research process. Some of the tools and knowledge developed by the BRT Centre are easily transferable and realistic to implement, while others may still need the participation of researchers in this process. Academic researchers can play a unique role in developing innovative solutions, underwriting the risk involved in the implementation process in those situations where such risks are unattractive to private firms.

Over the past five years we have developed methods for sharing our research outside the traditional academic journals. As discussed in Chapter Two, we have developed and now maintain a global database of BRT corridors that is open to all researchers and practitioners. We run a monthly webinar series to present results and open discussion on important topics. The Centre has relationships with public transport implementers around the world through the EMBARQ network and the SIBRT (the Latin American Association of Integrated Transport Systems and BRT). We also work with other centres of excellence supported by VREF, and actively participate in academic forums to advance international and interdisciplinary cooperation. We believe this model of academic–practitioner collaboration is critical in addressing the challenges we identify here.

A sense of urgency

This book is underpinned by the need to take a wide view of the urban transport problem. It cannot be separated from the growing crisis of climate change, the loss of biodiversity, and the challenges of poverty, health disparities, gender inequality and urban displacement. We need solutions that will reduce emissions, improve health and safety, increase social equity, and improve accessibility for the growing number of urban residents around the world. After five years of research we are confident that BRT is a critical part of these solutions.

We suggest that it is only with a sense of urgency that these problems will be solved. This urgency requires a dedication of resources. These resources should be the political capital necessary to implement projects, the funds needed for capital investments and operating subsidies, and the urban space needed for implementation.

BRT projects and public transport formalisation efforts are a challenge to the existing status quo, whether that be the domination of the private car in the use of existing financial resources and street space, or the limited role of government in the regulation and funding of urban public transport. A challenge to the status quo presents an opportunity to have a public debate about the use and prioritisation of resources and question the accepted realities. But overcoming those accepted realities is a huge challenge.

Despite the many challenges, we remain hopeful. We have observed a vast increase in BRT systems around the world in a very time short span, and the consideration of BRT as a valid alternative in many contexts. Much work remains to be done, but there is great potential for BRT to transform urban spaces to increase accessibility, to help build regional integrated public transport systems and provide sustainable urban environments which are inclusive. We recognise that this book is not a complete analysis of all the challenges facing BRT projects, nor do we provide conclusive solutions to all of the problems. But we do hope that this book has provided an interdisciplinary framework in which to understand the challenges and opportunities and has demonstrated some concrete results as a basis for moving forward.

This book is not the end of our work. Both individually and as the collective the BRT Centre has created, we will continue to advance research and build knowledge networks to solve the pressing issue of sustainable transport. We hope this book can help others join this effort and to see how their work fits into the larger vision moving forward.

Index

Entries from the Notes sections begin with 'n.'

Transjakarta 137–138
TransMilenio (Bogotá, Colombia)
  centralised control 334
  contracts for bus services 135–136,
  139
  enclosed stations 112
  express services 311
  as integrated system 36–38
  property value studies 183–185
  protests 136
  route choice (passenger) 242–244
TransOeste, Rio de Janeiro 363–365
Transport for London 34
travel passes 147–148, 156, 159
travel strategies 237–242
traveller behaviour research 209
trip assignment modelling 234
trip chain, importance of 103
trip linking 270
trip purpose 238, 249
trunk feeder networks
  Bogotá, Colombia 36
  BRTOD (bus rapid transit-oriented
  development) 202
  cost and level of service comparisons
  24
  versus direct trips 7, 282–284, 287,
  339
  as feature of BRT 4
  network design 282, 287
  Santiago 231, 253
  and vehicles 339
Turkey 20
  see also Istanbul

U

uncertainty, inevitability of 44
unemployed people fare discounts 150
unexpected events, dealing with 267,
  347–348
unions (bus worker) 56, 61, 281
United Kingdom
  bus service contracts 131, 132
  Cambridge 8, 23, 314 n.3
  integrated transport systems 32–33
  price elasticity for bus travel 149
  statistics on bus corridors 18–20
  see also London
United States of America
  BRTOD (bus rapid transit-oriented
  development) 185
  car use 102, 203
  Chicago 204 n.2
  Cleveland 8
  Eugene, Oregon 183
  gentrification 185
  integrated transport systems 33
  land use 182

light rail transit 210
Los Angeles 8, 184, 308
New Jersey 183
New York 17, 110, 117, 289, 355
Salt Lake City 210, 265
statistics on bus corridors 18–20
  see also Boston
urban design 202–203
urban development, and BRTOD
  187–207
users/ passengers
  complaints 6, 8
  consultation 43, 101–125
  customer classification 150, 275–276
  expectations 43, 255
  experience 306–313
  nonusers 219, 226, 373–374
  passenger needs 257
  passenger profiles 121
  passengers per kilometre 7
  perceptions 210–214, 267, 372
  preferences 209–229, 231–246,
  306–307
  satisfaction 166, 171, 173, 267
  user costs 294, 340, 346
  user data 148
  see also passenger information

V

value capture 91
value of time 167, 241, 245, 286, 293
vandalism 112
vehicles
  age of buses 37, 40, 54, 61–62
  automatic vehicle location systems
  (AVL) 263, 265, 267, 320
  average vehicle capacity utilization 59
  biarticulated buses ('bendy' buses)
  292
  both-sided doors 301, 339–340
  combibuses 61
  fleet size 295, 310, 338, 339, 341,
  343–344, 346
  microbuses 61–62
  minibus services 61
  modern vehicles, user preferences for
  219–221
  underutilisation of vehicles 283–284
  vehicle capacity, average utilisation 59
  vehicle injection 320
  vehicle management 339–344
  vehicle monitoring systems
  (automatic) 263, 265
  vehicle scheduling problem (VS)
  342–348
vertical versus horizontal coherence
  (policy) 74–78
vicious circle, car-public transport 306

Volvo Research and Educational
  Foundations (VREF) 10, 375

W

waiting spaces 234
waiting times
  automated data collection systems
    263, 272–273
  average waiting times 66
  contracts 132
  and corridor performance 307
  as externality in public transport 146
  and high versus low-frequency bus
    services 273
  holding in real time optimisation
    model (HRT) 322, 325, 330
  and passenger information systems
    247
  as performance measurement 266
  and route choice 233, 237–238,
    240–242
  search costs 146
  as user cost 151
  user preferences 234
  and vehicle management 341
  vehicle scheduling 344–348
walking, inclusion in BRT 103, 121
walking connection times
  automated data collection systems
    270–271
  as feature of BRT 7
  and route choice 240–241
  and station spacing 308
  Transantiago system (Santiago, Chile)
    67
  trunk and feeder versus direct trip
    configurations 283
  user preferences 233
  user versus operational costs 347
wayfinding *see* passenger information
wellbeing 182
wireless communication systems 320
women
  in citizen participation 121
  cyclists 110, 117
  as users of public transport 121, 219
word of mouth 249, 256
worker satisfaction 349
working conditions (drivers') 338,
    348–351
World Health Organization (WHO)
    355, 357

Z

zonal fares 147–148, 154–155, 265

Printed and bound by CPI Group (UK) Ltd, Croydon, CR0 4YY

23/04/2025

14661021-0004